D1499724

# THE LADDER OF SUCCESS
# IN IMPERIAL CHINA

STUDIES OF THE EAST ASIAN INSTITUTE

COLUMBIA UNIVERSITY

By PING-TI HO

明清社會史論

何炳棣自題

# THE LADDER OF SUCCESS
# IN IMPERIAL CHINA

*Aspects of Social Mobility, 1368–1911*

SCIENCE EDITIONS ®

John Wiley & Sons, Inc., New York

First Science Editions printing 1964

Science Editions Trademark Reg. U. S. Pat. Off.

Publication as a Science Editions paperback authorized
by Columbia University Press.

The East Asian Institute was established by Columbia University in 1949 to prepare graduate students for careers dealing with East Asia, and to aid research and publication on East Asia during the modern period. The research program of the East Asian Institute is conducted or directed by faculty members of the University, by other scholars invited to participate in the program of the Institute, and by candidates for the Certificate of the Institute or the degree of Doctor of Philosophy. Some of the products of the research program are published as Studies of the East Asian Institute. The faculty of the Institute, without necessarily agreeing with the conclusions reached in the Studies, hope with their publication to perform a national service by increasing American understanding of the peoples of East Asia, the development of their societies, and their current problems.

The faculty of the East Asian Institute are grateful to the Rockefeller Foundation and the Ford Foundation for the financial assistance which they have given to the program of research and publication.

*Dedicated to the Memory of My Father*

# FOREWORD

THIS volume is the first in a series of scholarly works in the social sciences through which Columbia University seeks to increase understanding of East Asia in recent times. The author, Professor Ping-ti Ho of the University of British Columbia, did a substantial part of the research on which the book is based while a Senior Research Fellow at the East Asian Institute of Columbia University in 1958–59, using the rich holdings of the Ming and Ch'ing periods in Columbia's East Asiatic Library.

The past two decades have seen a growing interest in China's social and economic history. With his pioneering works on "The Salt Merchants of Yangchou: A Study of Commercial Capitalism in Eighteenth-century China" (*Harvard Journal of Asiatic Studies* XVII [June, 1954], 130–68) and *Studies on the Population of China, 1368–1953* (Cambridge, Mass., Harvard University Press, 1959), to mention only two of his recent contributions, Professor Ho has been a leader in this movement to broaden the scope of modern research in Chinese history.

The nature and extent of social mobility in China have long interested historians and social scientists, since answers to these questions may provide a deeper understanding of the nature of Chinese society. The questions have strong political overtones, and the issues have been much debated during the past two decades. One may venture the assertion that Professor Ho's research on social mobility in Ming and Ch'ing times is the most comprehensive to date, covering as it does a period of nearly half a millennium and exploring systematically a far wider range of Chinese sources than has been used by other scholars who have dealt with the subject.

Professor Ho is interested in social realities. Convinced that Chinese legal texts do not always accurately reflect true social conditions, he has explored many types of literature contemporary with the period under review. Columbia's most unusual collection of genealogies, obituaries, and commemorative volumes is an example of the little-used materials he has employed.

Although the work is centered upon social mobility, it is no less a contribution to institutional history. In his effort to uncover social realities, Professor Ho deals—among many other topics—with the system of family-status registration in Ming times, certain less known aspects of the Ming-Ch'ing examination and academic-degree system, the working of community schools and private academies, and the origins of community chests which subsidized the travel of promising candidates for the civil service examinations. Much of his discussion of these and other topics is based upon local histories and other local materials which provide information unavailable in documents of national scope. A detailed knowledge of institutions and their regional variations is a prerequisite to the interpretation of numerical data.

That Professor Ho has been able to assemble such a large amount of numerical data for a period stretching back five hundred years may surprise students of European history. Data of similar quality and quantity probably do not exist for any European society before the nineteenth century.

C. MARTIN WILBUR
*Director, East Asian Institute*

*January, 1962*

# PREFACE

FOR students of Ming-Ch'ing social and institutional history there exists a sizable body of sources of unusual quality. The most systematic of these sources are the lists of *chin-shih* (holders of the highest academic degree who almost automatically became middle-ranking officials). These lists provide accurate information regarding candidates' ancestry for three generations. The forty-eight such lists available yield a total of 12,226 cases and cover reasonably well the whole period from 1371, when the first *chin-shih* examination was held under the Ming, to 1904, after which the time-honored civil service examination system was abolished. These supply the present study with the main body of its statistics but are supplemented by twenty lists of *chü-jen* and *kung-sheng* (holders of intermediate academic degrees who had the right to minor official appointment) of the last hundred years of the Ch'ing period, yielding a total of 23,480 cases, and by three lists of *sheng-yüan* (holders of the elementary academic degree who had no right to minor government appointment) of lower Yangtze. Two of the *sheng-yüan* lists cover the period from 1644 to 1904 and one the entire Ming-Ch'ing period from 1368 onward. A statistical study of socio-academic mobility at its elementary, intermediate, and higher levels forms the warp of this study.

The weft consists primarily of an evaluation of various types of qualitative evidence, such as government statutes, local histories, biographies, genealogies, social novels, works by contemporary observers of social and family affairs, and the like. Although most of them are non-quantifiable, they nevertheless throw important light on aspects of social mobility in general, such as the virtual absence of effective legal and social barrier to the movement of individuals and families from one status to another, the existence of a number of institutionalized and non-institutional factors which had a bearing on mobility, the long-range social and economic leveling of prominent families and clans, and the permeation of segments of the population with certain social concepts and myths conducive to social mobility. The major conclusions of this book, on socioacademic mobility as well as on general mobility, are drawn from the interpretation, appraisal, and integration of the _aggregate_ evidence, both statistical and qualitative.

While the subtitle of the book indicates my intellectual indebtedness to social sciences in general and to sociology in particular, I must make it clear that the emphasis of this study is upon certain organic aspects of social and institutional history rather than on historical sociology. It goes without saying that historical data, however good in quality and substantial in quantity, seldom are of the same kind as those required by contemporary sociological surveys. The historian cannot, like the sociologist, specify his data by designing elaborate questionnaires and by carrying out field surveys. Besides, the classification of statistics and the interpretation of a number of social phenomena require a detailed discussion of certain aspects of institutional history which, though it is likely to be laborious and tedious reading for social scientists, is vital to historians. As it turns out, this book deals as much with phases of social mobility as with institutional history, focusing, as it does, on the social composition of the officialdom. I have debated seriously whether the subtitle of the book should not be changed in order to prevent misunderstanding, but I have finally chosen to retain it chiefly because I have made use of the theoretical framework enlarged and improved upon during the past fifteen years by writers on social mobility.

Few topics are more challenging and revealing than a study of the blood circulation, so to speak, of a large and complex historical society over a span of five and a half centuries. Social composition of the ruling class and other more general aspects of social mobility have always had a high priority in my long-range research project on Ming and early Ch'ing history. The work on social mobility began in the late fall of 1954, almost as soon as I had found a preliminary explanation for a great historical puzzle, the growth of China's population during Ming-Ch'ing times.

In preparing the present study I have benefited throughout the years from discussion and association with scholars of various disciplines. I am indebted to my colleagues at the University of British Columbia, Mr. Neal Harlow, the Librarian, for securing general and rare materials indispensable to this study, Professors Harry B. Hawthorn, Cyril Belshaw, Kasper D. Naegele, and Bernard R. Blishen of the Department of Anthropology and Sociology for consultation during the formative stage, and Professor Marion B. Smith of the Department of English for editorial help. I must express my special thanks to Mr. T'ung-tsu Ch'ü, formerly of Columbia University, now of Harvard University, who has most fruitfully combined sociology with sinology, for a long series of discussions dating as far back as 1945, to Professor Bernard Barber of Barnard College and Dr. Elinor Barber for reading the first draft of the introductory chapter, to Professor Mary C. Wright of Yale University for reading the whole manuscript, and to Professor Sylvia L. Thrupp, editor of *Comparative Studies in Society and History*, and Professor Vernon K. Dibble, both of the University of Chicago, for their special articles commenting on my interim report on the subject, which have helped to clarify certain basic concepts. My thanks are also due Miss Elisabeth L. Shoemaker of Columbia University Press for her editorial work.

I owe much to the members of the Division of Orientalia of the Library of Congress, the East Asian Library of Columbia University, and the Harvard-Yenching Institute Library of Harvard University for their generous help. Dr. K'ai-ming Ch'iu, Director of Harvard-Yenching Library, has never failed to comply with my numerous interlibrary requests. I am also grateful to Mr. Chiang Fu-ts'ung, Director of National Central Library, and his associate Mr. Peter Ch'ang, and to Mr. Wang I-fei, Deputy-Director of the National Library of Peking, for the reproduction of some twenty extremely rare Ming and early Ch'ing *chin-shih* lists.

This study could not have been carried out without three grants for summer research from the President's Committee on Research of the University of British Columbia and a whole year's senior research fellowship which the East Asian Institute of Columbia University generously offered me. During my fellowship year at Columbia between September, 1958, and the end of August, 1959, I benefited greatly from constant association with Professor C. Martin Wilbur and other members of the Institute. I am especially grateful to Professor G. William Skinner, then at Columbia and now with Cornell, for his invaluable technical comments. I hope that this book may be a small memento of the happy and fruitful year I spent at my Alma Mater.

PING-TI HO

*May, 1961*
*Vancouver, B. C.*

# CONTENTS

# TABLES

*THE LADDER OF SUCCESS*
*IN IMPERIAL CHINA*

# CHAPTER I

# SOCIAL IDEOLOGY AND SOCIAL STRATIFICATION

IN its formative stage social ideology often reflects, in part, social realities. Since the major Chinese philosophical schools were all products of a late feudal age, the social ideologies which constituted an integral part of those schools were all more or less tinged with feudal ideals and shaped by a feudal environment. And, since the dynamic, many-sided changes in late feudal China created a wide range of problems which called for new solutions, the major schools, with their different attitudes towards the declining feudal order, came up with theories and proposals as diverse as the problems themselves. At one extreme, the Confucians harked back to the much idealized ancient kings and earnestly hoped to defend and strengthen the time-honored feudal system. At the other extreme, the Legalists endeavored to repudiate the existing order and to replace it with a unitary state and authoritarian society. While within the scope of the present study it is impossible to review in full the contents of the major ancient social ideologies, it is necessary to discuss a basic antithesis common to all.

## THE BASIC ANTITHESIS

Briefly stated, this antithesis consists of two fundamental oppositions. On one hand, society is necessarily hierarchical, that is, its component classes must have unequal rights and obligations, an essentially feudal concept which is derived from historical experience. On the other hand, a hierarchical society cannot survive indefinitely unless its inherent injustice is substantially mitigated if not entirely eliminated, a concept which transcends feudal boundaries. As will be seen, the eventual merger of the various ancient social ideologies and the attempts at resolving this basic antithesis have profoundly influenced the character and structure of Chinese society during the past two thousand years.

Unlike that of the ancient Greeks, who had democratically governed city-states in one stage of their political and social evolution, the outlook of the ancient Chinese was shackled by their feudal heritage. The concept of equality in its ancient Greek and modern Western sense is almost entirely lacking in feudal and post-feudal China. The point of departure in the Confucian social ideology is that all things, including human beings, are by nature unequal.[1] Confucius (551–479 B.C.) and his chief exponents believed that men differ greatly in intelligence, ability, and moral character. The natural hierarchy of men thus fitted in nicely with the feudal hierarchy of their times. They stressed the fundamental difference between gentlemen (*chün-tzu*), who are interested in only what is morally right, and inferior men (*hsiao-jen*), whose sole concern is self-interest. It was their opinion that the former should rule over the latter and that the differences between them in social functions, rights, obligations, and styles of life are therefore justified.

Mo-tzu (*ca.* 479–381 B.C.), a philosopher of humble social origin who attacked the Confucians and the hereditary privileges of the nobility, nonetheless saw the need of a hierarchical society. He said:

For the rulers to go to court early and retire late to listen to lawsuits and attend to government is their duty. For the gentlemen to exhaust the energy of their limbs and employ full wisdom of their minds to attend to court within and to collect taxes without from the passes, markets, and products from mountains, woods, and water and fields in order to fill up the granaries and the treasury is their duty. For the farmers to set out early and come back late, to sow seeds and plant trees in order to produce a large quantity of soy beans and millet is their duty. For the women to rise up at dawn and retire in night to weave and spin in order to produce much silk, flax linen, and cloth is their duty.[2]

The ideal state and society which Mo-tzu envisaged is one in which people of lowly status must obey absolutely the orders of their superiors.[3]

Another school of thought which had gradually been formulated since the time of the famous statesman Kuan-chung of the Ch'i state of the seventh century B.C. worked out a comprehensive theory of society and social classes. It is not easy to label this school of writers who in their attitudes towards the feudal society resemble the Confucians but who in their reliance on stratagems of political control heralded the coming of the Legalists. Their ideas eventually crystallized in the eclectic work *Kuan-tzu,* which is attributed to Kuan-chung but probably was not completed until the third century B.C. There can be little doubt, however, that certain chapters and passages, which with minor variations in wording are also found in the annals of the Ch'i state, reflected the social ideology of Kuan-chung's time.[4] Their advocacy of strict social distinctions may be illustrated by the following passages:

If the court is not respected, if the courtesies and distinctions between greater and inferior, and between age and youth are not observed, if just bounds are not kept, and if luxury of dress is not limited according to the rules for the classes; if everyone, chief and subjects, exceeds the limits of propriety, then respect for superiors and the government cannot be maintained.[5]

The book thus goes on to lay down elaborate sumptuary laws which define the rights, duties, and styles of life for various social classes.[6] The ideal society envisaged by Kuan-chung himself was the one in which the four major functional orders of commoners, namely, scholars, peasants, artisans, and merchants, should live in segregation and their status should be hereditary.[7]

With the passage of time the Legalist thinkers and statesmen of the fourth and third centuries B.C. took a social view vastly different from that expounded in the *Kuan-tzu.* The task of the Legalists was to abolish the various intermediate social classes between the ruler and the commoners and to deal a permanent blow to the hereditary feudal nobility. The aim was to create a unitary state, with all powers concentrated in the hands of the absolutist ruler. Although they brought an important new element into ancient Chinese political and social theories, namely, that all the people should have equal rights and duties as subjects of the ruler, the demarcation between the ruling and ruled classes became even sharper. For once the time-honored customary protections for the intermediate and lowly feudal classes were swept away, members of these classes were to be reduced to mere tools of the absolutist ruler and of those who assisted him in ruling. The Lord of Shang, one of the most successful of Legalist statesmen of the fourth century B.C., said: "Farming, trade, and office are the three permanent functions of the state. Farmers open up the soil, merchants import products, officials rule the people."[8] "The crowning phase of order," said Han Fei-tzu, the synthesizer of the Legalist school of the late third century B.C., should be found in a society in which "high and low do not trespass upon each other; the fool and the wise, each being content with his own lot, keep the scale and stand in perfect balance." [9]

It is clear, therefore, that neither the Confucian idealists, who hoped to defend the feudal order, the school of political strategists whose ideas crystallized in the book *Kuan-tzu,* the followers of Mo-tzu, who attacked certain feudal privileges but tried to salvage the rest, nor the Legalists, who did so much to hasten the death of feudalism, abandoned the idea of an unequal society. Although they differed widely in attitudes towards the various intermediate social classes, they all agreed on a sharp demarcation between the ruling and ruled classes. Even the Legalists' insistence on legal equality for commoners resulted in a most authoritarian state and society, which, if it theoretically did away with ancient estates and privileges, further polarized the governing and the governed and justified institutionalized inequality between the two. The only philosophical school that abandoned the idea of hierarchical society entirely was the Taoist. For the Taoist philosophers all things are equal metaphysically. As long as human beings, animals, plants, and rocks live in accordance with their own natures, the problem of high and low, right and wrong, large and small, powerful and humble does not exist.[10] Yet precisely because of their antisocial attitudes, which border on anarchism, they left no permanent imprint on traditional Chinese social ideology. It is likely that not until after the opening of China by the West in the 1840s did the Chinese for the first time come across the modern Western concept of social and political equality.[11]

In contrast to their diverse views on society as a whole, the theories and proposals by which the various schools attempted to resolve a common antithesis in their social ideologies are fairly similar. All of the schools realized that the feudal order which had long been in process of decay could not be salvaged unless the injustice inherent in the feudal system was effectively redressed. Confucius found that the natural hierarchy of men, based on differences in intelligence, ability, and moral character, came into direct conflict with the feudal hierarchy, based on status at birth. The means by which this conflict can be resolved, as he saw it, were two. First, the high and low alike must observe the principle of rectification of names. In other words, every status has its name as well as its actuality and the name must accord to its actuality. Thus a prince, in addition to holding princely status and privileges, must also fulfil the various obligations entailed by his princely status. The same should hold for other social classes. Failing this, a prince would disqualify himself as a prince and would be little different from a villein. When this theory is pushed to its logical extreme, we find Mencius' justification of a people's right to revolt against a tyrannical prince. This theory, however, rested entirely on a moral sanction which was known by events of Confucius' time to be largely ineffectual.

The second and in the long run more effective way to rationalize the hierarchical society, as Confucius suggested, was to select members of the ruling class on the basis of individual merit. For he believed that political and social disorder or degeneration usually starts from the top stratum of a state or society. The ruler and his officials can be likened to the wind and the commoners to the grass. When the wind blows, the grass bends. If *chün-tzu,* the morally superior men by Confucian definition, serve in government, peace, order, and justice will result. Although in his many references to the term *chün-tzu* he uses it in both the traditional sense, meaning people of high status, and the new sense, meaning people of superior knowledge and moral quality, there can be little doubt that he leans towards the latter.[12] In fact, when Confucius' whole system of thought is analyzed, it is obvious that he regards rule by the wise and virtuous as the very foundation of good government.

The question is therefore how to distinguish and select the intellectually and morally superior from the mediocre and mean-minded. That men are not born equal in intelligence and capacity is taken for granted by Confucius; but under feudalism most men, including many who were naturally gifted, lacked the opportunity for education. Confucius' proposal is therefore to offer the high and the low equal opportunity of education. For only thus can superior men be distinguished and selected from the rest. Hence Confucius' immortal saying: "In education there should be no class distinctions." [13] Mencius (371–289 B.C.), the foremost exponent of Confucius, citing ancient practices which being legendary were beyond proof, argued that it is the duty of the state to set up schools at various levels for the education of the people.[14] When it is remembered that up to his lifetime education had practically been a monopoly of the hereditary feudal nobility, Confucius, who endeavored to implement his doctrine by offering equal scholastic and moral instruction to all his disciples irrespective of their social origin, should indeed be credited with the first step towards social and intellectual emancipation. Thus, by attempting to perpetuate the feudal system, Confucius and his followers actually heralded the arrival of a new social order, based not on hereditary status but on individual merit. While upholding a hierarchical society, they concerned themselves with means to tackle its inherent injustice and bring about social equity mainly through education. This is why the Confucian social ideology transcends feudal boundaries and has remained useful long after the break-up of the feudal system.

During the two and a half centuries after Confucius' death, China underwent profound political, social, and economic changes. The break-up of the feudal system seemed impending. If the old order was to be partially salvaged, a more thoroughgoing theory of reform was required. Because of the changing times and his humble social origin, Mo-tzu offered a rationale which, if less subtle than Confucius', is more drastic and unqualified:

In administering the government, the ancient sage-kings ranked the morally excellent high and exalted the virtuous. If capable, even a farmer or artisan would be employed—commissioned with high rank, remunerated with liberal emoluments, trusted with important charges, and empowered to issue final orders. For, if his rank were not high, people would not respect him; if his emoluments were not liberal, people would not have confidence in him; if his orders were not final, people would not stand in awe before him. . . . Therefore ranks should be standardized according to virtue, tasks assigned according to office, and rewards given according to labour spent. When emoluments are distributed in proportion to achievements, officials cannot be in constant honour, and people in eternal humility.[15]

Thus the continued existence of a hierarchical society, with its sharp demarcation between the ruling and ruled, can be completely justified by the principle that status should be determined by achievement and virtue.

As compared with the age of Confucius when the interstate balance of power, chivalry, and social deference still lingered, the fourth and third centuries B.C. were a period of cutthroat struggle among seven Contending States, of growing Machiavellianism, and of increasing social mobility. There are famous instances of talented men of humble birth who became prime ministers and eminent statesmen. By this period the idea that social status should be determined mainly by individual merit had become deep-rooted. The Lord of Shang, for example, stated that "profits and emoluments, office and rank should be determined exclusively by military merit" and that "in neither high nor low offices should there be an automatic hereditary succession." The only other kind of merit to be recognized by the Legalist state was effort to enhance agricultural production which, like the army, would make the state self-sufficient and powerful.[16]

The sharply changing times brought about a marked change of tone within the Confucian school. Hsün-tzu, the leading Confucian thinker of the third century B.C., went so far as to say that "although a man is a descendant of a king, duke, prefect or officer, if he does not observe the rites of proper conduct and justice, he must be relegated to the common ranks; although he is a descendant of a commoner, if he have acquired learning, developed a good character, and is able to observe the rules of good conduct and justice, then elevate him to be minister, prime minister, officer, or prefect." [17] This was regarded by him as the very foundation of a "kingly government."

It is Hsün-tzu who, among ancient Chinese philosophers, had a deeper insight into sociological phenomena and formulated the most comprehensive theory in which the basic antithesis common to all the above-mentioned schools is resolved:

What is men's pleasure and purpose? To be honourable as the emperor, to be so wealthy as to own the country—this is what men's passions alike desire. But if men's desires are given rein, then their authority could not be endured, and things would not be sufficient to satisfy them. Hence the ancient Kings invented the rules of proper conduct and justice for men in order to divide them; causing them to have the classes of noble and base, the disparity between the aged and the young, and the distinction between the wise and the stupid, the able and the powerless; all to cause men to assume their duties and each one to get his proper position. This is the way of living in society and having harmony and unity. For when the benevolent man is in control, the farmers by their strength will be experts at the fields; the merchants by their knowledge of values will be experts at using wealth; all kinds of artisans by their skill will be experts at using tools; none of those above the grade of Officer and Prefect, up to the Duke and Marquis will fail to fulfil the duties of their office according to benevolence, generosity, wisdom and power—then this will be called the *ultimate equity*. Then whether a man's emolument is the whole empire, he will not think it too much for himself; or whether he is a gate-keeper, receiver of guests, keeper of gate-bar, or night watchman, he will not think it too little for himself. Hence it is said: Irregular but uniform, oppressive but favourable, unlike but alike—these are human relationships.[18]

By the third century B.C. at the latest, therefore, the various schools of thought, despite their prolonged mutual recriminations, had actually found a common formula in their social ideologies. Through the principle of individual merit their common antithesis is resolved. The only theoretical problem that remains to be briefly explained is how merit was defined by the various schools and how the diverse definitions for merit eventually merged.

Among the major schools only the Legalists clearly defined two kinds of merit, agricultural and military. The Confucians and followers of Mo-tzu were rather nebulous in their merit definitions. From their main teachings, however, it is possible to know the chief qualities which each of them esteemed. For the Confucians merit or virtue consisted mainly of learning, administrative ability, and such moral qualities as human-heartedness, righteousness, uprightness, and conscientiousness. For followers of Mo-tzu merit or virtue included such things as universal love, pacifism, frugality, and religious faith to deliver the mass of the people from want and misery. While it is true that the latter passionately attacked the former for their reluctance to practice universal love, justification of the pompous style of life of the upper classes, and emphasis on cultural rather than utilitarian values, yet because of the flexibility of the Confucian doctrine the difference between these two schools' merit concept is one of degree, not of kind. The Confucians, by grading love and by extending it through successive stages from oneself to the whole society, actually meet Mo-tzu's central doctrine of universal love more than halfway. For the Confucian human-heartedness is love between men, and conscientiousness means an extension of that love from close to remote relations. If the Confucians do not openly preach a doctrine of austere living, they at least advocate reasonable frugality for the ruling class and well understand that sufficiency in food and security of property are requisites to the cultivation of sense of honor and the maintenance of an orderly society. The only abiding difference is therefore between the Confucian humanists' appreciation of cultural values and Mo-tzu's deep religiosity, extreme austerity, and anti-cultural bias. It was partly because of the uncompromising stand of the followers of Mo-tzu that they gradually petered out as a school after China had become a unified empire.

For some time it seemed as though the school of Legalists was to triumph over other schools of thought. However, the first unified empire established by the Ch'in state, which had embodied Legalist teachings more fully than others, was of very short duration. After the founding of the long-lasting Han Empire in 206 B.C. the various schools of thought, particularly the Confucianist and the Legalist, tended to merge. While it was necessary for the unified empire to rely on the rule of law rather than on lofty Confucian moral principles, the harsh aspects of Legalism had to be softened and cloaked by Confucianism. On account of its common sense, humanism, catholicity, flexibility, and ability to assimilate useful teachings of other schools, Confucianism gradually overshadowed all its ancient rivals. Furthermore, its advocacy of a hierarchical society served the imperial government so well that during the period of intensified autocracy under Han Wu-ti (140–87 B.C.) Confucianism finally received imperial patronage and established its primacy over other schools. Since a strong centralized government took but limited cognizance of hereditary privileges, the Han rulers provided certain *ad hoc* means to recruit members of the ruling class, thus partially resolving the antithesis that had been a common feature of all major ancient social ideologies.

The merger of the merit concepts of various ancient schools may best be evidenced by the multifarious standards by which the Han government recruited officials, particularly local officials, through the recommendatory system. After 134 B.C. provincial and local authorities were regularly required to recommend meritorious men for government service. Occasionally central officials were also asked to recommend junior central officials. The major categories of men thus recommended or officially extolled were: (1) *hsiao-t'i li-t'ien,* men known for their filial piety, fraternal love, industry, and skill on the field, (2) *hsiao-lien,* men known for filial piety and incorruptibility, (3) *hsiu-ts'ai* or *mao-ts'ai,* men of unusual talent and ability, and (4) *hsien-liang fang-cheng* and *wen-hsüeh,* men known for their upright character capable of candid remonstrance, and men of literary attainments. In addition, some irregularly recruited minor categories included *ming-ching,* men with special knowledge of the classics, and those well versed in military affairs, cosmology, astrology, and such things as natural anomalies and calamities. During the brief interregnum of Wang Mang (9 B.C.–A.D. 24) several thousand men of "merit" were called to the imperial capital, among whom were astronomers, arithmeticians, musical experts, etymologists, historians, specialists in occult prognostics, herbalists, and natural historians.[19]

The merit concept remained very broad in scope during subsequent periods. For example, the systematic treatise on talents written by Liu Shao during the second quarter of the third century A.D. listed twelve categories of talents useful for government service, which were based on three basic qualities, namely, moral character, knowledge of the "laws," and proficiency in "methods" and "techniques" of political control and administration.[20] This is therefore a perfect mixture of Confucian and Legalist concepts. Between 657 and 828, as a learned late Ming scholar points out, there were no fewer than sixty itemized merits with which the imperial T'ang government recruited officials in order to supplement those chosen by the competitive civil-service examination system. Although such itemized merits were described very metaphorically, they were broadly related to moral character, literary training, administrative ability, and knowledge of military affairs. So broad was the T'ang merit concept that the state even wanted to recruit those proficient in musical principles, hermits with philosophical inclinations, and those extremely upright characters who would not hesitate to die as martyrs in case of necessity.[21]

With the passage of time, however, the merit concept appeared to become narrower until during a greater part of the Ming-Ch'ing period it boiled down to a knowledge of classics, stereotyped theories of administration, and literary attainments. The reasons for the long-range change in the concept of merit are complex but deserve a brief analysis.

First, the Han and post-Han recommendatory system, though theoretically based on a broad merit concept, more often than not failed to serve an important social and political function. The majority of those who entered government service through the Han recommendatory system were existing minor officials or descendants of officials and members of scholarly families. An exhaustive modern study shows that among those who entered government through the recommendatory channel and left biographical information rather few were of poor or non-scholarly families.[22] With the waning of central government authority and the ever-increasing influence of prominent local clans from the late second century A.D. onwards, the recommendatory system came to be more and more abused until it simply became a useful tool by which the powerful clans could perpetuate themselves.

Owing to its scandals and failure as a channel for social mobility the Han recommendatory system was discontinued for some time after the downfall of the Later Han Empire in 220 A.D. In its stead a new official, known as *chung-cheng* (literally "impartial and upright"), was appointed for each prefecture, whose function was to canvass and place talented men of the area into nine grades for the purpose of bureaucratic recruitment.[23] Although at first the new system aimed at rectifying the mistakes of the Han recommendatory system, it was soon abused to the extent that official grading was in general based on the candidate's family status.

After A.D. 316 North China was lost to the barbarians and the country was politically divided. Although some barbarian groups carried on a determined struggle against a number of prominent Chinese clans which chose to remain in the north and which were often armed for self-defense, the most successful of the aliens, such as the Ti people who founded the Ch'in state between 351 and 394 and the T'o-pa clan of the Hsien-pi people who founded the durable Northern Wei Empire (386–534), realized the importance of winning the support of powerful Chinese clans. Under the fundamental Northern Wei policy of racial and political compromise prominent Chinese clans shared spoils with the Hsien-pi tribal nobility and perpetuated themselves by holding high positions in civil administration.[24] The Chinese dynasties in the south (317–589) depended so much on the support of influential native southern clans and prominent northern clans which had migrated to the south since the beginning of barbarian invasion that the social order, particularly the upper strata, became hardened.[25] While it is true that even during the period of political domination by aristocratic clans in the north as well as in the south high positions were still not entirely closed against the humble, ambitious, and able,[26] for nearly three centuries high status was in general hereditary.

Second, after China was reunified under the House of Sui in 589, which was soon succeeded by the T'ang dynasty (618–907), there was the need to establish certain objective standards by which officials should be selected. The competitive civil-service examination system was therefore instituted.[27] In early T'ang times there were examinations for six different kinds of men, namely, *hsiu-ts'ai,* men of unusual talents and ability, *ming-ching,* men with a good knowledge of the classics, *ming-fa,* men well versed in legal matters, *ming-shu,* men skilled in calligraphy, *ming-suan,* men proficient in arithmetic, and *chin-shih,* literally "advanced scholars," who have usually been regarded by Western scholars as "doctors of letters." All except the last category can be traced back to Han times save for the fact that these titles or degrees now had to be earned through examination. The scope of the merit concept reflected by these examinations was not narrow. Moreover, recommendations of men of a very wide range of merit were made sporadically from time to time.[28]

Through trial and error, however, these were narrowed down to the *chin-shih* examination only, which was first established in the Ta-yeh period (605–618) and which perpetuated itself right down to 1904. There are several reasons for this change. For one thing, the early T'ang *hsiu-ts'ai* degree imposed such high standards of excellence on the candidates that very few could obtain it. It was discontinued sometime in the Chen-kuan period (627–649).[29] The examinations in arithmetic, calligraphy, and law were too specialized to serve as major channels of official recruitment. For a century or so after the founding of the T'ang the two important academic degrees were *ming-ching* and *chin-shih*. The curriculum for the *ming-ching* degree consisted of three tests. The first required the completion by the candidate from memory of ten test passages (*t'ieh*) from each of the following classics, namely, either the record of ritual *Li-chi* or the history of feudal states *Tso-chuan*, the treatise on filial piety *Hsiao-ching*, the Confucian analects *Lun-yü*, and the work on semantics *Erh-ya*. The candidate was given several words as a clue and could pass this first test by completing five or more of the ten test passages for each of the four classics. The second test consisted of oral interpretation of ten passages selected from classics, of which correct answers to six or more were required. The third test required a fairly lucid exposition in essay form of three assigned problems dealing with current affairs or aspects of administration, which was called *ts'e*. The main difference of the *chin-shih* curriculum was that it required less memorizing of the classics, two more essays on current affairs or administration, and the substitution for oral interpretation of the classics of an essay, a piece of rhymed prose (*fu*), and poems.

Professor Ts'en Chung-mien has explained satisfactorily the reasons why in the course of time *ming-ching* as an academic qualification failed to command respect and why the *chin-shih* degree alone came to be highly prized.[30] Briefly stated, the emphasis in the *ming-ching* curriculum was on mechanical memorization, while that in the *chin-shih* curriculum was on creative writing. Memorization was so much easier than imaginative literary writing that contemporaries soon likened *ming-ching* candidates to parrots. The oral examination for *ming-ching* candidates lacked objective standards and was prone to scandals or collusion. Since on the average not more than thirty *chin-shih* degrees were granted annually, a number which was much smaller than those of the *chin-shih* quotas of later periods,[31] the degree was very hard to get. It was so hard to get that contemporaries had the saying that one should be considered as lucky and "young" if he obtained the *chin-shih* degree at the age of fifty, while a person obtaining the much easier *ming-ching* degree at the age of thirty might indeed be regarded as "old." [32] So highly prized was the *chin-shih* degree that many members of the aristocracy who had other means of entering government service nevertheless vied with commoners in securing it. To mention an extreme case, a late T'ang emperor had made for himself a wooden tablet to be hung in front of his palace hall on which his personal name and the fictitious *chin-shih* title were inscribed.[33] Moreover, in spite of the changes in prose style, T'ang state documents were usually written in the highly exacting and sophisticated parallel style (*pien-t'i*). Since no other category of candidates required as high a standard of literary proficiency as *chin-shih,* it became apparent in the course of time that *chin-shih* had much better chances of rising to responsible or pivotal government positions. Thus of all early T'ang degrees only *chin-shih* commanded social prestige and was able to perpetuate itself in later periods.

Third, while superficially the T'ang and post-T'ang *chin-shih* curriculum seems to have been a drastic departure from the earlier merit concept, a closer scrutiny of the problems reveals that the difference was much smaller than is usually imagined. In the first place, in T'ang and Sung times the wide range of itemized merits on which men were recommended for state service served rather an ornamental than a real purpose, because not many men entered government through this channel. The only exception was the first seventy years or so of the Ming period (1368–1644) when the government demand for officials was almost insatiable. At this time the recommendatory system occasionally overshadowed the examination in importance as a means of selecting officials. But once the bureaucracy was saturated, the Ming government relied almost solely on the examination system for its routine recruitment of officials.[34] For whatever the limitations of the examination system, it was more objective and less open to particularistic influence than the recommendatory system. Moreover, ever since the rise of the *chin-shih* examination as a major channel of official recruitment there had been a long series of debates on the relative merits of examinations and other methods of selection. The issue was debated most thoroughly in the latter half of the eleventh century. While some prominent early Sung statesmen advocated drastic revision in the *chin-shih* curriculum or even its eventual abolition, no permanent change was brought about. By far the most balanced of the controversial views on educational theories and methods of selecting officials was expressed by the great poet Su Shih (1036–1101). He argued that from the strictly utilitarian point of view neither prose, poetry, nor essays on problems of statecraft (which were usually based on stereotyped ancient opinions) had anything directly to do with efficient administration, but within China's cultural tradition the *chin-shih* curriculum still remained the best that could have been designed. He pointed out that, in spite of the relative remoteness of the *chin-shih* curriculum from actual administrative needs, it had nonetheless produced many successful officials and prominent statesmen since its inception in Sui-T'ang times, an indication that it was a reasonably good method of selecting officials.[35] In fact, this late eleventh-century controversy so thoroughly exhausted the subject that no fresh opinions were expressed in subsequent periods until the inadequacies of the traditional studies in meeting the challenge of the West were fully exposed in the mid-nineteenth century. For in principle at least the range of knowledge required for passing the *chin-shih* examination was not actually narrow and the curriculum approximated fairly closely to the Confucian ideal of liberal education. Besides, while at its worst candidates with a touch of luck could pass it by parrotlike rehashing of highly stereotyped ancient principles and ideals, the sufficiently liberal education preparatory to taking the examinations not infrequently equipped candidates with common sense and sound judgment, qualities which were essential to the making of good administrators, especially in an age when comparatively simple administrative problems required no great amount of compartmentalized knowledge.

All in all, therefore, although the T'ang and post-T'ang examination system reflected a somewhat narrower concept of merit than the ancient recommendatory system, it achieved a far greater degree of objectivity than the latter. Professor Ts'en has conclusively shown that the perpetuation of *chin-shih* examinations was an outcome of empiricism rather than of the whims of certain T'ang rulers.[36]

After the competitive examination system became permanently institutionalized in T'ang times, the ancient principle that ruling-class membership should be determined on the basis of individual merit was firmly established in all subsequent periods. The only exceptions were the regional kingdoms founded by the alien Khitans and Juchens in North China between the late tenth and early thirteenth centuries and the Mongol Yüan dynasty (1260–1368). Even under the rule of these aliens the examinations were held, though irregularly.

In retrospect, although the various schools of thought all realized the importance of social equity in a society of unequal rights, the Confucian school alone tackled the problem at its base. For followers of Confucius were concerned not only with establishing merit as the basis of social status but with the creation of a just opportunity-structure for the poor and humble as well. As Confucius and his exponents realized, lack of educational opportunities often makes it impossible for poor men of superior native intelligence fully to demonstrate their worth. The truest form of social equity, the Confucian school believed, is educational equality, without which a society cannot in the long run justify the unequal rights, obligations, and functions assigned to its component classes.

As Confucianism established its primacy over other schools during the reign of Han Wu-ti, an imperial academy was set up in the national capital as a preliminary step towards the implementation of the true spirit of Confucianism. Save for a few prefectural and local schools established by some "model" officials, education in Han times was beyond the reach of the broad mass of the people. The situation remained essentially the same up to the eleventh century.[37] By the eleventh century more schools were established in large provincial and prefectural cities and a number of private academies began to appear, although in comparison with Ming-Ch'ing times the total number of schools was still rather small. At the beginning of the Ming period the Confucian ideal was carried a step forward by repeated imperial exhortations that a public (government) school be set up in every county and prefecture, except in aboriginal districts, and that elementary village schools be established through community effort. The continual improvement in the art of printing and the mushrooming growth of private academies in Ming times further broadened educational opportunities.[38] While it is true that in no period of Chinese history was the Confucian ideal of equality of educational opportunity fully realized, the Ming-Ch'ing period drew closer to it than all previous dynasties. As time went on, the basic social antithesis that had been tackled by various ancient schools of thought was more effectively, though still far from completely, resolved.

SOCIAL STRATIFICATION

While common social experience accounted for the similarity in principles of social stratification found in all major ancient schools of thought, the principle is best stated by the Confucians. As Confucianism established its orthodoxy from the late second century B.C. onwards, the Confucian theory of social stratification, most clearly and emphatically stated by Mencius, has served as a general guiding principle for the past twenty centuries. He says: "Some labor with their minds and some labor with their physical strength. Those who labor with their minds rule others, and those who labor with physical strength are ruled by others. Those who are ruled sustain others, and those who rule are sustained by others. This is a principle universally recognized." [39] With this sharp demarcation between the ruling and the ruled, based on mental and menial work, all major ancient schools of thought, such as the followers of Mo-tzu, the school of political strategists who expressed their ideas in the book *Kuan-tzu,* and the Legalists, concurred.

The exalted status of the ruling officialdom can be shown by a wide range of symbolic distinctions which differed in detail from one period to another but which always set it apart from the commoners. In the Ming-Ch'ing period these symbols extended to practically every aspect of an official's life, from the style of his garments, residence, horse carriage, sedan chair, and number of guards and servants when he was on the road, right down to the minute specifications for his funeral and grave. Within the hereditary nobility and bureaucracy such symbols were meticulously defined in accordance with rank. Moreover, members of the officialdom enjoyed other legal privileges. They were exempt from the labor services to which all commoners except degree-holders were liable. Theoretically they were supposed to live according to officialdom's code of honor, and hence were not subjected to the ordinary penal code and corporal punishments. Even in cases of violation of the law they could not be arrested without special imperial order. While many Ming-Ch'ing officials were imprisoned or sentenced to death, it is significant to note that the trial had to be preceded by an all-important ceremony in which they were deprived of their official ranks and therefore in theory relegated to the status of commoners.[40]

Below the ruling officialdom the nation at large was customarily classified into *ssu-min,* four major functional orders, namely, *shih,* scholars in a very loose sense, *nung,* those who engaged in agriculture, *kung,* artisans and craftsmen, and *shang,* merchants and tradesmen. This broad functional classification of commoners dates back at least to the late feudal age, as it is systematically expounded in *Kuan-tzu* and also in *Kuo-yü* (annals of feudal states).[41] As will be seen, this functional classification is too general to serve as a principle in social stratification.

Below the ordinary commoners there existed in Ming-Ch'ing times certain groups of "declassed" or "degraded" people who were numerically insignificant. They comprised the *yüeh-hu,* singers, dancers, and entertainers in Shansi and Shensi; the *kai-hu,* "beggars" in Kiangsu and Anhwei; the *to-min,* "lazy people" of Chekiang; the *tan-hu,* "boatmen" of Kwangtung; and the *shih-p'u,* "hereditary servants" of southern Anhwei. To these small regional "declassed" groups must be added the bonded servants of both sexes, prostitutes, actors and entertainers, and certain types of government runners who were scattered all over the country.[42] They were denied the rights given to ordinary commoners and intermarriage between them and ordinary commoners was legally prohibited.[43] They constituted, however, only a small fraction of one percent of the total population of the country and were legally emancipated by the edicts of the Yung-cheng Emperor (1723–35).[44] The completeness of their legal manumission may be evidenced by the right of their descendants, three generations after the enfranchisement, to take government examinations. Thus even the most serious of the discriminatory laws was removed and the main avenue of upward social mobility was opened for them. The fact that some of their descendants took full advantage of this social enfranchisement is shown by their purchase of Imperial-Academy studentships before the officially required period of transition expired.[45]

So much for the ideals of social order expressed in an array of juridical status. With regard to the actual application of the Mencian principle of social stratification, four basic considerations must be borne in mind. First, "the circumstance of a class being fairly stable in character, changing only slowly, may create a false impression that the membership is equally stable." [46] This is particularly true concerning the demarcation between the ruling bureaucracy and commoners. While at any given time the gulf separating the two seemed an awesome one indeed, the social composition of the former, especially after the competitive examination system became permanently institutionalized, was constantly changing. As will be demonstrated in subsequent chapters, distinctions of juridical status between the bureaucracy and commoners were merely lines of demarcation, lines that seldom constituted effective barriers to social mobility but could be crossed by men of ability and ambition.

Second, although the sequence of priority of the four major functional orders of commoners was legally defined, with scholars in the lead, followed by those engaged in agriculture, industries and crafts, and trade and commerce, it is extremely doubtful that it was strictly observed in any period of Chinese history. The relative importance of education, menial skill, and wealth as a determinant of social status is so complex that it deserves a systematic discussion in the following section.

Third, while the legal texts suggest that traditional Chinese society consisted mainly of two sharply opposed classes, namely, the ruling and the ruled, in actuality it was always a multi-class society. The ruling class was far from being socially homogeneous, as will be discussed later in this section. The quadruple functional division of commoners may have reflected in part late feudal ideals but is almost entirely useless for the stratification of post-feudal Chinese society. For example, in post-feudal China the term *nung,* which is often uncritically rendered as "peasants" or "farmers," actually included all those engaged in agriculture—large, medium, and small landlords, independent landowning peasants, peasants who owned very small parcels of land but had to rent additional land to be able to sustain their families, and tenants and agricultural workers. Similarly, the *kung* and *shang* categories must also be divided into various different status groups, ranging from small craftsmen to capitalist industrialists and from small tradesmen and peddlers to merchant princes. Commoners must therefore be stratified according to their occupation, wealth, income, education, style of life, and proximity to social prestige and power. Although the task of making a minute stratification of commoners is immensely complicated by the lack of systematic historical data on such multifarious criteria, it is obvious that the traditional Chinese society was always a multiple-class society.

Information is comparatively ample on the upper strata of commoners. The first academic degree conferred on the holder a privileged position as compared with the rest of commoners, as will be further discussed in more detail. In Ming-Ch'ing novels it was common for people to accord the polite address *yüan-wai* to a person of substantial property who might or might not be well educated or to refer to a family as *ta-hu* (large household) or *hsiao-hu* (small household) mainly though not exclusively on the basis of its economic standing. This shows that commoners themselves were class-conscious and that class distinctions were by no means based on the four legally defined functional orders. From 1451 onward the Ming state was compelled by financial necessity to confer honors on commoners who contributed grain or money for famine relief or for strengthening national defense. Those commoners who contributed several hundred *shih* (Chinese bushels) of grain were called *i-min* (philanthropic commoners). Because of their privilege of wearing a minor official's cap and attire and exemption from *corvée,* they gradually became *i-kuan* (philanthropic officials) in the eyes of commoners, although they were actually commoners.[47] Similarly, people of advanced age were officially honored and socially known first as *shou-min* (longevous commoners) and gradually as *shou-kuan* (longevous officials). Either age, personal integrity, wealth, or education could entitle a person to be honored by the local official as the main or secondary guest at the semiannual ceremonial banquet.[48] Thus within the vast body of commoners there was distinctly an "elite," which drew its sources from various functional orders, and the traditional Chinese society never consisted of only two polarized classes of the ruling and the ruled.

Fourth, in spite of the fact that officials were invariably those who labored with their minds, it is not true that all those who labored with their minds were members of the ruling bureaucracy. Indeed, the demarcation between those of the educated who entered government service and those of the educated who failed to break into the officialdom was no less fundamental than the gulf separating those who labored with their minds and those who labored with their physical strength. Since failure to distinguish these two categories of the educated has accounted for considerable confusion on the part of some modern writers when they attempt to describe the traditional Chinese stratification system and to define the "gentry" class, and since a major concern of the present study is mobility leading to officialdom, the composition of officialdom and the statuses of the two categories of the educated merit a systematic analysis.

In terms of privilege as distinct from political power the hereditary nobility stood at the apex of the society. It consisted of imperial clansmen and nonimperial noble houses created on account of meritorious services to the state or by special imperial favor and grace. In Ming times there were eight noble ranks for imperial clansmen. Only the eldest legitimate heir of the prince of the first or second rank inherited the title; the other sons were invested with a lower rank. From the third imperial noble rank downward even the eldest legitimate son could not maintain his father's rank and

was subject to a progressive descending scale. Under normal circumstances, therefore, the majority of imperial clansmen descended in
a matter of a few generations to the lowest noble rank, which entitled them to a modest annual stipend of 200 *shih* of grain, part of
which was paid in paper money that steadily depreciated in value.
In addition, it was fairly common for imperial clansmen to commit
crimes or misdemeanors, for which they were relegated permanently
to commoner rank. It was estimated by the famous official, historian,
and poet Wang Shih-chen (1526–90) that by the last quarter of the
sixteenth century the number of imperial clansmen had risen to
over 40,000, most of them social parasites.[49] While the relatively
few princes of the first and second ranks remained rich, powerful,
and not infrequently a menace to the people, a solution for the
problems of the majority of imperial clansmen was urgently needed.
After repeated requests from officials and imperial clansmen themselves the imperial descendants were eventually allowed in 1595
to take government examinations. It was not until 1622 that imperial clansmen produced their first *chin-shih*.[50]

The nonimperial Ming nobility did hardly better. So suspicious
were the early Ming rulers of the hereditary nobility and so cruel
the treatment they accorded it that by the late fifteenth century out
of six dukes and twenty-eight marquises created at the beginning of
the dynasty only one ducal family retained its title. In 1492, therefore, by special imperial grace the descendants of six meritorious
early Ming nobles were sought out and restored to their ranks.[51]

The imperial Ch'ing nobility was divided into twelve ranks and
subjected to a declining descent rule similar to that of Ming times.
When the son of a noble reached the twelfth and lowest rank, the
title ceased to be hereditary. The exceptions were that a very few
princes were given the right of perpetual inheritance and that the
descendants of princes of the top four ranks were protected by an
imperial edict of 1774 from descending below the seventh, eighth,
ninth, and tenth ranks respectively.[52]

These considerations, however, could not in the long run prevent
the imperial clansmen from slipping in the economic and social
scale. Their number had been multiplying constantly, and the majority of them had to be given opportunities for government service.

In 1724, therefore, special schools were established for them and students were given monthly stipends. In 1744 the better students were given the privilege of taking the metropolitan, or highest, examination without other requisites. They could either take the easier examination for translators (needed because Manchu government documents were written in both Manchu and Chinese) or the regular civil-service examination. Even when they took the latter their special curriculum was much simpler than that prescribed for ordinary candidates. This channel of mobility was closed in 1752 because of the fear of the Ch'ien-lung emperor (1736–95) that they might be so attracted by the prospect of an official career as to lose their martial tradition. However, his successor, the Chia-Ching emperor (1796–1820), realized the futility of the various half-hearted attempts to preserve Manchu nativism and issued a decree in 1799 permitting imperial clansmen once again to take the examination. In lieu of the ludicrously easy degrees which commanded no social respect conferred on them in the early Ch'ien-lung era, the law now provided that they had to take the provincial, or intermediate, examination first. When the metropolitan Chihli province held its examination in 1801 imperial clansmen were given a preferential quota of one successful candidate for every nine participants. The curriculum remained somewhat simpler than that for Chinese but a post-examination written test held in the palace prevented outright scandal. Since imperial clansmen had long been susceptible to Chinese cultural influence, the examination for translators was virtually abolished from 1819 onward.[53] Thenceforth a limited number of imperial clansmen entered government service through examinations.

Imperial clansmen could also enter government through *Tsung-jen-fu*, the Imperial Clansmen Court, as *bithesi*, or clerks. The entrance was easy because most of these clerical posts could be bought. By stages *bithesi* could be promoted to be censors of the circuits or supervisory censors of the six central administrative boards. But this channel was relatively narrow and crowded. An imperial edict of 1799 made it a permanent rule that the six boards should earmark small quotas of three grades of secretaries for imperial clansmen.[54] From these positions they could be transferred to provincial and local posts. In the main, therefore, imperial clansmen were better treated than in Ming times, and cases of downright self-degradation, rampant during the previous dynasty, were relatively few. But the broadened opportunities for government service by no means kept pace with the ever-increasing numbers of clansmen, nor did they basically alter the parasitic nature of their existence. This became obvious during the last hundred years of Manchu rule.

The nonimperial Ch'ing nobility, which was created mostly in reward for distinguished military service, consisted of nine ranks, the upper seven of which were each subdivided into three degrees. The duke, marquis, earl, and viscount roughly corresponded in status to the first rank in the officialdom. The baron corresponded to the second official rank, and the other four noble ranks to the third, fourth, and fifth official ranks.[55] All the noble ranks, except the ninth and lowest, were hereditary during a specified number of generations, ranging from twenty-six for a duke of the first degree to one for a noble of the eighth rank. In addition, the direct heirs of Confucius and a few other sages and worthies of the past were also given noble ranks. However, this small class of hereditary nobility did not command as much respect as high-ranking officials; a statute of the Board of Rites explicitly stated that "marquises, earls, viscounts, daughters of imperial princes of the first rank and their consorts cannot be compared in importance to first- and second-ranking officials of charge." Consequently, their sons were not given special quotas in the provincial examinations which had been customarily granted to sons of high officials.[56] In brief, the hereditary nobility in Ming-Ch'ing times should not be placed on an equal footing with traditional European aristocracy and must be regarded as a separate class of sinecure holders.

The bureaucracy proper can be divided into three strata. The upper stratum consisted of officials of the first, second, and third ranks who, among other things, had the power of recommending their subordinate officials and whose descendants had the *yin* (hereditary) privilege. The *yin* privilege, as will be discussed in detail in chapter IV, was normally limited to one descendant only and was not likely to go beyond two or three generations. The upper official stratum included the grand secretaries and associate grand secretaries (prime ministers in Ch'ing times), presidents and vice-presidents of the six boards, presidents, associate presidents and vice-presidents of the Censorate, and a number of other senior officials of the central government, governors general, governors, financial commissioners, and judicial commissioners of the provinces. Military officers of comparable ranks usually did not have the same power and status as their civil counterparts. This was especially true in Ming times.[57]

The middle stratum of the bureaucracy consisted of all officials from the seventh rank up to the fourth, ranging from heads of junior central courts and bureaus, censors, and secretaries of various central organs to intendants, prefects, and magistrates of departmental and ordinary counties. The lack of the right to recommend subordinate officials and the lack of *yin* privilege for their families marked them off from the top stratum, but they were officials of considerable responsibility and importance. The function of the seventh-ranking county magistrate, for example, included local fiscal and legal administration, maintenance of law and peace, and even supervision of local education. He was, so to speak, the "parent of the people."

The lower stratum of the bureaucracy consisted of all officials of the eighth and ninth ranks, such as assistant magistrates, deputy magistrates, submagistrates, county police-masters, jail wardens, etc. To a large host of these must be added unclassed clerks or sub-officials who could ascend to the lower classed ranks through seniority or special tests. The promotion of unclassed clerks and sub-officials was regarded as one of three "orthodox" avenues to bureaucracy in Ming times.[58] Officials of the eighth and ninth ranks were usually called *tso-tsa*, literally "auxiliary and miscellaneous." The directors and subdirectors of prefectural and county schools, though holding comparable ranks, were regarded as officials of "purer" status. The advantage of their "purer" status was somewhat offset by their meager emoluments and by their inability, as compared with the *tso-tsa,* to tap semi-legal or illegal sources of income. When in the nineteenth century the imperial government was forced by financial straits to sell offices, official ranks, and titles on a grand scale, the *tso-tsa* and subofficials were the main beneficiaries. In modern times, therefore, the line between the main body of officials and subofficials became increasingly blurred.

From this oversimplified description of the various strata of the bureaucracy it becomes clear that the officialdom was far from being a homogeneous body. Many of the members of the lower official stratum were actually men of comparatively modest circumstances.

The official class in the broad sense must also include retired officials, expectant officials, and certain types of degree-holders who were potential officials. The inclusion of retired officials is justified because an official's rights and special status did not terminate with the tenure of his office. For example, in the Sung-chiang area around Shanghai in the sixteenth century it was customary for retired officials to requisition domestic servants and sedan-chair carriers from local governments as if they were still on active duty.[59] Once an official, one always lived in the style of an official and was recognized as such by the society. This further reflects the sharp and abiding division between officials and commoners. There is abundant evidence that in Ming-Ch'ing times a greedy retired official and his family could still lord it over the countryside and encroach upon commoners' property without fear of intervention from local authorities.

The third or highest examination degree, *chin-shih,* won only by passing the metropolitan examination and palace examination, almost automatically placed a person in the middle stratum of the officialdom. Even when in the late Ch'ing period the bureaucracy became increasingly glutted because of the growing number of expectant officials who had purchased offices and ranks, *chin-shih* as a group invariably had the highest priority on office and was vulgarly called the *lao-hu-pan,* literally "the tiger class." No initial qualification for office was better or more esteemed than the *chin-shih* degree.

The second or intermediate degree, *chü-jen,* won by passing the provincial examination, also entitled a person to an eventual minor official appointment. In early Ming times *chü-jen* who failed to obtain the *chin-shih* degree were promptly appointed as directors and subdirectors of prefectural and county schools. The appointment was usually so immediate that many *chü-jen* preferred to enroll in the Imperial Academy so as to have better facilities for further studies and better chances of passing the metropolitan examination.[60] After the middle and lower strata of the bureaucracy began to become glutted by the middle of the sixteenth century the Board of Civil Appointments made various efforts to reserve a certain ratio of vacant offices for *chü-jen*. Moreover, from late Ming times onward examinations were held at twelve-year intervals by commissions of selection which placed a number of *chü-jen* in the posts of county magistrates, directors and subdirectors of schools, and other comparable offices. In fact, the term *chü-jen* means an "established man" or "elevated man," that is, a person who was established both academically and officially; whether or not he was rewarded with an immediate office is immaterial.

The *chü-jen* status was a crucial one in the stratification of Ming-Ch'ing society. This can be shown from social novels, which will be cited below, and biographies. To give one of the many examples, Chang Shih-i (1506–61) of Hua-t'ing County, a part of modern Shanghai, was forced by economic necessity to engage in trade in order to support his family and his elder brother, a struggling scholar. After becoming well-to-do, he hired a famous local scholar to teach his two sons. There was no tangible change in his subjective status evaluation during the years in which his two sons were *sheng-yüan*, holders of the first or elementary degree. Not until his second son passed the provincial examination in 1558 did he and his wife exclaim in ecstasy: "Now we can get ourselves out of this trade business!" [61] The sudden categorical elevation in status was obviously not economic but social, for he had long been well-to-do. Neither his sons' previous *sheng-yüan* degrees nor their later *chin-shih* degrees and high office could compare with the family's first *chü-jen* degree in its crucial significance for upward mobility.

*Kung-sheng* was also a crucial academic degree, for, along with *chü-jen*, it served as a demarcation between the potential officials and commoners. The term *kung-sheng* literally means "tribute students," that is, those of the holders of the first degree who were chosen for further studies at the Imperial Academy or for eventual minor official appointment. They were at first chosen on the basis of seniority but later also on that of merit. The difference between *kung-sheng* and *sheng-yüan* was a fundamental one. The latter were "undergraduates" subject to periodic tests supervised by provincial educational commissioners; as "undergraduates" they had no opportunity of official appointment. Those holding the *kung-sheng* degree were, on the other hand, considered as having "graduate" status, were not subject to periodic tests, and were entitled to eventual minor official appointment.

The number of *kung-sheng* never amounted to more than a fraction of the number of *sheng-yüan*. From 1441 onward the quotas for *kung-sheng* became fixed, being one for every prefectural school annually, two for every school of a department county triennially, and one for every county school biennially. Those chosen in this routine fashion were called *sui-kung-sheng*, literally "annual tribute students." From 1568 onward extra quotas were granted as a gesture of imperial grace. Henceforth on occasions of imperial celebration the regular local quotas were doubled and those on extra quotas were called *en-kung-sheng*, literally "tribute students by virtue of imperial grace." [62]

Since many of the regularly promoted *kung-sheng* were men approaching middle age and not necessarily men of special merit, throughout Ming times there were two special methods of selecting *kung-sheng*. First, owing to the shrinking opportunities for official appointment available to *kung-sheng* as a status group, from mid-Ming times onward special commissions were set up to select *kung-sheng* for immediate appointment. Shortly before the turn of the sixteenth century these selections began to become institutionalized, being held at a twelve-year interval. Successful candidates were called *pa-kung-sheng*, usually assigned to seventh and eighth ranking posts. The second type of special selection was open to *sheng-yüan* who, from early Ming times, were sporadically tested on the basis of literary attainments. Successful ones were given *kung-sheng* status and called *hsüan-kung*, literally "specially selected *kung-sheng*," a term which after 1628 was changed to *yu-kung-sheng*, literally "tribute students of special merit." The latter type of selection remained sporadic until 1764, after which the tests were regularly held once every three years. Not until 1863 did the *yu-kung-sheng* have opportunities of immediate official appointment through the further test of a special commission. The total number of *yu-kung-sheng* triennially selected was very small, being between sixty and seventy for the entire country. It was observed by contemporaries that among all types of tribute students the *yu-kung-sheng* as a group produced the highest percentage of eminent men because the basis of selection was strictly literary accomplishment.[63]

The fifth category of tribute students consisted of *fu-pang* or *fu-kung-sheng* who, though having failed in the provincial examination, were specially recommended by examiners as candidates of considerable literary attainments. This category appeared rather late in the Ming period, for not until the T'ien-ch'i period (1621–27) did the system of selecting one *fu-pang* for every five *chü-jen* begin to become institutionalized. The *fu-pang* were thenceforth given the status of *kung-sheng,* hence the name *fu-kung-sheng.*[64] The Ch'ing government perpetuated the Ming practice.

All these five types of *kung-sheng* were regarded as having attained an "orthodox" qualification for minor official appointment. They were all "regular" *kung-sheng*. That their legal status was fully recognized by the society is easily shown. First, although by early Ming practice only *chin-shih* and *chü-jen* were entitled to the erection at their residence of a flagpole on which was hoisted a red silk flag bearing the academic degree written in gold, in later Ming times it became a nationwide custom for all types of *kung-sheng* to display the same symbolic evidence of their special status.[65] Second, from early Ming times *chü-jen* and *kung-sheng* were often examined together for immediate official appointment and their difference in status lost significance with the passage of time. By Ch'ing times it had become so blurred that *chü-jen* and *kung-sheng* who passed special examinations usually compiled lists in which concise information was given on their ancestry for three preceding generations. That they all provided information on their ancestry was because of their institutionally and socially recognized status. Being "established" in status, they had the right as well as obligation to honor their ancestors. Third, practically all local histories have tables for local regular *kung-sheng* who, together with *chin-shih* and *chü-jen,* were recognized as higher degree holders and members of the bureaucracy in the broad sense.

The beginning of the Ming practice of selling the *kung-sheng* title is only dimly known. Unlike the sale of Imperial Academy studentships, the sale of *kung-sheng* titles is not clearly mentioned in Ming documents. However, the unusually well-informed late Ming scholar, Shen Te-fu, testified to three things. First, in the late sixteenth century at the latest only *ling-sheng*, that is, those senior *sheng-yüan* who received government stipends, were legally allowed to buy the graduate *kung-sheng* status. Second, since the graduate *kung-sheng* status enabled a person to enter government service and conferred on him other academic and social rights, many ordinary *sheng-yüan* who had not attained *ling-sheng*'s seniority falsified their status to buy the *kung-sheng* title. Third, these "irregular" *kung-sheng* also erected a flagpole at their residences to distinguish themselves from *sheng-yüan* and non-degree-holding commoners.[66] There can be little doubt about the accuracy of Shen's account, for some of the earliest Ch'ing *chin-shih* listed *ling-kung-sheng*, that is, *ling-sheng* who bought the *kung-sheng* title, among their ancestors.[67] The Manchu war against the rebellious southern feudatories forced the government from 1675 onward to sell, among other things, the *kung-sheng* title to *ling-sheng* and two other junior categories of *sheng-yüan* for some two hundred taels of silver.[68]

The fact that these irregular *kung-sheng* attained their title through purchase has led a modern writer to regard them as being inferior in status to the five categories of regular *kung-sheng*. He finds the status difference between the regular and the irregular *kung-sheng* so great that he places the former in the "upper gentry" and the latter in the "lower gentry." [69] Disregarding for the moment the validity of the terms "upper gentry" and "lower gentry," the true legal and social status of the irregular *kung-sheng* justifies careful investigation.

We may supplement that writer, whose sole reason for giving an inferior status to irregular *kung-sheng* seems to rest on their purchased origin, by pointing out that there was a theoretical difference between the legal statuses of these two main categories of *kung-sheng*. Whereas the regular *kung-sheng* were free from the supervision of the provincial educational commissioner because of their graduate status, the irregular *kung-sheng* were supposed to be under the joint supervision of the commissioner and local authorities. The difference was, however, more apparent than real. For example, while a statute of 1757 provided once more that the irregular *kung-sheng* should be duly supervised by the educational commissioner and local authorities, it frankly admitted that up till then the educational commissioner had seldom known where to check the names of the irregular *kung-sheng* of the province.[70] It is obvious that they had in reality been regarded as "graduates"; as such their names had been customarily withdrawn from the educational commissioner's registers. A statute of 1863 further clarifies the true legal status of irregular *kung-sheng*. It says:

> From now on those who have purchased the *kung-sheng* title and Imperial Academy studentships should still be subjected to the supervision of local authorities, in accordance with the statutory provisions of the Ch'ien-lung [1736–95] period. In case they and *sheng-yüan* create trouble, [the local authorities] should inquire in conjunction with the directors of local schools. . . . Regarding the rest, the directors of schools should not intervene.[71]

It is to be noted that the entire lack of mention of the provincial educational commissioner reveals that irregular *kung-sheng* had long ceased to be even theoretically supervised by him; that the fact that they were still supposed to be supervised by local authorities and local directors of schools was related only to possible cases of misconduct; and that their actual "graduate" status and legal rights as *kung-sheng* were never affected by these half-hearted statutes.

This being the case, the various editions of *chin-shen ch'üan-shu*, that is, directories of officials, of the eighteenth and nineteenth centuries list numerous minor officials, sometimes middle and high-ranking officials, who entered the bureaucracy on the qualification of irregular *kung-sheng*. The social status of irregular *kung-sheng*, which differed in no way from that of regular *kung-sheng*, is shown by the fact that they too had customarily erected flagpoles at their residences since late Ming times. It was not until 1863, when the volume of sale had already gotten beyond the control of the imperial government, that a lukewarm statute forbade the new purchasers to continue the practice.[72] There is little reason to believe that during a period of rapid, drastic decline of dynastic prestige

and central power the new statute could have been effectively enforced, especially when the majority of local officials entered government service through purchase and naturally had a group sympathy toward irregular *kung-sheng*.[73] Indeed, so deep-rooted had
been the common notion that irregular *kung-sheng* were legitimate
potential officials that scholar-officials of Ch'ang-shu in southern
Kiangsu, a county which had an unusual record of academic success,
regarded a purchased *kung-sheng* as an "orthodox" qualification
for government service.[74] All in all, therefore, it is ill-advised to
regard irregular *kung-sheng* as being inferior in status to regular
*kung-sheng*.

There was yet another large category of first degree holders called
*chien-sheng*, that is, students of the Imperial Academy. In early
Ming times hundreds of them were appointed to offices, sometimes
to high offices, without their having to acquire a more advanced
degree. The Imperial Academy in early Ming times was therefore
an even more important channel for bureaucratic recruitment than
the *chin-shih* examinations, especially when the latter quotas were
small. Even without the benefit of immediate official appointment
*chien-sheng* still enjoyed the best library and tutorial facilities in
the country. This can be shown by the fact that out of a total of
12,272 *chin-shih* degrees granted in forty-four examinations between
1406 and 1574 no less than 6,453 of the recipients, or 52.6 percent,
were originally students of the Imperial Academy. In 1499 and 1508
students of the Imperial Academy monopolized all the three first-
class honors and the honors of being placed first in the metropolitan
examinations.[75] Small wonder, then, that many *chü-jen* who failed
to pass the metropolitan examination preferred enrolling in the
academy to accepting an immediate minor office. In Ming times the
status of the *chien-sheng* as a potential official can hardly be doubted,
for special recommendations, *chin-shih* and *chien-sheng*, and the
promotion of government clerks and subofficials were known as the
three major orthodox avenues toward membership in the bureaucracy.[76]

The status of *chien-sheng* underwent important changes in Ming
times. The landmark was the serious Mongol invasion of the Peking
area in 1449 which resulted in the capture of the reigning Ming

emperor and which forced the government to sell offices, and official titles. Starting in 1451, a series of imperial decrees allowed at first *sheng-yüan,* but later also men without an academic degree, to purchase the Imperial Academy studentships with grain or horses.[77] The sale was suspended after the northern defense had been strengthened but was sporadically revived in times of serious natural calamity. By the last quarter of the fifteenth century several tens of thousands of studentships had been sold.[78] Since the purchased *chien-sheng* title also entitled a person to minor official appointment, the lower stratum of the bureaucracy began to be glutted. In 1488 Wang Shu, one of the most upright presidents of the Board of Civil Appointments of the Ming period, testified that the average *chien-sheng* now had to wait almost twenty years for a real office.[79] The glut in the lower bureaucracy seems to have been somewhat eased in the early sixteenth century as the volume of sale of studentships was brought under control. Figures for the Imperial Academy's total enrollments and those of the students who entered the Academy by purchase are available for nineteen years of the period 1545–81. Of a total nineteen-year enrollment of 16,070, 6,869 or 42.6 percent purchased the *chien-sheng* title.[80] It ought to be pointed out that the figures are far from complete because a much larger number of people who purchased the title stayed home and did not enroll in the academy. While it is true that the volume of sale was much smaller than that of the Ch'ing period, the sale did much to affect the status of *chien-sheng* and their opportunities for official employment. By the turn of the sixteenth century it was not uncommon for the holders of purchased studentships to be pushed around and insulted by local authorities. In some cases their social status hardly differed from that of commoners.[81] But it is important to bear in mind that right down to the very end of the Ming period *chien-sheng* were legally and institutionally entitled to government office; as such they as a group should be regarded as potential officials.

More drastic changes in the status of *chien-sheng* occurred after the founding of the Ch'ing empire in 1644. The Imperial Academy had but a nominal existence under the new dynasty. The total enrollment seldom exceeded 300, which was a far cry from its heyday under the Ming when the enrollment exceeded 10,000.[82] The sale of *chien-sheng* titles was continually increased, and during the thirty years of the reign of the Tao-kuang emperor (1821–50) 315,825 student-ships were sold for a total revenue of 33,886,630 taels of silver, not including those sold by the central government in the metropolitan Chihli province. The number of studentships sold between 1799 and 1820 was at least equally large, for even excluding Chihli and Shansi provinces the government received a total revenue of 40,-724,169 taels from sales during these twenty-one years.[83] It would not be an exaggeration to say that in Ch'ing times practically any-body who could afford a little over 100 taels could obtain the *chien-sheng* title and the right to wear the scholar's gown and cap. In the history of the famous trading area, Hui-chou prefecture in southern Anhwei, for example, almost all of the numerous biographical sketches of local tradesmen who donated to local philanthropy are prefaced by the term *chien-sheng*.[84]

A perusal of various Ch'ing statutes shows that, except for a very small number of *chien-sheng* who actually studied in Peking and who could take special selective tests for lowly ranking clerks and copyists after their failure in the Chihli provincial examination, *chien-sheng* as a rule were unable to enter government service with-out further purchase of official titles. In the light of their much deteriorated legal status and rights as compared with those enjoyed during the greater part of the Ming period, it seems reasonable to exclude them from the group of potential officials of the Ch'ing period. On the other hand, *chien-sheng* constituted a privileged group among the commoners. They were exempt from labor serv-ice and from the routine tests of the provincial educational com-missioner because of their theoretical "graduate" status. In addition, for the well-to-do commoners the *chien-sheng* title was a requisite for further purchase of official titles.

We now turn to the largest group of degree holders, the *sheng-yüan*. The legal and social status of *sheng-yüan,* who along with *chien-sheng* constitute what Chang calls "lower gentry," likewise deserves a systematic analysis. While undoubtedly even the lowest academic degree still had some significance in the Ming-Ch'ing so-ciety, failure to understand its full institutional and social connotations inevitably results in a fundamental misconception as to the anatomy of the traditional Chinese society and its key class, commonly and loosely called the "gentry."

It is worth reiterating that the Mencian principle of social stratification, as cited above, is a very general one and that not all those who labored with their minds were necessarily members of ruling class. This basic fact is older than Mencius, for the book of *Kuan-tzu* had already clearly stated that scholars, peasants, artisans, and merchants were the four major groupings of commoners. Various ancient Confucian classics clearly explained that in the late feudal period there were three grades of *shih* (scholars) in government service but also *shih* who, together with peasants, artisans, and merchants constituted the commoners. The latter type of scholar was called *shih-min,* literally "scholar-commoners."[85] This contrast between official-scholars and scholar-commoners persisted through more than two thousand years of post-feudal China. Indeed, the contrast between these two categories of scholars was no less fundamental than the demarcation between people who labored with their minds and those who labored with their physical strength. For example, the famous economic statesman Sang Hung-yang (152?–80 B.C.) more than once expressed his scorn for nonofficial scholars during the court debates in 81 B.C. and the original thinker Wang Ch'ung (A.D. 27-*ca.* 100) pointed out that "the public is wont to esteem the officials and despise the scholars." [86]

There can be little doubt that in Ming-Ch'ing times *sheng-yüan* were scholar-commoners. But being holders of the first degree, they were regarded by law and society as the leading group among the commoners. Their degree also gave them a touch of gentility, as may be evidenced by the way in which a *sheng-yüan* was politely addressed as *hsiang-kung,* that is, "mister," which was different from the vulgar way of addressing a *chü-jen* as *lao-yeh,* that is, "your honor." [87] Like higher degree holders, *sheng-yüan* were exempt from labor service. Before the sale of Imperial Academy studentships their degree was the only requisite for higher degrees and statuses. For all these reasons they and Ch'ing *chien-sheng* constituted a privileged class among commoners and an important social "transitional" group.

On the other hand, they had no opportunity for official employment, a basic fact which set them apart from holders of the *kung-sheng* or higher degree. While their elementary academic degree was a thing to be desired, it was never so important as to justify the compilation of their class lists. Local histories completely overlooked them because they were "undergraduates" and "unestablished." Although toward the end of the imperial era scholars of a few localities compiled lists for them partly out of sympathy for their prolonged toil without reward and partly for fear that their names would fall completely into oblivion, such lists contain no information on their ancestry because as scholar-commoners they had no valid reason to honor their forebears.

Owing to their "unestablished" status in both the legal and the social sense, they had to eke out a meager living whenever and wherever possible if their families were not rich. The majority of them taught in village schools or served as family tutors, often at subsistence wages. Such a career was commonly described as *pi-keng* or *yen-t'ien,* literally "ploughing with a writing brush or with an inkslab." For the Ming-Ch'ing periods the examples are legion. A few are given in the Appendix.

A *sheng-yüan,* if need be, would even do sundry jobs derogatory to his scholarly status. In the famous social novel *An Unofficial History of the Literati,* for example, K'uang Ch'ao-jen had for years made bean curd to support his ailing father. After collecting a few strings of congratulatory money from neighboring small men when he acquired his *sheng-yüan* degree, he ceased to sell bean curd but still had to make a living as a peddler. His friend Ching Lan-chiang, a *sheng-yüan* and poet, made his living by operating a turban and cap store. In Nanking a *sheng-yüan* by the name of Ma supported himself by selling beef cattle. The prolonged scorn and humiliation which he had suffered from neighbors made him willing to die as a martyr when the city fell to the Taiping rebels in 1853.[88] The poor and good-for-nothing *sheng-yüan* who allied themselves with local government underlings and bullied village illiterates are a common curse in social novels.

In fact, so great was the pressure of living and so commonly did *sheng-yüan* and Ch'ing *chien-sheng* "degrade" themselves that a long series of statutes in the 1793 and 1812 editions of the *Complete Statutes Relating to Examination Affairs* forbade them to work as store bookkeepers, clerks of local irrigation projects, petty local brokers, local government runners, etc.[89] These statutes do not seem to have been effective, for so many *sheng-yüan* and *chien-sheng* preferred a more practical living to the comfortless dignity of a "purer" status that Hu Lin-i, governor of Hupei, requested in 1855 that they be allowed to engage in brokerage, a request which was refused by the imperial government.[90] Thus a substantial number of *sheng-yüan* and *chien-sheng* in Ch'ing times failed to live up to the legal and social status expected of them by the state. The bulk of evidence from various biographical series bearing on the frequency with which *sheng-yüan* and *chien-sheng* forsook their métier to become small tradesmen indicates that even in their subjective evaluation their status was by no means an exalted one.[91]

When the legal status and social realities of the *sheng-yüan* are understood, it is difficult to accept the view that they constituted the "lower gentry." If any doubt remains, the great social satirist Wu Ching-tu (1701–54) dispels it for modern students. In his description of the elaborate funeral for old lady Fang, mother of a very rich salt merchant who had an official title, the local *shen-shih* or "gentry" who marched in the front "solemnly and respectfully" included active and retired officials, *chin-shih, chü-jen, kung-sheng,* and *chien-sheng,* while *sheng-yüan* followed in the rear "hurriedly and sheepishly." [92] Seldom have the compositions of "gentry" and "non-gentry" and their contrast in social status been more minutely and precisely delineated.

His definition for the composition of "gentry" is almost exactly the same as our definition for the class of officials and potential officials except on one technical point. Whereas we regard *chiensheng* as potential officials in Ming times only, this great Ch'ing novelist listed them among "gentry." This difference, however, might very well be unreal, for Wu's satire on the *Literati* was hypothetically set against the background of Ming times. Being a member of a distinguished scholar-official family, he sometimes purposely shows off his intimate knowledge of history and Ming institutions.[93] For defining the composition of Ming "gentry," Wu's delineation

is flawless and entirely supported by actual Ming customs and practice. For example, the famous statesman and philosopher Wang
Yang-ming, shortly before his death in 1528, ordered the people of
Kwangsi to contribute varying amounts of grain for famine relief
according to their social status. It was provided that *hsiang-kuan* or
"gentry," *chü-jen,* and *chien-sheng* families should each contribute
three bushels, *sheng-yüan* families two bushels, and ordinary commoner families one bushel.[94]

Although it is impossible to prove definitely that in this particular instance concerning *chien-sheng* Wu twisted social facts a bit
to make them fit in with the Ming background, another great early
Ch'ing novel helps us to solve this puzzle. This is *A Marriage that
Awakens the World* by P'u Sung-ling (1640–1715). Its background,
too, is supposedly set in Ming times, but we can be sure that P'u
portrays faithfully the society of his own times. One of the novel's
main characters, Ti Hsi-ch'en, a rich man's son and hen-pecked
husband, purchased a *chien-sheng* title early in his life. But to have
any hope of retiring as a member of the country gentry with leisure
and with perfect social security, he had to purchase a further official title.[95] It thus becomes abundantly clear that in early Ch'ing
times the *chien-sheng* title was no longer in itself sufficient to qualify
a person for membership in the local elite. The composition of the
local elite or "gentry" given in social novels therefore agrees completely with our definition of the class of officials and potential
officials.

Chang's inclusion of *chien-sheng* and *sheng-yüan* in nineteenth-
century "gentry" is defensible only if the broad and loose term
*shen-shih* is taken strictly literally. *Shen* is an abbreviation of the
time-honored terms *chin-shen, hsiang-shen, hsiang-kuan,* and *hsiang-
huan,* which all mean officials—active, retired, and potential. *Shih*
or *chin* means scholars, or more precisely nonofficial scholars. In
chapter 13 of the 1792 edition of the history of Shao-hsing prefecture, a highly cultured and academically successful area in Chekiang,
the local population was classified into four major categories of
households, namely, *shen-hu, chin-hu, min-hu,* and *tsao-hu. Chin-hu,*
or households of holders of the first degree, were clearly differentiated from *shen-hu,* or "gentry" households and ranked above the

ordinary common and salt-producer households. This reflected the difference in status between *shen* and *chin* or *shih* and also the fact that the latter, being nonofficial degree holders, were a significant social transitional group which among the commoners was the nearest to the source of power and prestige. This is why many traditional writers lump the *shen* and the *shih* or *chin* together. But it is vital that modern students search out the full institutional and social connotations of these terms and define them more precisely. The most interesting observation is that even when *shen* and *shih* are put together by traditional writers, the combined term *shen-shih* often means the former without the latter. The names and titles of local *shen-shih* who provided leadership in establishing schools or expanding school property are sometimes available. They are worth analyzing.

TABLE 1

SAMPLE MEMBERSHIP OF *SHEN-SHIH*

| Year | Locality | Total number | Titles held by shen-shih |
|------|----------|--------------|--------------------------|
| 1867 | Shang-jao (Kiangsi) | 8 | 1 expectant official, rank 4a<br>4 *chin-shih*<br>3 *chü-jen* |
| 1876 | Lo-t'ing (Chihli) | 5 | 1 *chü-jen*, active central official, rank 5a<br>1 *chü-jen*, expectant central official, rank 5a<br>1 *chü-jen*, expectant magistrate, rank 7b, with a brevet of 5th rank<br>1 *ling-kung-sheng*, expectant official, rank 5b, with a brevet of 4th rank<br>1 *ling-kung-sheng*, expectant official, rank 5b |
| 1896 | Hsin-hua (Hunan) | 16 | 1 holder of a brevet of 4th rank<br>1 central official, rank 6a<br>2 county magistrates, rank 7b<br>4 directors of schools, rank 8a<br>1 sub-director of county school, rank 8b<br>4 *chü-jen*<br>3 *kung-sheng* |

Sources: *Lo-t'ing Tsun-tao shu-yüan lu*, 1876; *Hsin-chiang shu-yüan chih*, 1867; and *Hsin-hua hsüeh-t'ien chih*, 1896.

The striking common feature is that even the loose term *shen-shih* does not include any *chien-sheng* or *sheng-yüan*, which constitute the bulk of Chang Chung-li's "lower gentry."

Since in the field of Chinese studies the term "gentry" has become very popular in recent years, a brief discussion of the term itself is necessary. As is well known, gentry is a typically English term which from Tudor times onward acquired rather concrete social, economic, and political connotations. In the sixteenth, seventeenth, and eighteenth centuries members of the English gentry owned large landed estates, controlled or dominated county administration, and, from the late eighteenth century onward, were mostly Tory in their political sympathies. Some keen contemporary French observers of English society could find no French or continental European analogy to these English gentry, whom they called "nobiles minores," an appellation with an aristocratic aroma.[96] Within certain limits it is of course permissible to borrow a foreign term, but when the realities behind the borrowed term are so remote from the social, economic, and political contexts of the original, there is strong reason to reject the term altogether. Since the most important determinant of English gentry status was landed property and sometimes other forms of wealth, there is danger in borrowing it as a generic term for the Chinese class of officials and potential officials who, during a greater part of the Ming-Ch'ing period, owed their status only partly to wealth but mostly to an academic degree. Furthermore, it is difficult to equate broadly the Chinese class of officials and potential officials with the English gentry because many of the officials and potential officials of the lower bureaucratic stratum were actually men of relatively modest circumstances and a far cry from "nobiles minores." They should be regarded as a key class only in the peculiar context of the Ming-Ch'ing society.

To sum up the composition of the official class in its broad sense, in Ming times it includes officials, active, retired, expectant, and potential; subofficials, *chin-shih*, *chü-jen*, *kung-sheng*, both regular and irregular; and *chien-sheng*. The Ch'ing period official class is the same except for the *chien-sheng*, which is excluded. *Sheng-yüan* are regarded for the whole Ming-Ch'ing period as a significant socially transitional group among commoners. While no demarcation between the broadly defined official class and commoners can be completely free from arbitrariness, the many-sided evidence presented above, and much else that would be repetitious, shows that our demarcation is in the main justified in terms of both legal and social stratifications.

## EDUCATION AND WEALTH AS DETERMINANTS OF SOCIAL STATUS

Although the statuses of the various strata of officialdom as legally defined by the Ming and Ch'ing governments coincide remarkably well with their social statuses, in our study of the stratification of commoners we find a certain amount of discrepancy between the legal and social statuses of various major commoner groups. The traditional Chinese state was at once a Confucian and a "physiocratic" state; as such it had its strong legal biases. Being Confucian, it ascribed a status to scholar-commoners superior to those ascribed to other main categories of commoners. This is easily understandable because the scholars were the lone group of commoners who labored with their minds. Being "physiocratic," the state regarded peasants as primary producers of wealth on whose labor the nation, especially the governing class, depended for sustenance. Hence the peasants, though manual workers, suffered comparatively little from the discriminatory laws and were always entitled to take civil-service examinations. Even the book of *Kuan-tzu,* which contains certain social concepts at least as old as those of Confucius and which advocated strict hereditary professions and statuses for commoners, welcomed the ascendancy of the gifted sons of peasants into the scholarly and eventually the feudal bureaucratic ranks.[97] The artisans and merchants, on the other hand, were regarded by the traditional Chinese state as secondary producers of wealth and as middlemen. As such they were subjected to sumptuary and discriminatory laws among which the most serious was the denial by the state of their right of entry into the official class. Up to the end of the Sung period the law forbade artisans and merchants and their families to take government examinations. The common impression that Chinese society traditionally looked down upon and discriminated against artisans and merchants has persisted to modern times.

An examination of historical social realities, however, reveals a different picture from the one shown in legal texts. The capitalist merchants, money-lenders, and industrialists of the Former Han period not only defied sumptuary laws by conspicuous consumption but traveled with large retinues and were treated almost as social equals by the vassal kings and marquises.[98] They were so formidable a menace to the small men and ordinary consumers that they were called by contemporaries *su-feng,* literally "untitled nobility." Many rich merchants and artisans in T'ang times successfully evaded the sumptuary laws and assumed a style of life prescribed only for the socially superior.[99] Although Sung laws forbade merchants to take examinations, there is definite evidence showing that many officials and frustrated candidates openly engaged in trade and that not a few members of merchant families managed to pass the national examination and become officials.[100] Many great *se-mu* (non-Mongol and non-Chinese peoples from Central Asia and beyond) merchants dominated the domestic and international trade, and even governmental fiscal administration, in Yüan times.[101] The removal of the most serious discriminatory laws against merchants and artisans during the Ming-Ch'ing period may be regarded as a belated recognition by the state of their increasing power.

This leads us to another fundamental problem of social stratification in Ming-Ch'ing China, namely, the relative importance of education (or its more concrete expression: opportunities for government service) and wealth as determinants of social status. Since government statutes and documents deal mainly with legal stratification, subtler social realities must be sought in social novels and private literary writings. Granted that some of the cases given below are perhaps too extreme to be accepted as a reflection of the general social truth, such extreme cases will nevertheless help to sharpen our theoretical perception of the relative importance of an office or a potential office and of wealth as determinants of social status. We will arrive at a more balanced view after these extreme cases are interpreted against some statistics which reflect the general social pattern.

We are fortunate in having a most revealing and realistic social novel *An Unofficial History of the Literati,* a work which is indispensable for the study of that key social class in Ming-Ch'ing society. One of the many illuminating episodes concerns an indigent southern scholar, Fan Chin, who for years lived partially at the mercy of his father-in-law, a bullying and cursing butcher. When the news that he had passed the provincial examination arrived, he was so stunned and choked with emotion that he temporarily lost his senses. Since the butcher had previously inflicted physical pain on Fan to bring him back to his senses, some neighbors suggested that he should do it again. But the butcher no longer dared because he believed that his son-in-law, now a *chü-jen,* must have been the reincarnation of one of the stars in heaven. This second degree, which entitled Fan to an eventual office, was charismatic in more than one way; it completely transformed his economic and social status overnight. A local retired county magistrate, himself a holder of the *chü-jen* degree, immediately called and offered Fan a large house and some ready cash. Soon the smaller men of the locality offered Fan either a part of their land, shares of their stores, or themselves as domestic servants—all in the hope of gaining his favor and protection.[102]

An episode in another social novel, *The Marriage that Awakens the World,* differs only in minor detail. It is about the sudden change of fortune of Ch'ao Ssu-hsiao, for years a *sheng-yüan* and man of limited property. After having failed repeatedly to attain the *chü-jen* degree he eventually became a *kung-sheng* through seniority. This graduate status enabled him to take a special examination for minor government office. He passed it and was to be appointed a county magistrate. This news was sufficient to induce some of the local poor to offer themselves as his domestic servants, certain local "middle-class" people to transfer to him the title deeds of their property, and money-lenders to make loans to him with nominal or no interest.[103] The Ch'ao family suddenly became one of the richest and most powerful in the district. These two episodes, given independently by a southern and a northern novelist, indicate that a higher degree often led to sudden elevation in both economic and social status.

That wealth itself might not be an ultimate source of power in Ming-Ch'ing China can be further illustrated. From mid-Ming times at the latest, the merchants of Hui-chou prefecture in hilly southern

Anhwei were one of the richest commercial groups in the country. They could boast of many merchant princes whose fortunes exceeded one million taels of silver. A highly instructive case is given in *Wu-tsa-tsu,* a famous miscellany in five parts by the extensively traveled and unusually observant Hsieh Chao-che, *chin-shih* of 1592 and later governor of Kwangsi, a work which became in Tokugawa Japan a most popular guide on late Ming China. He mentions the case of Wang Tsung-chi, a millionaire merchant of Hui-chou. Being so rich, Wang traveled with a large retinue of servants and female entertainers. Once his retinue affronted a local official by failing to make way promptly enough, and the result was prolonged litigation which brought about his bankruptcy.[104] It is impossible to ascertain whether Wang had obtained a degree or an official status through purchase, but it is clear that wealth alone was not equal to bureaucratic power.

The case of the Wu family of Hui-chou is even more illuminating. The family fortune was built on the salt trade in the early sixteenth century. By the late sixteenth and early seventeenth centuries the family was so rich that it contributed heavily to local philanthropy, including the establishment of a private academy and the printing of sixteen classics for free distribution to needy students. By patronizing scholars the Wus had long been accepted as members of the local elite, a fact which under normal circumstances would have afforded the family effective social protection. Moreover, the family was so realistic as to have contributed 300,000 taels to the imperial coffer with the result that six of its male members obtained the titles of seventh-ranking central officials. This newly acquired formal official status, coupled with its wealth, enabled the family to appropriate timberland of the Huang Mountain without difficulty. In 1626, however, a perfidious servant passed on to a greedy and powerful eunuch a much exaggerated version of the family's encroachment upon public mountain land. Not only was the entire family property in the Hui-chou area seized by the government; its various investments in the salt trade and its pawnshops in Tientsin, Honan, Yang-chou, and Hang-chou were all investigated and subsequently confiscated.[105] Even rich merchants with official rank were, under special circumstances, helpless before the bureaucracy.

These cases are by no means confined to the Hui-chou area and the late Ming period. In the first half of the eighteenth century, as is also vividly described in *An Unofficial History of the Literati,* there was the case of Wan Hsüeh-chai, one of the head salt merchants of Yang-chou, a cultural center and city of conspicuous consumption, situated near the junction of the Yangtze and the Grand Canal. Even by Yang-chou standards of spending, the way in which Wan entertained famous men of letters would be regarded as extravagant. His fifth concubine, a woman of some literary gift and great social ambition, had sponsored a poetry club. In spite of his elite status he fell victim to the ravenous appetites of local officialdom. After prolonged deliberation with his favorite concubine he decided to spend 10,000 taels out of his rapidly dwindling fortune to buy without delay a real office of a fourth-ranking prefect in the remote province of Kweichow. Only by buying an immediately available office of the highest rank permitted by law did he manage to escape from what he and his concubine had thought to be imminent death.[106] Commenting on the Wan case, Wu Ching-tzu cited a common Chinese saying of the day which contains a fundamental social truth: "The poor should never antagonize the rich and the rich should never antagonize the officials."

Li Chih, better known by his pen-name Li Cho-wu (1527–1602), a onetime local official and an intellectual rebel, made this general observation: "Merchants, carrying a large amount of cash and bearing all the hazards of a long journey, are often subjected to extortion by customs officials and subofficials. They have to swallow a great deal of humiliation if their business transactions are to be pushed through. To realize profit and to avoid harm, they must make friends with the nobility and officials." [107] This was why in Ming-Ch'ing times merchants sometimes erected stone monuments as an expression of their gratitude to some compassionate local officials who duly protected them against the bullying and exploitation of local government subofficials and underlings.[108]

On the ultimate source of power in Ming-Ch'ing society, a late-nineteenth-century social novel, *A Revelation of the True Countenance of the Bureaucracy,* says in its preface:

The official's status is exalted, his name distinguished, his power great, and his prestige incomparable—this is well known even to youngsters. In ancient times the commoners were divided into four major functional orders, namely, scholars, peasants, artisans, and merchants, each engaging in its own occupation and each performing its own function. . . . Since the introduction of the examination system . . . scholars have forsaken their studies, peasants their ploughs, artisans their crafts, and merchants their trades; all have turned their attention to but one thing—government office. This is because the official has all the combined advantages of the four without requiring their necessary toil. . . . Speaking of the official, he may not be capable of assisting the emperor, but he is more than resourceful in oppressing the commoners.[109]

The above illustrations and observations no doubt contain considerable social truth. They should not, however, distort our sense of proportion. For one thing, cases of rich merchants, rendered bankrupt by extortionate officials, though illuminating, are exceptional rather than normal. Second, although wealth as a determinant of social status was in theory overshadowed by a higher academic degree or an office, its real power steadily grew as time went on. Prior to 1451, wealth at best could only help to acquire a better education and facilitate the eventual attainment of higher degrees and office, for until then officials had been recruited exclusively through regular civil-service examinations or special recommendations, or from among students of the Imperial Academy, subofficials, and government clerks. The serious Mongol invasion of the Peking area in 1449 forced the Ming government to sell official ranks and titles and Imperial Academy studentships, a step which opened up an important new channel of social mobility for the rich. In the long run the sale of offices, titles, and studentships had far greater effect on social mobility than did the institution of *la Paulette* in France under the *ancien régime,* which facilitated the ascent to the aristocracy of the *bourgeoisie.*[110]

From partial statistics and testimonials of contemporary scholars and officials we know that during the Ming period the sale of offices, titles, and studentships was generally held within bounds. After the fall of Peking in the early spring of 1644 a Ming prince assumed the imperial title in Nanking and carried on the struggle against the Manchus. His chief means of raising funds was the sale of offices and titles on a grand scale.[111] This runaway sale of offices was halted with the capture of Nanking by the Manchus in 1645, but it had a significant bearing on early Manchu policy. Throughout the 1660s and 1670s the Manchu government was in dire need of money, first to pay for the maintenance of the three powerful southern feudatories and then to finance the war to suppress their rebellion. Indeed, between 1678 and 1682 the Manchu government not only sold offices and titles on a large scale but resorted to the almost un-precedented practice of selling the *sheng-yüan* degree throughout the country.[112] The sale of the *sheng-yüan* degree was discontinued permanently after the final pacification of all China including For-mosa in 1683, but the sale of offices and titles was subsequently resorted to at times of military campaigns, major natural calamities, and public works programs.[113]

The volume of sales of offices and titles during the first half of the Ch'ing period is not exactly known, but a rare list of 1798 reveals that in that year 1,437 central offices and 3,095 provincial and local offices were sold, not including the numerous lowly offices with the rank of 9b and unclassed posts. The 1,258 assistant county magis-tracies sold formed the largest single category, followed by 547 *bithesi,* which constituted the largest group of central offices. There were several cases in which offices were bought for boys under ten years old so that after a period of expectancy they could receive their offices early in life.[114] Although the sale was far from an annual affair, the total number of 4,532 offices sold exceeded the aggregate of ranked offices of the central government by at least one third. These figures, together with the volume of sale of *chien-sheng* titles between 1799 and 1850, indicate at least that in a greater part of the mid-Ch'ing period it was far easier than during the Ming for money to be directly translated into high social status.

The proportions of officials who entered government service by purchase can be known by an analysis of two types of systematic data which yield information on officials' initial qualifications for office. The first type consists of various editions of *chüeh-chih ch'üan-lan,* or handbooks on official ranks and emoluments. The earliest ones available in North America are of the third quarter of the eighteenth century and there is a rather abundant group for the nineteenth century. A sampling of them reveals that for more than a century changes were relatively slight in the percentage distribution of central officials of orthodox (higher degrees and *yin*) and unorthodox (by purchase, etc.) origins. This is because certain categories of central offices were conventionally reserved for officials of orthodox and unorthodox origins respectively. For example, high offices and academic posts were as a rule filled by men of high academic qualifications, and certain kinds of offices, particularly the *bithesi* or Manchu writers, were reserved for and bought by Manchu, Mongol, and Chinese Bannermen. The distribution of the three grades of secretaries of the six boards and a few other central organs also followed a certain ratio. The gradually increasing number of secretaries through purchase was usually accompanied by a corresponding increase in the number of extra-quota junior secretaries, called *e-wai-chu-shih*, posts earmarked for new *chin-shih*. On balance, in the central government officials of orthodox qualifications always outnumbered officials of unorthodox origins by a modest margin.

The changing ratio between officials of orthodox and unorthodox backgrounds can be better shown by an analysis of the initial qualifications of local officials. Since a full analysis of the innumerable *tso-tsa*, or local officials of the two lowest ranks, is extremely time-consuming, and since the majority of them, during the nineteenth century at least, owed their positions to purchase, the analysis is confined to the class of local officials between the seventh and the fourth ranks, the backbone of local administration. The dates of the official directories are so selected to represent the latter half of the eighteenth century, the first half of the nineteenth century, and the post-Taiping period, which witnessed a drastic increase in sale of offices.

In 1764, when the Ch'ing empire was at the peak of peace, prosperity, and orderly administration, over seventy percent of the local officials in this particular list were holders of degrees of regular *kung-sheng* or above. In 1840, when the country was still at peace, the percent increase of officials of unorthodox origins had been modest. But the Taiping rebellion of 1851–64 forced the government to sell offices on a scale hitherto undreamt of. After its pacifi-

TABLE 2

PERCENTAGE DISTRIBUTION OF LOCAL OFFICIALS'
INITIAL QUALIFICATIONS

| Year | Total officials[a] | Regular degree | Yin | Purchase | Miscellaneous[b] |
|------|------|------|------|------|------|
| 1764 | 2,071 | 72.5 | 1.1 | 22.4 | 4.0 |
| 1840 | 1,949 | 65.7 | 1.0 | 29.3 | 4.0 |
| 1871 | 1,790 | 43.8 | 0.8 | 51.2 | 4.2 |
| 1895 | 1,975 | 47.9 | 1.2 | 49.4 | 1.5 |

Sources: *Chüeh-chih ch'üan-lan* for the years 1764, 1840, 1871, and 1895.

[a] The total number is that of those officials who stated their initial qualifications.

[b] Miscellaneous includes those who were promoted from subofficial positions and those who were recommended by provincial authorities because of their military service or other merits.

cation the percentage of the unorthodox was invariably higher than that of the orthodox.

The information given by the above data is not complete. *Chüeh-chih ch'üan-lan* never specify whether officials of initial orthodox qualifications had ever used purchase as a secondary, or in many cases as a primary, means of facilitating their entrance or promotion. The second type of data given in *t'ung-kuan-lu,* or official directories of various provinces, is more satisfactory. Since most of them do not include the vast group of *tso-tsa,* we can only analyze the backgrounds of provincial and local officials of the seventh rank and above.

The 1886 edition of the official directory of Chekiang is particularly illuminating because of its completeness and its information on the *tso-tsa* and the directors and subdirectors of prefectural and county schools. The local school officials as a group offer a lone and therefore sad exception to the general rule that after 1850 money had become more important than academic attainments as a determinant of official status. Of the 90 educational officials, 60 were holders of regular degrees as against 26 who obtained offices through purchase and 4 by recommendation. But 26 of the 60 holders of regular degrees had resorted to purchase in order to get themselves appointed. All but 34 of a total of 272 *tso-tsa,* excluding a larger number of those who bought the rank 9b and unclassed offices, owed their positions to purchase alone.

TABLE 3

PERCENTAGE DISTRIBUTION OF QUALIFICATIONS
OF PROVINCIAL AND LOCAL OFFICIALS
$(A + C + D + E = 100; B + C + E = F)$

| Year | Province | Total officials | Regular degree | | Purchase (exclusive) | Miscellaneous without purchase | Miscellaneous combined with purchase | Purchase (exclusive and in combination) |
|------|----------|-----------------|------|------|----------------------|--------------------------------|--------------------------------------|------------------------------------------|
| | | | A | B[a] | C | D[b] | E | F |
| 1847 | Honan | 289 | 68.9 | 4.9 | 28.6 | 1.2 | 1.3 | 34.8 |
| 1859 | Shantung | 305 | 38.7 | 1.6 | 55.1 | 2.0 | 4.2 | 60.9 |
| 1871 | Anhwei | 150 | 32.0 | 9.4 | 46.6 | 13.4 | 8.0 | 64.0 |
| 1880 | Kiangsu | 425 | 20.4 | 9.4 | 65.4 | 10.0 | 4.2 | 79.0 |
| 1886 | Chekiang | 294 | 38.7 | 10.2 | 42.2 | 8.9 | 10.2 | 62.6 |
| 1893 | Honan | 160 | 43.1 | 15.6 | 51.9 | 1.9 | 3.1 | 70.6 |
| 1894 | Shensi | 294 | 44.2 | 4.9 | 45.0 | 6.5 | 2.3 | 52.2 |

Sources: *Chung-chou t'ung-kuan lu*, 1847 and 1893; *Shan-tung t'ung-kuan lu*, 1859; *Huan-chiang t'ung-kuan lu*, 1871; *Chiang-su t'ung-kuan lu*, 1880; *Che-chiang t'ung-kuan lu*, 1886; *Kuan-chung t'ung-kuan lu*, 1894.

[a] The percentage figures in column B are those of the officials whose main qualification was a higher degree but whose appointment or promotion was facilitated by purchase.

[b] To avoid too minute classification, small numbers of officials who entered service through *yin* are included.

What can be demonstrated from individual biographies but not by systematic statistics is that even before the sale of offices money, in a large number of cases, must have helped materially in the attainment of a good education, a higher academic degree, and eventually an official status. This fact was sometimes best explained by poor and struggling scholars. Shen Yao (1798–1840), a *yu-kung-sheng* of 1834 and an expert on historical geography, for example, made the following general observation:

[From Sung times onward] the scholars who had not yet entered government service had to have some landed property for self-sustenance before they could afford to concentrate on their studies. For this reason productive occupations, particularly trade and commerce, have become more and more important. Without their ancestors' management and bequest the descendants can seldom have opportunities to engage in serious studies and to become officials.[115]

From his own experiences and from those of his many gifted but frustrated friends, Shen came to the conclusion that "the god of money has reigned supreme." While his impressions were necessarily one-sided, exaggerated, and applicable in all probability only to the latter half of the Ch'ing period, they certainly help modern students to realize how exaggerated was the general belief in Ming-Ch'ing times that under the nationwide system of competitive examination individual merit alone determined one's social worth and status.

By way of summing up, it is clear from our illustrations and from general statistics that money in Ming-Ch'ing China was not in itself an ultimate source of power. It had to be translated into official status to make its power fully felt. From the founding of the Ming to the Mongol invasion of 1449 wealth could indirectly help in the attainment of a higher degree and an official appointment. The sporadic sales of offices after 1451 opened up a new channel of social mobility for the well-to-do and made money an increasingly important factor in the determination of social status. But up to the outbreak of the Taiping rebellion in 1851 the state had always made the examination system the primary, and the sale of offices the secondary, channel of mobility. When after the outbreak of the Taiping rebellion the state began to lose its regulatory power, money overshadowed higher academic degrees as a determinant of social status.

In comparing social stratification in Ming-Ch'ing China with that of the early modern and modern West, we find that the difference is one of degree, not of kind. The demarcation between manual workers and those who labored with their minds may have been sharper in Confucian China than in the West, but such demarcation is found in practically all pre-modern and modern literate societies. Even in contemporary North America, which has a minimum of prejudice against manual work, one of the fundamental distinctions in the stratification system is that between white-collar and manual-labor occupations. Confucian tradition and values may have exerted greater pressure on the wealthy to gain entry into the ruling elite, but similar urges and social inferiority complexes are found in the *nouveaux riches* of most pre-modern and modern societies. Education, or more precisely a university degree, is becoming increasingly important in the stratification of the most "materialistic" North American societies. Even the meticulous legal regulations of the styles of life of various social classes in traditional China are not unique; they are shared by medieval and some postfeudal European societies.[116] What is unusual about Ming-Ch'ing society is the overwhelming power of the bureaucracy and the ability of the state, in all but the last sixty years of a five and a half century period, to regulate the major channels of social mobility more or less in accordance with a time-honored guiding principle.

# CHAPTER II

# THE FLUIDITY
# OF THE STATUS SYSTEM

SOCIAL movement is not limited to the vertical dimension. In any highly differentiated society, one expects to find a certain amount of movement among occupational roles which are more or less equally evaluated. Our understanding of vertical mobility, which requires measurement of upward or downward movement between statuses more or less highly evaluated within the stratification system, is increased by a study of movements among equally evaluated statuses. "Horizontal mobility is," writes a modern sociologist, "a datum in the analysis of vertical mobility." [1]

Yet there are serious technical difficulties in dealing exclusively with horizontal mobility in a historical society like that of Ming-Ch'ing China. It is sometimes impossible to differentiate non-quantifiable material on occupational mobility of a more or less horizontal nature from certain types of quantifiable data on mobility which was initially horizontal but eventually resulted in substantial gain or loss in status. Since the bulk of historical material at our disposal does not lend itself to scientific multiple-criteria analysis, it is often difficult to assess accurately whether occupational mobility initially horizontal in character also implies a certain degree of upward or downward mobility in status. For example, students of Chinese social history frequently come across cases illustrating mobility between scholarly and commercial roles; many are the poor scholars who forsook their métier for trade, and no less numerous are the tradesmen who, after accumulating a certain amount of saving, gave up trade for studies. In theory, the legal and social status of even a poor scholar should have been superior to that of a substantial tradesman in the traditional Chinese society. Yet the poor scholar alone was the best judge of his own interests, including the likely gain or loss in social status consequent on his change of occupation. Modern students can only surmise that to give up one's scholarly career involved something of a loss in social status, but we have no reliable means of assessing whether or not a substantial improvement in economic status adequately compensated for his theoretical initial loss in social status. Since it is impossible to know his subjective "felicific calculus," we can never be sure in such cases whether the mobility involved was merely horizontal or simultaneously vertical.

Instead of dealing exclusively with horizontal mobility, therefore, we will treat in this chapter an aspect of mobility which is considerably broader in scope, namely, the fluidity of the status system. Specifically, we will discuss the lack of effective legal barriers preventing the movement of individuals and families from one status to another; statistics which, though most directly relevant to vertical mobility, imply initial occupational and horizontal mobility; the fluidity of the status system reflected in contemporary literature, genealogies, and biographies; and the permeability of the Confucian social ideology. It is hoped that the broad treatment given to social mobility in this chapter, together with detailed illustrations in the Appendix, will provide the meaningful context needed for interpreting the statistical data presented in subsequent chapters.

## THE ABSENCE OF EFFECTIVE LEGAL BARRIERS TO STATUS MOBILITY

With the passing of feudalism in the late third century B.C., classes and statuses ceased to be hereditary. There were, however, two exceptions. First, each dynasty had its imperial and nonimperial nobility which was numerically insignificant and often did not amount to more than a small class of hereditary sinecurists. It need not concern us here. Second, during certain periods of Chinese history the state's need for labor service made necessary the registration of segments of commoners as hereditary special status groups. Individuals in these hereditary special status groups, in theory at least, were not allowed to change their status. It is the aim of this section to trace the history of such special status groups in Ming times and to explain the reasons why they failed to be real barriers to status mobility.

The early Ming registration of special hereditary status groups was a continuation of the Mongol Yüan practice. Under the unusually oppressive Mongol rule, commoners were registered as *min* (ordinary commoner), *ju* (scholar), *i* (medical practitioner), *yin-yang* (astrologer), or as members of one or another of the many special status groups which were required by law to perform various types of service vital to the state, such as *chün* (soldier), *t'un* (military agricultural colonizer), *chiang* (artisan), *yen* or *tsao* (salt producer), *k'uang* (miner), *chan* (postal worker), etc. Many of the special statuses were minutely subdivided.[2] Without an extensive examination of Yüan sources it is impossible to say whether the Mongol government succeeded in strictly maintaining such special-service statuses, but there is evidence suggesting that change of status was by no means uncommon. One of the best sources for the study of status changes in Yüan times is the list of *chin-shih* of the year 1333, the only one of its kind extant for the period.[3] In it we find, for example, that Li Ch'i, the winner of the highest honors among the Chinese candidates, gave his originally registered family status as "artisan" but listed both his grandfather and father as officials. A few other Chinese candidates from families of supposedly hereditary special-service statuses listed one to three generations of officials among their paternal ancestors. Practically all the Mongol candidates who gave their family statuses were from families of Mongol garrisons.

The system of family status registration remained essentially the same under the early Ming. The laws of 1369 and 1370 provided for the registration of families according to their original or compulsorily assigned occupational status and for the punishment of any subsequent illegal changes in status.[4] The majority of commoners, however, were broadly classified under *min*, which included families engaged in agriculture, commerce, trade, and any other professions outside the special-service categories.

Had these regulations been stringently enforced, they would have constituted real barriers to status mobility, and Ming society would have approached the ideal envisaged by the ancient Ch'i statesman Kuan-chung, namely, hereditary and permanently segregated occupational groups. In reality, however, the early Ming state was mainly concerned with the maintenance of minimal quotas of personnel so that certain kinds of service vital to the state could be performed when needed. There was never any wish to freeze the society permanently nor did the dynastic founder Ming T'ai-tsu (1368–98) and his successors fail to realize that a certain amount of status mobility was necessary if the society was to achieve stability. Besides, the occupational range of the largest status group *min* was so wide that even if the laws concerning special status groups had been strictly enforced it would still have been possible for the majority of commoners to change their occupations and attendant social statuses.

Information on the three major special-service statuses, namely, those of artisan, soldier, and salt producer, is relatively full. First, the history of the changes within the artisan status should be briefly summarized. At the beginning of the Ming dynasty artisans were classified into two main categories, namely, *pan-chiang*, or those artisans of various provinces who were required to report to work at the nation's capital for a limited number of days at regular intervals of between one and five years, and *chu-tso jen-chiang*, or those artisans and families who were required to take up permanent residence in the metropolitan area so that they might always be available to meet the construction needs of the imperial government. Both categories of artisans were registered with, and brought under the jurisdiction of, the Board of Public Works. The quota for the former, first fixed at 230,289, in 1393, underwent little change in subsequent reigns. The quota for the latter, which received government stipends, fluctuated between 15,000 and 12,000. After the national capital was moved from Nanking to Peking in 1421, most of the latter took up permanent residence in the metropolitan Peking area.[5]

Since the early Ming state was concerned with maintaining rather than increasing the number of artisans, later statutes left considerable leeway as to the number of adult males of an artisan family to be formally registered as artisans. A statute of 1426, for example, provided that if an artisan household had two or three adult males only one should be registered as artisan. Two out of every four or five, and three out of six or more, adult males of an artisan household should stay in the quota. All the other adult males, the sick, maimed, orphaned, and extremely poor of artisan households were released from the official quota. This statute, no doubt, enabled many members of artisan households to change their occupation and status.

Depending on the craft and the distance between their native districts and the capital, many artisans reported to the capital city only once every three, four, or five years. Their length of stay in the capital was generally determined by the principle that no one should work for the government more than a month each year. Even adding the time spent on travel to their net working time of between three and five months in the capital city every three to five years, the majority of artisans still had ample opportunity to earn their living the way they liked. The comparatively lenient replenishment system and the reasonable working schedule made occupational and status mobility possible for substantial numbers of the artisan population.

Furthermore, in the course of time not all newly recruited artisans proved to be as proficient at their crafts as their forebears. From the early fifteenth century on it became increasingly common for members of artisan households to evade service and even the registered family status itself. The steady development of the Ming economy also made it desirable for the state to experiment with commutation of artisan service. Starting in 1485 a series of statutes provided that *pan-chiang* in the remote southern provinces and in some northern provinces could commute at will. By 1562, when decades of trade with the Portuguese and Japanese had brought about a substantial increase in the nation's silver stock,[6] commutation was made compulsory on a national scale. Thenceforth some 80 percent of the artisans who were classified as *pan-chiang* were virtually, though not technically, freed from their status. They still had to register under the artisan status for purely fiscal reasons.

Information is scantier on those artisans and families who permanently resided in the two capital cities of Peking and Nanking.

Ming statutes testified to their frequent desertion and the almost progressive deterioration of their standards of skill and performance.[7] Since they subsisted on government pay, their numbers in the two capital cities were purposely kept low. Their deplorable conditions can be learned from a special work on the history of the residential artisans of Nanking who were responsible for shipbuilding. By the middle of the sixteenth century these artisans were a far cry from their ancestors who had built the large and sturdy ocean-going fleets which the famous eunuch-admiral Cheng Ho in the early fifteenth century used for naval expeditions to southeast Asia, the Indian Ocean, and the East African coast. Most of these artisans in the sixteenth century "no longer have the skill" and "not even one or two out of a hundred know their craft." Many of them had been reduced to abject poverty, working as agricultural tenants for neighboring landlords who had encroached upon the property originally allotted to their ancestors as an auxiliary source of sustenance.[8] Small wonder, then, that a statute of 1534 provided that all adult males of residential artisan households of the metropolitan Peking area who were outside the formal quota had only to register their names with the Board of Public Works and to make an annual payment of three tenths of a tael of silver each. The revenue from this source was to be used by central government offices for hiring private artisans. This was a partial commutation of services for residential artisans. Although the detailed history of Ming residential artisans remains to be written, the complete abolition of the artisan status by the Manchu government in 1645 indicates the extent to which the residential artisan status had already become obsolete in Ming times.[9]

It is interesting to note that families of artisan status in Ming times produced many prominent men. Wu K'uan, for example, who won the highest honors in the metropolitan and palace examinations of 1472 and became president of the Board of Rites, was from an artisan family of Ch'ang-chou County, part of Su-chou in southern Kiangsu. He was famous for his literary attainments and nationally admired for his integrity and benign character. While a *sheng-yüan* he had to bribe county government underlings to free his family from regular service as textile weavers. His family history provides us with an example of comparatively early occupational and status mobility in that during his youth his family had already acquired several hundred *mu* of land. The income from agriculture, rather than from crafts, enabled him to engage in serious studies and to become prominent.[10] It is even more interesting to note that one of the most successful of Chinese clans in Ch'ing times, the Changs of T'ung-ch'eng in southern Anhwei, produced its first *chin-shih* Chang Ch'un in 1568 while still registered under the artisan status. Thanks to the gradual commutation of artisan service after 1485, the Chang family had acquired considerable landed property and begun to educate its youths since the time of Chang Ch'un's grandfather.[11]

Among the special-service statuses the most important was *chün-chi*, military status. In early Ming times some 2,700,000 adult males from slightly less than 2,000,000 households were so registered. Approximately one out of every six households was liable to military service. Such a large force was necessary to cope with the continual wars against regional contenders after the founding of the Ming in 1368 and to safeguard the northern borders from the Mongols and other tribes. Owing to the importance of national defense, statutory regulations for maintaining *chün-chi* on a strictly hereditary basis were more stringent and minute than those for other statuses. For the purpose of military administration the Ming empire was divided into a number of *wei*, garrison headquarters, each of which consisted theoretically of 5,600 enlisted men. Each *wei* was divided into five *so*, garrison posts, of 1,120 men each. These *wei* and *so* were established in the metropolitan area, along the northern boundary, and in the vast interior of the country. In order to make the metropolitan area the political and military center of gravity, early Ming emperors stationed some 800,000 men there, of whom 380,000 belonged to the metropolitan battalions, the remainder being periodically called to duty from provincial garrisons.[12]

At first all those who were drafted into the armed forces were allotted land and raised their own food as state tenants in time of peace. The heavily garrisoned northern posts, which could not possibly achieve self-sufficiency, were supplied through an ingenious government policy whereby merchants who shipped grain to such frontier posts were given salt certificates which they could exchange for government salt in the coastal areas. To save the cost and labor of transporting large quantities of grain to the northern posts, many resourceful merchants carried out commercial agricultural colonization in the northerly areas, taking on the poor people of the locality as tenants. Theoretically speaking, therefore, the early Ming military system was financially almost self-sufficient and the military status hereditary and inalienable.

Before very long, however, it was becoming increasingly difficult for the government to maintain such a self-perpetuating army. The main reasons were as follows. First, from the early fifteenth century onward it was not uncommon for generals and other officers to exploit soldiers for their private ends, as domestic servants, tenants, or manual workers whose income the former partially or totally appropriated. The metropolitan battalions were probably the worst exploited because they were brought under the command of powerful eunuchs during and after the Ch'eng-hua period (1465–87). The upper ranks were usually filled with members of the eunuch clique or of rich courtier families. The increasingly large-scale palace construction after 1500 further reduced metropolitan soldiers to a position little different from that of compulsory unskilled workers. Second, officers generally shared the profit of "squeeze" by appropriating among them a part of army rations and supplies, with the result that many soldiers could not live without supplementary earnings from sundry lowly jobs. Third, officers often utilized the procedure for replenishing the original regional *chün-chi* quota to enrich themselves. Bribery and blackmail were rampant. In 1477 in Kiangsu, for example, on the occasion of replenishing a group of 66,000 soldiers some 200,000 or 300,000 innocent commoners who did not belong to the *chün-chi* were the victims of extortion.

By far the most important factor in the government's problem was that people under *chün-chi* had a universal desire to divest themselves of their status by every possible means. This is easily conceivable because of the bleakness of their life, their utter lack of personal freedom in comparison with other commoner groups, and the constant exploitation and abuse to which they were subjected. Besides, they bore a definite social stigma because it was the early Ming practice to swell the army ranks with convicts of various kinds.[13] Whatever their original legal status as defined in the statutes, by the first half of the fifteenth century they had already become the most oppressed social group, often despised by ordinary commoners. Ming writers well knew that "none of the social groups have suffered more from their services and been more eager to get rid of their status than the *chün-chi* people." [14]

The consequence of these and many other scandalous practices was disastrous. Desertion was common and often reached serious dimensions. As early as 1428 the scale of army desertion made it necessary for the government to order a nationwide *chün-chi* reregistration.[15] Statutes of 1438 and 1479 and those of the Ching-t'ai period (1450–56) repeatedly forbade *chün-chi* people from surreptitiously changing their status.[16] The laws were, of course, of no avail. By about 1520 the metropolitan battalions, which originally boasted of 380,000 men, had less than 140,000, of whom only some 20,000 were physically fit for military service. Desertion was in fact not seriously combated by generals and officers; so long as widespread desertion was not discovered by special government inquiries ordered from above at fairly long intervals, they were able to appropriate the deserters' share of rations and supplies.

Desertion among provincial and frontier garrisons must have been equally rampant. In the middle of the sixteenth century, by which time the entire China coast was harassed by the Japanese pirates and the Chinese scoundrels who guided them, inquiries were made about the state of coastal garrisons. Only then was the scale of desertion discovered. The actual garrison forces along the coast amounted to a mere 32 percent of the legal quota in Liao-tung, 57 percent in Shantung, 22 percent in Chekiang, 44 percent in Fukien, and 23 percent in Kwangtung.[17]

Throughout the second half of the sixteenth century a series of memorials by high officials urged the government drastically to overhaul the military organization and its draft system. Some went so far as to suggest commutation of military service. The government's lack of initiative, coupled with the seriousness of the problem itself and of the importance of northern and coastal defense, precluded a legal abolition of *chün-chi*. But these memorials were eloquent testimonials to its almost total collapse. By the late Wan-li period (1573–1619) the rank and file of the metropolitan forces had become anything but an army. Drill and discipline were gone. The ranks earned their livings by peddling or craftsmanship and contributed a part of their earnings to their superiors. At inspection the ranks and onlookers talked and laughed, for everybody knew that the army was a joke. The regular provincial hereditary army had also become, by the middle of the sixteenth century at the latest, a mere shadow of its former self and its duties were increasingly performed by mercenary troops raised *ad hoc* to meet national and regional emergencies.[18] The total abolition of *chün-chi* in 1645 was a belated recognition of a long accomplished fact.

Because of the wide discrepancy between the laws which attempted to keep the army permanently on a hereditary basis and the actual practices described above, it is not surprising that *chün-chi* people achieved occupational and status mobility throughout Ming times. Like the artisan status, therefore, *chün-chi* failed to be an effective barrier to status mobility. It should be mentioned in passing that *chün-chi* began to produce *chin-shih* from as early as the first examination held in 1371. It produced its top honors men in 1438 and boasted many prominent statesmen and officials. Li Tung-yang, for example, who won fourth highest honor in the palace examination of 1468 before he turned eighteen, was a descendant of garrison soldiers near Peking. One of the most powerful prime ministers of the late fifteenth century, he was the first Ming official to receive the most coveted posthumous title *wen-cheng*, "Cultured and Upright." [19]

The third major special-service status group comprised salt producers of both coastal and inland provinces. A variety of terms was used in Ming times to describe salt-producing households, but the most generally applied were *yen-hu* or *tsou-hu*. Since salt is vital to human life and the importance of the salt gabelle to state income ranked next only to the land tax, the government began to register salt-producing households two years after the founding of the dynasty in 1368. During the large-scale wars and rebellions attendant upon the downfall of the Yüan dynasty, many of the original salt-producing households had deserted their assigned profession or *corvée* duty. From 1370 on, some *min-hu* or ordinary commoner households along the coast or near the inland salt lakes were forced to register as salt producers. Sometimes convicts were also assigned to the same *corvée* task.[20]

At first, salt-producing households were allotted land and marshes as their means of sustenance and also as sources of fuel for boiling brine. The quota of salt to be produced by each household was originally fixed in accordance with its economic ability and man power. In the course of time, however, the property of salt producers of small means was encroached upon by the rich, and many petty producers were reduced to abject poverty. The hapless salt producers resorted either to seeking the protection of powerful local clans or to outright desertion. In 1529 a salt censor testified that more than one half of the salt producers under the jurisdiction of the Liang-huai Salt Administration, which had its salterns both north and south of the Huai River, had deserted. Hsü Tsan, prime minister and concurrently president of the Board of Civil Appointments (died in 1548) also said: "The poor [salt producers] have deserted, the rich illegally purchased release from their status, and the whole quota become vastly different from that of earlier times." [21] Despite the increasingly minute regulations of compulsory replenishment and the severe penalties imposed for desertion and surreptitious change of status, salt producing as a hereditary status simply could not be maintained. By the late sixteenth century the Ming government belatedly accepted the inevitable by putting salt production on a laissez-faire basis. Thereafter, only those who could make a profitable living out of salt making or those who did not have means to leave it stayed, as salt producers or hired hands of the well-to-do. The time-honored laws of compulsory hereditary recruitment were virtually abandoned.[22]

Unlike other special-service hereditary statuses of the Ming period which were swept away by the Manchu government in 1645, salt producers remained after the change of dynasty as a special and theoretically hereditary status. However, in view of the economic principle that governed salt production the Manchu government wisely continued the laissez-faire policy of the late Ming period. From time to time attempts were made to redistribute salt producers' landed property and marshes, but such attempts were usually unsuccessful. In fact, the forces of rising capitalism continued to disrupt the planned hereditary society of salt producers. In the Liang-huai area, for example, by the middle of the eighteenth century much of the land, marshes, and salterns originally owned by salt producers had become the property of wealthy factory salt merchants. Many salt producers had become wage earners, entirely dependent on the capitalist factory merchants.[23] This process went on until 1831, when salt production was formally put on a free contractual basis, governed by the laws of demand and supply. The time-honored *yen-chi* and *tsao-chi* became little but a fiction.

Biographical material reflects the gradual change described. At the beginning of the Ming period, for example, Yüeh Chi of Ting-hai on the Chekiang coast was forced to register under *yen-chi*, although both he and his father were erudite scholars. Being legally a salt producer, Yüeh Chi had no alternative but to perform the arduous task of making salt until his untimely death in 1390.[24] The famous philosopher Wang Ken (1483–1541), a leading radical exponent of the neo-Confucian philosopher Wang Yang-ming (1472–1528), had a paternal great-great-grandfather who served as a headman of salt producers in T'ai-chou, Kiangsu. Although by Ming laws all male members of a salt-producing household (including juveniles) must be registered as salt producers, he once accompanied his father on a trading journey to Shantung. Despite poor and often-interrupted schooling, he carried the Confucian Classics in his sleeves and asked to be enlightened whenever possible. Thanks to his aspirations and especially to his strength of character and genius, he created a profound impression on Wang Yang-ming, whom he met in 1511, an encounter which marked the beginning of this famous teacher-disciple relationship.[25] Wang Ken's subsequent career as a dynamic thinker need not concern us here,[26] but it is significant to note that the authorities did not forbid him and his descendants to forsake their status as salt producers.

Because of the difficulty of strictly maintaining hereditary statuses and also because many salt producers were well-to-do, there were at least 388 *chin-shih* produced by *yen-chi* and *tsao-chi* during the Ming period. Under the laissez-faire Ch'ing policy families of this status continued to produce higher degree holders and officials. Sometimes even a poor salt producer could become prominent. The well-known scholar Ling T'ing-k'an (1757–1809) of northern Kiangsu coast, who became a *chin-shih* in 1790, provides an example.[27]

From the above survey of the history of the three major special-service statuses of the Ming period, it becomes clear that all these hereditary statuses broke down in the course of time. Since the majority of the nation was lumped under the broad *min* status whose rights to occupational and status mobility were never interfered with by the state, and since the Ch'ing government abolished all special-service statuses except the *yen-chi* or *tsao-chi*, it may be said that throughout a span of five and a half centuries the legal barrier to occupational mobility was more apparent than real.

It should also be remembered that even during the early Ming period, when special hereditary statuses were more strictly maintained, the imperial government and officials were in general lenient and sympathetic toward members of such statuses who had aspiration and ability. The case of Wang Ken is indicative. Some earlier and more extreme cases are even more so. Lu Chung, to mention one of the early instances, was recommended by provincial officials as a learned scholar suitable for an educational post. He was granted an audience by Emperor Hsüan-tsung (r. 1426–35). Officials of the Board of Civil Appointments reminded the emperor that Lu was registered under *chün-chi* and ought to enroll in the army, for so stringent were the statutory regulations that in theory no member of a soldier household could rid himself of his hereditary status unless he became the president of the Board of War. Upon hearing the officials' reminder, the emperor said: "It would be better for our schools to have one more good teacher than for our army to have another private." Lu was thus appointed as deputy director of studies of T'ai-p'ing prefecture in southern Anhwei.[28] Disregarding statutory regulations, Emperor Hsüan-tsung granted special dispensation to a number of *chün-chi* scholars recommended for government service in 1431.[29] The able and compassionate prime minister Yang Shih-ch'i (1365–1444), who himself came from a poor family and had lost his father, was instrumental in persuading the emperor to adopt a lenient attitude toward people of humble statuses who aspired to move up the social ladder. Thanks to his long premiership, even descendants of decapitated political offenders were allowed to take examinations and to become officials.[30]

The case of Chou Hui, who flourished in the mid-fifteenth century, is perhaps most illuminating. While serving as a private in the garrison forces at Lan-chou in Kansu, he had an opportunity to hear a lecture on *The Great Learning,* a Confucian primer, and was deeply moved. Studying during his off-duty hours he finally became a scholar of regional renown. A general and marquis dispatched a messenger to ask Chou to be his family tutor. On the grounds that as a garrison soldier the summons could be construed only as a call to duty by a commanding general, Chou at first refused. But he stipulated that if he were to be treated properly as a family tutor, the marquis should send his sons to him. The marquis complied. Thenceforth Chou attracted students from far and wide, from prominent families as well as from lowly and ostracized statuses. Among students of humble social origins were the brothers Cheng An and Cheng Ning, both hereditary musical entertainers in the household of an imperial prince. Their aspirations won a special dispensation from the prince, and they rid themselves of a status which would otherwise have permanently segregated them from ordinary commoners.[31]

These cases were by no means exceptional. In the early fifteenth century at least three humble men of the Su-chou area in southern Kiangsu were known to have performed compulsory *corvée* duties in their youth but to have secured special dispensation from sympathetic local officials. They were Wu Hui, who served as an envoy to the state of Champa in Indochina, and Liu Yü and Wu K'ai, who both eventually became secretaries of the Board of Punishments. Liu Yü was originally drafted as a local-government underling, a rather despised status.[32] More cases like these would have been known had people of other localities been as enthusiastic as people of Su-chou in compiling biographies for those natives who succeeded in moving up the social ladder but failed to achieve fame.

It would be unfair, however, to present just one side of the picture. Unavoidably there were cases in which officials refused to allow men of lowly origins to change their status. Lu Shen, for example, a *chin-shih* of 1505 who held several educational posts including the presidency of the Imperial Academy of Nanking,[33] defied the wishes of Prince Chin of Shansi that the son of one of the latter's musical entertainers be kept in the local school roster. Lu was known to have said: "It would be better for our schools to have one less student than for them to be polluted by one man." But this refusal was related to the change of a status which was statutorily and customarily regarded as morally impure and may not apply generally to the change of status of special-service groups. There is reason to agree with Ho Liang-chün, a scholar and minor official of Lu's native Shanghai, that Lu's inflexibility was "probably unique in recent times." [34]

To conclude our discussion on the absence of an effective legal barrier to status mobility, it should be pointed out that, however stringent legal regulations on the maintenance of hereditary special-service statuses might be, early Ming rulers and officials in general lacked the determination literally to enforce them. On the contrary, their unusually sympathetic attitude toward ambitious and talented men of humble status, their surprisingly flexible and broad merit concept,[35] and their realization of the necessity of a certain amount of social mobility in order to make the state and society stable were perhaps among the most important factors in the increasing obsolescence of the rigidly defined hereditary statuses. In fact, it was precisely during the early Ming when the legal barrier to status mobility appeared to be the most formidable that the ruling class exhibited the most sympathy toward the humble and poor. This sympathetic attitude toward status mobility was maintained by the majority of the ruling class during the greater part of the sixteenth century, thanks to the nationwide influence of the teachings of Wang Yang-ming, which imply a belief in the intrinsic equality of men.[36]

STATISTICS ON MING *chin-shih* FROM SPECIAL STATUSES

The absence in Ming times of an effective legal barrier to the free movement of individuals and families from one status to another may best be shown by the proportion of *chin-shih* who came from families of special-service statuses which were supposed to be hereditary.

TABLE 4

*CHIN-SHIH* FROM SPECIAL STATUSES, 1371–1643

| Status | 1371–1445 | 1448–1484 | 1487–1523 | 1526–1562 | 1565–1604 | 1607–1643 | Total |
|---|---|---|---|---|---|---|---|
| *Ju* (scholar) | 79 | 34 | 18 | 15 | 7 | 7 | 160 |
| *Chün* (soldier) | 250 | 1,010 | 1,339 | 1,149 | 1,185 | 676 | 5,609 |
| *Kuan* (army officer) | 18 | 165 | 222 | 197 | 204 | 99 | 905 |
| *Yen* or *Tsao* (salt producer) | 7 | 51 | 82 | 79 | 94 | 75 | 388 |
| *Chiang* (artisan) | 29 | 161 | 198 | 211 | 189 | 66 | 854 |
| *Chan* (postal service) | 3 | 3 | 9 | 6 | 0 | 1 | 22 |
| *Mu-so* (horse breeder) | 0 | 0 | 0 | 4 | 2 | 2 | 8 |
| *T'ai-i* (medical official) | 0 | 10 | 8 | 8 | 4 | 2 | 32 |
| *I* (private medical practitioner) | 3 | 17 | 18 | 7 | 4 | 2 | 51 |
| *Ch'in-t'ien-chien* (official astronomer) | 0 | 2 | 3 | 0 | 0 | 0 | 5 |
| *Yin-yang* (private astrologer) | 0 | 0 | 1 | 0 | 0 | 0 | 1 |
| *Fu-hu* (rich family) | 5 | 15 | 4 | 3 | 1 | 0 | 28 |
| *Kuang-lu-ssu-ch'u* (official cook) | 0 | 1 | 0 | 4 | 1 | 0 | 6 |
| *P'u-hu* (hunter) | 0 | 0 | 0 | 1 | 0 | 0 | 1 |
| *Shang* (salt merchant) | 0 | 0 | 0 | 0 | 0 | 1 | 1 |
| *Tsung-shih* (imperial clansman) | 0 | 0 | 0 | 0 | 0 | 4 | 4 |
| Total (special statuses) | 394 | 1,469 | 1,902 | 1,684 | 1,691 | 935 | 8,075 |
| Total (all *chin-shih*) | 1,465 | 3,588 | 4,311 | 3,999 | 4,674 | 4,567 | 22,577 |

Sources: Li Chou-wang, *Kuo-ch'ao li-k'o t'i-ming pei-lu ch'u-chi* (1746 ed., revised from original 1721 ed.), part 1, on the Ming period. For the three examinations of 1418, 1421, and 1427 no family statuses are given. The numbers of *chin-shih* of these years are excluded. Family statuses for the year 1400, missing from the listing, have been supplied from *Chien-wen erh-nien tien-shih teng-k'o lu* (list of candidates who passed the palace examination of 1400).

It ought to be mentioned that the number of special statuses as recorded in Ming *chin-shih* lists far exceeds that shown in the table. For example, there are at least five or six subcategories of soldiers, including noncommissioned officers and widow-households of the Nanking imperial gendarmerie, which in the table are included in *chün-chi*. *Kuan-chi*, which literally means "official status" is likely to mislead the unwary. Actually *kuan* as a status term in Ming times applied only to army officers and their families.[37] There were several kinds of artisans, including textile weavers and others con-scripted into the army as artisans, salt producers, boatmen and horsemen in the postal service, and horse breeders, which have been amalgamated in the table. The status *fu-hu*, or rich family, was established when during the reigns of Ming T'ai-tsu and Ming Ch'eng-tsu (1403–24) several tens of thousands of rich households of the country, especially of the wealthy northern Chekiang and southern Kiangsu areas, were forced to take up permanent residence first near Nanking and then in the metropolitan Peking counties of Wan-p'ing and Ta-hsing. Many of them became bankrupt under heavy fiscal and *corvée* burden. In the course of time the status of rich family bore little semblance to its name. Imperial clansmen were not allowed to take examinations until 1595 and the reasons why they did not produce their first *chin-shih* until 1622 have never been explained in Ming documents. Possibly the right of impover-ished imperial clansmen to earn their living or office was recognized in 1595 only as a broad principle.

Salt merchants were not specially registered until 1600, when *shang-chi*, literally "merchant status," was created for salt mer-chants of Chekiang.[38] This status never applied to merchants in general. Unlike other special-service statuses of Ming times which partook of the nature of *corvée*, *shang-chi* was theoretically an im-perial favor bestowed upon the richest and most resourceful of the merchant groups. Members of salt merchant families were entitled to take pre-*sheng-yüan* and *sheng-yüan* examinations under special *shang-chi* quotas, which were often, though not always, a useful channel of initial social mobility.[39] After 1600 *shang-chi* student quotas were established in Kiangsu, Shantung, Chihli, Shansi, Shensi, Kansu including Ninghsia, and Kwangtung. But some salt-produc-ing provinces, such as Liao-tung (Fengt'ien in Ch'ing times), Fukien, and Yunnan, never had *shang-chi* quotas. Szechwan, a significant salt-producing province, did not have a *shang-chi* student quota until 1858.[40]

Because of its late creation, *shang-chi* produced only one *chin-shih* during the entire Ming period. But it is important to bear in mind that prior to 1600 salt merchant families had actually produced several hundred *chin-shih* who were officially classified under *min-*

*chi.* Fortunately, some Ch'ing works on various salt administrations list *chin-shih* of the Ming period who originated from salt merchant families and had attained the *chin-shih* degree before the inception of *shang-chi.* The numbers of Ming *chin-shih* from salt merchant families given in Ch'ing works are necessarily incomplete because up to 1492 the nature and organization of the salt trade differed drastically from that of late Ming and Ch'ing periods. Up to the end of the fifteenth century there were technically no full-time salt merchants. Those who wished to engage in the salt trade had to ship grain to frontier posts along the Great Wall in exchange for the *yin* (a standard weight unit in salt trade) certificates with which they received salt in the main salt-producing areas along the coast. In fact, such merchants were usually called *pien-shang,* "frontier merchants," rather than *yen-shang,* "salt merchants."[41] After 1492 merchants could receive salt in the coastal area by simply making a monetary payment instead of transporting grain to the northern borders. It took more than half a century to reorganize the salt trade and the major salt administrations.[42] Because of these complex changes over a long period, figures for pre-1500 *chin-shih* from frontier salt merchant families are incomplete. Even incomplete figures indicate that a high degree of academic success was achieved by members of a comparatively small number of salt merchant families, and help to correct the misleading impression given by table 4.

As we see from table 4, out of a total of 22,577 *chin-shih* of the entire Ming period who gave their family statuses, only 160, or less than 7.1 percent, came from families of registered scholar status. There were 7,915 candidates of special statuses ranging from army officer, medical official, and rich family down to garrison soldier, salt producer, and artisan. If our incomplete figure for candidates from salt merchant families is added, the aggregate of candidates from special statuses amounted to 8,104 or 35.9 percent of the total. The remaining 64.1 percent came from families classified under the broad category *min,* which represented the large majority of the nation and was made up theoretically of those engaged in agriculture, trade, commerce, and other unspecified occupational groups. The *min* category also included civil officials, for it was Ming prac-

TABLE 5

HIGHER DEGREE HOLDERS FROM SALT MERCHANT
FAMILIES IN MING TIMES

| Salt administration | Period[a] | Number of chin-shih | Period[a] | Number of chü-jen |
|---|---|---|---|---|
| Liang-huai | 1371–1643 | 106[b] | 1371–1642 | 133[b] |
| Liang-che | 1568–1643 | 12 | 1558–1642 | 23 |
| Ch'ang-lu | 1521–1640 | 13 | 1441–1641 | 17 |
| Shantung | 1493–1643 | 13 | 1369–1642 | 19 |
| Ho-tung | Ming (unspecified) | 45 | Ming (unspecified) | 146 |
| Total | | 189 | | 338 |

Sources: *Liang-huai yen-fa chih* (1806 ed.), ch. 47; *Liang-che yen-fa chih* (1801 ed.), ch. 24; *Ch'ang-lu yen-fa chih* (1726 ed.), ch. 13; *Shan-tung yen-fa chih* (1725 ed.), ch. 13; *Ho-tung yen-fa chih* (1727 ed.), ch. 8.

[a] The periods are those on which specific information is available in the works on various salt administrations.

[b] Those candidates whose family status was *tsao-hu* or whose native places were *ch'ang* (salt factory) are excluded because they were probably members of salt-producer families.

tice that officials must retain their original registered family status. The sudden and drastic decline in numbers of candidates from special statuses in the subperiod 1607–43 is mainly accounted for by the fact that such statuses had long lost their original meaning and been merged into the broad *min* category. In the light of our knowledge of the increasing difficulty in maintaining the hereditary statuses, it seems likely that the trend toward the merger of certain special statuses with the ordinary commoner status had started comparatively early.[43] Indeed, we may doubt whether there is any real hiatus in institutional history; the increasing obsolescence of family-status registration in the latter half of the Ming led to its almost total abolition in early Ch'ing times.

From these figures it is fairly safe to say that in Ming times there was a great deal of occupational mobility which eventually resulted in status mobility. It is almost certain that the amount of occupational mobility which was more or less horizontal and which involved upward mobility not radical enough to be indicated in table 4 was much greater. Unfortunately, the Ch'ing government discontinued the Ming practice of family-status registration so that a comparison between Ming and Ch'ing is impossible. It seems reasonable to suggest, however, that with the removal of almost all remnants of legal barriers to free occupational and status mobility in Ch'ing times, the trend that had been clearly indicated during the Ming could hardly be reversed. This will become clear when the accounts of contemporary observers and biographical material are examined.

Social phenomena which cannot be shown in statistics impressed contemporary observers. Ming and early-Ch'ing commentators on institutional and social matters have left a body of evidence which shows that men from various humble walks of life were appointed to offices in the first half century of the Ming without their having to attain a higher academic degree.[44] While it is true that this unusual practice was stopped after the second quarter of the fifteenth century, it had helped greatly to establish the principle of "li-hsin wu-fang," that the selection of talents should be based on no hard and fast rules.[45]

A hitherto little noticed institutional factor which also helped people of "miscellaneous" statuses to ascend the social ladder was the provision in early Ming laws that the two metropolitan provinces of Pei-Chihli and Nan-Chihli should reserve five *chü-jen* degrees within their respective quotas for provincial candidates from these statuses. No exact definition for "miscellaneous" was given, but it is clear that "miscellaneous" meant sundry statuses which, if not legally debilitating, were at least regarded by contemporaries as "impure." [46] These included, for example, unclassed local and central government clerks, copyists, computers, waiters, and sometimes eunuchs' adopted sons. There is reason to believe that these provincial quotas for people of "miscellaneous" statuses were minimal rather than maximal, for in 1453 alone there were at least twenty-five *chü-jen* degrees awarded to candidates of "miscellaneous" statuses out of a total Pei-Chihli quota of 250.[47] The flexibility of the status system is epitomized by the extraordinary fact that the three first-class honors men of the palace examination of 1448 were a Confucian scholar, a one-time Taoist monk-apprentice, and a one-time protégé of a Buddhist monk.[48]

FLUIDITY OF THE STATUS SYSTEM SEEN IN SOCIAL LITERATURE

The lack of effective legal barriers to status mobility and the general fluidity of the status system were reflected in social literature, genealogies, and biographies. Kuei Yu-kuang (1506–71), the famous scholar and prose writer of lower Yangtze, for example, observed: "In ancient times the four functional orders of commoners had their distinct functions, but in later times the status distinctions between scholars, peasants, and merchants have become blurred." [49] Wang Tao-k'un, *chin-shih* of 1547, a pedantic prose writer and descendant of tradesmen, gives a vivid description of the strategy followed by people of his ancestral Hui-chou area to assure social success:

Hui-chou, with approximately one scholar out of every three merchants, is a highly cultured area. For just as merchants seek after handsome profit, scholars strive for high honors. It is not until a man is repeatedly frustrated in his scholarly pursuit that he gives up his studies and takes up trade. After he has accumulated substantial savings he encourages his descendants, in planning for their future, to give up trade and take up studies. Trade and studies thus alternate with each other, with the likely result that the family succeeds either in acquiring an annual income of ten thousand bushels of grain or in achieving the honor of having a retinue of a thousand horse-carriages. This can be likened to the revolution of the wheel, with all its spokes touching the ground in turn. How can there be a preference for any one profession? [50]

As will be seen, this realistic social strategy was by no means confined to the actively trading Hui-chou area or to the Ming-Ch'ing period. It reflected the social reality which had been profoundly changed by the permanent institutionalization of the competitive civil-service examination system since T'ang times. It was in general based on three fundamental considerations. First, since at least Sung times, when examination became the most important channel of social mobility, a higher degree or an office had been the goal for most commoner families. Second, the transition from commoner status to membership in the ruling bureaucracy was often a gradual process during which the average family had to face economic realities. Third, in spite of the social premium which Confucian society placed on scholarship, there was little deep-seated social prejudice against non-scholarly productive occupations which were frequently carried on simultaneously or in alternation with basic studies. The average family in its initial stage of social transition often regarded adequate living as more fundamental than higher aspirations.

For example, Yüan Ts'ai, the famous writer on family affairs who flourished in the late twelfth and early thirteenth centuries, while recommending that a family should encourage its gifted members to pursue a scholarly and eventually an official career, emphasized at the same time the necessity of providing the less gifted of its members with skills needed to earn a living. He argued that so long as one could earn his livelihood without bringing disgrace to his ancestors, any occupation from fortune-telling, geomancy, and medicine to agriculture, trade, and craft should be regarded as respectable.[51] *Chü-chia pi-pei,* one of the most popular family guides compiled by Ch'ü Yu (1342–1425), upheld the common Sung view that "the talented should study and prepare for examinations but the mediocre must be taught a useful trade to earn their living." [52]

This social realism found its way into clan instructions and covenants of many Ming and Ch'ing genealogies and other writings on family management. While some families preferred a simultaneous pursuance of studies and agriculture (an occupation which yielded lower returns but gave greater stability),[53] many others mentioned no preference but insisted that their members earn an honest living before higher social goals could be reached. Still others, like the Ho clan of northern Anhwei which had various branches dispersed in Kiangsu, Kiangsi, Honan, Fukien, Hupei, Hunan, and Kwangtung, were so realistic as to admit openly: "Although studies and earning a livelihood may complement each other, at times they also hinder each other." The Ho clan's instructions pointed out that if one's modest natural endowment failed to enable him to go very far in his studies or if one could not afford prolonged studies, there was nothing wrong in foregoing further study and taking up agriculture or trade.[54]

In examining social literature, modern students cannot fail to be impressed by the number of cases in which a commoner labored with both his mind and his physical strength in the process of attaining a minimal qualification for an office. There were numerous cases of Ming and Ch'ing scholars and officials who in the early stage of their social metamorphosis ploughed the fields and studied the classics at the same time. One of the many, Kung I-ch'ing of I-wu county in the heart of Chekiang, as a youth "bared his legs, carried food in a straw basket, studied hard after a full day's work in the field." He became a *chin-shih* in 1574.[55] Yang Chi-sheng, *chin-shih* of 1547, was the son of a landowning peasant of Yung-ch'eng in west central Hopei. From the time he was seven years old by Chinese reckoning, he daily pastured the family ox. After hearing neighbor boys recite classics he entreated his older brother to allow him to study. Until he acquired his first degree before he reached eighteen he had performed *corvée* duty in his brother's stead. Becoming a boarder in a Buddhist monastery, he often studied till the small hours. After repeated failures in higher examinations he eventually became a *chin-shih*. His courageous censure of the powerful prime minister Yen Sung, which cost him his life in 1555, made him one of the most famous martyrs of Ming times.[56]

Since the majority of the Chinese lived on the land and many officials came from farming households, *keng-tu*, or "plough and study," were usually regarded as parallel and occasionally convertible undertakings. The first major philosopher of Ming times, Wu Yü-pi (1381–1469), for example, a native of Kiangsi and the son of a president of the Imperial Academy, decided not to take examinations while a young man but "to sustain himself with the plough." Although during his prime he attracted students from afar, "he wore a thatched cloak, worked with his ploughshare amidst rain, and discussed metaphysics with them." [57] Liu Ta-hsia (1436–1516), one of the famous presidents of the Board of War, taught his sons not to forget the family's humble origin. One of his favorite disciplines instituted at home was that his sons should work in the fields on a rainy day.[58] Chang Mao (1437–1522), a famous president of the Imperial Academy who eventually became president of the Board of Rites at Nanking, insisted that his sons should all earn their living by cultivating the family's modest acreage.[59] An extreme case is that of Shan Fu of Ch'üan-chou on the southern Fukien coast, who, after retiring from a county magistracy in the 1560s, became an agricultural tenant because his family had originally been poor and his upright character had made it impossible for him to accumulate savings while in office.[60] Granted that these cases are not typical of the Ming period, in which incorruptible officials were less rare than during the Ch'ing, they illustrate the common notion that plough and studies should go together. My ancestral hall in Chin-hua in the heart of Chekiang was named, as thousands of others were, *Keng-tu-t'ang*, "the Hall of Plough and Studies."

Evidence is not lacking to show that in the initial stage of social transition crafts and studies were frequently taken up simultaneously. Wu Chung-liang of Hsiu-ning in Hui-chou made his living as a blacksmith during the day, while studying at night. Being constantly annoyed by mosquitoes in summer nights, he soaked his feet in a tub of water so that he could concentrate on his studies. After acquiring the *chü-jen* degree in 1593, he entered government service and eventually became a magistrate of a department county in Hunan. He was nicknamed "the blacksmith *chü-jen*." [61] A shoe-repairer, Ch'ien Chin-jen of Su-chou, spent his meager savings on books which he studied by himself. Thanks to his native intelligence and perseverance, he eventually mastered the basic classics, philosophies, and Buddhist and Taoist literature. Upon hearing of this unusual shoe-repairer, scholars of Su-chou were at first highly suspicious but after repeated queries they became convinced of his sound scholarship. Ch'ien eventually became a family tutor and was generally called by the populace "the shoe-repairer scholar." [62] Many spinners and weavers of the lower Yangtze of late Ming and early Ch'ing times became well-to-do and climbed up the social ladder. Chang Han, for example, *chin-shih* of 1535 who reached the high office of president of the Board of Civil Appointments in the early 1570s, was the grandson of a silk weaver of Hang-chou, capital city of Chekiang, whose modest fortune had been built on a single loom.[63]

Families of still more lowly occupations have been known to encourage their members to study. Shang Lo, for example, who had the unique distinction of placing first in provincial, metropolitan, and palace examinations and retired as prime minister in 1477, was the grandson of an indigent hunter and firewood gatherer.[64] The case of the Hsü family of Ch'ien-t'ang, one of the twin cities which made up Hang-chou, is also worth noting. The ancestors of its first successful member, Hsü Ch'ao (1647–1715), *chin-shih* of 1673 who later became president of the Board of Civil Appointments, were fishermen. He was named Ch'ao (literally, "tide") because he was born in the family fishing boat at the time of a rising tide.[65] His son, Hsü Pen (1683–1747), *chin-shih* of 1718, served as prime minister from 1736 to 1744. Since then the family has produced two governors, one sub-chancellor of the Grand Secretariat, and many higher degree holders and officials, and has ranked among the most prominent clans in a province of unusual academic success.[66]

By far the largest body of evidence showing the interchangeability of statuses during various stages of social transition is that devoted to merchants and tradesmen. This situation is understandable since, as pointed out so long ago by the great Han historian Ssu-ma Ch'ien, trade and commerce yielded much higher returns than agriculture and crafts. Although this may not have been equally true in the various periods of Chinese history, we do know that the largest fortunes in Ming-Ch'ing times were as a rule built on trade and international commerce. While a systematic study of the methods and processes of capital accumulation in Ming-Ch'ing times yet remains to be written, there is substantial evidence showing that the formation of large fortunes did not necessarily require large initial capital. Some merchants were originally rich or allied themselves with officials from the beginning so that they were able to enter such lucrative government-controlled trades and industries as salt, tea, timber, liquor, mining, smelting, and import and export. Many others, however, started in a humble way, as peddlers, retailers, small interlocal merchants, shop apprentices, or bookkeepers who were gradually admitted into large partnerships on the strength of personal character and ability.[67]

The pattern of social mobility of rich merchant families, for which records are sometimes relatively abundant, was such that gifted members were encouraged to study and often succeeded in becoming higher degree holders and officials while the majority of the other members became bibliophiles, art connoisseurs, or patrons of scholars and men of letters, or otherwise helped to dissipate the family wealth in conspicuous consumption and debauchery. The general direction of their social mobility was toward the elite, and the merchant element in such families became less and less prominent.[68] As to small merchants and humble tradesmen, the available material is too fragmentary to warrant any broad generalization. But there is enough evidence to indicate that in Ming and early Ch'ing times at least—when the growing population was not yet too large to affect adversely standards of living and when the continual influx of silver had almost incessantly stimulated industries, crafts, trade, and interregional exchange of commodities—there were ample opportunities for small men with meager capital but plenty of business skill to improve their economic and eventually their social status.

Contemporary social novels abound in the success stories of such small men. Some may have been somewhat exaggerated, but the case of the loyal servant-merchant Ah Chi can be entirely authenticated and can serve as an illustration. He was a servant of the Hsü family of Ch'un-an in hilly west-central Chekiang. The family property had been divided by the two grown-up brothers, one of whom was his master. After his master's death the widow and her five children were hard pressed by the other branch of the family. His mistress pawned all her jewelry for twelve taels of silver, which were handed to Ah Chi to invest. He went to the mountains to buy lacquer and sold it wherever the local supply was low and the price favorable. Within a year he made a threefold profit. In twenty years' time he made a fortune of several tens of thousands of taels exclusively out of interlocal trade. The widow's three daughters were amply provided with dowries and the two sons were given elaborate weddings. A family tutor was hired to teach the sons, who also bought Imperial Academy studentships. Owing to the loyalty and good management of the servant, the widow became one of the richest persons in a comparatively poor district.[69]

In all likelihood, with a touch of luck a small tradesman might in a relatively short period of time acquire more means and leisure than a hard-working landowning peasant or an artisan. Since his profession required a certain degree of literacy, the tradesman was more likely than the peasant or artisan to pursue basic studies if he had social ambition. Of fairly numerous cases we may mention a few famous ones. Ch'en Chi of Wu-chin in southern Kiangsu was a merchant's son. After selling goods in Hang-chou he spent one half of the profit buying books. He borrowed books which he could not afford to buy and copied them in his spare time. After more than ten years of sudy he had mastered the classics, histories, and philosophical works. When Ming Ch'eng-tsu set up a commission for the compilation of the famous encyclopedia *Yung-lo ta-tien,* he was appointed the director although he had not attained even the first academic degree.[70]

The well-known scholar and bibliographer Wang Chung (1745–94) of Yang-chou was orphaned at seven. The family was so poor that he was forced to become an apprentice in his teens. He worked in book stores and took advantage of the ample opportunities for study which they provided. After he had placed first in the local *sheng-yüan* examination in 1769, his assiduity and literary talents won the respect of many scholars and officials. Although he failed to obtain a higher degree because of what he admitted to be nervousness, his various works, particularly a series of essays on classics, philosophy, and etymology entitled *Shu-hsüeh,* were held in high regard by contemporaries, and he earned an entry in the *Draft History of the Ch'ing Dynasty.*[71] Wang Shih-to (1802–89) of Nanking was forced by poverty to work in his teens as an apprentice, first in a secondhand clothes store, then in a bakery. Whether working or unemployed, he studied the four basic Confucian Classics and practiced calligraphy. His diligence and perseverance impressed his maternal grandfather, who gave him occasional funds with which to pursue his studies. Between 1821 and 1858 he earned his living by teaching the children of private families; in this way he made the acquaintance of a number of scholars and officials and gained access to fine private libraries. The attainment of the *chü-jen* degree in 1840 did not disrupt his pattern of life. He continued to work on historical geography and the compilation of local prefectural histories. His scholarly achievements were finally brought to the attention of the imperial government, which bestowed upon him the honorary title of preceptor of the Imperial Academy in 1885.[72] It should be mentioned that both Wang Chung and Wang Shih-to were of Hui-chou descent and came from families which for generations had members who alternated between trade and studies.

The alternation between and convertibility of trade and studies is nowhere better shown than in the voluminous biographical chapters of the 1827 edition of the history of Hui-chou perfecture. Most of the brief sketches of those known for local charitable contributions, filial piety, fraternal love, and care for poor kinsmen are prefaced with the title of student of Imperial Academy, a designation which they bought years after they had been forced by economic necessity to quit studies and take up trade.[73] The fluidity of the status system is also manifest among Shensi merchants, who in Ming and early Ch'ing times ranked with Hui-chou merchants as a leading commercial group. Wen Ch'un, a member of a Shensi salt merchant family which established its business in Yang-chou, who became a *chin-shih* in 1565 and later a president of the Board of Civil Appointments, described in detail the histories of many Shensi families which either engaged in agriculture, trade, and sudies simultaneously or moved up into the bureaucracy after acquiring wealth through farming, usury, or the cloth and salt trade.[74] The process whereby poor scholars gave up their métier for trade and the reverse process whereby tradesmen took up studies are fully shown in a mid-Ch'ing work especially devoted to those unknown commoners who after years of occupational zigzags were still unsuccessful in their attempt to climb the social ladder.[75]

The fact that status-consciousness was often blurred not only among commoners but also between commoners and elite groups can be amply illustrated. A few examples will suffice. Chou Yün, a small rice merchant of early Ch'ing who eventually became a poet of note in the highly cultured Chia-hsing area in Chekiang, in his old age wrote a poem to describe his life:

> Like a scholar, but I am without a degree,
> Like a peasant, but I have studied,
> Like an artisan, but I know of no craft,
> Like a tradesman, but I don't run [after profit].

Yet a man of his social status was admitted into the local elite.[76] A few men of very humble circumstances in Yang-chou in the late seventeenth and eighteenth centuries, such as a small rice dealer, a small brewer, a small candle and incense maker, and a peasant, associated themselves with members of the local elite.[77] The great

late-Ch'ing Hunan scholar Wang K'ai-yün had among his disciples
a Buddhist monk, a maker of bamboo baskets, a blacksmith, a carpenter, and a buffalo boy. What is even more revealing is that the
carpenter, Ch'i Po-shih (1863–1957), who became a great painter,
was in his early struggling days admitted into the poetry club sponsored by members of two prominent local clans.[78]

Another interesting social phenomenon to be observed is that in
Ming-Ch'ing times many officials and their families were engaged
in trade. Despite a statute of 1394 which prohibited dukes, marquises, earls, and civil and military officials of the fourth rank and
above from allowing their family members or servants to engage
in trade,[79] the censor-general Li Ch'ing presented to the throne in
1407 a memorial stating that "nobles and generals frequently have
their sons and domestic servants engage in the salt trade, with the
result that they have become a real menace to the interest of the
government and the people." [80] The government's subsequent difficulties in enforcing the law of 1394 indicate the strength of the
social tendencies which counteracted it.[81] The law of 1394 could
not but have far-reaching implications, for never according to Ming
law were nobles of ranks lower than those of duke and marquis and
officials below the fourth rank actually forbidden to engage in trade.
Huang Hsing-tseng (1490–1540), a scholar of Su-chou, testified in
his interesting notes on the social customs of his native lower
Yangtze that many official families had been engaged in iron smelting, warehouse business, usury, pawnbroking, and the wholesale
or retail selling of novelty goods, and had amassed fortunes which
sometimes exceeded one million taels. He also observed that in the
suburbs of the nation's capital many officials had set up pawnshops,
money-lending establishments, and stores dealing in salt, wine, and
liquor.[82] Ho Liang-chün, a scholar of Shanghai who printed his
miscellaneous notes in 1579, was struck by the same phenomenon
in his native Sung-chiang prefectural area.[83]

The early Ch'ing government generally connived at this practice.
One of the well-known cases was that of the powerful Manchu
Mingju (1635–1708), prime minister between 1677 and 1688. His
trusted Korean servant An Shang-i was a leading salt merchant in
Chihli who, because of his master's political influence, almost suc-

ceeded in establishing a monopoly in the Ch'ang-lu salt administration. His salt business was carried on by his son An Ch'i, nationally known as a patron of scholars and an art connoisseur. A Chinese, Chang Lin, served as Mingju's business agent. Entering the government by purchasing an office, he eventually became financial commissioner of Fukien and Yunnan. His two sons, Chang Huan and Chang Hsün, carried on the salt trade at Tientsin, both became *chü-jen* in 1693, and later served as secretaries of the Imperial Patent Office. They left several volumes of prose works and poetry.[84] That Mingju and his protégés were not the only officials of the time who engaged in the salt trade became apparent in the famous trial of 1710, which was instituted by other Ch'ang-lu salt merchants to meet the An family's threat of establishing a monopoly. The case had to be hushed up, for had it been pressed too hard many former Chihli officials would have been implicated.[85]

Indeed, it may be said that in Ch'ing times the social distinction between officials and rich merchants was more blurred than at any other time in Chinese history except for the Mongol Yüan period. The most lucrative of trades, such as salt and import and export, were usually farmed out to those who could afford to underwrite tax payments in advance. As the price of their business monopoly, these merchants had to consent to being constantly squeezed by such officials as the salt censors and the commissioner of maritime customs at Canton, vulgarly known to Europeans as Hoppo. The holders of these lucrative official posts were Manchu, Mongol, and Chinese Bannermen and members of *Nei-wu-fu* (Imperial Household Department) who, after milking the merchants, were themselves milked, for it was customary for them to contribute to the department's coffers when their tenure of office expired. These rich merchants were thus the government's invaluable agents in an ingenious network of milking and profit-sharing.

The value of the rich merchants to the government was enhanced by their almost incessant monetary contributions to the central treasury. The Liang-huai salt merchants, for example, contributed 36,370,963 taels to the government between 1738 and 1804, not counting the 4,670,000 taels spent on the Ch'ien-lung emperor's southern tours and numerous smaller contribuions to salt officials.

Although the recorded contributions of the thirteen Co-hongs of Canton between 1773 and 1832 amounted to only 3,950,000 taels, it was widely known that the Wu family alone contributed to government and non-government agencies at least 10,000,000 taels in three generations. For their contributions the salt and Co-hong merchants were rewarded with official titles and ranks, some as high as that of financial commissioner (rank 2b). The Ch'ien-lung emperor stayed in several salt merchants' villas and gardens during his six southern tours and took a personal interest in the family affairs of not a few merchants.[86] All this was a far cry from the high-handed measures which the first and third emperors of the Ming applied to rich families of the lower Yangtze; it reflected a basic change in the attitude of the imperial government toward rich merchants.

By translating their wealth into academic-bureaucratic success the rich merchant families could further command social respect. Their success can be partially demonstrated by figures. The numbers of higher degree holders produced by major regional salt merchant groups between the founding of the Ch'ing and the turn of the eighteenth century are shown in the following table.

TABLE 6

HIGHER DEGREE HOLDERS FROM SALT MERCHANT
FAMILIES IN CH'ING TIMES

| Salt administration | Chin-shih | | Chü-jen | |
|---|---|---|---|---|
| | *Period* | *Number* | *Period* | *Number* |
| Liang-huai | 1646–1802 | 139 | 1645–1803 | 208 |
| Liang-che | 1649–1801 | 143 | 1646–1800 | 346 |
| Shantung | 1646–1805 | 47 | 1645–1804 | 145 |
| Ch'ang-lu | 1646–1802 | 64 | 1648–1804 | 232 |
| Ho-tung | 1646–1771 | 33 | 1645–1788 | 71 |
| Total | | 426 | | 822 |

Sources: *Liang-huai yen-fa chih* (1806 ed.), ch. 48; *Liang-che yen-fa chih* (1801 ed.), ch. 24; *Shan-tung yen-fa chih* (1808 ed.), ch. 19; *Ch'ang-lu yen-fa chih* (1805 ed.), ch. 17; *Ho-tung yen-fa pei-lan* (1789 ed.), ch. 10.

Thanks to the mention of the numbers of salt merchants in some Ch'ing works on the salt administrations and to one modern study, the comparative advantage enjoyed by salt merchant families in competitive examinations can be roughly shown. The Liang-huai salt administration probably did not have more than 230 or 250 licensed merchants at any given time between the founding of the Ch'ing and 1800.[87] The Liang-che salt administration, which boasted of some very rich merchants who individually supplied seven or eight percent of the salt quota of the entire area, probably did not have more merchants than Liang-huai.[88] A complete list of salt merchants of the Shantung salt administration for the year 1805, fortunately available, yields a total of only 129.[89] For the year 1789 we know that the Ho-tung salt administration had 57 transport merchants and 379 *tso-shang,* or "residential merchants."[90] The latter were actually independent salt producers, men whose resources were substantial but limited compared with those of the capitalist factory merchants of Liang-huai. Even the transport merchants of Ho-tung were often men of limited means.[91] The number of Ch'ang-lu merchants is not mentioned, but in view of the comparatively small area under Ch'ang-lu jurisdiction and of the fact that in the late seventeenth century a few salt merchants almost succeeded in squeezing the others out, the total number of merchants was probably considerably smaller than that of Liang-huai.

The right to engage in the salt trade was in general hereditary, although we have to take into account the vicissitudes of salt merchant families. Some of them declined in a matter of two or three generations and were replaced by new men and some lasted longer. But it seems rather unlikely that the cumulative number of salt merchant families in these five groups could have exceeded 2,000 during the century and a half between the founding of the Ch'ing and 1800. The total number of *chin-shih* granted during the same period was 15,000 in round numbers. We thus find that the two richest groups of salt merchants of Liang-huai and Liang-che, which had probably an aggregate of less than 1,000 families, produced 282 *chin-shih,* or 1.88 percent of the national total. This should be compared with the minimal national total of 20,000,000 households at the beginning of the Ch'ing and the minimal total of 50,000,000 households by 1800.[92] The astounding academic success of the five groups of salt merchants may be more conveniently gauged from the fact that during the entire 267 years of the Ch'ing period less than a dozen highly cultured, urbanized, and densely populated prefectures could produce more than 400 *chin-shih*.[93] Yet these five groups produced 426 in 156 years.

Qualitatively, the academic-bureaucratic success of salt merchant families was even more impressive. The Chekiang group produced prime ministers Wang Yu-tun (1692–1758) and P'an Shih-en (1770–1854);[94] the Liang-huai group, one of the most powerful of prime ministers, Ts'ao Chen-yung (1775–1835); and the Shantung group, prime ministers Kao Hung-t'u (died in 1645) and Li Chih-fang (died in 1694). In addition, they produced several dozen officials of the third rank and above.[95]

The correlation between wealth and academic success can also be shown by statistics from the actively trading Hui-chou area. This hilly prefecture comprised six counties, the population of which increased from slightly more than 500,000 in Ming times to probably 1,500,000 in the early nineteenth century. It would have been considerably larger if many of its native sons had not permanently settled elsewhere. Between 1646 and 1826 the area produced 519 *chin-shih* and 1,058 *chü-jen,* including a number of scholars who took up residence elsewhere. It is certain that its *chin-shih* productivity was many times higher than that of comparable areas. What was even more remarkable was that of a national total of 225 *chin-shih* with first-class honors between 1646 and 1826 as many as 29, or 13 percent of the national total, were natives of Hui-chou or were of Hui-chou descent.[96] There was a great deal of truth, therefore, in the generalization of the poor but gifted scholar Shen Yao that whereas in ancient times scholars mostly came from scholarly families, from Sung times onwards a disproportionate number of scholars originated in merchant families.[97]

This being the case, from the early Ch'ing onward rich merchant families commanded an ever increasing social prestige. Some salt merchant families which produced officials called themselves *kuan-shang,* or "official-merchants." Although such an appellation was legally banned in 1724, the purpose was merely to prevent such merchants of exceptional prestige from partially evading their tax payments.[98] In social practice, however, the distinction between officials and rich merchants became dimmer and dimmer. It is well known that the Co-hong merchants of Canton were addressed by both Chinese and Westerners as *qua* (Cantonese corruption of *kuan*, or official) in the eighteenth and nineteenth centuries. It is also common knowledge that in late Ch'ing times *kuan* or *shen* (officials, retired officials, and prominent local leaders) were increasingly lumped together with *shang* (merchants) during fund-raising campaigns.

## THE PERMEATION OF SOCIETY BY CONFUCIAN IDEOLOGY

One of the basic yet most difficult problems in social mobility studies is to assess the extent to which the prevalent social ideology of a given society has permeated the various social strata. The difficulty confronting us is greater because the object of our study is a historical society to which no sampling survey can be applied. Like other major societies both historical and modern, the Ming-Ch'ing society had its own ideological precepts, mottoes, proverbs, and myths which may or may not embody substantial truth but without which the majority of people would lack the necessary incentive for self-advancement. The permeation into all strata of the prevalent social ideology is in a sense a requisite to a substantial amount of mobility.

As has been discussed in chapter I, the Confucian social ideology at once justified social inequality and upheld the principle that social status should be determined by individual merit. This ideological dualism was better resolved after the competitive civil service examination system became a permanent institution in T'ang times, and particularly after the establishment of government schools at the county, prefectural, and provincial levels and of a rudimentary but nationwide scholarship system in the beginning of the Ming period. The effect of the examination system on social mobility became more and more apparent after the mid-T'ang period, and during the last thousand years there gradually arose a long series of proverbs and myths which were based on the Confucian social ideology and reflected an important new social phenomenon: the fact that academic success and subsequent position in the bureaucracy were no longer necessarily dependent on family status. We need mention only a few such proverbs. "Golden mansions and Yen Ju-yü [since Han times an abstract paragon of female beauty and charm] are both to be found in books." "Generals and ministers were not originally blue-blooded, and so a man of ambition should aim high." "A bequest of chests of solid gold is not as valuable to your descendants as teaching them a basic classic." All these, and many others, suggest the American myth found in the books of Horatio Alger except that the goal is academic-bureaucratic success which, while it implies material success, cannot be precisely equated with it.

Biographical material enables us to know whether the Confucian social ideology reached the lower strata of Ming-Ch'ing society. The brief illustrative material given in the preceding section and the more detailed information given in the Appendix show that in many cases it did. Neither the famous Ming martyr Yang Chi-sheng, a northern peasant's son who aspired to study while pasturing the family ox, nor the blacksmith Wu Chung-liang, who became a *chü-jen* and local official, was unique. Indeed, Ming-Ch'ing biographies yield many parellels. For example, the early life of the famous scholar and painter Wang Mien of Chekiang, the hero of the first chapter of the great social novel *An Unofficial History of the Literati,* who was eventually called to government service by Ming T'ai-tsu, is almost an exact description of the early life of Yang Chi-sheng.[99] The courageous censor Yang Chüeh, a poor peasant of Shensi who became *chin-shih* in 1529; Lu Shu-sheng, a small holder in the neighborhood of Shanghai who placed first in the metropolitan examination of 1541; and Liu Chih-lun, *chin-shih* of 1636, a poor Szechwan peasant who had to gather and sell firewood to help the family make ends meet but who as a youth aspired to be a sage, all reflected the pervading influence of the post-T'ang Confucian social ideology among the rural poor.[100] A landless agricultural tenant, the father of the famous admiral P'eng Yü-lin (1816–90) of Heng-yang in southern Hunan, knew that for a poor man the only way to bring about a marked change in social status was through the study of Confucian Classics.[101]

Confucian social ideology also penetrated into the lower strata of urban craftsmen and tradesmen. T'u Ch'ao of Su-chou, for example, though a silver miner, used all his savings to enable his younger brother to concentrate on studies in the hope of eventually revolutionizing the family status.[102] Shih Ching, also of Su-chou, who had to be a peddler to support his family of hereditary silk weavers, studied hard, became a *chü-jen* in 1480, and later served as a local official.[103] Shih P'an, who won the highest honors in the palace examination of 1438; Wang Hsing, the well-known early-Ming scholar recruited into government service; Chiang Eng, who served as lieutenant-governor of Fukien in the late fifteenth century, and Wang Chüeh-lien, *chin-shih* of 1739 and later a palace tutorial official, were all sons of small tradesmen who early in life begged their reluctant parents to allow them to give up trade for studies.[104] The last-named, a native of the most backward province Kweichow who dared to go counter to his parents' wishes at the tender age of five, is particularly indicative of the degree to which the Confucian social ideology had permeated. When a substantial tradesman's own sons were mediocre, he would sometime choose as his future son-in-law a studious neighbor boy to whom he gave financial aid and constant encouragement.[105] Even the enfranchised declassed people were so eager to avail themselves of the Confucian belief in individual merit that in the latter half of the eighteenth and the early years of the nineteenth centuries they used every means to acquire the first degree before the expiration of the legally required transitional period of three generations.

The Confucian social ideology by no means influenced the male sex only. Ming-Ch'ing biographies show a large number of cases in which the widowed mother held fast to the prevalent social belief and strictly supervised her son's scholastic work. She herself might be semiliterate or completely illiterate, but she would weave, spin, and undergo prolonged privation, just to make it possible for her son to concentrate on his studies. We need mention only some outstanding cases. Li Po (1630–1700), one of the three nationally famous early-Ch'ing Shensi scholars, as a youth was saddened by the downfall of the Ming and decided never to seek any degree or office under the alien Manchu rule. But his widowed mother forced him to take the examination.[106] Li Tao-nan's mother, widow of an impoverished salt merchant, on her deathbed said to her son: "[Despite poverty] it is still better to study." Li Tao-nan thereupon named his study after his mother's last words and became a *chin-shih* in 1759.[107] The grandmother of Yen Ch'en, a *chin-shih* of 1859, rousing herself out of a coma, suddenly opened her eyes and said to Yen Ch'en's parents: "The wisest thing in life is to study." [108]

While all this, and much else, unmistakably indicates the remarkable extent to which the prevalent social ideology pervaded the lower social strata, there would be danger of exaggeration if another side of the picture were not examined. From the literary works of successful men we gather the impression that not all members of their families cared for the prolonged ascetic scholastic work so necessary for academic success. For example, Chang Han, a descendant of silk weavers, who became president of the Board of Civil Appointments in the early 1570s, testified that both his father and his second elder brother were concerned neither with family management nor with serious studies; they preferred easy living.[109] The same can be said of many members of some of the most prominent Ming-Ch'ing clans[110] and of certain very wealthy families who not infrequently indulged in "music, women, dogs, and horses." [111] More examples are given below in chapter IV, "Downward Mobility." There is no way of knowing even approximately what portion of the population (for economic or other reasons) remained unaffected at any given time by this Confucian social ideology, although it is obviously unfair to assume that the complete lack of any biographical record for the majority of the people implies that they rejected the prevailing ideology.

After both sides of the problem have been weighed, it may still be said that the Confucian social ideology probably spread reasonably widely and deeply into the various social strata. Three main reasons seem to support our impression. First, to a large extent the system of values and goals in traditional China, at least in Ming-Ch'ing society, was more monolithic and less class-specific than those of modern industrial societies. Unlike complex modern societies in which higher social goals may be reached through business, industry, specialized professions, art, the theater, and even sports, Ming-Ch'ing society's one ultimate status-goal was attainable only through academic-bureaucratic success. The value-monolith can best be shown by the stark realism of Ma Ch'un-shang, one of the most interesting characters in *An Unofficial History of the Literati*, who made his living by editing examination essays. To an illustrious official's descendant who had no ambition for a career, he said:

From ancient times everybody has striven to enter the civil service. Confucius, for example, lived in the Ch'un-ch'in period when officials were selected on the strength of their wise sayings and good conduct. This is why Confucius said: "Make few false statements, do little that you may regret, and you will find your emoluments." This was the civil service of Confucius' time. By the period of Contending States eloquence of speech became the road to officialdom. This is why Mencius orated so tirelessly to one prince after another. This was the civil service of Mencius' time. . . . Under the reigning dynasty officials are selected by the best possible criterion—essays. If even Confucius were living today, he would have been studying the technique of essay writing and preparing himself for examinations. He certainly would not have said: "Make few false statements, do little that you may regret." Why? Because that kind of talk would get him nowhere, for nobody would give him an office.[112]

To the indigent scholar K'uang Ch'ao-jen, who had ailing parents to support, Ma gave the following advice:[113]

After you return home you should consider practicing essays and passing examinations the best way to honor your parents. There is nothing else in this world by which you can better establish yourself. It goes without saying that fortune-telling and divination [your present occupation] is a lowly profession. Even teaching or joining an official's private staff is no solution. Only by passing successive examinations and acquiring your *chü-jen* or *chin-shih* degree can you instantaneously bring honor to your ancestors.[113]

Thus one set of values pervaded the length and breadth of the whole Ming-Ch'ing society, although only those of the poor who had unusual intelligence and determination could avail themselves of such values.

Second, the monolithic value system found its full expression in various social symbols which could not fail to serve as a powerful psychological challenge to many of the humble and relatively humble. The vastly different rights, obligations, and styles of life of the ruling and the ruled were there for everybody to observe. Besides, shortly after 1400 it became a social custom for various localities to erect arches or gateways to honor their native sons who became *chü-jen* and *chin-shih*. The purpose was to arouse the ambition of the local populace so that the district could maintain or improve its academic and social success. From the latter half of the fifteenth century on, arches and gateways on a more elaborate scale were built by an increasing number of localities for native sons who reached high office.[114] In the course of time even a *kung-sheng* was entitled to erect a flagpole to show off his "established" status. In Ch'ing times some localities went so far as to build community temples where tablets of past local higher degree holders were kept. When descendants of those worshiped in community temples passed higher examinations, new flagpoles were erected as a further honor to the departed and as an inspiration to the living.[115] It was very hard indeed for most men in Ming-Ch'ing China not to be aroused by these elaborate social symbols to feelings of envy, humiliation, indignation, or frustration. Concrete examples of the psychological impact of academic achievement as the dominant factor of successful upward mobility will be given in the Appendix.

Third, there were many channels through which the Confucian social ideology was disseminated. The clan and family system was one. Ever since the rise of the clan system in Sung times various writers on clan and family affairs, impressed by the fact that inept descendants of distinguished people fell into complete oblivion and that studious young men from ordinary commoner families often rose to prominence, emphasized the importance of education and persistence as the chief means to social success. Clans in Ming-Ch'ing times usually had among their instructions a typically Chinese moral exhortation that wealth and honor were inconstant and that a man could rely only on his scholastic effort and ambition. The establishment at the beginning of the Ming period of a nationwide school and scholarship system and the growth of private academies after 1500 further helped to propagate the Confucian social ideology. In fact, so monolithic was the value system that it was perpetuated not only through institutionalized channels but also by the words of parents, relatives, neighboring elders, and even village storytellers.

CHAPTER III

# *UPWARD MOBILITY:*
# *ENTRY INTO OFFICIALDOM*

ENTRY into officialdom is perhaps the most important of the many aspects of social mobility in Ming-Ch'ing China. There can be little doubt that traditional Chinese society considered entry into the ruling bureaucracy the final goal of upward social mobility. From the standpoint of the modern researcher, this aspect is also the most rewarding, because the quality and quantity of the best type of available data allow meaningful quantification and statistical analysis. When properly classified and interpreted according to their historical, institutional, and social contexts, these statistical data will answer one of the basic questions in the study of traditional Chinese society and institutional history, namely, whether the Ming-Ch'ing ruling class was recruited from a reasonably broad social base and whether there are grounds for the conventional impression that during the last two dynasties of China's *ancien régime* career was open to merit. When these statistics are appraised and correlated with the aggregate evidence of this study, as will be done in the concluding chapter, they will go a long way toward explaining the fundamental nature and character of the Ming-Ch'ing society.

A BRIEF CRITICISM OF SOURCES

Chinese historical sources are rich in biographical material. The bulk of the twenty-six dynastic histories consists of biographies. In addition to these officially or occasionally privately compiled dynastic histories, for the Ming-Ch'ing period there are over a hundred privately compiled biographical series, the most famous and voluminous of which are Chiao Hung's *Kuo-ch'ao hsien-cheng lu,* printed in 1616, and Li Huan's *Kuo-ch'ao ch'i-hsien lei-cheng,* printed in 1880. Furthermore, most of the known editions of local histories contain biographical chapters.[1] For the purpose of social mobility studies, however, all these biographical series are sources of limited, sometimes dubious, value for two main reasons. First, the full data about the biographies necessary for classification according to social origin are often lacking. Second, the selection of biographies is often biased.

Their deficiencies as sources for social mobility studies are not far to seek. Biographies in dynastic histories often completely overlook an individual's family background except when his ancestor or ancestors were officials of high and middle ranks or otherwise known for their special talents or achievements. Although the account of a prominent person in a privately compiled biographical series frequently includes an official record of his career, one or more nonofficial biographical essays usually of a eulogistic nature, and a detailed epitaph based on the biographer's association with the deceased or on information supplied by the deceased's descendants or relatives, the treatment of ancestry and early processes of social mobility in such accounts is far from uniform or specific. There were often certain aspects of the life and background of a prominent person which his biographer-friend, paid biographer, or descendants wanted to magnify or to hide. Biographical material in local histories, being usually very sketchy, is an especially risky source for social mobility studies.

Since the value of any statistical study depends on the quality of the sources it uses, and since the mobility data in Chang Chung-li's *The Chinese Gentry* are based entirely on local histories and are more extensive than earlier studies on the subject, it seems pertinent to make a brief assessment of his data. A large-scale check would require too much time and effort because only a small number of the individuals included in local histories can be found in national biographical series, or other better types of sources, or can

be checked against our *chin-shih* ancestral data. Only a sample
check is made on a few prominent individuals whose ancestries the
present author is able to supply offhand.

### TABLE 7

#### A SAMPLE CHECK ON THE ACCURACY OF FAMILY
#### BACKGROUND DATA OF LOCAL HISTORIES

| | | Family background | |
| Name | Major achievement | Sources used by Chang Chung-li | Other sources |
| --- | --- | --- | --- |
| T'ao Chu | *Chin-shih*, 1802; governor general | No information[a] | Family very rich, later impoverished; T'ao's father a *sheng-yüan*[b] |
| Cheng Ping-t'ien | *Chin-shih*, 2d highest honor, 1822 | No information[c] | Cheng's great-grandfather a *sheng-yüan*[d] |
| Lu Chien-ying | *Chin-shih*, 1822; governor general | No information[e] | Lu's great-grandfather a *sheng-yüan;* his grandfather a student of Imperial Academy[d] |
| Wang Ming-hsiang | *Chin-shih*, highest honor, 1833 | No information[c] | Wang's great-grandfather a *sheng-yüan*[f] |
| Wei Yüan | *Chin-shih*, 1844; famous historian and geographer | No information[a] | Family very rich, later impoverished; Wei's father a low-ranking official[g] |

[a] *Hunan t'ung-chih* (1887 ed.).
[b] T'ao Chu, *T'ao-wen-i-kung ch'üan-chi* (printed some time after 1839), ch. 47, which is entirely devoted to his family history.
[c] *Kiangsi t'ung-chih* (1881 ed.).
[d] *Tao-kuang jen-wu t'ung-nien ch'ih-lu* (*chin-shih* list of 1822).
[e] *Mien-yang chou-chih* (1894 ed.).
[f] *Tao-kuang kuei-ssu-k'o hui-shih t'ung-nien ch'ih-lu* (*chin-shih* list of 1833).
[g] *Shao-yang Wei-fu-chün shih-lüeh* (undated, written by Wei's son).

Since the *sheng-yüan* degree is an indication of Chang-li's "gentry"
status, the validity of his "gentry" mobility data collected from
local histories is very much open to doubt.[2]

The most fundamental defect of the above types of biographical
material is that the criteria for inclusion in them are seldom explicit, but almost invariably subjective, and even then are never

followed with consistency, much less with exhaustiveness. For the Ming period a good illustration is Kuo T'ing-hsün's *Kuo-ch'ao ching-sheng fen-chün jen-wu k'ao,* a gigantic biographical series arranged prefecturally in 115 chapters printed in the T'ien-ch'i period (1621–25). Since he was educational commissioner of Kiangsu and Anhwei, which constituted the southern metropolitan province, he devoted 31 chapters to these provinces alone, as compared with 15, 13, and 6 chapters devoted to the academically unusually successful provinces of Chekiang, Kiangsi, and Fukien. Very few chapters were given to northern provinces and only one chapter each to three southwestern provinces. There is not a single biography devoted to the prominent men of Ch'üan-chou prefecture along the southern Fukien coast, which was academically unusually successful and one of the most socially mobile areas in the country. The longest biographies run to over 100,000 words, while the brief ones consist of a few dozen, sometimes only a few, lines. Su-chou prefecture in southern Kiangsu, for example, an area known for its local custom of writing biographies even for the poor and humble,[3] leads all the prefectures with a total of 201 "prominent" men, whereas its close neighbors, Ch'ang-chou and Sung-chiang prefectures, both extremely successful academically, are given only 86 and 73 "prominent" men respectively.[4]

To give an example of a Ch'ing biographical series, in Li Huan's voluminous *Kuo-ch'ao ch'i-hsien lei-cheng,* which deals with 5,986 "prominent" Chinese (if we exclude several hundreds of imperial clansmen and Manchu and Mongol Bannermen), the achievement criteria were twisted and distorted to satisfy the compiler's local patriotism. In spite of the fact that Hunan, Li's native province, produced the largest number of generals and provincial officials during and after the Taiping rebellion, it ranked very low in *chin-shih* productivity, which was an important factor in the production of prominent men. Owing to Li's subjective standards, however, Hunan ranked second in his compilation and ahead of the highly cultured Chekiang as the second largest producer of "prominent" men. The risk of using this largest Ch'ing biographical series for statistical purposes can be roughly shown by the following comparison with another biographical series of similar though less biased nature and with the objective and exhaustive series on Ch'ing *chin-shih.*

TABLE 8

PRODUCTIVITY OF PROMINENT MEN IN CH'ING TIMES
*(by provinces)*

| | Series A | | Series B | | Series C | |
|---|---|---|---|---|---|---|
| *Province* | *Percent* | *Ranking* | *Percent* | *Ranking* | *Percent* | *Ranking* |
| Kiangsu | 23.53 | 1 | 21.24 | 1 | 10.93 | 1 |
| Chekiang | 14.92 | 3 | 17.30 | 2 | 10.43 | 2 |
| Chihli | 4.98 | 5 | 6.54 | 4 | 10.13 | 3 |
| Shantung | 5.18 | 4 | 6.21 | 5 | 8.45 | 4 |
| Kiangsi | 3.24 | 10 | 5.64 | 7 | 7.08 | 5 |
| Honan | 4.59 | 7 | 3.36 | 10 | 6.33 | 6 |
| Shansi | 3.59 | 8 | 2.75 | 13½ | 5.34 | 7 |
| Fukien | 3.44 | 9 | 5.59 | 8 | 5.23 | 8 |
| Bannermen | — | — | — | — | 4.86 | 9 |
| Hupei | 1.84 | 15 | 2.89 | 12 | 4.53 | 10 |
| Anhwei | 4.75 | 6 | 6.92 | 3 | 4.44 | 11 |
| Shensi | 2.29 | 14 | 2.98 | 11 | 4.22 | 12 |
| Kwangtung | 2.34 | 12 | 4.74 | 9 | 3.78 | 13 |
| Szechwan | 3.01 | 11 | 2.75 | 13½ | 2.86 | 14 |
| Hunan | 15.93 | 2 | 6.16 | 6 | 2.71 | 15 |
| Yunan | 1.59 | 17 | 1.18 | 16 | 2.59 | 16 |
| Kweichow | 0.93 | 18 | 0.99 | 17 | 2.24 | 17 |
| Kwangsi | 0.42 | 19 | 0.74 | 18 | 2.13 | 18 |
| Kansu | 1.61 | 16 | 1.94 | 15 | 0.95 | 19 |
| Manchuria | 2.30 | 13 | — | — | 0.68 | 20 |
| Total | 99.48 | | 99.93 | | 99.96 | |

Sources: Series A is from Li Huan, *Kuo-ch'ao ch'i-hsien lei-cheng;* Series B is from *Ch'ing-shih lieh-chuan;* both tabulated in Chu Chün-i, *Chung-kuo li-tai jen-wu chih ti-li fen-pu.* Series C is based on *chin-shih* lists collected and tabulated in Chang Yüeh-hsiang, "Ch'ing-tai chin-shih chih ti-li ti fen-pu," *Hsin-li,* IV (no. 1, March), 1926. It should be noted that Chang's *chin-shih* figures are not too accurate because of some omissions. For more accurate figures and provincial rankings, cf. table 28.

The biographical series A and B, being based on subjective multiple achievement criteria, are not cross-sectional. Series C, which includes all Ch'ing *chin-shih,* is based on a single achievement criterion. For purposes of sociological inquiries there can be little doubt that series C is by far the most valuable, because a *chin-shih* almost invariably began his official career in the middle strata of the bureaucracy and was a member of the national elite in that his name was inscribed on stone tablets erected in front of the Imperial Academy. It goes without saying that he was considered a prominent man by people of his ancestral locality. Moreover, only series C is cross-sectional, being based on a uniform objective standard of achievement. Although its definition for achievement is narrower than those of series A and B, there must have been a fairly close relationship between academic success and social prominence, viewed as such by contemporaries, in the Confucian society.

Some of the variations between series A and B and series C can be explained. For example, Kansu and Manchuria, which produced the smallest numbers of *chin-shih* but proportionately larger shares of military men, naturally rank higher in series A and B than in series C. Hunan and Anhwei, the two provinces which produced the largest numbers of generals and provincial officials during and after the Taiping rebellion, rank very much higher in series A and B than in series C. But however much military men might have contributed to the degree of "prominence" to these two provinces in the last 60 years of a 267 year period, their rankings in series A and B are highly suspect. Proportionately, some of the variations among the three series are even more serious. For example, Kiangsu produced but slightly more *chin-shih* than Chekiang and Chihli, yet its share of "prominent" men is 1.57 times that of Chekiang and 4.92 times that of Chihli in series A and 1.22 times that of Chekiang and 3.25 times that of Chihli in series B. It is manifestly absurd to imagine that Hunan, which produced but 25.7 percent of the number of *chin-shih* produced by Chekiang should have surpassed the latter in "prominence" ranking. Leaving the quality of individual biographies aside, we must recognize that these commonly used biographical series are capable of serious statistical distortion.[5]

Superior in quality to the types of biographical series mentioned above are the examination booklets of successful candidates. In Ming and especially in Ch'ing times it became an almost nation-wide custom for *chin-shih*, *chü-jen*, *pa-kung-sheng*, and *yu-kung-sheng* to reprint their examination essays and poems for distribution to examiners whom they regarded as "patrons" and "teachers," to certain officials with whom they hoped to curry favor, and to relatives, friends, and acquaintances. This was also the occasion for them to receive congratulatory money or gifts from people of their locality who, generally speaking, could not fail to recognize them as the newly established. Since originally *chin-shih* booklets were stamped with a seal in vermilion ink, they were commonly called *chu-chüan* (vermilion booklets). *Chü-jen* and *kung-sheng* booklets were stamped with a seal in black ink, and were called *mo-chüan* (black booklets). In the course of time this technical difference was neglected and the two types of examination booklets were commonly called *chu-chüan*.[6] They are invaluable for the study of candidates' ancestry because they provide precise information as to whether the families had produced holders of academic degrees or offices during the three preceding generations. It is regrettable, however, that the small numbers of these booklets known to be extant and their extremely uneven chronological and geographic coverage greatly curtail their value as sources for social mobility studies.[7]

The main body of sources for our study of the social composition of the bureaucracy and of entry into officialdom consists of over seventy lists of *chin-shih, chü-jen,* and two special categories of *kung-sheng*, namely, *pa-kung-sheng* and *yu-kung-sheng*. There are two types of *chin-shih* lists available. One type gives only the names of *chin-shih* and other miscellaneous information of non-biographical nature and is usually entitled *Hui-shih lu,* that is, List of successful candidates of the metropolitan examination. Lists of this kind are useless for our purpose.

This study relies exclusively on lists of the second type which provide precise information on candidates' ancestry. The titles of such lists underwent several changes in Ming-Ch'ing times. All except three of the extant Ming *chin-shih* lists which contain useful information on candidates' family backgrounds are entitled *Chin-shih teng-k'o lu,* that is, lists of those who were formally granted the *chin-shih* degree. These words are invariably preceded by the year in which the metropolitan and palace examinations took place. The technical difference between these lists and *hui-shih lu* is that although those who had passed the metropolitan examination were already *de facto chin-shih*, their *de jure* status as *chin-shih* was conferred only after they had taken the final palace examination, in which everybody passed as a matter of course. Only after they were formally "graduated" (*teng-k'o*) could they be correctly called *chin-shih;* only then were they required to compile formal lists of their names, birth dates, registered places of residence, ages, brief *curricula vitae,* spouses, children, and paternal ancestors of the past three generations, and offices or degrees, if any, held by them. Since *teng-k'o lu* were submitted to the throne, their arrangement is very formal, with all candidates listed in the order of their placement at the final palace examination, led by the three first-class honors men, followed by second-class and third-class *chin-shih.*

Textually *teng-k'o lu* are excellent because they were compiled at a time when all successful candidates, save for the very few who for reasons of illness or urgent family matters could not wait for the palace final, were present in the nation's capital. For this reason and particularly because of the solemnity of the occasion *teng-k'o lu* contain information of a high degree of accuracy. The only bias in the information given in these lists concerned age, sometimes falsified by certain candidates because age was occasionally a secondary factor in government's consideration for a candidate's initial appointment. But even this minor falsification was highly risky and infrequently resorted to because the age factor could be checked against a candidate's earlier *curriculum vitae* filled out at the time of the *sheng-yüan* and *chü-jen* examinations.

Since *teng-k'o lu* were primarily a source of reference for the imperial government, in the course of time candidates themselves preferred the compilation of a different type of list for their own private circulation. The earliest known extant list of this new type is the *Chin-shih t'ung-nien pien-lan lu* (List of *chin-shih* classmates for private reference) for the 1553 class. Since classmate relationship was customarily regarded as almost an extension of kinship and often obliged classmates to stand by and help one another, this and subsequent similar lists all stress the "fraternal" element. Members of the class were listed not according to their rankings in the palace examination but according to seniority in age. Thus members of the class called each other "brothers," and this peculiar kinship extension often passed on to the next generation. The need for and the many benefits of this extended kinship made it increasingly desirable for candidates to compile informal lists. The last extant Ming *chin-shih* list (for the class of 1610) and all extant early Ch'ing lists are entitled either *Chin-shih lü-li pien-lan* (*Curricula vitae* of *chin-shih* for private reference) or *Chin-shih san-tai lü-li pien-lan* (*Curricula vitae* of *chin-shih* with information on three preceding generations for private reference). The contents are, however, exactly the same, for the former type also gives ancestry records, despite its shorter title. After 1800, *chin-shih* lists were invariably compiled privately and entitled *Hui-shih t'ung-nien ch'ih-lu* (Lists of successful metropolitan candidates by order of seniority in age).

This gradual change in the system of compiling *chin-shih* lists has created a textual problem for modern researchers. In contrast to *teng-k'o lu* which were compiled during the interval between the metropolitan and final palace examinations, and edited and printed shortly after the results of the palace examination were known, *t'ung-nien ch'ih-lu* were usually compiled years after the original examinations had been held. In one or two cases the lists were not printed until after a lapse of more than twenty years. The longer the interval, of course, the greater the likelihood that some members of the original class might have died or been lost track of by one or more editors, invariably members of the class. It was rather common for some later Ch'ing lists to have gaps of information on the family background of a number of candidates.

Cases in which the names of the candidate's paternal ancestors are not given must be excluded from our tabulation as being textually defective. Even when the names of the candidate's ancestors are complete, special pains must be taken to ascertain whether they indeed had held no degree or office. There are usually certain clues in the lists with which candidates' ancestral background can be checked. For example, the list for the class of 1822 was not printed until 1833. After a lapse of eleven years the editor was able to give the exact positions and ranks held by members of the original class in 1833. Cases in which members of the original class seem at first to have come from humble families but are mentioned in the list as having "formerly" held certain offices are excluded as well, because the lack of ancestral record might be due to the death of the informant. Only those members from families without holders of degree or office who were in active government service in 1833 are counted in this study as having originated from ordinary commoner families.

The compilation of national lists of *chü-jen,* who numbered well over 1,000 each triennium and were scattered all over the provinces, was a much more difficult task. For one or two national *chü-jen* lists of the nineteenth century the lacunae in information on candidates of certain provinces are so great that these provinces have to be excluded entirely from our tabulation. Whether those *chin-shih* and *chü-jen* whose names are retained in their lists but whose family background is blank came from humble and obscure families cannot be ascertained. For statistical purposes we have no alternative but to exclude all the textually defective cases from our tabulation. Fortunately, the great majority of the available Ming and early Ch'ing *chin-shih* lists are textually of high quality, and the aggregate number of *chin-shih* of these early lists amounts to well over one half of the available cases of the entire Ming-Ch'ing period. The margin of error due to omission of textually defective cases, when expressed as a percentage, is not likely to be serious.[8]

In addition to the textual problem in later Ch'ing lists, our available sources in general may have two other theoretical defects. On close scrutiny, however, they do not seem to affect much of the quality of our data. The first theoretical defect is that although our lists provide by far the most precise information on the candidates' lineal ancestry, only later Ch'ing lists yield more specific information on the candidates' close collaterals. Thanks to the meticulous and exact regulations by which the Ming and Ch'ing governments granted honorific titles to officials' lineal ancestors, both living and deceased,[9] it is almost always possible to tell whether a candidate had close collaterals who had been officials. Two examples will suffice to demonstrate how the true ancestral statuses of the candidate are determined.

### EXAMPLE 1

Name of candidate: Lo Wen-chün.
Degree: *chin-shih,* ranking third in the palace examination of 1822.
Initial appointment: second-class compiler of the Han-lin Academy, rank 7a.
Ancestral and family record:

Great-grandfather: no title, no degree.
Grandfather: second-class compiler of the Han-lin Academy, title post-
humously bestowed by the Imperial Government.
Father: same as grandfather
Two uncles: no title, no degree.
Three brothers: no title, no degree.

Drawn from *Tao-kuang jen-wu t'ung-nien ch'ih-lu* (*Chin-shih* list of 1822,
printed in 1833).

Typical of later Ch'ing lists, the one for the class of 1822, from
which the above example is drawn, was printed many years later.
Had it been compiled and printed in the year of the examination,
no honorific title would have been shown for any of the candidate's
lineal ancestors. This is because according to Ming-Ch'ing practice,
after an official had completed his first term of office he was entitled
to request the imperial government to bestow upon his grandfather
and father the same rank and title he actually held at the time. This
concise family and ancestral record thus shows that all his lineal
ancestors and close collaterals had never held an academic degree
or office. The candidate must be classified as one from an ordinary
commoner family.

### EXAMPLE 2

Name of candidate: Li Chen-chu.
Registered family status: *min* (commoner).
Degree: *chin-shih,* class of 1610, third class.
Ancestral record:
Great-grandfather: president of the Board of War, title posthumously
bestowed by the Imperial Government.
Grandfather: same as great-grandfather.
Father: no title, no degree.
Two brothers: army officers.

Drawn from *Wan-li san-shih-pa-nien keng-hsü-k'o hsü-ch'ih lu* (*Chin-shih*
list of 1610).

Here we can see that none of the candidate's lineal ancestors had
held any actual office. The exalted honorific titles posthumously
bestowed on his great-grandfather and grandfather cannot be the
consequence of the candidate's recent academic success; for if so his
father should have been equally honored. The honorific titles must
have been due to the fact that one of the candidate's uncles had

served at least one term in the high office of president of the Board of War, he was thus able to honor his grandfather and father. What the concise family and ancestral record shows is that none of the lineal ancestors of the candidate had held any real office or degree, but that he had a distinguished uncle, who, owing to the format of *chin-shih* lists of the time, is not mentioned. But the vital information on the most significant close collaterals is implied, which enables us to speculate that the candidate's academic success and the career of his two brothers as minor army officers are likely to have been due in part to the help of their distinguished uncle. Although all the candidate's lineal ancestors were ordinary commoners without any academic degree, he must be classified as one originating from a high-ranking official family.

The lack of information on collaterals in Ming and early Ch'ing *chin-shih* lists is therefore not a serious defect, for what is needed for determining a candidate's true ancestral statuses is always implied. It should be mentioned that many later Ch'ing *chin-shih* lists yield so much information on ancestry, including close and sometimes even remote collaterals, that they almost amount to abridged genealogies.

As to the lack of information on remote collaterals in Ming and early Ch'ing *chin-shih* lists, the important thing to remember is that, in spite of the existence of the clan system in many parts of China, the "family" or at most the "extended family," that is, husband, wife, children, and sometimes one or both of the husband's parents, almost always constituted a unit of common consumption.[10] From local histories we learn that it was customary in most parts of China for married brothers to live separately. The aging parent or parents usually lived with one of their married sons, commonly the eldest. Thus the majority of "families" were not even necessarily "extended." This may best be evidenced from the average size of the "family" in 1393, which consisted of 5.68 persons, and that of the average family in fourteen provinces in 1812, which consisted of 5.33 persons.[11] Neo-Confucian teaching on practicing mutual help among kin makes it legitimate for modern students to assume that a struggling young man could probably receive financial or other forms of aid from his successful uncles, granduncles, and older first cousins, but it is extremely doubtful that he could owe his success mainly to the help and influence of his remote collaterals.

The second theoretical defect of our sources is the lack of information on the economic status of the candidate's family. This defect may be a real one for the period from the founding of the Ming in 1368 to 1450, when examinations and recommendations by high officials were the only two major channels of socio-political mobility. But owing to the serious Mongol invasion of the Peking area in 1449, which resulted in the capture of the reigning emperor, the Ming government was forced to sell minor official titles, offices, and the title of student of the Imperial Academy. As has been stated in chapter 1, during the latter half of the Ming and the entire Ch'ing period men of above average economic means almost invariably purchased at least an Imperial Academy studentship, if not higher title or rank. While it is true that during the latter half of the Ming the sale of Imperial Academy studentships was several times suspended temporarily, the sale of minor official titles and ranks was on a significant scale during times of famine or national emergency. For the greater part of the five and a half centuries under our study, therefore, our data actually imply some information on the economic status of the candidate's family.

To be fair, historical data can seldom be ideal for sociological purpose; in fact, even studies on the social origin of certain elite groups of modern and contemporary societies are based on data which provide information only on the occupations of the fathers of elite members, not all of which can be precisely classified.[12] In terms of the numbers of generations covered, explicit and implied information, chronological coverage, and quantity, the Ming-Ch'ing *chin-shih* data can compare favorably to similar data of any large historical society.

The forty-eight *chin-shih* lists presented in table 9 below represent practically all that are known to me to be extant in China and North America. With the exception of the very first list of 1371, which has been preserved in a modern collectanea, the other sixteen Ming lists are all rare items in the possession of the National Central Library at Taipei, Taiwan, and the National Library of

Peking. The former has nine, two of which are also available in the original in the Library of Congress, and the latter has seven, which are all available in microfilm in the Library of Congress. By far the rarest lists are those of the early Ch'ing period. Of the nine early Ch'ing lists eight have been supplied by the National Library of Peking and one by the National Central Library. For reasons that cannot easily be discovered, no *chin-shih* lists of the Yung-cheng (1723–35), Ch'ien-lung (1736–95) and Chia-ch'ing (1796–1820) periods are known to be extant. The system by which leading sinological libraries generally list as rare only works printed before the change of dynasty in 1644 makes it impossible for me to prove that *chin-shih* lists of these three Ch'ing reign periods are definitely nonexistent, despite negative replies from leading Chinese libraries to my inquiries. For the post-1820 period twenty *chin-shih* lists have been located in the Library of Congress and the libraries of Columbia and Harvard Universities and two were kindly supplied me personally by Mr. Fang Chao-ying. Under existing international circumstances it may be said that in searching for statistical data for this study few turnable stones have been left unturned.[13]

The 4,790 cases for the Ming period amount to slightly less than 20 percent of the Ming *chin-shih* total. The 7,436 cases for the Ch'ing period constitute nearly 28 percent of the Ch'ing *chin-shih* total. Quantitatively these lists are significant. Altogether they yield a total of 12,226 cases and are fairly representative of all subperiods except the eighteenth century, for which only the list of 1703 is available. To make up for the deficiency in statistical data for the eighteenth century, the best we can do is to supplement the lone *chin-shih* list of 1703 with a national *pa-kung-sheng* list and three provincial *chü-jen* lists.

For the study of socioacademic mobility at the intermediate provincial level, we rely mainly on national *chü-jen* lists, for provincial *chü-jen* lists exist only in rather limited quantity, and then contain only small numbers of candidates. National *chü-jen* lists are known to be extant only for the nineteenth century. Altogether nineteen such lists have been located in North America but three of them are textually too defective to be included in our tabulation. In order to give a better chronological coverage, the sixteen useful national *chü-jen* lists have been supplemented by four lists dealing with special categories of *kung-sheng*. All told, these twenty lists of intermediate degree holders of the nineteenth and early twentieth centuries give a total of 23,480 cases, almost twice as many as those yielded by the forty-seven Ming-Ch'ing *chin-shih* lists. For the post-1800 period, therefore, our statistical data are rather rich and the problem of entry into officialdom can be systematically tackled at two different levels.

The aspect of socioacademic mobility which is most difficult to ascertain statistically is the entry of commoners of nonscholastic families into the vast *sheng-yüan* body, for these holders of the elementary degree were nowhere socially recognized as being established. Local histories do not as a rule even contain their name lists, let alone any information on their ancestry. Although late in the Ch'ing period special *sheng-yüan* lists were compiled by scholars for more than half a dozen lower-Yangtze counties, only three of them yield brief but vital information on *sheng-yüan* ancestry. The list of Nan-t'ung Department County on the north shore of lower Yangtze covers the entire Ming-Ch'ing period. The list of the neighboring Hai-men County covers the Ch'ing period only. The most bulky part of the list of all types of degree holders of Ch'ang-shu County in southern Kiangsu deals with *sheng-yüan* of the entire Ch'ing period. By way of family background all these three lists give two types of *sheng-yüan*, one with his name only but no other information, one with his name and also a brief reference to his being the great-grandson, grandson, grandnephew, son, or nephew of somebody else. After painstaking checking it has been found that the latter was invariably a holder of the elementary or higher degree. Although the information on ancestry is much briefer than that given in lists of higher degree holders, it actually covers the same number of generations, and it enables us to establish whether a *sheng-yüan* originated from a scholastic family or from an ordinary commoner family which had not previously produced any degree holder. What enhances the value of these two unusual lists is that the information on ancestry extends to collaterals. If quantitatively they do not enable us to generalize on the social composition of *sheng-yüan* for the entire country, they nevertheless yield some invaluable clues on the socioacademic mobility near its grass-roots level.

## STATISTICS

Before presenting statistics on the family background of Ming-Ch'ing *chin-shih* and nineteenth-century *chü-jen* and *kung-sheng*, it is necessary to explain briefly our criteria of classification. In the light of the power structure and the value and prestige system peculiar to Ming-Ch'ing society, which have all been systematically discussed in our introductory chapter, we classify these three types of higher degree holders into four categories.

Category A consists of candidates whose families during the three preceding generations had failed to produce a single holder of the elementary degree, let alone any office or official title. When it is remembered that even successful small tradesmen during late Ming and Ch'ing almost invariably adorned themselves with a title of student of the Imperial Academy purchased for between 100 and 200 taels, and that the vast majority of *sheng-yüan* had to eke out their meager living by teaching or doing clerical or sometimes even manual work, a family which for three generations had failed to produce a single holder of the elementary degree may reasonably be regarded as one of humble and obscure circumstances. Since Category A candidates rose from obscurity to membership in the broadly defined ruling bureaucracy during their own lifetime, they represent cases which, in the context of Ming-Ch'ing society, may be regarded as examples of rising "from rags to riches."

Category B consists of candidates whose families during the three preceding generations had produced one or more *sheng-yüan* but no holder of a higher degree or office. In the light of our detailed discussion of *sheng-yüan's* legal and social status and mode of life in the preceding chapters, it should be apparent that the great majority of the candidates from *sheng-yüan* families were relatively humble or even poor. That *sheng-yüan* families should be regarded as a significant social transitional group at all can be justified only by remembering the premium that the Confucian society attached to bookish knowledge and student status. Category B includes also those candidates of the Ch'ing period whose families had produced

one or more *chien-sheng,* or holders of the title of student of the
Imperial Academy, during the three preceding generations. The
reason why Ming *chien-sheng* have to be classified differently is that
in Ming times they had a right to minor official appointment. As
explained in detail in chapter I, *chien-sheng* in Ch'ing times hardly
differed from *sheng-yüan* at all save for their nominal "graduate"
status, which was not, however, accompanied by a right to minor
government service. While the average Ch'ing *chien-sheng* was
probably from a family of above average means, his family's economic status must not be overestimated. For the title could be
bought for a small sum of money and the truly rich or well-to-do
man was likely to purchase a higher title or minor official rank so
as to join the local elite. Candidates of the entire Ming-Ch'ing
period who came from *sheng-yüan* families and candidates of the
Ch'ing period who came from *chien-sheng* families should be regarded as emanating from families which were already in the process
of partial upward mobility. By definition, however, they were still
of commoner origin.

Category C consists of candidates whose families during the three
preceding generations had produced one or more holders of higher
degrees or offices. By higher degree is meant a degree that was higher
than *sheng-yüan.* For the Ming period this category includes *chien-
sheng* and for the entire Ming-Ch'ing period all types of *kung-sheng.*
To these should be added families with subofficials or ancestors
who had purchased official titles and ranks. Altogether they constituted the class of officials and potential officials, or a bureaucracy
in a very broad sense. It ought to be pointed out that, although
their legal and social status differed from that of commoners, many
families of the lower stratum of this broadly defined bureaucracy
were actually of relatively limited prestige, privilege, and economic
means.

Category D, which is a subdivision of Category C, consists of candidates whose families within the three previous generations had
produced one or more high officials, that is, officials of the third rank
and above. Since officials of the upper three ranks had, among other
things, the *yin* privilege, their families may be regarded as nationally
"distinguished." To these should be added those candidates who

came from families which belonged to the upper ranks of the imperial and nonimperial hereditary nobility which, much like the high-ranking officials, enjoyed hereditary privileges. Lower noble ranks are excluded from this category but included in Category C because such ranks were merely in the nature of minor sinecures.

The criteria for Category A are very strict and those for Category C very lenient. If our criteria must have a certain bias, the bias should be on the safe side, especially when the highest status among the candidate's ancestors for three generations decides the candidate's family status. In other words, our percentage figures of candidates from humble and obscure families are not likely to be inflated except by textual incompleteness which has failed to be detected.

It must be emphatically pointed out that our percentage figures based on the above criteria of classification are far from being able to tell the whole story about the long and complex process of socioacademic mobility. Our figures would convey different impressions to those who have gone through these lists themselves and those who are inclined to treat statistics abstractly. While the individual ancestry records often reveal considerable vicissitudes within the families, our figures cannot adequately demonstrate such changes and tend to generalize the family status by the highest status produced in three preceding generations. In other words, the mobility rates shown in the following tables are invariably *minimized*.

For example, despite our qualification that Category C families actually varied a great deal in standing, our broad classification still suggests a large degree of homogeneity among them. It is not unlikely that without further explanation Category C candidates would be generally taken to represent cases of little or no mobility. On the contrary, there was considerable fluctuation in a Category C family within three, including the candidate himself, four generations. A few concrete examples will bear this out.

Ch'en Sung, a *chin-shih* of 1835, may serve as an illustration. His great-great-grandfather migrated to Szechwan as a tenant farmer. Not until his grandfather's day did the family become substantial. Consequently, for two generations his immediate ancestors both obtained the *kung-sheng* status.[14] The actual amount and degree of mobility in the family during five generations are more than our statistics can show. Wu Huai-ch'ing, a *chin-shih* of 1890, is representative of scores of candidates whose families had been for generations rather poor and humble until their fathers barely qualified for our Category C. Wu was born in 1863 in a poor Shensi county. From his great-great-grandfather to his grandfather no one obtained the lowest degree. His grandfather was forced by poverty to give up the hope of becoming a degree holder, and eked out a meager living by teaching village pupils. The family's continued poverty compelled his father to give up his studies and to practice medicine for many years. After saving up a little, his father purchased the lowest official rank, 9b.[15] While by our definition his family must be classified as Category C, it is obvious that this is a case of very substantial upward mobility which cannot be shown in our figures.

If these and many similar cases represent the long processes of upward social mobility within our Category C, many other families of the same category had actually been in process of downward mobility for generations until the candidates halted the trend by obtaining the *chin-shih* degree. Cheng Te-shu, for instance, a *chin-shih* of 1586, had a successful great-grandfather who reached the post of a prefect, rank 4a. His grandfather and father barely managed to obtain the *sheng-yüan* degree. Wu Tao-kuang, a member of the same class, had a comparable great-grandfather, but his grandfather and father failed even to obtain the *sheng-yüan* degree.[16] Even our table 14, which subclassifies the families of Category C candidates, cannot possibly reflect the actual range of the mobility among generations within the supposedly homogeneous Category C families.

Nor can our figures on Categories A and B candidates adequately indicate the actual processes of the family's initial and preparatory mobility that was essential to the candidate's eventual success. Late Ch'ing *chin-shih* lists often yield information on such multi-generation changes in occupation and status, particularly on the alternation between productive occupations and studies, which corroborate our aggregate evidence on the fluidity of the status system presented in the preceding chapter.

All in all, therefore, owing to our lenient criteria for Category

C but very strict criteria for Category A, and especially because the highest status of three preceding generations determines the candidate's family status, the mobility figures shown in the following tables are considerably below the truth.

For the entire Ming-Ch'ing period we find that Category A accounted for 30.2 percent of the total candidates, Category B for 12.1 percent, and Category C for 57.7 percent. The sum of Categories A and B, which by definition represented candidates from commoner families, was 42.3 percent. With the exceptions of the classes of 1655, 1682, and 1703, candidates from high-ranking official families never exceeded 10 percent of the total and the over-all average of Category D during the whole five and a half centuries was a mere 5.7 percent. Detailed figures are given in table 9.

The significant changes in the percentage distribution of Categories A, B, and C during various subperiods are shown in table 10 on page 114. Because of its small numbers and relatively few changes, Category D is omitted.

While a systematic explanation of the various factors which affected socioacademic mobility rates must await chapter V, it seems pertinent to point out briefly here that the combined circumstances in early Ming were unusually favorable to the humble and obscure, who constituted a majority during our first subperiod, 1371–1496. In the course of time, however, the various advantages enjoyed by members of official families could not fail to prevail. In the sixteenth century Category C steadily gained ground and outnumbered commoner groups by a small margin. The most crucial change occurred from the late sixteenth century onward, when Category A dropped drastically to below 30 percent, a drop which was, however, partially compensated for by a sharp rise in Category B. These two phenomena seem to indicate that socioacademic mobility was becoming increasingly difficult for the commoners, many of whom required an inter-generation preparation to attain the final goal of mobility. This trend continued for a while shortly after the change of dynasty in 1644, when the Manchu government purposely set up unusually large *chin-shih* quotas in order to attract the service of the newly subjugated Chinese. After the Manchu empire became stabilized under the K'ang-hsi emperor (1662–1722), *chin-*

## TABLE 9

### SOCIAL COMPOSITION OF MING-CH'ING *CHIN-SHIH*[a]

(*The sum of A, B, and C = 100 percent*)

| Year | Total number of chin-shih[b] | Category A | | Category B | | Combined percent of A and B | Category C | | Category D | |
|---|---|---|---|---|---|---|---|---|---|---|
| | | Number | Percent of total | Number | Percent of total | | Number | Percent of total | Number | Percent of total |
| 1371 | 28 | 21 | 75.0 | — | — | 75.0 | 7 | 25.0 | — | — |
| 1412 | 106 | 89 | 84.0 | — | — | 84.0 | 17 | 16.0 | 9 | 8.5 |
| 1457 | 294 | 182 | 61.8 | — | — | 61.8 | 112 | 38.2 | 9 | 3.0 |
| 1469 | 248 | 149 | 60.0 | — | — | 60.0 | 90 | 40.0 | 11 | 4.5 |
| 1472 | 250 | 137 | 54.8 | — | — | 54.8 | 113 | 45.2 | 13 | 5.2 |
| 1496 | 298 | 140 | 47.0 | — | — | 47.0 | 158 | 53.0 | 14 | 4.6 |
| 1505 | 303 | 126 | 41.6 | — | — | 41.6 | 177 | 58.4 | 12 | 4.0 |
| 1521 | 330 | 156 | 47.3 | — | — | 47.3 | 174 | 52.7 | 13 | 3.9 |
| 1535 | 329 | 154 | 47.0 | — | — | 47.0 | 175 | 53.0 | 22 | 6.9 |
| 1538 | 317 | 154 | 48.6 | 1 | 0.3 | 48.9 | 162 | 51.1 | 23 | 7.3 |
| 1544 | 312 | 151 | 48.4 | 2 | 0.6 | 49.0 | 159 | 51.0 | 24 | 8.0 |
| 1553[c] | 384 | 182 | 47.4 | 24 | 6.2 | 53.6 | 178 | 46.4 | 15 | 3.9 |
| 1562 | 298 | 133 | 44.6 | — | — | 44.6 | 165 | 55.4 | 17 | 5.7 |
| 1568 | 405 | 203 | 50.1 | — | — | 50.1 | 202 | 49.9 | 17 | 4.2 |
| 1580 | 302 | 134 | 44.4 | — | — | 44.4 | 168 | 55.6 | 12 | 4.0 |
| 1586 | 356 | 105 | 29.5 | 54 | 15.1 | 44.6 | 197 | 55.4 | 18 | 5.0 |
| 1610 | 230 | 61 | 26.5 | 40 | 17.4 | 43.9 | 129 | 56.1 | 18 | 7.8 |
| 1652 | 366 | 85 | 23.2 | 48 | 13.1 | 36.3 | 233 | 63.7 | 30 | 8.2 |
| 1655 | 401 | 112 | 28.2 | 65 | 16.2 | 44.2 | 224 | 55.8 | 48 | 11.7 |
| 1658 | 407 | 126 | 30.7 | 58 | 14.2 | 44.9 | 223 | 55.1 | 25 | 6.1 |
| 1659 | 358 | 124 | 34.6 | 32 | 8.9 | 43.5 | 202 | 56.5 | 27 | 7.5 |
| 1661 | 373 | 112 | 29.7 | 57 | 15.2 | 44.9 | 204 | 55.1 | 36 | 9.6 |
| 1673 | 138 | 37 | 26.8 | 22 | 15.9 | 42.7 | 79 | 57.3 | 5 | 3.6 |
| 1682 | 151 | 12 | 8.0 | 17 | 11.3 | 19.3 | 122 | 80.7 | 18 | 11.9 |
| 1685 | 169 | 30 | 17.6 | 33 | 19.2 | 36.8 | 106 | 63.2 | 15 | 8.9 |

| Year | Total number of chin-shih[b] | Category A | | Category B | | Combined percent of A and B | Category C | | Category D | |
|---|---|---|---|---|---|---|---|---|---|---|
| | | Number | Percent of total | Number | Percent of total | | Number | Percent of total | Number | Percent of total |
| 1703 | 104 | 10 | 9.6 | 20 | 19.2 | 28.8 | 74 | 71.2 | 17 | 16.3 |
| 1822 | 210 | 23 | 10.9 | 52 | 24.8 | 35.7 | 135 | 64.3 | 12 | 5.3 |
| 1829 | 223 | 46 | 20.6 | 49 | 22.0 | 42.6 | 128 | 57.4 | 10 | 4.4 |
| 1833 | 226 | 30 | 13.3 | 62 | 27.4 | 40.7 | 134 | 59.3 | 16 | 7.1 |
| 1835 | 243 | 26 | 10.7 | 54 | 22.2 | 32.9 | 163 | 67.1 | 17 | 7.0 |
| 1844 | 200 | 31 | 15.5 | 53 | 26.5 | 42.0 | 116 | 58.2 | 7 | 3.5 |
| 1859 | 191 | 52 | 27.2 | 35 | 18.3 | 45.5 | 104 | 54.5 | 7 | 3.6 |
| 1860 | 146 | 35 | 24.0 | 33 | 22.5 | 46.5 | 78 | 53.5 | 6 | 4.1 |
| 1865 | 228 | 36 | 15.8 | 49 | 21.4 | 37.2 | 143 | 62.8 | 13 | 5.7 |
| 1868 | 228 | 25 | 10.9 | 50 | 21.9 | 32.8 | 153 | 67.2 | 13 | 5.7 |
| 1871 | 280 | 45 | 16.0 | 66 | 23.5 | 39.5 | 169 | 60.5 | 7 | 2.5 |
| 1874 | 228 | 15 | 6.6 | 52 | 22.8 | 29.4 | 161 | 70.6 | 9 | 3.9 |
| 1876 | 216 | 30 | 13.9 | 49 | 22.7 | 36.6 | 137 | 63.4 | 5 | 2.3 |
| 1877 | 276 | 40 | 14.9 | 46 | 16.7 | 31.6 | 190 | 68.4 | 16 | 5.6 |
| 1880 | 276 | 31 | 11.2 | 49 | 17.7 | 28.9 | 196 | 71.1 | 13 | 4.7 |
| 1883 | 245 | 31 | 12.6 | 40 | 16.3 | 28.9 | 174 | 71.1 | 9 | 3.6 |
| 1886 | 263 | 29 | 11.0 | 55 | 20.9 | 31.9 | 179 | 68.1 | 15 | 5.7 |
| 1889 | 251 | 40 | 15.9 | 41 | 16.0 | 31.9 | 170 | 68.1 | 12 | 4.8 |
| 1890 | 234 | 24 | 10.3 | 44 | 18.4 | 28.7 | 166 | 71.3 | 8 | 3.5 |
| 1892 | 239 | 31 | 12.9 | 45 | 18.8 | 31.7 | 163 | 68.3 | 13 | 5.4 |
| 1895 | 181 | 30 | 16.6 | 27 | 14.9 | 31.5 | 124 | 68.5 | 6 | 3.2 |
| 1898 | 142 | 33 | 23.2 | 22 | 15.5 | 38.7 | 87 | 61.3 | 5 | 3.5 |
| 1904[c] | 243 | 88 | 36.2 | 25 | 10.3 | 46.5 | 130 | 53.5 | 4 | 1.7 |
| Total or Average | 12,226 | 3,696 | 30.2 | 1,471 | 12.1 | 42.3 | 7,059 | 57.7 | 691 | 5.7 |

[a] For complete listing of these 48 *chin-shih* lists, see Section I of the Bibliography. They are chronologically arranged there and the exact title for each list can be identified by the year.

[b] The total numbers of *chin-shih* of various years are those of the candidates whose ancestral records are given. For textual reasons certain numbers of successful candidates have to be excluded from later Ch'ing lists.

[c] For this year information is available for only two preceding generations instead of the usual three.

TABLE 10

CHANGING SOCIAL COMPOSITION OF *CHIN-SHIH*
IN VARIOUS SUBPERIODS
(*in percent*)

| Period | Category A | Category B | Categories A and B | Category C |
|--------|-----------|-----------|--------------------|-----------|
| 1371–1496 | 58.2 | — | 58.2 | 41.8 |
| 1505–1580 | 46.9 | 0.9 | 47.8 | 52.2 |
| 1586–1610 | 28.5 | 16.0 | 44.5 | 55.5 |
| Ming average | 47.5 | 2.5 | 50.0 | 50.0 |
| 1652–1661 | 29.2 | 13.6 | 42.8 | 57.2 |
| 1673–1703 | 15.8 | 16.4 | 32.2 | 67.8 |
| 1822–1904 | 15.5 | 20.0 | 35.5 | 64.5 |
| Ch'ing average | 19.1 | 18.1 | 37.2 | 62.8 |

*shih* quotas were drastically reduced. The reduced quotas, coupled
with the persistent fact that academic competition had become increasingly acute, brought about a further drop in Category A percentage. As will be shown in table 22 in chapter V, K'ang-hsi's
restrictive *chin-shih* quota policy was continued by his grandson,
the Ch'ien-lung emperor (1736–95). Had significant numbers of
eighteenth-century *chin-shih* lists been available, it is not unlikely
that we should find Category A figures even somewhat smaller than
the average of the K'ang-hsi period. This estimate can be partially
gauged from our supplementary eighteenth-century data tabulated
in table 12. All in all, therefore, it would appear that because of
the lack of data for the eighteenth century the Category A average
for the entire Ch'ing period may be slightly too high. If so, the
actual Category A average for the entire Ch'ing period should probably be very close to those of the K'ang-hsi era and of the nineteenth
century. In other words, the Ch'ing Category A percentage is likely
to be slightly over one fourth of that of the early Ming. It is important to bear in mind, however, that the drastically lower Category A percentage during the Ch'ing was partially mitigated by a
sustained rise in Category B, which, except during the first two
decades of the Manchu dynasty, exceeded the percentage for Category A.

The social composition of *chü-jen* and *kung-sheng* of the nineteenth and early twentieth centuries is shown in table 11.

Although the average percentage figures for Categories A and B of late Ch'ing *chü-jen* and *kung-sheng* are all higher than the corresponding figures for *chin-shih* of the same period, the most remarkable feature of these two independent statistical series is their general compatibility. A comparison of these two series indicates that it was somewhat easier for men of nonofficial families to acquire the intermediate degrees than the advanced *chin-shih* status. This seems all the more reasonable as competition at the level of the metropolitan examination must have been keener and more difficult for the commoners than at the levels of *chü-jen* and *kung-sheng* examinations.

There is, however, one seemingly erratic feature in the last two lists which should be explained briefly. The Category A figures for the lists of 1906 and 1910, being 33.6 and 41.7 percent respectively, are substantially higher than the total average, which is 20.1 percent, and seem to break the uniform pattern of fluctuation within a narrow range. There are two major reasons for this unusual phenomenon. First, the list of 1906 is one of *yu-kung-sheng,* which differs somewhat from other lists. *Yu-kung-sheng,* selected on the basis of literary merit exclusively, traditionally boasted a higher proportion of poor talented scholars than did other categories of *kung-sheng* and *chü-jen*.[17] Second, the 1910 list is also a special list of those *chü-jen* and *kung-sheng* who had passed a court examination. The reason for this special court examination was that, since the examination system had been permanently abolished in 1905, those intermediate degree holders who had obtained their degrees before 1905 had to be given an opportunity for minor appointment. In fact, ever since the abortive "One Hundred Days of Reform" of 1898, the abolition of the examination system had been in the offing, and an increasing number of office aspirants had either purchased minor offices or begun to study modern subjects in Japan, in the West, and in modern types of schools in China. The higher percentage of men of humble circumstances in the 1906 and 1910 lists was therefore partly a reflection of the sad state of those who, after having invested so much in Confucian classics, could not easily adapt themselves to the rapidly changing circumstances. The

## TABLE 11

### SOCIAL COMPOSITION OF LATE-CH'ING *CHÜ-JEN* AND *KUNG-SHENG*[a]
(The sum of A, B, and C = 100 percent)

| Year | Total number of candidates | Category A | | Category B | | Combined percent of A and B | Category C | | Category D | |
|---|---|---|---|---|---|---|---|---|---|---|
| | | Number | Percent of total | Number | Percent of total | | Number | Percent of total | Number | Percent of total |
| 1804 | 1,021 | 235 | 23.0 | 322 | 31.5 | 54.5 | 464 | 45.5 | 23 | 2.2 |
| 1807[b] | 1,109 | 211 | 19.0 | 281 | 25.3 | 44.3 | 617 | 55.7 | 25 | 2.2 |
| 1808 | 1,133 | 237 | 20.8 | 414 | 36.5 | 57.3 | 482 | 42.7 | 45 | 4.0 |
| 1816 | 1,052 | 187 | 17.7 | 396 | 37.6 | 54.5 | 469 | 44.7 | 35 | 3.3 |
| 1821[b] | 1,402 | 268 | 19.1 | 404 | 28.1 | 47.2 | 730 | 52.8 | 39 | 2.7 |
| 1828 | 1,175 | 239 | 20.3 | 322 | 27.7 | 48.0 | 614 | 52.0 | 25 | 2.1 |
| 1831[c] | 930 | 198 | 20.2 | 243 | 26.1 | 46.3 | 489 | 53.7 | 36 | 3.9 |
| 1832[b] | 1,192 | 247 | 21.4 | 269 | 22.5 | 43.9 | 676 | 56.1 | 34 | 2.9 |
| 1834 | 1,064 | 194 | 18.2 | 259 | 24.3 | 42.5 | 611 | 57.5 | 37 | 3.5 |
| 1835 | 1,130 | 247 | 21.9 | 314 | 27.8 | 49.7 | 569 | 50.3 | 32 | 2.8 |
| 1843 | 1,106 | 212 | 19.1 | 314 | 28.4 | 47.5 | 580 | 52.5 | 41 | 3.7 |
| 1844 | 1,094 | 259 | 23.6 | 298 | 27.2 | 50.8 | 537 | 49.2 | 31 | 2.8 |
| 1849[d] | 1,751 | 302 | 17.2 | 424 | 24.2 | 41.4 | 1,025 | 58.6 | 38 | 2.2 |
| 1855 | 1,311 | 254 | 19.3 | 368 | 27.3 | 46.6 | 689 | 53.4 | 24 | 1.4 |
| 1870 | 1,752 | 335 | 19.1 | 386 | 22.0 | 41.1 | 1,031 | 58.9 | 57 | 3.2 |
| 1879 | 1,314 | 225 | 17.1 | 286 | 21.7 | 38.8 | 803 | 61.2 | 34 | 2.6 |
| 1885[d] | 1,649 | 303 | 17.8 | 281 | 17.0 | 34.8 | 1,065 | 65.2 | 34 | 1.4 |
| 1897 | 1,694 | 334 | 19.7 | 232 | 13.7 | 33.4 | 1,128 | 66.6 | 31 | 1.8 |
| 1906[e] | 354 | 119 | 33.6 | 37 | 11.0 | 44.6 | 198 | 55.4 | 4 | 1.1 |
| 1910[f] | 247 | 103 | 41.7 | 27 | 10.9 | 52.6 | 117 | 47.4 | 4 | 1.6 |
| Total or Average | 23,480 | 4,709 | 20.1 | 5,877 | 25.0 | 45.1 | 12,894 | 54.9 | 619 | 2.6 |

[a] For complete listing of sources, see Bibliography, Section I, B. The exact title of each list can be identified by the year.
[b] One province excluded.
[c] Three provinces excluded.
[d] *Pa-kung-sheng.*
[e] *Yu-kung-sheng.*
[f] Special examination to select *chü-jen* and *kung-sheng* for minor appointments.

substantially higher Category A figure in the 1904 *chin-shih* list may be similarly explained.

Since the lacunae in our otherwise systematic *chin-shih* data are caused by the scarcity of information on the eighteenth century, the lone *chin-shih* list of 1703 will be compared with four extant lists of intermediate degree holders in table 12.

Of these lists the one of the 1703 class of *chin-shih*, which yields information on 104 of a total of 166 candidates, is suggestive though textually imperfect. The *chü-jen* list of Fukien for the class of 1752 covers only 72 cases, a number too small to be accepted as typical of the southeastern provinces in the eighteenth century. The one partial and one complete *chü-jen* list of metropolitan Chihli province, where in Ch'ing times official families congregated, show Category C figures which are likely to be somewhat higher than those of other provinces. The only list that has some value in indicating the mobility pattern of the century is that of the 1789 class of *pa-kung-sheng*, which covered the entire country and is textually of high quality. Its Category A figure of 16.6 percent is slightly smaller than those of two *pa-kung-sheng* lists of the nineteenth century. While several factors affecting mobility rates of the eighteenth century must await discussion in chapter V, our available data here suggest that this century was probably a period of shrinking mobility rates for the poor and humble, whose chances of attaining the advanced *chin-shih* degree are likely to have been particularly slim.

From tables 9 and 10, candidates from official families constituted exactly 50 percent in the Ming and 63.2 percent in the Ch'ing, giving an over-all average of 57.8 percent for the entire period covered by our study. While during the greater part of the Ming-Ch'ing autocracy officials and potential officials had to conform to the state-subscribed ideology, they must not be assumed to have been homogeneous in their social and family background. As has been discussed under Social Stratification in chapter I, the lower stratum within our leniently defined official class consisted of *chü-jen* and *kung-sheng* who were expecting minor office, officials of the eighth and ninth ranks who were vulgarly called the "auxiliary and miscellaneous," and sub-officials who could ascend to the ranked office

TABLE 12

SOCIAL COMPOSITION OF CANDIDATES OF THE EIGHTEENTH CENTURY

| Year | Total number of candidates | Category A | | Category B | | Combined percent of A and B | Category C | | Category D | |
|---|---|---|---|---|---|---|---|---|---|---|
| | | Number | Percent of total | Number | Percent of total | | Number | Percent of total | Number | Percent of total |
| 1703[a] | 104 | 10 | 9.6 | 20 | 19.2 | 28.8 | 74 | 71.2 | 17 | 16.3 |
| 1752[b] | 72 | 16 | 22.2 | 24 | 33.3 | 55.5 | 32 | 44.5 | 2 | 2.8 |
| 1789[c] | 1,149 | 190 | 16.6 | 372 | 32.2 | 48.8 | 587 | 51.2 | 29 | 2.5 |
| 1794[d] | 85 | 12 | 14.1 | 20 | 23.5 | 37.6 | 53 | 62.4 | 9 | 10.6 |
| 1800[e] | 193 | 28 | 14.5 | 33 | 17.0 | 31.5 | 132 | 68.5 | 17 | 8.9 |
| Total or Average | 1,603 | 256 | 16.0 | 471 | 29.4 | 45.4 | 876 | 54.6 | 74 | 4.6 |

[a] *K'ang-hsi ssu-shih-erh-nien kuei-wei-k'o san-tai chin-shih lü-li* (1703).

[b] Fukien *chü-jen* list, entitled *Ch'ien-lung jen-shen-k'o Fu-chien hsiang-shih t'ung-nien ch'ih-lu* (1752).

[c] National *pa-kung-sheng* list, entitled *Ch'ien-lung chi-yu-k'o ke-sheng hsüan-pa t'ung-nien ch'ih-lu* (1789).

[d] An incomplete list of *chü-jen* of Chihli, entitled *Ch'ien-lung chia-yin en-k'o Shun-t'ien hsiang-shih t'ung-nien ch'ih-lu* (1794).

[e] A complete *chü-jen* list of Chihli, entitled *Chia-ch'ing keng-shen en-k'o Shun-t'ien hsiang-shih t'ung-nien ch'ih-lu* (1800).

by various means including routine promotion. They differed greatly from the high- and middle-ranking functionaries in power, prestige, and wealth. The middle stratum consisted of central, provincial, and local officials between the seventh and the fourth rank who did important secretarial and administrative work in the capital and formed the backbone of provincial and local administration. The upper stratum consisted of officials of the three top ranks who among other things enjoyed the hereditary *yin* privilege. If we know the range of rank in which the careers of the majority of *chin-shih* were likely to end, our analysis of the background of *chin-shih* from official families will afford us a means of roughly gauging the intergeneration upward and downward mobility within this large group.

First, let us find out where the majority of *chin-shih*, most of whom started out as seventh-ranking officials, were likely to wind up. A number of local histories mention the final positions attained by *chin-shih* of their localities, but there is some risk of incomplete or inexact information. Fortunately, we have at our disposal a late Ming *chin-shih* list which was compiled with meticulous care by a descendant of a member of the class half a century after the examination had been held. It contains precise information on the final standings of members of the original class. We also have a late Ch'ing list which was compiled by a member of the class more than twenty years after graduation. It provides information on members' standing at that time, the vast majority of which are likely to be final. These will be analyzed in table 13.

While admittedly the information given in the 1868 list, which was printed at least twenty-two years later, may not be final for a small number of members of the class, it is extremely unlikely that those who eventually attained the three top ranks could reach 10 percent of the total. Although the lack of similar information for *chin-shih* of other classes makes a systematic statistical study impossible, these two lists confirm in general our impression that it was much more difficult for *chin-shih* to attain high official rank during the Ch'ing than during the previous Chinese dynasty. One of the main reasons was that the total number of high posts during the Ch'ing was substantially reduced for the Chinese, who had to share them with the Manchus and Mongols, and also with Chinese

TABLE 13

FINAL RANKS ATTAINED BY *CHIN-SHIH*

| Class | Total number in the class | High rank | | Middle rank | |
|---|---|---|---|---|---|
| | | Number | Percent of total | Number | Percent of total |
| 1592 | 307 | 75 | 24.4 | 232[a] | 75.6 |
| 1868 | 275 | 19 | 7.0 | 256 | 93.0 |

Sources: *Wan-li jen-ch'en-k'o chin-shih lü-li pien-lan* (1592; compilation completed in 1646); *T'ung-chih ch'i-nien hui-shih t'ung-nien ch'ih-lu* (1868; printed sometime after 1890).

[a] Five of these 232 never actually served in the government because of sickness or premature death.

Bannermen. As the 1868 list shows, only 68 members, or 31.6 percent of the class, had reached the fifth and fourth ranks by 1890. This being the case, from the standpoint of inter-generation mobility within official families, it may fairly safely be said that the majority of *chin-shih* of high official ancestry were likely to end up lower in the official hierarchy, that the majority of those of middle official ancestry were likely to register no gain in official status, and that only those of lower or potential minor official ancestry, by virtue of their advanced degree alone, were definitely on the ascent.

Since a full analysis of all forty-eight lists would be too time-consuming, we deal with a dozen lists only. The following lists are selected partly for their textual excellence and partly for better chronological coverage. Because crucial change in the social composition of *chin-shih* occurred first in the late Ming and then in the K'ang-hsi period, it seems necessary to include the last Ming lists of 1610 and two of the three available lists of the K'ang-hsi period. Although the 1703 list is textually incomplete, it is the only one of its kind available for the eighteenth century. So far as information on the ancestry of individual *chin-shih* is concerned, it is of good quality.

Table 14 reveals certain important facts which the previous tables of this chapter have not clearly indicated. First, in any given three-generation period 23.7 percent of *chin-shih* from low official and potential low official families, on the strength of their advanced

TABLE 14

SUBCLASSIFICATION OF *CHIN-SHIH* FROM OFFICIAL FAMILIES

*Members from official families*

| Class | Total number of the class | Percent of members from commoner families | Low[a] | | Middle | | High | |
|---|---|---|---|---|---|---|---|---|
| | | | Number | Percent of class total | Number | Percent of class total | Number | Percent of class total |
| 1469 | 248 | 60.0 | 34 | 13.7 | 54 | 21.8 | 11 | 4.5 |
| 1472 | 250 | 54.8 | 55 | 22.0 | 45 | 18.0 | 13 | 5.2 |
| 1538 | 317 | 48.9 | 61 | 19.3 | 78 | 24.5 | 23 | 7.3 |
| 1562 | 298 | 44.6 | 73 | 24.5 | 75 | 25.2 | 17 | 5.7 |
| 1610 | 230 | 43.9 | 58 | 25.2 | 53 | 23.1 | 18 | 7.8 |
| 1655 | 401 | 44.2 | 83 | 20.8 | 93 | 23.3 | 48 | 11.7 |
| 1682 | 151 | 19.3 | 38 | 25.2 | 66 | 43.6 | 18 | 11.9 |
| 1703 | 104 | 28.8 | 14 | 13.2 | 43 | 41.7 | 17 | 16.3 |
| 1822 | 210 | 34.3 | 61 | 29.0 | 65 | 31.0 | 12 | 5.7 |
| 1860 | 146 | 46.5 | 39 | 26.7 | 33 | 22.7 | 6 | 4.1 |
| 1876 | 216 | 36.6 | 68 | 31.2 | 64 | 29.9 | 5 | 2.3 |
| 1892 | 239 | 31.7 | 83 | 34.8 | 67 | 28.1 | 13 | 5.4 |
| Total or Average | 2,810 | 42.9 | 667 | 23.7 | 736 | 26.2 | 201 | 7.2 |

Data drawn from table 9.

[a] For the years 1469, 1472, 1538, 1562, 1610, 1655, and 1682 *chien-sheng* is regarded as a potential low official. Although by definition *chien-sheng* should be excluded from the Ch'ing potential official group, a small number of early Ch'ing *chin-shih* had *chien-sheng* among their ancestors who lived in Ming times and who by definition of potential officials of the Ming period should be included. *Chien-sheng* is excluded from the official class in all post-1700 lists.

degree, had already ascended to the middle rungs of the bureaucracy. At the same time, in addition, an average of 42.9 percent of *chin-shih* came from commoner families. When almost two thirds of new *chin-shih* came from commoner families or from families of low-ranking active and potential officials, we may say that the composition of the officialdom was constantly in a state of flux. Second, a relatively small percentage of *chin-shih* of high official ancestry were subject to a sort of almost built-in descending mechanism which made it difficult for top-ranking families to maintain their exalted status in the long run. Third, despite the constant recruiting of new blood, the bureaucracy nevertheless could maintain internal continuity and balance because on the average about one third of the new *chin-shih* were from middle and high official families, a fact which made feasible the thorough and leisurely assimilation of newcomers from commoner stock and from low official families. By rewarding the socially ambitious and by maintaining the stability of the bureaucracy, the civil service examination system served an important political and social purpose. It is important to bear in mind that in spite of these facts revealed by table 14, the actual amount and degree of upward and downward inter-generation mobility within the Category C families must have been considerably more than can be shown statistically because the highest status of the candidate's three lineal ancestors determined his family status.

In our statistical study of upward socioacademic mobility there is one aspect for which information is very hard to obtain, namely, the social composition of the vast body of *sheng-yüan*. Since the attainment of the *sheng-yüan* status marked the formal beginning of the long process of the socioacademic climb, any material which indicates the social composition of holders of the elementary degree will shed light on a critical level in the upward mobility process. The only three extant *sheng-yüan* lists which contain ancestral records deserve a detailed analysis.

The details on the *sheng-yüan* quota system will be given at the beginning of chapter V. It suffices to say here that the general trend conforms by and large to the long-range changes shown in table 9 on *chin-shih* social composition, except that, right down to the late Ch'ing, *sheng-yüan* were still recruited from a rather broad social base. The smallest percentages of students from commoner families without degree holders are found in the Hsien-feng period (1851–61), a decade of intense Taiping wars which seriously disrupted the lower Yangtze area. In spite of the fact that our data cover only three lower Yangtze localities, they are highly significant for several reasons. First, they show that even in a highly cultured district like Ch'ang-shu, which boasted many first-class *chin-shih* and nationally distinguished families, ordinary commoners still had a fair chance of achieving this critical initial social transition. Second, the three series of local figures help us to interpret the implications

## TABLE 15

### FAMILY BACKGROUND OF SHENG-YÜAN

| Period | Ch'ang-shu County Total number | Sheng-yüan from families without degree holder Number | Percent of total | Hai-men County Total number | Sheng-yüan from families without degree holder Number | Percent of total | Nan-t'ung County Total number | Sheng-yüan from families without degree holder Number | Percent of total |
|---|---|---|---|---|---|---|---|---|---|
| 1368–1487[a] | — | — | — | — | — | — | 267 | 263 | 98.6 |
| 1488–1505 | — | — | — | — | — | — | 88 | 78 | 88.6 |
| 1506–1521 | — | — | — | — | — | — | 143 | 120 | 83.9 |
| 1522–1566 | — | — | — | — | — | — | 444 | 332 | 74.8 |
| 1567–1572 | — | — | — | — | — | — | 35 | 22 | 62.9 |
| 1573–1620[b] | — | — | — | — | — | — | 549 | 375 | 68.3 |
| 1621–1627 | — | — | — | — | — | — | 195 | 138 | 70.8 |
| 1628–1644 | — | — | — | — | — | — | 303 | 186 | 61.4 |
| Total (Ming) | — | — | — | — | — | — | 2,024 | 1,514 | 74.8 |
| 1644–1661 | 507 | 338 | 66.7 | 47 | 38 | 80.9 | 286 | 162 | 56.6 |
| 1662–1722 | 1,050 | 671 | 63.9 | 333 | 200 | 60.0 | 811 | 462 | 57.0 |
| 1723–1735 | 267 | 189 | 70.8 | 78 | 36 | 46.2 | 218 | 117 | 53.7 |
| 1736–1795 | 1,142 | 663 | 58.1 | 424 | 230 | 54.2 | 1,071 | 658 | 61.4 |
| 1796–1820 | 464 | 224 | 48.3 | 180 | 76 | 42.2 | 494 | 258 | 52.2 |
| 1821–1850 | 608 | 293 | 48.2 | 207 | 86 | 41.6 | 534 | 229 | 42.9 |
| 1851–1861 | 227 | 78 | 34.4 | 62 | 20 | 32.3 | 177 | 71 | 40.0 |
| 1862–1874 | 408 | 173 | 42.4 | 95 | 42 | 44.2 | 350 | 146 | 41.7 |
| 1875–1904[c] | 851 | 357 | 42.0 | 210 | 103 | 49.0 | 403 | 198 | 49.1 |
| Total (Ch'ing) | 5,524 | 2,986 | 54.5 | 1,636 | 791 | 48.4 | 4,344 | 2,301 | 53.0 |

Sources: *Kuo-ch'ao yü-yang k'o-ming lu* (printed some time after 1904); *Ching-hsiang t'i-ming lu* (1933); *T'ung-hsiang t'i-ming-lu* (1933).

[a] The periods are reign periods. The very small numbers of student ranks granted up to 1487 make it convenient to combine several early Ming reign periods.

[b] Includes the short reign of Ming Kuang-tsung in 1620.

[c] For Nan-t'ung County the list ends in 1891.

of our more extensive data on higher degree holders. Since the examination system was highly selective and *chin-shih* represent only the apex of a vast pyramid of degree holders, the fact that, even during the Ch'ing period, when Category A *chin-shih* averages dropped to between one third and one quarter of the early Ming average, more than 50 percent of *sheng-yüan* originated from non-degree-holding commoner families would imply a much wider opportunity-structure for ordinary commoners at the pyramid's broad base. Without these Ch'ang-shu, Hai-men, and Nan-t'ung figures we could only speculate; with them our speculation is at least partially validated. Third, the fact that *sheng-yüan* from degree-holding families gradually rose from an insignificant fraction of the total in the early Ming to a narrow majority in the latter half of the Ch'ing must not be taken to mean that local families of scholarly tradition were increasingly able to perpetuate their success in local examinations. Summing up the invaluable but highly complex table of *sheng-yüan* arranged according to local clans, the editor of the Nan-t'ung list thoughtfully observed that few local clans had succeeded in producing even one *sheng-yüan* each generation for more than a few generations. A similar table and a similar editorial comment are found in the *sheng-yüan* list of the neighboring Hai-men County.[18] The fact that on the average nearly three quarters of *sheng-yüan* during the Ming and more than one half during the Ch'ing came from obscure commoner families without previous elementary degree holders would indicate that the social composition of the large *sheng-yüan* body, even more than that of the much smaller *chin-shih* group, was in a constant state of flux.

To conclude, the most important feature shown in the statistical series is the persistent downward trend of Category A *chin-shih* figures from the late sixteenth century to the very end of the Ch'ing period. This persistent decline, interpreted in its social context, would indicate the increasing difficulty and frustration of the humble and obscure in ascending the socio-bureaucratic ladder. While its effect was partially ameliorated by the steady rise of the Category B series, actually the difficulty and frustration of the humble and obscure were all the greater because our statistics in this chapter do not show the increasing power of money which during the greater part of the Ch'ing was easily translated into ruling-class membership and which glutted the market for bureaucratic office. Reasons for the long-range downward trend in the Category A series and for the changing opportunity-structure will be systematically discussed in chapter V. In the final chapter a further attempt will be made to integrate the main statistical data presented in this chapter with the aggregate evidence of our study.

# CHAPTER IV

# DOWNWARD MOBILITY

IN social mobility studies long-range downward mobility is sometimes implied but seldom systematically investigated. This is because data showing downward mobility are much harder to collect than those on other types of mobility. Some recent studies of social mobility in modern Western industrialized societies contain data on change in occupational status between fathers and sons based on sample surveys,[1] but little information is available for changes in occupational status over a number of generations. In the present study the only useful data for research on downward mobility are genealogies, which usually contain information on academic degrees, offices, and official titles held by kinsmen. Therefore our data differ in nature from modern Western data.

Unlike data on ancestry given in lists of successful civil-service candidates, which are precise and cross-sectional, genealogical records are very bulky and must be carefully sifted to be useful. For one thing, the clan system was not well developed in all parts of China in Ming-Ch'ing times. The majority of genealogies available are of Yangtze provinces. Moreover, since the average clan was a far from socially homogeneous body, the proportion of holders of higher academic degrees or offices is relatively small. For the majority of the members of the average clan, therefore, there is no information whatever on their social, occupational, and economic statuses.

For these reasons we choose the histories of four clans as illustrations of the general processes of social leveling. The four clans so selected were among the most prominent in late Ming and Ch'ing times. They are the Wang clan of Hsin-ch'eng, near the capital city

Chi-nan of Shantung; the Chang clan of T'ung-ch'eng in southern Anhwei; the Chi clan of Wu-hsi in southern Kiangsu; and the Ch'en clan of Hai-ning in northeastern coastal Chekiang. There is no formal genealogy of the first clan available in North America, but it is possible to marshal systematic information by generation on the academic-bureaucratic statuses of its male members and also considerable highly revealing information on the ancestral instructions which accounted for its unusual success. For the other three clans formal genealogies are available in the Columbia University Libraries and in the Library of Congress, which enable us to compute the intergeneration change in academic-bureaucratic prominence. It is hoped that the records of these extraordinary clans will sharpen our understanding of the processes of long-range downward mobility in general. If the decline of these most prominent clans was inevitable in the course of a number of generations, it is fairly safe to generalize that the processes of downward mobility of the average successful clan must have been less gradual.

In addition to summarizing statistically the records of these sample families, we shall also attempt to explain the environmental, educational, institutional, and economic factors which had a bearing on downward mobility.

SAMPLE GENEALOGICAL RECORDS

THE WANG CLAN. The ancestor of the Wang clan in Hsin-ch'eng was Wang Kuei, who attained his majority in the late Yüan period. Originally a native of Chu-ch'eng County in Shantung, he had to emigrate because of lack of economic opportunity in his ancestral village and also for fear of the possible reprisal of local bandits whom he and other villagers had repulsed. Wang Shih-chen (1634–1711), one of his most famous descendants, testified that in his newly adopted place, Hsin-ch'eng County, he first worked as a tenant for a great landlord, Ts'ao.[2] One day during a violent dust-storm a young maiden sought refuge in the Ts'ao household. It was found that she was from Wang Kuei's ancestral village. With the landlord as the matchmaker, Wang Kuei took her for bride, and she gave birth to five sons. Hard work and frugal living enabled him eventually to buy some property. His economic status was further improved by intensive farming and by lending grain and money at the conventional high interest rates.

Little is said about Wang Wu (Wang the Fifth), the youngest of Wang Kuei's five sons, who sired all the later famous Wangs. From the brevity of the account and particularly from his personal name "the Fifth," an ordinal designation which is commonly given to illiterate peasants or people of lower orders, he probably did not receive a good education. It is likely that he carried on farming with continued success, because he began to donate to local charities. Two of his four sons became degree holders. The eldest son, Wang Lin, obtained his first degree at the age of thirteen and later became a *kung-sheng*, which qualified him as a deputy director of a county school. He finally reached the post of director of the school of the Ying-ch'uan Principality in Honan. One of his younger brothers was a *sheng-yüan*.

Wang Lin, the most successful of the third generation, was perhaps typical of many substantial landowning peasants' sons in the process of upward social climb which was not without cost. The fact that he had four uncles and three brothers would suggest that the share of land he inherited must have been rather small in comparison with the size of the total property at the death of his grandfather Wang Kuei. His small property, coupled with his scholarly occupation, involved him in recurrent financial difficulties. Although it is impossible to determine the length of time between his passing the first local examination and his attainment of the *kung-sheng* status, it is likely to have been considerable because the conferring of *kung-sheng* was generally based on seniority. From time to time he had to depend on his maternal uncle to make ends meet. Even after attaining the *kung-sheng* level, he had a small income and persistent economic worries. It was by no means certain that the next generation would be able to climb higher in the social scale.

Unlike families of similar circumstances which failed to continue the upward climb, Wang Lin was fortunate in having an unusually studious and ambitious son, Wang Ch'ung-kuang (1502–58). When the latter was eight years old, Wang Lin once ordered him to quit his studies partly because of economic difficulty and partly as a test of his perseverance. The lad demonstrated his determination by placing two big characters, *chin-shih,* on his desk. Thanks to his father's prolonged tutoring, Wang Ch'ung-kuang became a *chin-shih* in 1541. The crucial change in family fortune therefore took place in the fourth generation.

Wang Ch'ung-kuang, the first really successful member of the clan, finally reached the position of *ts'an-i* (assistant to the governor, rank 4b) of Kweichow, where he died in a campaign against aborigines. During the seventeen years he served in various local and provincial posts he corresponded regularly with his sons and advised them on what to read, and particularly on the techniques of composing examination essays. For him and his sons the primary goal in life was to pass the highest examination. His instruction to his sons is as follows:

> What you cherish must be a righteous heart,
> What you do must be righteous deeds,
> What you befriend must be men of learning,
> What you discuss must be useful scholarly subjects.

This instruction was subsequently inscribed on a stone tablet erected in the courtyard of the ancestral hall. It was Wang Ch'ung-kuang who first laid down the pattern of family instruction which was a mixture of Confucian puritanism and social realism. Realizing how much he owed his success to his early psychological challenge, he inculcated in the minds of his sons and grandsons the importance of ambition as a factor in social and academic success. One of his favorite topics of family conversation with his pre-teen-age grandsons was how they thought they would rank in future examinations.[3]

The family tradition was well preserved by some distinguished members of the fifth and sixth generations. Wang Chih-yüan, the second son of Wang Ch'ung-kuang, *chin-shih* of 1562, who later reached the high office of vice president of the Board of Revenue, tirelessly taught his younger brothers, sons, and nephews that energy must not be dissipated and that true wisdom lay in non-entanglement in court politics. Since the mid-Ming and late-Ming period witnessed a long series of factional strifes and many prominent officials were severely punished for their "party" affiliations, this career man's prudence no doubt helped to prolong the family's success.

He further laid down the rule that all male youths must stay within the family compound, devote themselves to the preparation of higher examinations, and refrain from discussing politics.[4] Basing his instructions on his own experience, he summarized for the reference of the whole family the main government regulations on examination affairs and the techniques of writing the "eight-legged" style of composition.[5] The wisdom and austere practicality of family tradition crystallized in a couplet made by his younger son, Wang Hsiang-ch'ien, *chin-shih* of 1602, who later became governor of Chekiang. This couplet, like the sayings of Wang Ch'ung-kuang, was inscribed in the ancestral hall. It reads:

> To receive ancestors' one wise heritage: Be diligent and be thrifty;
> To show posterity two orthodox avenues: To study and to plough.

The excellent tradition of the Wang clan was well known to contemporaries. Niu Hsiu, a scholar of the late seventeenth century, testified to the psychological challenge to which the Wang youths were constantly subjected:[6]

The Wang family of Hsin-ch'eng has for generations risen to preeminence since Wang Ch'ung-kuang. This success is due to its strict family instruction. On occasions of family gatherings, such as weddings and funerals, new years and festivals, or ancestral worship, every member of the family must wear attire proper to his status before the ceremony is held. Not until a male member's name has been entered in the registers of the educational commissioner is his wife allowed to wear silver jewelry or to don a silk garment. Otherwise he and his wife have to wear humble attire all their lives. Those who have attained official ranks are resplendent in official hats and sashes, those who have failed in examinations are doomed to wear short [commoners'] jackets. This sharp contrast in status makes the laggards ashamed. Therefore the father instructs his son, the wife urges her husband that everybody must study hard and make good in examinations and officialdom. This is why the Wang clan has produced so many holders of higher degrees and officials and has become a clan of national renown.

After explaining the main reasons for the family's early success we are in a position to analyze the list of the Wangs for whom records are available.[7]

From table 16 it is evident that the Wang clan reached the apex of its success during the sixth generation, which produced 9 *chin-shih*, 1 *chü-jen*, and 3 *kung-sheng*. Of the nine *chin-shih*, four reached high official ranks. Although reasons for its gradual decline are nowhere systematically explained, there are significant forebodings that after the sixth generation its unusual academic success may not easily be maintained. Wang Shih-chen testified:[8]

After my great-great-grandfather [Wang Ch'ung-kuang] rose to prominence by obtaining the *chin-shih* degree in the mid-Chia-ching period [1522–66], my family reached the height of success during the late decades of the Ming. Every generation produced its prominent men. When the Ming government was torn by factional strife, none of them was involved. My late grand-uncle the grand preceptor [Wang Hsiang-ch'ien], who for sixty years served alternately as high minister and commanding general, was no exception. However, one of my grand-uncles, the senior secretary of the Board of Civil Appointments [Wang Hsiang-ch'un], became a prominent member of the Tung-lin party. Though gifted, he was superficial and imprudent. This was the first change in our family tradition.

While members of the Tung-lin party were in general men of integrity and high ideals,[9] they courted disaster by prolonged and excessive attacks on the inner cabinet controlled by powerful eunuchs. By joining the Tung-lin party Wang Hsiang-ch'un certainly deviated from his ancestral instruction, which is aptly described by the old Chinese saying that "the wise should be primarily concerned with self-preservation." By associating with Tung-lin men of letters, many of whom were intemperate or openly flaunted their literary skills, Wang Hsiang-ch'un was the first member of the clan who dissipated his energies.

In fact, Wang Hsiang-ch'un was not the only one who failed to conform to the family pattern of realistic career officials. The clan, being nationally prominent during its sixth generation, could no longer subject all its male members to the austere scholasticism and self-discipline which had so far accounted for its unusual success. For some members, the time had come to enjoy the fruits of family success. Wang Hsiang-hsien, for example, was without an academic degree but "careless and nonconformist, indulged in wine, and skilled in the cursive style of calligraphy." Wang Hsiang-ming, also of the sixth generation, likewise failed to obtain a degree but managed to earn a place in local history on account of his poetic gift and calligraphic skill.

The trend towards easier living, artistic and literary hobbies,

## TABLE 16

### PROMINENT MEMBERS OF THE WANG CLAN

| Generation | Name | | Degree, official rank, or other accomplishment | Holders of higher degrees and offices (each generation) | | | | Total of high officials (each generation) |
|---|---|---|---|---|---|---|---|---|
| | | | | Total | Chin-shih | Chü-jen | Kung-sheng | |
| 1st | Kuei | 王貴 | — | — | | | | — |
| 2d | Wu | 伍 | — | — | | | | — |
| 3d | Lin | 麟 | kung-sheng; 7b | 1 | 0 | 0 | 1 | — |
| 4th | Ch'ung-kuang | 重光 | chin-shih (1541); 4b | 1 | 1 | 0 | 0 | — |
| 5th | Chih-yüan | 之垣 | chin-shih (1562); 2a | 6 | 3 | 1 | 1 | 2 |
| | Chih-fu | 輔 | chü-jen (1561); 5a | | | | | |
| | Chih-ch'eng | 城 | kung-sheng; 5a | | | | | |
| | Chih-yu | 猷 | chin-shih (1567); 3a | | | | | |
| | Chih-tung | 棟 | 7b | | | | | |
| | Chih-tu | 都 | chin-shih (1595); 4a | | | | | |
| 6th | Hsiang-k'un | 象坤 | chin-shih (1565); 2a | 15 | 9 | 1 | 3 | 4 |
| | Hsiang-ch'ien | 乾 | chin-shih (1572); 1b | | | | | |
| | Hsiang-chin | 晉 | chin-shih (1604); 2a | | | | | |
| | Hsiang-meng | 蒙 | chin-shih (1568); 4a | | | | | |
| | Hsiang-tou | 斗 | chin-shih (1595); 6a | | | | | |
| | Hsiang-chieh | 節 | chin-shih (1592); 7b | | | | | |
| | Hsiang-heng | 恒 | chin-shih (1595); 2a | | | | | |
| | Hsiang-ch'un | 春 | chin-shih (1610); 5a | | | | | |
| | Hsiang-yün | 雲 | chin-shih (1625); 4a | | | | | |
| | Hsiang-fu | 復 | 5a | | | | | |
| | Hsiang-tui | 兌 | kung-sheng; 8b | | | | | |

| Generation | Name | | Degree, official rank, or other accomplishment | Holders of higher degrees and offices (each generation) | | | | Total of high officials (each generation) |
|---|---|---|---|---|---|---|---|---|
| | | | | Total | Chin-shih | Chü-jen | Kung-sheng | |
| | Hsiang-hsien | 咸 | 8b; fond of wine and skilled in calligraphy | | | | | |
| | Hsiang-t'ai | 素 | *chü-jen* (1573) | | | | | |
| | Hsiang-ken | 艮 | *kung-sheng*; 5a | | | | | |
| | Hsiang-i | 益 | *kung-sheng*; 8b | | | | | |
| | Hsiang-ming | 明 | skilled in calligraphy and poetry | | | | | |
| 7th | | | | 6 | 2 | 2 | 2 | 0 |
| | Yü-k'uei | 輿 | *chü-jen* (1612) | | | | | |
| | Yü-yin | 蘷 | *chin-shih* (1628); 5a | | | | | |
| | Yü-hui | 胤 | *sheng-yüan* | | | | | |
| | Yü-tuan | 慧 | skilled in poetry and painting | | | | | |
| | Yü-chiu | 端 | skilled in poetry | | | | | |
| | Yü-sheng | 玖 | skilled in literature | | | | | |
| | Yü-mei | 盛 | *kung-sheng*; 7b | | | | | |
| | Yü-chieh | 美 | *sheng-yüan*; donor to local charities | | | | | |
| | Yü-ch'ih | 階 | *kung-sheng*; never holding office | | | | | |
| | Yü-hsiang | 叔 | *chin-shih* (1659); 7b | | | | | |
| | Yü-i | 襄 | *chü-jen* (1661) | | | | | |
| 8th | | | | 5 | 4 | 1 | 0 | 1 |
| | Shih-ch'un | 士純 | skilled in painting and poetry | | | | | |
| | Shih-lu | 祿 | *chin-shih* (1655); 5b | | | | | |
| | Shih-chi | 驥 | *chin-shih* (1664); 7b; skilled in poetry | | | | | |
| | Shih-yü | 鼇 | *chü-jen* (1651); fond of wine; skilled in poetry; well versed in Buddhist classics | | | | | |

TABLE 16 (*Continued*)

| Generation | Name | | Degree, official rank, or other accomplishment | Holders of higher degrees and offices (each generation) | | | | Total of high officials (each generation) |
| --- | --- | --- | --- | --- | --- | --- | --- | --- |
| | | | | Total | Chin-shih | Chü-jen | Kung-sheng | |
| | Shih-t'i | 士騠 | skilled in string instrument *ch'in*, poetry, and well versed in Buddhist classics | | | | | |
| | Shih-yu | 祐 | *chin-shih* (1670) | | | | | |
| | Shih-chen | 禛 | *chin-shih* (1655); 1b; bibliophile, connoisseur, and a foremost poet | | | | | |
| 9th | Ch'i-wo | 啓沃 | *chin-shih* (1676); 7b; known for painting skill during long retirement | 3 | 1 | 1 | 1 | 0 |
| | Ch'i-lei | 磊 | skilled in calligraphy and painting | | | | | |
| | Ch'i-shu | 湅 | *kung-sheng* by purchase; 8a; skilled in poetry, painting and calligraphy | | | | | |
| | Ch'i-ta | 大 | *chü-jen* (1669); 8a; skilled in poetry and calligraphy | | | | | |
| 10th | Chao-tsan | 兆瓚 | expectant 8b | 5 | 0 | 3 | 1 | 0 |
| | Chao-kao | 杲 | *kung-sheng*; skilled in calligraphy | | | | | |
| | Chao-lung | 隆 | *chü-jen* (1788), imperially bestowed because of advanced age | | | | | |
| | Chao-hsin | 信 | *chin-sheng*; known for local charity | | | | | |
| | Chao-tan | 郯 | *sheng-yüan*; filial son | | | | | |
| | Chao-hung | 宏 | *chü-jen* (1799) | | | | | |
| | Chao-k'un | 錕 | *chü-jen* (1799) | | | | | |

| Generation | Name | | Degree, official rank, or other accomplishment | Holders of higher degrees and offices (each generation) | | | | Total of high officials (each generation) |
|---|---|---|---|---|---|---|---|---|
| | | | | Total | Chin-shih | Chü-jen | Kung-sheng | |
| 11th | Tsu-hsi | 祖緹 | 7b | 5 | 0 | 3 | 0 | 0 |
| | Tsu-yung | 緺 | *chü-jen* (1801); 7b (1802); all imperially bestowed | | | | | |
| | Tsu-hsi | 熙 | *chü-jen* (1756); 8b; fond of wine and travel; skilled in painting | | | | | |
| | Tsu-yü | 鈺 | *chü-jen* (1753); 8a | | | | | |
| | Tsu-su | 肅 | *sheng-yüan*; 4a; through successive purchases | | | | | |
| 12th | Ch'en-feng | 宸俸 | military *chin-shih* (1761) | 6 | 1 | 5 | 0 | 0 |
| | Ch'en-tzu | 仔 | *chü-jen* (1771); 7b | | | | | |
| | Ch'en-chieh | 佶 | *chin-shih* (1752); 7a | | | | | |
| | Ch'en-tsan | 儧 | *chü-jen* (1783); expectant 7b | | | | | |
| | Ch'en-sui | 綏 | *chü-jen* (1794); 8a | | | | | |
| | Ch'en-yang | 揚 | *chü-jen* (1762) | | | | | |
| 13th | Yün-kuan | 允灌 | *chin-shih* (1836); 7b | 4 | 2 | 2 | 0 | 0 |
| | Yün-ch'u | 楚 | *chin-shih* (1805) | | | | | |
| | Yün-tsun | 犉 | *chü-jen* (1810) | | | | | |
| | Yün-po | 柏 | *chü-jen* (1819) | | | | | |
| 14th | Wei-jung | 維榮 | *chü-jen* (1825) | 2 | 0 | 2 | 0 | 0 |
| | Wei-tu | 度 | *chü-jen* (1888); 8b | | | | | |

Sources: *Hsing-ch'êng Wang-shih chia-sheng* (undated, probably late 17th century); *Hsin-ch'êng hsien-chih* (1693 and 1933 eds.), chapters on degree holders and biographies; Wang Shih-chen, *Ch'ih-pei ou-t'an*, various accounts on Wang ancestry.

wine and music became more noticeable during subsequent generations. The seventh generation failed to produce a single man
of national prominence, and the eighth only one—Wang Shih-chen.
Wang Yü-ch'ih, father of Wang Shih-chen, constantly led his sons to
compose poetry and practice archaic styles of writing. In the light of
the clan's temporary though drastic decline in prominence, some
relatives suggested to Wang Yü-ch'ih that he should rather supervise his sons in more utilitarian scholastic work such as practicing
examination essay writing, but he resolutely refused.[10] While it is
true that in spite of the gradual deviation from early family tradition the eighth generation produced one president of the Board of
Rites and two other *chin-shih,* the seeds for the clan's decline in
academic-bureaucratic success were further sown by its most famous
member. From his initial appointment as judge of Yang-chou prefecture in 1659 to his death in 1711, Wang Shih-chen achieved national fame almost exclusively through poetry, nationwide literary
and artistic association, and a career as a connoisseur and bibliophile.[11] In fact, by his lifetime the prevailing mode of life of the
Wang clan had changed so much that, of the seven members of his
generation recorded in local history, five took poetry, literature,
painting, music, and Buddhism as lifelong avocations. Even a maternal relative, Hsü Yüan-shan, cared for nothing except literature,
philosophy, and art and eventually became one of the four famous
hermits of the locality.[12]

In all likelihood the Wang clan had been multiplying throughout the generations. What is not mentioned in local history is perhaps even more important than what is recorded. There must have
been an increasing proportion in each generation of members of
the clan who could neither obtain a higher degree nor achieve
artistic or literary distinction. They were nevertheless all members
of the leisured class, living on inherited property and ancestral
glory. With the lone exception of Wang Tsu-su of the eleventh
generation, who finally attained the position of prefect through
successive purchases of rank, none of the progressively fewer higher
degree holders reached an office higher than the seventh rank. It is
not unlikely that they preferred comfortable living as retired minor
officials to strenuous government service. The increasingly minute

division of property must also have brought economic difficulties to many members of the clan. In any case, the fact that Wang Shih-chen's descendants became poor and obscure was well known, and one of them in the early nineteenth century demeaned himself and his illustrious ancestors by earning his living as a local government runner—a not uncommon social phenomenon which constituted the theme of a poem of lamentation by a Kiangsi scholar.[13] The famous late-Ch'ing scholar Miao Ch'üan-sun also testified to the impoverishment of Wang Shih-chen's descendants, who had sold practically all the books, curios, paintings, and calligraphic works that had made Wang Shih-chen nationally famous.[14]

THE CHANG, CHI, AND CH'EN CLANS. These three clans were among the most distinguished of Ch'ing times. The Chang clan of T'ung-ch'eng and the Chi clan of Wu-hsi each produced a prime minister in two consecutive generations. The Ch'en clan of Hai-ning surpassed them by producing a prime minister in three consecutive generations. The Chang clan, whose remote ancestors were registered under *chiang-chi* (artisan status) but owned considerable land, rose to national prominence during the ninth genealogical generation which produced its first prime minister, Chang-Ying (1638–1708), who established for all his sons a strictly ultilitarian program of studying the techniques of writing examination essays.[15] His second son, Chang T'ing-yü (1672–1755), one of the most powerful Chinese prime ministers of the entire Ch'ing period, achieved the unique honor of having his name entered posthumously in the imperial ancestral temple. The Chi family during its fourth genealogical generation produced its first prime minister, Chi Tseng-yün (1671–1739), whose unusual success was repeated by his second son, Chi Huang (1711–94). The family, which for three generations prior to the rise to prominence had produced several scholars and one minor official, was a typical case of "ploughing with the writing brush." The Ch'en clan of Hai-ning was descended from a poor young man who married into the family of an owner of a bean-curd store.[16] The three prime ministers were Ch'en Chih-lin (1605–66) of the ninth generation, Ch'eng Yüan-lung (1652–1736) of the tenth generation, and Ch'en Shih-kuan (1680–1758) of the eleventh generation. Legend had it that even the great Ch'ien-lung emperor was a member of the Ch'en clan, which is of course absurd but is indicative of its extraordinary record of academic-bureaucratic success. The Chang clan during Chang T'ing-yü's lifetime reached such an unprecedented height that in 1742 Liu T'ung-hsün (1700–73), the upright censor-general who soon became one of the famous prime ministers, stated in a memorial that the Changs and their maternal relatives the Yaos of the same T'ung-ch'eng area accounted for almost one half of the *chin-shen* ("gentry") of all China.[17] Obviously an exaggeration, this statement reflected the fact that the Chang clan's record of success was probably unique in the entire Ming-Ch'ing period. Dazzled by their fortune and honors, contemporaries were willing to believe in the Ch'en and Chang family legends that their prolonged prominence was due to geomancy.[18]

Since a genealogy of a "common descent group" is a very bulky work, we will analyze the mobility trend of only the most successful branches of these three clans. Our purpose here being a study of downward mobility, we treat Chang Ying, Chi Tseng-yün, and Ch'en Yü-hsiang (1545–1628), the nearest common ancestors of the three Ch'en prime ministers, as the "founders" or the first generations.

A technical analysis of these genealogical data can be deferred until our discussion in the following sections of institutional and noninstitutional factors which were related to downward mobility. A general examination of the genealogical records here shows a common long-range decline in academic-bureaucratic success, which was both quantitative and qualitative. It cannot be explained satisfactorily why this long-range decline was also partially biological. The Chi family from the fifth generation onward failed to reproduce itself biologically and a similar biological decline began to take place in the Ch'en clan from the tenth generation onward. In both cases the process of biological decline was accelerated by the Taiping rebellion, which exacted a heavy toll of human lives in southern Kiangsu and northern Chekiang. While on the surface the Chang clan was able, till the compilation of its new genealogy in 1890 at least, to reproduce itself biologically, qualitatively the biological loss had already been very heavy during the third generation. Chang

## TABLE 17
### DOWNWARD MOBILITY OF THE CHANG, CHI, AND CH'EN CLANS

| Generation | Total male descendants | Degrees | | | | | | Officials | | | | Percent of degree holders in total male descendants | Percent of officials in total male descendants |
|---|---|---|---|---|---|---|---|---|---|---|---|---|---|
| | | Yin | Chin-shih | Chü-jen and Kung-sheng | Sheng-yüan | Chien-sheng | Total | High | Middle | Low | Total | | |
| **DESCENDANTS OF CHANG YING** | | | | | | | | | | | | | |
| 2d | 6 | — | 4 | 2 | — | — | 6 | 3 | 1 | 1 | 5 | 100 | 83.3 |
| 3d | 14 | 1 | 4 | 8 | — | 1 | 14 | 3 | 8 | — | 11 | 100 | 78.6 |
| 4th | 38 | 3 | 1 | 15 | 2 | 16 | 37 | 1 | 14 | 15 | 30 | 97.3 | 79.0 |
| 5th | 77 | 1 | 2 | 6 | 10 | 28 | 47 | — | 10 | 13 | 23 | 61.0 | 30.0 |
| 6th | 101 | — | 1 | 5 | 9 | 22 | 37 | — | 12 | 21 | 33 | 36.5 | 32.6 |
| 7th | 113 | — | 2 | 6 | 6 | 20 | 34 | — | 11 | 11 | 22 | 30.0 | 19.4 |
| **DESCENDANTS OF CHI TSENG-YÜN** | | | | | | | | | | | | | |
| 2d | 8 | 1 | 1 | 3 | — | 3 | 8 | 2 | 4 | 1 | 7 | 100 | 87.5 |
| 3d | 25 | — | 1 | 1 | 1 | 20 | 23 | — | 11 | 6 | 17 | 92.0 | 68.0 |
| 4th | 56 | — | — | 2 | 4 | 27 | 33 | — | 9 | 13 | 22 | 60.0 | 39.4 |
| 5th | 63 | — | — | 3 | 2 | 15 | 20 | — | 2 | 15 | 17 | 31.7 | 27.0 |
| 6th | 49 | 1 | — | 1 | 2 | 8 | 12 | — | 2 | 6 | 8 | 24.5 | 16.3 |
| 7th | 28 | 1 | — | 1 | 1 | 3 | 6 | — | 1 | 3 | 4 | 21.4 | 14.3 |
| 8th–9th | 16 | — | — | — | — | 4 | 4 | — | — | 3 | 3 | 25.0 | 18.8 |
| **DESCENDANTS OF CH'EN YÜ-HSIANG** | | | | | | | | | | | | | |
| 2d | 5 | — | 2 | — | 1 | 2 | 5 | 1 | 1 | — | 2 | 100 | 40.0 |
| 3d | 11 | — | 1 | 6 | 2 | 2 | 11 | 1 | 2 | — | 3 | 100 | 27.3 |
| 4th | 38 | 1 | 6 | 7 | 7 | 12 | 33 | 4 | 9 | 2 | 15 | 86.8 | 39.5 |
| 5th | 67 | — | 7 | 18 | 7 | 15 | 47 | 3 | 20 | 5 | 28 | 70.0 | 41.8 |
| 6th | 173 | 2 | 1 | 23 | 20 | 68 | 114 | — | 41 | 14 | 55 | 65.8 | 31.8 |
| 7th | 260 | 1 | 2 | 16 | 39 | 75 | 133 | — | 23 | 31 | 56 | 51.2 | 21.5 |
| 8th | 268 | 2 | 5 | 18 | 23 | 68 | 114 | 2 | 16 | 51 | 69 | 42.9 | 25.7 |
| 9th | 299 | 1 | — | 10 | 15 | 41 | 67 | 2 | 13 | 36 | 49 | 22.4 | 13.4 |
| 10th | 224 | — | — | 10 | 32 | 23 | 64 | — | 8 | 18 | 26 | 28.6 | 11.6 |
| 11th | 157 | 2 | — | 8 | 22 | 11 | 43 | — | 7 | 11 | 18 | 27.5 | 11.5 |
| 12th | 82 | — | — | 1 | 9 | — | 10 | — | — | 1 | 1 | 12.2 | 1.2 |

Sources: *T'ung-ch'eng Chang-shih tsung-p'u*, *Hsi-shan Chi-shih tsung-p'u*, and *Hai-ning Po-hai Ch'en-shih tsung-p'u*.

T'ing-yü's branch was without doubt the most successful. Of his four sons three died relatively young. The eldest, Chang Jo-ai (1713–46) was scholastically the most brilliant. He had in fact won first-class honors in the palace examination of 1733 but was relegated to *ch'uan-lu* (first of the second class) because of the petition of his prudent father, who was afraid that his son's academic distinction would arouse further jealousy and adverse criticism. Chang Jo-ai's excellent command of literature and his skill in calligraphy and painting made him one of the Ch'ien-lung emperor's favorite young officials. Shortly after he had reached the much-coveted position of sub-chancellor of the Grand Secretariat and concurrently of vice president of the Board of Rites, his extremely promising official career was suddenly cut short at the age of thirty-three. Chang T'ing-yü's second son, Chang Jo-ch'eng (1721–70), who attained the *chin-shih* degree in 1745, died in the post of vice president of the Board of Rites at the age of forty-nine. The third son, Chang Jo-shu (1727–60), who entered government through *yin,* died at the age of thirty-three without having had the opportunity to climb higher than his initial post of second-class secretary of a central board. But for the extraordinary favor bestowed by the Ch'ien-lung emperor on the youngest son Chang Jo-t'ing (1728–1802), who eventually reached the high office of president of the Board of Punishments, the decline of the Chang family would have come sooner.

In the absence of systematic scientific explanation the best we can do is to speculate that prolonged academic-bureaucratic success inevitably brought about a change in the mode of life of members of successful clans. It is possible that two or three generations after the initial success many young members of the family took to sensual or sensuous pleasures, or to various forms of sophisticated dissipation which gradually sapped their vitality. After the pinnacle of success was reached it was not uncommon for many of the promising members of the clan to die young. Genealogies usually give dates of births and of deaths, but the laborious work of tabulating life spans of members of distinguished clans must await future research.

In any case, our records show that these three distinguished clans failed in the long run to reproduce themselves academically and socially. In the Chang clan the last member who managed to attain the third official rank was Chang Tseng-i (1747–97), son of Chang Jo-t'ing, thanks again to the Ch'ien-lung emperor's remembrance of the services of his grandfather and father. For the Chi clan none from the third generation onward could reach the third official rank. The Ch'en clan ceased to produce high officials after the eighth generation, or four generations after the apex of success was reached. Further analysis shows that two or three generations after the height of prominence, by far the majority of the degree holders of these clans were the lowly *sheng-yüan* and especially the purchased *chien-sheng*.

The economic foundation of the Chang family may have remained sound three or four generations after reaching its apogee, despite successive divisions of the common property. This was because the large clans of the T'ung-ch'eng area (Chang Ying's clan in particular) had always preferred investment in landed property to other types of investment.[19] Land, as Chang Ying pointed out in a famous essay, gave a lower yield on investment, was an immobile asset, and was hence harder for descendants to sell.[20] Probably because of this long family tradition and also owing to the size of the family fortune accumulated during the first three generations, a few Changs of later generations could still buy their way into middle official ranks. The Chi clan was much less fortunate in that both Chi Tseng-yün and Chi Huang were known for their incorruptibility, and their savings from official emoluments did not amount to very much. A grandson of Chi Tseng-yün testified that the properties which the two prime ministers bequeathed were "less than that of a middle-class person's."[21] This may have been an exaggeration, but there can be little doubt that in spite of its unusual success the family was not actually rich. By the eighth and ninth generations the whole Chi clan could produce only four students of the Imperial Academy and three holders of lowly titular official ranks. Many obscure clans in process of upward climb could have done better.

HUMAN ENVIRONMENT

The gradual but inevitable long-range downward mobility of these most prominent clans would suggest that the same process was at work within ordinarily successful families. Within the scope of the present study it is impossible to analyze a significant number of bulky genealogies. There are, however, many keen contemporary observers of family vicissitudes whose theory of human environment as a factor in downward mobility is worth our examination.

As has been explained earlier, post-T'ang society differed in nature from pre-T'ang and early-T'ang society in that there were few institutional means whereby prominent clans could perpetuate themselves. By Sung times the civil-service examination system replaced family prestige as the most important determinant of social status. Already some Sung social observers fully recognized this increasing fluidity in the status system and the consequently more drastic rise and fall of family fortunes. Yüan Ts'ai, the famous writer on family affairs of the late twelfth century, generalized:

World affairs constantly change. This may indeed be regarded as a law of nature. Nowadays people often think that in view of their present prosperity they should have nothing to worry about for the rest of their lives. Actually, however, many of them sink in almost no time. Generally speaking, along with the change in calendrical order each decade,[22] human fortunes are also bound to change. Without having to look far back, we can easily see from what has happened in our vicinity during the past ten or twenty years that human success and failure, rise and fall can never be static.[23]

His over-all conclusion was that changes in human fortune were determined primarily by human environment and family education.

After lifelong observations, Yeh Tzu-ch'i, the noted scholar of the late Yüan and early Ming periods, made this generalization:

If the ancestor's wealth and honor were first obtained by serious studies, the descendants, being accustomed to a life of ease, are bound to look down upon studies. If a family acquired its fortune through hard work and frugality, its descendants, with a fortune at their disposal, generally forget about diligence and thrift. This is the basic reason why there are so many declining and declined families. May this be a warning to all of us! [24]

The reasons for the corruption of the youths of official families and for their inevitable decline were explained at first hand by a Ch'ing local official:

There is little that one can do when one's sons and grandsons are mediocre. It is important, however, that the scholastic family tradition should be preserved so that even if they are poor they can still make a living by teaching village pupils. It is a good thing if they are content with coarse clothes and straw shoes and refrain from going to the cities. . . . My late father used to say that, from his twenty years' experience as an official in Fukien and from his twenty years' observation at home, out of some one hundred former official colleagues only the sons of one or two men could surpass them in an official career and only ten or twenty percent of the descendants could keep up their original family standings through hard work and prudent living. Is it because local officials' descendants are naturally bad? [The reason is that] wealth and comforts had weakened their ambitions; even if they did not live an extravagant and dissipated life they were already good for nothing. In the event that their fathers lost their official posts and were forced to retire to their ancestral homes, they could do practically nothing because of their lack of special skills. The result was that they could only sit and eat away their family resources. Moreover, while being brought up in their fathers' official residences, they were subjected to various tempting traps laid by bad associates and flattering servants. Unless they were unusually wise and strong-willed, they were sure to succumb. Besides, their fathers, being themselves local officials, were occupied with legal and fiscal matters; so occupied as a rule that they could barely manage to deal with the high and low and had no time or energy to supervise their children. Although the youths had acquired bad habits no one would frankly advise their fathers. There were cases in which the family had already become insolvent while the father was still on active official duty. When citing several such instances my father sighed and grieved. He warned my brothers and me about this repeatedly when we were young. Fortunately, when we grew a little older we were sent back to our ancestral home, thus avoiding such traps and bad environmental influence. We all began by teaching village schools and then served as clerks after building up a little reputation. We worked even harder than indigent scholars and hence were able to establish ourselves. Unfortunately I myself have once more become a local official. During the past five or six years I have constantly reminded myself of my father's words, lest my own children should turn out to be loose. For five generations starting from my great-great-grandfather, we have managed to perpetuate our local official career. This is because of our wise ancestral instructions. At first thought we should congratulate ourselves, but the second thought makes me shudder.[25]

All the above and many other peculiarly Chinese human environmental explanations of the rise and fall of family fortunes are sound and are borne out by ample biographical evidence. A few examples suffice to show how some of even the most illustrious official families fell into oblivion in one or two generations because of lack of proper family education. Yang Shih-ch'i (1365–1444), one of the most famous early Ming prime ministers, whose wisdom and moderation won the utmost confidence of four emperors, was shocked by censors' reports that his son Yang Chi had committed in the ancestral district a number of atrocities including manslaughter. Although the Emperor Ying-tsung withheld the charges from the ailing statesman, Yang Shih-ch'i was rudely awakened to the consequence of his failure as a father and soon died in grief.[26] His son was subsequently executed. The descendants of his two famous colleagues Yang Jung and Yang Fu were hardly better. The former's son Yang Kung, who entered government as a middle-ranking official through *yin*, was relegated to a commoner because of his encroachment upon villagers' properties. Another son, Yang Hua, and a grandson, Yang T'ai, were executed and their properties confiscated because they had committed murder. Yang Fu's grandson barely escaped exile for killing a domestic slave. The son of Hu Kuang, another distinguished early Ming official, paid with his life for manslaughter.[27] While Liang Ch'u was a prime minister, one of his two sons exterminated in 1513 more than thirty families totaling some three hundred lives, because they had refused to surrender their properties. His second son, who was entitled to enter government service through *yin*, died young.[28] So frequently did kinsmen of prominent Ming officials commit excessive crimes that the famous historian Chao I devoted a special article to the subject.[29]

Granted that the descendants of the majority of prominent officials did not disgrace their families by outrageous crimes, their various forms of dissipation and debauchery nevertheless brought their families' eventual downfall. A late Ming work, rich in anecdotes, gives the following account of the life of the eldest son of Wang Ao (1450–1524), a famous prime minister and leading man of letters:

Wang Ao's son Wang Yen-che was by nature extravagant. He built a huge mansion in which to house his collection of female entertainers and concubines. When his children went out they were followed by tens of servants of both sexes, all in resplendent attire. His jewels, curios, ancient bronzes, porcelains, calligraphic specimens, and paintings were worth hundreds of thousands of taels. At a New Year's Eve banquet he invariably hung up a lantern made of pearls. All wine cups were ancient and made of jade. When he returned home, his sedan chair was first placed in front of the middle gate. After the gate was opened, it was carried inward by buxom female servants. He was usually surrounded by some twenty concubines, each of whom was waited upon by two maids. Everybody got drunk. When sufficiently stimulated, he rubbed women's shoulders and retired to an inner chamber, with an orchestra leading the way. In the chamber he drank once more until he fell asleep.[30]

Wang Ao's other three sons may not have been equally notorious; they were all connoisseurs and bibliophiles.[31] It seems more than coincidental that so little is known about Wang Ao's later descendants except that one of his ninth-generation descendants was so poor that he became a store apprentice. Although with the help of maternal relatives he eventually became a *sheng-yüan* and married at the late age of thirty, his prolonged hardship and malnutrition accounted for his premature death at thirty-one.[32]

The Hsü clan of K'un-shan in southern Kiangsu, which in early Ch'ing times produced three *chin-shih* with first-class honors, namely, Hsü Ch'ien-hsüeh (1631–94), president of the Board of Punishments, Hsü Ping-i (1633–1711), vice president of the Board of Rites, and Hsü Yüan-wen (1634–91), prime minister, serves as an illustration of a somewhat different type of downward mobility. Although the Hsü family was known to have encroached upon neighbors' property, it had a long and distinguished scholarly tradition. There was no sign of sudden decline, as all Hsü Ch'ien-hsüeh's five sons became *chin-shih* and for two or three generations the Hsüs dominated the local rosters of higher degree holders. But their expensive tastes and hobbies as bibliophiles and connoisseurs and their patronage to scholars were perpetuated in the family and their descendants acquired a disdain for any productive occupation. In the course of time one of Hsü Ch'ien-hsüeh's great-great-grandsons was compelled to earn his living as a local government runner at the age of thirteen. The very fact that none of his kinsmen had prevented him from demeaning the family shows that most if not all branches of the family had been economically leveled off. He later eked out a meager living by story-telling near a local temple. When people asked him about his family background he pretended to be deaf and answered with a forced foolish smile because he did not want to disgrace his illustrious ancestry. After his mother's death he disappeared forever. Local people believed that he had drowned himself. He was remembered as Hsü, the filial son.[33]

Even without noticeable depravity or evidence of being spoiled, descendants of distinguished officials might still sink if they were not studious or were otherwise inept. Take the descendants of Huang Huai (1367–1449), a famous early Ming prime minister, for example. His prudence, foresight, and power to analyze all sides of a problem once won the high praise of Emperor Ch'eng-tzu. Since from 1427 on he enjoyed twenty-two years of retirement in his ancestral home in Yung-chia in southern coastal Chekiang, it is unlikely that he should have neglected the proper education of his descendants as many of his colleagues did. Yet, by the early sixteenth century, if not earlier, his descendants had become so impoverished that a Chekiang scholar-official testified to the unbelievable fact that they sold even the stone tablets of their ancestral graves.[34] The descendants of Pien Kung, *chin-shih* of 1496, who eventually reached the high office of president of the Board or Revenue of Nanking, furnish another example. Since Pien Kung was a native of Chi-nan, the capital city of Shantung, and a noted poet of the mid-Ming period, Wang Shih-chen, himself an outstanding poet of the K'ang-hsi era, was eager to collect information on Pien and his descendants when he was compiling an anthology of the Chi-nan prefectural area. Wang took special pains to locate Pien's descendants and eventually found out that Pien's eldest son had received the *yin* privilege and served as a middle-ranking official and that his second son was a poet of local renown. Afterwards his descendants fell into complete oblivion. The two surviving descendants discovered after long inquiry, who belonged to the seventh and eighth generations respectively, were both illiterate landless tenants, whose only proud possession was Pien Kung's portrait, handed down through the generations.[35]

While it was fairly common for the Chinese to share folk beliefs attributing unusual academic-bureaucratic success to geomancy or to something supernatural and predestined, actually the Confucian stress on education and human effort always prevailed. Ch'en Mao-jen, who served as a local official of Ch'üan-chou prefecture in southern coastal Fukien between 1603 and 1605, was typical of the basically rational scholar-officials. He commented:

Outside the east gate of the prefectural city of Ch'üan-chou are public hills covering an area of several square *li*, a place for the burial of the poor. Graves in this public cemetery are crowded like a chessboard with no spaces vacant. But often the specimens of high academic success stand out prominently among them. Is this because at times of burials their families studied geomancy? It is rather because, on the one hand, though propertyless, the ancestors were of spotless virtue, and, on the other hand, while without inheritance, the descendants naturally warded off wordly temptations and concentrated on their studies in order to stand up on their own. We often hear that rich families sometimes wait more than ten years to bury their parents because of the shortage of good spots. Yet after they have eventually buried their forebears, the descendants have become progressively impoverished and sunk socially. Is this because they did not emphasize geomancy or failed to choose auspicious locations? [36]

Contemporary accounts and biographical materials make it difficult for modern students not to accept the close, perhaps causal, relationship between human environment and the rise and fall of family fortunes.

### THE COMPETITIVENESS OF THE EXAMINATION SYSTEM

In searching for the implications of our data on the social composition of *chin-shih*, given in table 9, we find it striking that, save for the years 1655, 1682, and 1703, the distinguished families failed to produce more than 10 percent of the *chin-shih* at each examination. Taking the over-all average for the entire Ming-Ch'ing period, they accounted for only 5.7 percent of the total candidates. It is true that the distinguished families constituted only a small portion of official families, but their aggregate number during any given average three-generation period must have been considerably larger than the total *chin-shih* quota of any specific examination. The fact that in spite of their incomparable advantages members of distinguished families failed to dominate *chin-shih* examinations, in sharp contrast to the prolonged monopoly of political power by a few hundred aristocratic families in eighteenth-century England, goes far to testify to the general effectiveness of the competitive examination as a factor in the social-leveling process and to the inability of wealthy and top-status families in the long run to maintain their position.

Other available avenues such as purchase of official ranks or *yin* aside, the majority of descendants of distinguished officials and wealthy men still had to compete successfully in higher-level examinations to qualify for an official post. In Ming-Ch'ing times it was by no means certain that even the studious, intelligent, and unspoiled members of distinguished families could pass higher examinations, for there was always the element of luck. To this, the pathetic case of Yeh Liang-ts'ai, a great-grandson of Yeh Sheng (1420–74), an able and incorruptible official and a famous bibliophile who reached the high office of vice president of the Board of Civil Appointments, is an eloquent testimony. His maternal uncle Wang Shih-chen (1526–90) of T'ai-ts'ang in southern Kiangsu gave the following biographical sketch:

Children of our two families shared the same habits and education and got along beautifully with one another. When Mr. Yeh first came to live with us as a maternal relative, he was still in his teens but already a *sheng-yüan*. His literary compositions impressed us all. His maternal relatives, who cherished high hopes for him, whispered to each other that he was indeed a chip off the old block, the one who would duplicate the splendid career of Wen-chuang [Yeh Sheng's posthumously canonized title]. Mr. Yeh in his routine reviewing tests supervised by the educational commissioners seldom failed to place first. For this reason he was very confident of himself and frequently discussed ways to become a statesman. It never occurred to him that the attainment of the *chin-shih* degree could be difficult. After many years, however, he still failed to pass higher examinations. . . . [As a last resort] he was on the point of accompanying me to Peking to take a special examination in order to qualify as a county magistrate. As he said, his life would be wasted should his name fail to enter posthumously into the biographies of model officials. How pathetic that he failed even to make this modest hope materialize! [37]

Owing to its highly competitive nature, the examination system brought about a greater degree of both upward and downward movement than is usually found in modern industrial societies, where, in the light of some recent studies, inter-generation vertical mobility is in most cases rather gradual.[38]

As compared with the hereditary privileges of T'ang and Sung officials, the *yin* for Ming-Ch'ing officials was greatly curtailed in scope. At the very beginning of the Ming period all officials from the seventh rank up could secure *yin* for one of their heirs after serving a required initial period of office satisfactorily. The relative leniency of the early Ming *yin* system was, however, partially offset by the accompanying regulations that such heirs could enroll only in the Imperial Academy and that they could receive office only after passing special examinations.[39] Soon afterwards special examinations were no longer required, but the *yin* privilege was confined to direct heirs of officials of the third rank or above.[40] For practically the whole of the Ming-Ch'ing period the *yin* regulations were such that a son of a first-rank official could enter government service without examination as a fifth-ranking official and, through a descending scale, a son of a third-rank official received an office of the seventh rank.

Some concrete examples will make clear the working of the *yin* system and the effect of special imperial favor. Chang T'ing-yü, for instance, secured a maximum of *yin* and other special privileges for his sons. His eldest son Chang Jo-ai had received the minor noble rank of *ch'ing-chü tu-wei* before he passed the *chin-shih* examination in 1733 with distinction. After he had entered government service through examination this low noble rank, which was more honorific than useful, was of little significance. Chang T'ing-yü's unique position secured for his second son, Chang Jo-ch'eng, the regular *yin*. But in 1745 Chang Jo-ch'eng became a *chin-shih* and thus found it unnecessary to utilize this privilege. Thanks again to Chang T'ing-yü's intimate relations with the emperor, the *yin* was allowed to pass on to the third son, Chang Jo-shu. Because of his early death in the office of second-class secretary of a central Board (rank 5b), the *yin* privilege ceased. Consequently the youngest son, Chang Jo-t'ing, had to enter government by purchasing a rank after failing to obtain a degree higher than *kung-sheng*.[41]

It must be pointed out that the privileges received by Chang T'ing-yü's sons and one grandson far exceeded the scope of ordinary *yin.* Chang Jo-t'ing, who lived to the advanced age of seventy-four, turned out to be the main recipient of special imperial favors. In 1786 he was made quite unprecedentedly a subchancellor of the Grand Secretariat, an office which as a rule was filled by a man with a distinguished academic background. A special imperial edict was issued stating that this appointment was due exclusively to the emperor's remembrance of Chang T'ing-yü and must not be made a precedent.

What is to be noted is that although both Chang Jo-ai and Chang Jo-ch'eng eventually reached the second official rank they died without having served the required period. They thus failed to secure *yin* for their heirs. As it turned out, the elder of Chang Jo-ai's sons started out by purchasing a *chien-sheng* title, later attained the *chü-jen* degree, and eventually became a fifth-ranking secretary of a central board. The younger son, after passing a *pa-kung* examination, entered government as a copyist and ended his career as a lowly assistant county magistrate (rank 8a). Chang Jo-ch'eng's only son died while holding a *chien-sheng* title. Not only did these three subbranches of the family fail to receive any real *yin* benefit; the drop in status was very drastic.

Of Chang Jo-t'ing's eight sons only the seventh entered government service by virtue of *yin* but soon died in his initial post of third-class secretary of a central board (rank 6a). The *yin* first acquired by Chang T'ing-yü and extended by Chang Jo-t'ing thus became extinct. The most successful of the eight sons of Chang Jo-t'ing was Chang Tseng-i (1747–97), who, also owing to his distinguished grandfather, finally became judicial commissioner of Chekiang (rank 3a), thus extending *yin* for one more generation. The other sons all purchased first Imperial Academy studentships and then some minor offices. Only one of them reached rank 7b. From the third generation after Chang T'ing-yü's death, therefore, the few middle-ranking officials of the family owed their position to examination and purchase.

In the Chi family only Chi Tseng-yün's second son actually benefited from *yin* and eventually became a prefect (rank 4a). By the late eighteenth century the emperor, remembering the services of the two Chi prime ministers, bestowed on the sixth-generation heir of the eldest line the lowest noble rank of *en-ch'i-wei*, which, through ordinarily nonhereditary, was made hereditary for one generation. The two recipients of *yin* listed in table 17, one of the sixth and one of the seventh generation, enjoyed nothing more than small sinecures. Without special imperial favor which actually lay outside the proper scope of ordinary *yin*, the *yin* privilege would have ceased with the third generation. From table 17 and from a sampling of biographies in the Chi clan genealogy, it appears that the *yin* system actually had almost no effect on the clan's progressively downward mobility.[42]

There is reason to believe that *yin* regulations during Ch'ing times were more strict than those of the Ming period. For one thing, throughout the greater part of the Ming period powerful eunuchs and ministers were able to secure special favors for their descendants or relatives. But their abuse of power often courted disasters which more than nullified the transient and broadened *yin* privilege. By and large Ch'ing officials were more prudent, and cases of perverted abuse of family privilege among their descendants were much fewer. Moreover, if he could later enter government service by some other avenue, the first recipient of *yin* was permitted by Ming regulations to transfer his *yin* to his brother or heir. There is evidence that Ch'ing regulations in general forbade *yin* transference, which was granted only by special imperial grace. For example, Ts'ao Chen-yung (1755–1835), one of the most powerful prime ministers of the mid-Ch'ing period, secured *yin* for his eldest son, who died young. Only his intimate relations with the Tao-kuang emperor (1821–50) made possible the tranference of *yin* to his second son, Ts'ao En-ying (1808–54). Ts'ao En-ying, who had repeatedly failed to pass the higher examinations, eventually reached the post of commissioner of the Office of Transmissions (rank 3a).[43] The *yin* was therefore extended for another generation.

The difficulty of *yin* transference was further attested by the historian Chao I (1727–1814), whose intimate knowledge on Ch'ing institutions was derived from his service on the private secretarial staff of the prime minister Wang Yu-tun (1692–1758) and subsequently as a secretary of the Grand Council. Wang Yu-tun secured *yin* for his eldest son, who died in 1760 without receiving an actual appointment. "Since then," Chao said, "none of my late teacher's (i.e., Wang Yu-tun's) sons has been able to enter the government roster." Then one day Chao recalled that Wang had once mentioned that it was proper for a high minister's heir to take a special trip to Peking to thank the emperor personally if any posthumous honor had been bestowed on his father. Chao thereupon suggested to Wang's two surviving sons, both Chao's former students, that they come to Peking to thank the Ch'ien-lung emperor for his routine funeral essay and other token gifts bestowed posthumously on Wang long ago in the hope that this might revive his remembrance of a former faithful minister. Thanks to Chao's clever plot with Fu Heng, the Manchu noble, statesman, and confidant of the emperor, the Wang sons were given two brief audiences which resulted in the appointment of one as a sixth-ranking secretary and the award to the other of a *chü-jen* degree. It is worth pointing out that prior to these audiences many of Wang's former colleagues and subordinates had been cool to Wang's sons, for they knew only too well the futility of seeking *yin* transference. After that time the example was followed by the descendants of a few high ministers as an extra means of securing special imperial favor.[44] From these examples it is evident that normally the regular *yin* privilege could seldom be extended beyond two generations.

Fortunately for our quantitative study of the working of the *yin* system, seven lists of *yin* recipients, which are dated 1821, 1851, 1862, 1875, 1889, 1894, and 1904, are available in the Columbia University Libraries, in the Library of Congress, and in Kyoto. The first four dates are years of imperial accessions. The year 1889 was one in which the Kuang-hsü emperor attained his majority and an imperial wedding took place. The last two dates marked the sixtieth and seventieth birthday anniversaries (by Chinese count) of the Empress Dowager Tz'u-hsi. It seems that the number of *yin* recipients given in the list of 1821 represents the total cumulative number of *yin* holders still alive and that the number given in each subsequent list is likewise the cumulative number of the intervening period. These seven lists cover therefore roughly the entire nineteenth century, although because of deaths the actual total number of *yin* granted is likely to have been somewhat larger than the aggregate shown in the following table.

TABLE 18

LATE-CH'ING *YIN* RECIPIENTS

| Period | Number |
|---|---|
| Up to 1821 | 614 |
| 1821–1851 | 119 |
| 1852–1862 | 80 |
| 1863–1875 | 93 |
| 1876–1889 | 25 |
| 1890–1894 | 48 |
| 1895–1904 | 43 |
| Total | 1,022 |

Sources: *Tao-kuang yüan-nien en-yin t'ung-nien lu* (1821); *Hsien-feng yüan-nien en-yin t'ung-nien ch'ih-lu* (1851); *T'ung-chih yüan-nien en-yin-sheng t'ung-nien ch'ih-lu* (1862); and *Kuang-hsü yin-sheng t'ung-nien ch'ih-lu* (compiled in 1904), which contains the lists of 1875, 1889, 1894, and 1904.

It ought to be mentioned that the above lists deal with holders of regular *yin* and *en-yin* (*yin* through special imperial grace) only. They do not include *nan-yin* (*yin* conferred on the descendant of one who had died in a civil or international war in loyal service to the state). The number of the latter during the post-Taiping period is likely to have been not insignificant. The *nan-yin* privilege, however, at best amounted to a minor sinecure held in most cases for life only.

In brief, impressed by the wide scope and the express purpose of the pre-Ming *yin* system, some modern scholars, who have yet to consult Ming-Ch'ing legal texts, let alone family histories and biographies, have made exaggerated and distorted generalizations about the social effect of the *yin* system in China from 500 to 1900. From our illustrations of the working of the *yin* system in some distinguished families and from our general figures, it seems reasonable to conclude that *yin* had little real effect on the long-range downward mobility of high official families during Ming-Ch'ing times.

DILUTION OF WEALTH

It has been explained in chapter I that academic degree and wealth were the two important determinants of social status and that from 1451 onward wealth in general could be translated into academic-bureaucratic success. The problem of progressive dilution of wealth, which had so much to do with the long-range downward mobility of prominent families, must therefore be systematically discussed in terms of their mode of life and the working of the family system.

*Mode of Life of the Leisured Class.* The leisured class in Ming-Ch'ing China consisted of active and retired officials, scholars from families of independent means, and *nouveaux riches,* who, after making their fortunes in trade or elsewhere, joined the ranks of the elite. In spite of being occupied with administrative duties, officials had their due share of leisure which was not infrequently devoted to the cultivation of scholarly hobbies. Opportunities for avocational activities were ample when officials were on long leaves caused by the death of a parent or an administrative blunder. Retired officials and scholars of means had almost unlimited leisure, as did *nouveaux riches.* In fact, the common status symbols of members of the elite were a leisurely mode of life and the pursuance of sophisticated hobbies.

It is true that not all officials were scholars. But many of them had developed a genuine interest in literature, classics, history, philosophy, or art before they became officials. The comparatively simple curriculum required by the examinations could hardly satisfy their intellectual needs. Since avocations are rewarding as sources of personal pleasure and socially important as status symbols, many Ming-Ch'ing officials engaged in expensive hobbies as bibliophiles and art connoisseurs. The list of those officials, scholars, and *nouveaux riches* who achieved national fame as bibliophiles and connoisseurs is a very long one.[45] Suffice it to say here that from imperial princes down to nonofficial scholars the collecting of books and objects of art became a very common avocation. Many men of the leisured class devoted their lifetimes to building up their collections, and such avocations were in most cases carried on by their descendants. Even those who had no genuine interest in literary and artistic research went into these hobbies for prestige purposes. The scope of elite hobbies broadened after the opening of the sixteenth century, as giant strides were made in printing[46] and the production of fine stationery, ceramics, copper and bronze castings, lacquer work, and ivory and jade carvings, things which answered the growing demands of the elite.

After a brief respite caused by wars of banditry and the change of dynasty in the middle decades of the seventeenth century, China's material culture continued to develop during the prolonged period of peace and prosperity and to enhance the enjoyment of the elite. The vogue of cultivating scholarly hobbies extended even to the Manchu imperial court and its nobles.[47] The craze for books and art reached its zenith during the Ch'ien-lung era. This pleasure-loving emperor must rank among the world's foremost art connoisseurs. He greatly expanded the imperial collection of calligraphic specimens and old paintings, and added to it numerous works by contemporary scholar-official artists. The amount and range of the imperial collection may be evidenced by the three series of catalogues which run to a total of 240 *chüan*.[48] With the emperor setting the example, an increasing number of officials and *nouveaux riches* pursued their advocations with redoubled passion.

Within certain limits these expensive elite hobbies were most rewarding to the individual and did not necessarily cause immediate financial insolvency. But a continued indulgence in such activities over a period of several generations could not help becoming a heavy drain on family resources. This may be evidenced by the frequency with which famous libraries and art collections changed hands.[49] In fact, it was fairly common before the rise of great bibliophiles and connoisseurs in the sixteenth century for wealthy families of the lower Yangtze region to become bankrupt because of their elite hobbies.[50] After the sixteenth century instances of bankruptcy caused by avocational passions greatly multiplied. Take the very large fortune of An Ch'i (born in 1683?) as an example. After making his huge fortune in the salt trade first in Ch'ang-lu and then in Liang-huai, he built up a private collection of paintings and calligraphic masterpieces which overshadowed all previous private collections with the possible exception of that of the greatest Ming connoisseur, Hsiang Yüan-pien (1525–90) of Chia-hsing, Chekiang. It was known that the items in An Ch'i's collection came mostly from four prominent sources, namely, the declined Hsiang family; Sun Ch'eng-tse (1593–1675), vice president of the Board of Civil Appointments and author of the famous descriptive catalogue of paintings *Keng-tzu hsiao-hsia lu;* the prime minister Liang Ch'ing-piao (1620–91); and Pien Yung-yü (1645–1712), longtime governor of Fukien and eventually vice president of the Board of Punishments. By the 1720s the cummulative effect of An Chu'i's extravagant living and lifelong passion for art began to tell and he was compelled to sell his collection.[51]

While An Ch'i was an exceptional case, a more typical example of the effect of elite hobbies on the dilution of wealth is provided by the K'ung family of Canton, descendants of Confucius who had made a fortune in the salt trade and become famous scholars and officials.[52] During the second quarter of the nineteenth century the K'ung family's collection of paintings and calligraphic specimens became nationally famous. But by 1892, when the family's most famous connoisseur, K'ung Kuang-t'ao, eventually printed an annotated catalogue of the family art collection, a scholar-official friend and author of the postscript stated that the K'ung family had already been forced by financial necessity to disperse its collection which had been built up over three generations.[53]

The sad end of the fairly rich scholarly family of Ch'ien may be typical of many families which failed to become connoisseurs of national renown:

Mr. Ch'ien Lü-t'an of Wu-chin [southern Kiangsu] was noted for his skill in painting plum trees and for the art of seal carving. He was particularly good at authenticating ancient calligraphic works and paintings, and things of archaeological interest. He and his elder first cousin [Ch'ien] Lu-ssu were all well known to high officials. To enjoy themselves, they designed their own garden by digging ponds, shaping up artificial rocks, and planting trees and flowers. . . . Their house used to be filled with guests. . . . In 1806 Lü-t'an died in Su-chou. A few years later Lu-ssu also passed away. The latter's son became so poor that he could not survive. He finally drowned himself in the fifth month of 1820. This was not quite ten years after his father's death. The beautiful garden and the family's art collection had all disappeared.[54]

Granted that not all connoisseurs and bibliophiles were spend-thrifts, still there is reason to agree with the wise and moderate Wang Shih-chen as to the truth in the old Chinese saying: "Avoca-tional passion kills higher ambitions." If Wang's craze for books and taste for art did not cause him immediate insolvency, it cer-tainly prevented him from improving his family's economic status. Besides, scholarly hobbies were contagious and imperceptibly sapped the aspirations of many younger kinsmen. Perhaps it was this belated realization of the insidious effect of avocations that made him cite himself as a warning to descendants.[55] The list of sons and grand-sons of successful late Ming and Ch'ing officials who, owing to family avocational pursuits, took up calligraphy, painting, literary pastimes, scholarly research, or the collecting of books, art objects, stone inscriptions, and bronzes as an engrossing lifelong devotion and achieved permanent fame thereby is a very long one. They may have had a full enjoyable life, but what happened to their descend-ants in another generation or two is not too hard to imagine. In-deed, Ch'ien Yung (1759–1844), the noted painter of the lower Yangtze region who had observed so many connoisseur families during his long life, generalized: "If a poor scholarly or declined ex-official family produces a young man skilled in practical manage-ment, he will almost certainly make the family rich. If a rich or landowning family has a son who loves literature, art, and music, he will almost surely impoverish the family." [56] The prudent Chang T'ing-yü said: "Descendants who inherited ancestral wealth often could not manage it and were likely to indulge in music, women, or curios. Those who indulged in music and women caused bank-ruptcy during their own lifetime. Almost none of those who in-dulged in curio collection could keep his collection for two genera-tions. I am constantly warned by so many such cases which I have seen personally." [57]

Expensive hobbies, however, were but one aspect of the mode of life of the leisured class. The necessity of living in a grand style, the maintenance of a large number of domestic servants, the obligation of supporting less fortunate kinsmen, the constant and often lavish entertainments among members of the elite were not conducive to saving. Despite traditional teachings on the wisdom of frugality, the social and cultural milieu made it difficult for members of the leisured class not to live according to its norms.

Everything officials and well-to-do scholars did, the *nouveaux riches* were bound to outdo. This was partly due to the fact that, although successful officials were reasonably affluent, by far the largest fortunes were made in trade. The social inferiority complex of the newly rich also prompted them to go to extremes. The unusually observant and well-traveled Hsieh Chao-che of the late Ming period noticed how rich merchants "squander gold like dust" on "concubines, prostitutes, and lawsuits" and how their eagerness to break into the elite made them an easy prey for curio and art forgers.[58]

Conspicuous consumption reached new heights in eighteenth-century Yang-chou, where the great Liang-huai salt merchants congregated. *Yang-chou hua-fang lu,* a contemporary guidebook to that beautiful city, gives the following vivid account:

The salt merchants of Yang-chou vied with one another in extravagance. Each wedding or funeral, with all its expenses for food, clothing, and carriages, could cost several hundred thousand taels. There was one merchant who insisted on having more than ten meticulously prepared dishes every meal. At dinner time he and his wife were waited upon by a host of servants who served everything from tea and noodles to vegetable and meat plates. They only needed to shake their heads to have the undesired dishes removed and more appetizing ones brought in. There was a lover of horses, which he raised by several hundreds. Each day a single horse's maintenance ran to several tens of taels. In the morning they were taken to the outskirts of the city and in the evening they were taken back. So rich was their coloring that the onlookers' eyes dazzled. There was a lover of orchids, who planted them everywhere from the gate to inner studios. There was one who erected wooden nude female statues in front of his inner halls, all mechanically controlled, so as to tease his guests. In the beginning, An Ch'i was the most notorious. His notoriety was surpassed by that of later comers. There was one who wished to spend ten thousand taels in one day. One of his guests suggested that he buy gold foils. From the top of the Golden Hill he threw down the gold foils which, carried by the wind, soon scattered midst trees and grass and could not be gathered again. There was another who spent three thousand taels buying *pu-tao-weng* [a kind of bottom-heavy doll in the form of an old man that cannot be toppled over] from Su-chou to be floated on water. So numerous were these dolls that the stream was choked. There was one who loved beautiful things. From the gate-keepers to the kitchen-maids his household consisted of only good-looking young persons. On the other hand, there was one who was fond of ugly things. [Once an applicant], being convinced from looking at the mirror that he was not ugly enough, smeared his face with soy sauce and exposed it to the sun. There was yet another who loved big things. He designed for himself a huge bronze urinal container five or six feet tall. Every night he climbed up to relieve himself. For quite some while these people vied with one another in novelties and eccentricities which were too numerous to be described in full.[59]

While the vulgar and untutored of the *nouveaux riches* squandered their wealth in the most perverted manner, the cultured and refined went to another extreme by patronizing scholars and poets or by cultivating the expensive hobbies of the bibliophile and the art connoisseur. The Rainbow Bridge Garden of the Hung family had been adorned with a galaxy of scholars and artists since the late seventeenth century. From the second quarter of the eighteenth century onward the Little Translucent Mountain Cottage of the Ma family, the Bamboo Garden of the Ch'eng family, and the Garden of Repose of the Cheng family ranked among the nation's foremost literary salons, where periodic poetry contests were held, with lavish entertainments and rich monetary rewards. The Ma brothers, Ma Yüeh-kuan (1688–1755) and Ma Yüeh-lu (1697–1766?), both gifted poets and bibliophiles, made their residence a year-round luxurious hostel for various categories of men of letters. With the help of expert bookdealers they built up one of the finest collections of rare Sung and Yüan editions which were housed in the Ts'ung-shu-lou, a library also known for its collection of paintings, calligraphic masterpieces, and stone rubbings, which was generally recognized as the best north of the Yangtze. In 1772, when by imperial order the board for the compilation of the monumental *Ssu-k'u ch'üan-shu* was set up, the son of Ma Yüeh-lu submitted a large number of rare books of which 776 titles were transcribed by the Imperial Manuscript Library.[60]

These men were not unique. Of the seven intimate library-owning families of the metropolitan Hang-chou five had originally come from Hui-chou and made their fortunes in commerce and the salt trade, namely, the Wu, the three different Wangs, and the Pao.[61]

The most famous of them were Wang Ch'i-shu (1728–99?) and Pao
T'ing-po (1728–1814). In 1772 the former contributed 524 rare books
for transcription by the Imperial Manuscript Library and he was
famous also for his collection of ancient and modern seals, the specimens of which were printed in four series between 1745 and 1757
under the title *Fei-hung-t'ang yin-p'u*. The latter contributed 626
rare works in 1772 and ranked among the foremost private printers
of Ch'ing times. During and after his lifetime as many as thirty
series of rare works were printed as a collectanea, entitled *Chih-pu-
tsu-chai ts'ung-shu*, exclusively out of family funds.[62]

These cultural expressions of the *nouveaux riches* were not confined to the lower Yangtze area. In nineteenth-century Canton,
where some of the largest family fortunes were located, the two
richest Co-hong families, Wu and P'an, refused to be overshadowed
by those lower Yangtze merchant princes of the previous century.
The Wu family, during the late years of the famed Howqua III
(Wu Ch'ung-yüeh, 1810–63), and shortly after his death, published
thirty installments of a gigantic collectanea, entitled *Yüeh-ya-t'ang
ts'ung-shu*. The most cultured of the P'an family, P'an Shih-ch'eng,
who in 1832 was rewarded by the emperor with a *chü-jen* degree
for his generous contribution to famine relief, followed with the
printing of a smaller but highly useful collectanea *Hai-hsien-shan-
kuan ts'ung-shu*.[63]

It hardly need be said that, like the Liang-huai merchants of Yang-
chou, the rich merchant families of Hang-chou and Canton built
their luxurious villas, collected art, patronized scholars, and entertained guests on a lavish scale. It is easily understandable that after
one had become rich additional wealth did not beget additional
prestige. On the contrary, only conspicuous spending for cultural
purposes could secure more prestige. Modern students may perhaps
raise the point that if these families had managed their businesses
and invested their money wisely, their wealth might still have
lasted in spite of heavy spending. The truth is that the social milieu
in Ming-Ch'ing times was hardly conducive to the development of a
genuine capitalistic system such as characterized the Europe of the
seventeenth, eighteenth, and nineteenth centuries.

In the first place, by far the easiest way to acquire wealth was to buy the privilege of selling a few staples which enjoyed a universal demand, like salt and tea, which were under government monopoly. The right was hereditary and could not easily be expanded at the expense of other licensed merchants. The activities of the salt, Co-hong, and other powerful merchant groups all partook of the nature of tax farming rather than of genuine private enterprise. In the second place, outside these few monopolies opportunities for profitable investment were rather limited. Third, business management was usually an extension of familism, permeated with nepotism, inefficiencies, and irrationalities which in the long run brought about the decline of such monopoly trades. Moreover, after receiving their monopoly from the government, families were in turn subjected to constant milking by the government.[64]

Contemporary accounts of the decline of such *nouveaux riches* families are necessarily much more scarce than those describing their prosperity. It is still possible, however, to know that many of them declined or became bankrupt eventually. Li Tou, the author of that famous guidebook to Yang-chou, for example, mentioned briefly that not a few of the luxurious villas owned by rich merchants had changed hands before the end of the eighteenth century.[65] The painter Ch'ien Yung, who lived till 1844, testified to more cases of bankruptcy.[66] Several decades after the deaths of the Ma brothers a scholar was saddened by the sight of the once famous Little Translucent Mountain Cottage, which had become run down and had been sold.[67] We know in more detail how the famous bibliophile and scholar-official Ch'eng Chin-fang (1718–84), a member of a leading salt-merchant family which owned the Bamboo Garden, was forced to sell his library of 50,000 *chüan* and that he owed the poet Yüan Mei (1716–98) a debt of 5,000 taels at the time of his death.[68] A more detailed case study of the dissipation of a very large family fortune is given in the Appendix, case 12.

THE FAMILY SYSTEM

The operation of the Chinese family system was one of the fundamental factors which in the long run leveled off family wealth. Although large clans are known to have existed throughout Chinese history, people in post-feudal periods usually lived in extended conjugal families. Despite the strengthening of the clan system since the rise of Neo-Confucianism in Sung times, the actual economic unit was the family, not the clan, which consisted of all patrilineal common descendants.[69] The effect of the "common descent group" on social mobility in general will be discussed in the next chapter. Here we should deal with the aspect of the family system which had the most to do with the dilution of wealth, namely, the absence of primoginiture.

Primogeniture, which was the core of the ancient feudal noble clans, outlasted feudalism by some two centuries. After the founding of the Former Han empire in 206 B.C. a number of vassal kingdoms were created for sons of emperors, and fiefs and noble ranks conferred on ministers and generals of meritorious service who were not members of the imperial clan. There was therefore a partial revival of feudal practice within the framework of a centralized empire. Through high-handed measures of the central government most of the nonimperial noble houses had lost their fiefs by the last quarter of the second century B.C., but the vassal kingdoms were not subjected to progressively minute division until the gradual abolition of the rule of primogeniture from 127 B.C. onward.[70]

For the past two thousand years, therefore, the high and the low have usually divided up family property at the death of the head of the family. The fact that in dynastic histories a few clans whose members for generations lived and shared property together were invariably hailed as paragons of virtue reflects the permanent effect of the absence of primogeniture.[71] "In fact," concludes a modern Chinese sociologist, "the average family in traditional China did not succeed in keeping more than three generations together but underwent a perpetual splitting process."[72]

It is true that cries for the revival of the ancient clan system and of primogeniture became audible in Sung times, when men in general had to rely on their own merit to move up the social ladder and when great hereditary families were things of the past. Neo-Confucian philosophers like Ch'eng I (1033–1107) and Chu Hsi (1130–1200) advocated the revival of primogeniture and the exaltation of the status of *tsung-tzu* (eldest heir of the eldest line) in the hope that the integrity of ancestral property might thus be perma-

nently maintained and that the clan as a whole might not decline.[73]
In actual social practice, however, the *tsung-tzu* was almost always
a titular figure, entitled neither to greater authority over the rest of
the clan nor to a greater share of property.[74] A recent study, based
on an extensive analysis of traditional Chinese clan rules, makes the
following summary of the practice of dividing the family inheritance:

> The principle of giving each son an equal share of inheritance varied
> somewhat with local custom. In some places, the eldest son received a
> double share of inheritance either on the ground of his having more
> grown-up offspring than his younger brothers, or in partial imitation of
> the ancient feudal rule of primogeniture. Sons of the wife usually got
> more than the sons of a concubine. But many localities allowed none of
> these deviations from the principle [of equal inheritance].[75]

Although detailed descriptions of the division of family property
are rather scarce because Neo-Confucian and more ancient teachings did not favor the keeping of such accounts, a few concrete examples will make the economic effect of such divisions clear. Chi
Chin, for instance, the fourth son of Chi Tseng-yün, who eventually
became an intendant and acting financial commissioner of Hupei,
died before he reached middle age. While his widow was still alive
his property was divided into five shares of more than 200 *mu* each,
one share going to each of the four sons, and the fifth share going to
the perpetual clan sacrificial land. Although the testimonial of Chi
Wen-fu, a great-grandson of Chi Tseng-yüan, that legacies left by
the family's two prime ministers "did not amount to that of a
middle-class person's" was undoubtedly exaggerated, it may well
have been a true description of the share which he actually received.[76] Take as another example P'eng Yün-chang (1792–1862),
who eventually became prime minister. Among his distinguished
ancestors were P'eng Ting-ch'iu (1645–1719), who placed first in the
palace examination of 1676, and P'eng Ch'i-feng (1701–84), who
placed third in the palace examination of 1727 and reached the
high office of president of the Board of War. After the division of
family property by the brothers and sisters in 1800 the share received by P'eng Yün-chang was so small that it barely enabled him
to carry on his studies and to prepare for higher examinations. By

1826 he was forced to take a special examination to qualify for a lowly teaching post in order to support his family.[77] But for his eventual success in the *chin-shih* examination and in reaching the top of officialdom the P'eng family would have continued its downward trend.

The great-great-grandfather of the famous diarist Wang K'ai-yün (1833–1916) had accumulated more than 10,000 *mu* of fertile paddies in Hsiang-t'an in lowland Hunan and ranked among the richest men of the locality. His property was divided up by five sons. Owing to subdivision over three generations and also to free spending, Wang K'ai-yün's father was forced to earn his living by becoming a small tradesman and his uncle by teaching village pupils.[78] A struggling man like Wang Hui-tsu (1730–1807), who became a *chin-shih* in 1775, was able to buy out of his lifetime savings 90 *mu* of land, of which 40 *mu* went to the clan sacrificial land and 10 *mu* each was left to his five sons. Two of the five sons whose mother was a concubine had to live in the country as small landowning peasants.[79]

The custom of more or less equal inheritance frequently gave rise to property disputes among brothers and sometimes remoter kinsmen. This unsavory fact is reflected in the large number of clan rules which forbade contention or lawsuits over inheritance.[80] Widows with minor sons often found it impossible to ward off the encroachment of rapacious brothers-in-law or more distant kinsmen.[81] It need scarcely be said that the rate at which family property was diluted was proportionate to the population of each branch. What the Southern Sung writer Yüan Ts'ai noticed—that the customary division of property accelerated the decline of those branches with a large number of children or dependents—must be equally valid for the Ming-Ch'ing period.[82]

Unlike the ruthless efficiency of the English family system based on the rule of primogeniture, which, in the witty words of Professor Tawney, "if it did not drown all the kittens but one, threw all but one into the water," [83] the Chinese family system was constantly subjected to the process of economic leveling. The relationship between the progressive dilution of property and the inability of high-status families to perpetuate themselves is nowhere more poignantly pointed out than by Ke Shou-li (1505–78), a famous censor-general, noted for his conservatism and integrity. After retiring from official service he contributed one thousand *mu* of land to his clan and provided that it should never be divided or alienated. On that occasion he said: "When [the ancient] clan system of which primogeniture formed the core cannot be revived, the world can have no hereditary families; when the world has no hereditary families, the imperial court can have no hereditary ministers." [84] Small wonder, then, that Ming-Ch'ing China could not have "predestined parliament men" as eighteenth-century England had as a matter of course, for "predestined parliament men" were possible only because through primogeniture and entail the aristocracy had preserved the integrity of its landed estates which, in the last analysis, were the most important source of political power before the age of reform.[85]

SUMMARY

Long-range downward mobility of high-status families could take place because of any one of the following factors: failure to provide children with a proper education, the competitive nature of the examination system which was based in the main on merit rather than on family status, the limited *yin* privilege of high officials, the mode of life and cultural expressions of the leisured class, and the progressive dilution of wealth due to the absence of primogeniture. While the first four are variables, the last is almost a constant. It is important to note that within a small number of generations usually two or more such factors were simultaneously at work and, if not arrested by new academic success, would further accelerate the descending process.

Although downward mobility data as systematic as those on *chinshih* ancestry are nonexistent, the unusually well-informed Wang Shih-chen (1526–90) culled the following partial data from his vast knowledge of Ming institutions. From the founding of the Ming dynasty to the late years of his life, over a period of more than two centuries, only twenty-two families were able to produce a president of a central board in two consecutive generations. Thirty-three families were able to produce a central official of the third rank or above in two consecutive generations. Out of these thirty-three only three families produced a central official of the third rank or above for three consecutive generations. The Lin family of Fu-chou, Fukien, won the unique distinction of producing a president of a central board for three consecutive generations. In the whole empire only two families, the Chiang of Hang-chou and the Liu of Pa-hsien in Szechwan, produced *chin-shih* for five consecutive generations.[86]

There is reason to believe that the few most prominent Ch'ing clans overshadowed the Ming records of family prominence. For six generations including that of Chang Ying himself, for example, his clan succeeded in producing at least one *chin-shih* each generation who attained the additional honor of being selected as member of the Han-lin Academy. But when genealogical records are examined the long-range downward mobility becomes statistically evident.

An unusually thorough monograph on prominent clans deserves our attention. Professor P'an Kuang-tan, a leading Chinese social geneticist, in his painstaking study of 91 prominent clans of Chia-hsing prefecture, Chekiang, of Ming-Ch'ing times, challenges the commonly accepted saying which dated back to the feudal times of primogeniture: "A gentleman's [i.e., a feudal lord's] grace becomes extinct in five generations." From his information, which is culled from genealogies, biographies, and local histories, we see that, on the average, a clan's "prominence" lasted a little over eight generations.[87] On the surface, therefore, his conclusion is not only at variance with that of this chapter but also with the statistics of a modern methodical study of the descendants of Former Han nobility, which prove that the famous ancient saying was too optimistic.[88] The different conclusions are, however, accounted for by different viewpoints and criteria. Professor P'an approaches his problem from the point of view of genetics, which is more concerned with a clan's biological perpetuation than with its social prominence. His criteria are such that whenever a relative's name is found in a wide range of sources he counts as one generation of "prominence," whatever his social status. As is well known, a "common descent group" usually consisted of dozens if not hundreds of males. It frequently happened that although a clan as a whole had long been in process of decline, one or two subbranches might still produce one or two men who managed to leave their records locally. As a rule, one did not have to acquire a degree higher than *kung-sheng* to get his name included in a local history. The fact that even by such extremely lenient standards for "prominence" the average clan fell into complete oblivion in some eight generations would rather seem to confirm the present findings based on a sociological and quantitative point of view.

Some late Ch'ing general impressions which differ in time and nature from Wang Shih-chen's partial data for the Ming period are also worth a brief mention. Of a handful of *sheng-yüan* lists available, two are arranged according to local clans. The two localities in which these clans lived are T'ung-chou in southern Kiangsu and the neighboring Hai-men sub-county. Both editors remarked in their introductions how comparatively difficult it was for a clan to continue to produce holders of this elementary degree for more than a few generations.[89] The statesman Tseng Kuo-fan (1811–72), despite his extraordinary successful career and marquisate, is known to have said that he would be immensely gratified if in each generation his descendants could do no better than acquire the lowly · *sheng-yüan* status.[90] Judging from our findings his wishes were indeed not unduly modest.

# CHAPTER V

# FACTORS AFFECTING
# SOCIAL MOBILITY

A NUMBER of institutionalized and noninstitutional factors had an important bearing on social mobility in Ming-Ch'ing times. A systematic analysis of these factors will help us to understand the changes in the opportunity-structure during various subperiods and to explain the reasons for the long-range changing mobility trend shown in chapter III. All factors relevant to social mobility, save for those related exclusively to downward mobility which have been explained in chapter IV, will be discussed in this chapter.

## EXAMINATION AND STATE SCHOOLS

From the seventh century onward the effect of the competitive civil service examination system on social mobility became tangible. It was the examination system that gradually broke up the political monopoly of the early T'ang northwestern aristocracy, an amalgam of the Chinese and non-Chinese nobility which had played a key role in reunifying China in 589. While it is impossible to measure even approximately the amount of sociopolitical mobility in T'ang times, the political *parvenus* who owed their official position to their academic success soon developed a strong group solidarity and vied for power with the aristocracy which, though it became less able to maintain its political monopoly, continued to enjoy paramount social prestige until the very end of the T'ang period. The final decline and extinction of many T'ang noble houses amidst the wars and turmoil of the Five Dynasties (907–60) created further opportunities for plebeians to enter the service of the subsequent Sung government, although it is doubtful whether commoners of truly poor, humble, and nonscholastic families had much chance of academic-political success up to the end of the Northern Sung in 1126.[1]

Although the permanent institutionalization of the examination system was a partial application of the Confucian principle that ruling-class membership should be determined by individual merit, yet for more than three centuries after the examination system had become permanently institutionalized the state was mainly concerned with using it as a channel for bureaucratic recruitment rather than to provide educational facilities for those who aspired to become officials. In other words, from the seventh century to early Sung times the state did not regard public education as one of its vital functions except for the maintenance of the venerable institution of the Imperial Academy, which for some time had had but a nominal existence.[2] Education was very much a private affair, depending almost entirely on the individual's family background and personal opportunity. But after the founding of the Sung the basic dynastic policy gradually led the state to tackle the problem of public education. In order to curb and eliminate the influence of the remaining regional military governors, the early Sung state greatly enhanced the prestige and power of civil officials and made the examination system an increasingly important channel of sociopolitical mobility. This in turn led some conscientious provincial and local officials to grapple with a problem more fundamental than the examination system itself, namely, the establishment of publicly supported schools as a training ground for examination candidates. For without public schools the true Confucian ideal of offering equal educational opportunity to all could not be realized and the examination system would benefit only those who could afford to receive education. The principle of public education was incontrovertible, because a very limited number of public schools had been sporadically created by some "model officials" since the late second century B.C.[3]

So far as can be ascertained from Sung records, the earliest public school of the Sung period was founded in 1022 in Yen-chou in southwestern Shantung on the initiative of the prefect. It became the first formal prefectural school of the country in the following year when the emperor allocated a limited amount of land for its maintenance. A few officials soon followed suit, but the problem of public education did not receive serious government attention until the reforming statesman Fan Chung-yen became prime minister in 1043.[4] The outcome of a court discussion in 1044, presided over by the emperor himself, was an imperial decree which stated briefly that the lack of public educational facilities had prevented many gifted men from serving the state and ordered that schools be established in every province and prefecture. From private Sung literary works, however, we are able to surmise that the discrepancy between the goal set in 1044 and the reality was a wide one and that throughout the remainder of the Sung period good public schools were exceptions rather than the general rule.

The reasons are manifold. First, the imperial government failed to develop a sustained interest in public education because it was soon torn by a prolonged factional strife of unusual intensity and was forced to migrate to the south after the fall of the capital city K'ai-feng in 1126. Second, the lack of permanent funds and endowments made it difficult for the average prefecture or county to set up public schools. The existence of the few successful prefectural schools depended almost solely on official initiative and local response. Even in the few localities where people donated generously for educational purposes, the endowed property often dwindled or was appropriated by unscrupulous local magnates. Third, the decree of 1044 was a half-hearted measure, for it failed to provide fixed regulations for the creation, selection, and maintenance of teaching staffs. Even in a few prefectures which did establish public schools the tutors were, for a long time after the issuance of the decree, subordinate officials of the prefects who could at best devote only a part of their time to teaching and school supervision. Although a decree of 1078 ordered the provinces and prefectures to appoint full-time school teachers with official ranks, the total number of teachers was only 53 in an empire of some 1,000 counties. Even when the selection of school teachers was comparatively strict, the teachers were often forced by their low rank and pay to do sundry jobs to make ends meet.[5]

An unexpected by-product of this arrested Sung educational

campaign was the improvement of the Imperial Academy, which gradually changed from a nominal institution to the foremost school of the land with a peak enrollment of 3,800 and 1,700 before and after the fall of the northern Sung in 1126.[6]

Although Sung people well understood the logical link between examinations and public schools, they failed to integrate the two. From early Ming times onward the examination and school systems became inseparable. In 1369 the Ming founder T'ai-tsu issued orders that a school be set up in every prefecture and county, staffed by government-appointed teachers and permanently supported by state funds. Before his long reign ended in 1398, approximately 1,200 schools had been established in areas within his effective jurisdiction.[7] More schools were established for a number of *wei*, or military garrison headquarters, during the first half of the fifteenth century.[8] With the continual expansion of China's inner frontier and the sinicization of the hitherto aboriginal areas, the number of state schools increased to 1,741 in 1812 and 1,810 in 1886.[9] By the early Ming regulation every prefectural school was to have a director and four subdirectors and every county school a director and two subdirectors. Thus there were several thousand school officials in the empire.[10] Despite the comparatively low ranks and emoluments, school officials were held in high regard by early Ming rulers, who not infrequently appointed famous scholars to school posts and promoted meritorious school officials to high positions.[11] It is true that gradually school posts came to be reserved almost exclusively for deadwood *chü-jen* and *kung-sheng*, who from mid-Ming times onward began to glut the lower stratum of officialdom, and the value of the schools as local centers of serious studies became less and less. But throughout the Ming-Ch'ing period state schools served several important functions. First, they supervised *sheng-yüan*'s routine work and administered government scholarships or stipends. Second, for poor and secluded districts schools were often the only places which provided minimal library facilities. Third, through schools the state controlled the vast body of undergraduates, or *sheng-yüan*, from whom higher degree holders and officials were selected. Thus the school and examination systems were well integrated.

Through the integrated school and examination system the Ming and Ch'ing states attempted to regulate the volume of socioacademic mobility at its three different levels—local, provincial, and national. The state's regulatory policy varied according to its needs at the time and to its will to control, and its effect on mobility differed from one period to another. Generally speaking, the state was more concerned with the final stage of socioacademic mobility, which was symbolized by the attainment of the *chin-shih* degree and which had a direct bearing on the demand and supply of officials, than with the intermediate *chü-jen, kung-sheng,* and initial *sheng-yüan* stages. We may also make the generalization that the state policy gradually changed from one of extreme leniency and sympathy toward humble commoners at the very beginning of the Ming to one of unusual restriction at the height of Manchu power, roughly the period from 1683 to 1795. The gradual change in state policy coincided in the main with the long-range changing mobility trend shown in table 9, that is, the persistent drop in the percentage figures of Category A *chin-shih* from the late sixteenth century onward.

State regulations of the initial stage of socioacademic mobility should be reviewed first. Almost as soon as the Ming dynasty was founded, the government provided that those who could pass a series of local examinations were to be granted the *sheng-yüan* degree, which was made a formal qualification for taking the provincial examination. *Sheng-yüan* quotas were fixed at ratios of 60 for each metropolitan prefectural city, 40 for each ordinary prefectural city, 30 for each large county (*chou*), and 20 for each ordinary county (*hsien*). All *sheng-yüan* were enrolled in prefectural or county schools and subjected to instruction, periodic reviewing tests, and the discipline of school officials. They were exempt from *corvée* duty and were entitled to free board and a monthly stipend of six tenths of a *shih* (Chinese bushel) of rice, which was increased to a whole *shih* in 1382.[12] This Ming innovation was important for two reasons. First, it marked the beginning of the system of three formal academic degrees and qualifications, namely, *sheng-yüan, chü-jen,* and *chin-shih,* which lasted till the final abolition of the examination system in 1905. Second, it marked the beginning of a rudimentary but nationwide scholarship system based on the Confucian principle of individual merit. In an age of simple needs a modest stipend of a *shih* of rice a month was generally sufficient to enable a struggling young man to concentrate on his studies, and the exemption from *corvée* duty for himself and for two other adult males of his family (if there were any) materially reduced the whole family's fiscal burden.

In spite of the fact that the Ming-Ch'ing system of *sheng-yüan* recruitment is generally regarded as a matter of common knowledge by students of Chinese history, actually the changes in the system in Ming times are not clearly recorded in Ming statutes and there is a fundamental difference between early Ming and Ch'ing regulations. While in Ch'ing times the quotas were those for *sheng-yüan* to be admitted in each examination year, early Ming quotas were those for the total cumulative numbers of *sheng-yüan* of various localities. Assuming that by about 1400 the total number of schools was around 1,200 and that the subsequent increase of schools for military garrison headquarters and in the southwest pushed the total upward to 1,300 around 1450, and further assuming that the average school had a total enrollment of 25, we get a national total of only 30,000 and 32,500 *sheng-yüan*, when the national population was increasing from a previous total of more than 65,000,000.[13] To meet the popular demand for larger quotas, the government created in 1385 a new category of students, *tseng-kuang-sheng-yüan*, commonly called by its contraction *tseng-sheng* (additional *sheng-yüan*), without fixed quotas. The technical difference between the original *sheng-yüan* and *tseng-sheng* was that the latter were not entitled to government stipends, although after passing local qualifying examinations they had the same right as the former to take the provincial examination. After that time *sheng-yüan* on government scholarships were commonly called *ling-sheng* and regarded as the senior and meritorious group in the expanding student body. In 1428 quotas were set for *tseng-sheng* at the same ratios as those for *ling-sheng*, thus theoretically doubling the original student quotas. In 1447, upon the request of a prefect, a statute provided that in localities where there were more educated youths than local quotas could accommodate, a new category of junior students, *fu-hsüeh-sheng-yüan*, commonly called by its contraction *fu-sheng* (supplementary *sheng-yüan*), was created, without fixed quotas.[14]

Along with the repeated enlargement of *sheng-yüan* quotas, however, the early Ming state maintained a very strict school discipline and constantly attempted to reduce the cumulative numbers of students. Starting in 1391 a long series of statutes provided that those *sheng-yüan* who failed to pass the provincial examination within five, six, or ten years after having obtained their degree were to be dismissed from the schools and relegated to the status of local government clerks or ordinary commoners.[15] This harsh treatment was justified because local student quotas were limited and only by constant screening could there be vacancies for fresh talents. Through piecemeal selection of the new and merciless pruning of the old the total number of *sheng-yüan* was kept very small. The president of the Board of Rites in Nanking reported in a memorial of 1438 that throughout the country there were only slightly over 30,000 *sheng-yüan*. By making the first academic degree difficult to obtain and by strictly adhering to the principle of individual literary merit the early Ming state succeeded in preventing over-congestion at higher-level examinations and subsequent excessive wastage of social effort.[16]

Meanwhile, the national population was steadily growing and the nation at large became increasingly aware of the importance of education as the main avenue of upward social mobility. The early Ming policy of keeping the student body small could not be maintained for very long. After their abolition in 1450, the quotas for *tseng-sheng* were restored and made permanent in 1467. As a reflection of the popular sentiment of the time there was a sarcastic saying in the metropolitan area that "while Buddhist monks can be freely recruited on the principle of universal salvation, the hapless *hsiu-ts'ai* [vulgar name for *sheng-yüan*] remain subjected to limited quotas." [17] In spite of the fact that information on changes in the Ming system of *sheng-yüan* recruitment is fragmentary at best, we gather from scattered statutory evidence that from the late fifteenth century onward the government had to make original student quotas more flexible so as to accommodate the growing demands of the nation.

Shortly after 1500 the old laws, whereby *sheng-yüan* of over a certain number of years' standing were constantly pruned, were gradually relaxed. In 1532 a censor who advocated a more lenient policy toward *sheng-yüan* of long standing received imperial endorsement.[18] Four years later a statute allowed *sheng-yüan* fifty years old and over, who had repeatedly failed in higher examinations and wanted to retire from the school rolls, to retain the privilege of *corvée* exemption and to wear students' caps and gowns as a mark of distinction from ordinary commoners.[19] This more lenient policy toward *sheng-yüan,* together with the fact that unquotaed *fu-sheng* had gradually become a permanent feature of the system, must have accounted for large increases in their cumulative numbers. For example, whereas the populous and highly cultured Wu-shi county in southern Kiangsu had only 62 *sheng-yüan* in 1424, the number rose to 239 in 1572.[20]

Furthermore, from 1436 onward the creation of the post of provincial educational commissioner[21] gradually brought about an important change in regulations regarding *sheng-yüan* admission. Although the admission of new *sheng-yüan* remained on a very strict and piecemeal basis for a considerable time after the creation of this new office, we learn that by 1575 quotas were set for new *sheng-yüan* to be admitted in each examination year at ratios of 20 for a prefectural school, 15 for a county school, and 4 or 5 for a school of a small and culturally backward county. Another statute of 1583 further provided that the educational commissioner must see to it that these quotas were annually filled and that in populous and highly cultured localities the quotas could be doubled.[22] There is reason to believe that these two statutes merely laid down a broad principle and that actual practices still varied from place to place.

Of late Ming local histories, the 1607 edition of the history of Pao-ting Prefecture in the northern metropolitan province Pei-Chihli yields the most specific figures.

Several technical points should be observed. First, in spite of the

TABLE 19

STUDENT QUOTAS OF PAO-TING PREFECTURE AS OF 1607

A. PAO-TING PREFECTURAL SCHOOL
(*Total cumulative quota: 400*)

| Category | Number |
| --- | --- |
| Ling-sheng | 40 |
| Reinstated ling-sheng | 10 |
| Tseng-sheng | 40 |
| Reinstated tseng-sheng | 3 |
| Fu-sheng | 280 |
| Total | 373 |

B. CH'ING-WAN COUNTY SCHOOL
(*Total cumulative quota: 226*)

| Category | Number |
| --- | --- |
| Ling-sheng | 20 |
| Reinstated ling-sheng | 2 |
| Ling-sheng deprived of stipend | 4 |
| Tseng-sheng | 20 |
| Reinstated tseng-sheng | 2 |
| Fu-sheng | 157 |
| Total (excluding 10 fu-sheng dismissed from school) | 205 |

C. AN-SU COUNTY SCHOOL
(*Total cumulative quota: 197*)

| Category | Number |
| --- | --- |
| Ling-sheng | 20 |
| Reinstated ling-sheng | 7 |
| Ling-sheng deprived of stipend | 3 |
| Expectant ling-sheng | 4 |
| Tseng-sheng | 20 |
| Expectant tseng-sheng | 6 |
| Fu-sheng | 116 |
| Total (excluding 11 fu-sheng dismissed from school) | 176 |

Source: *Pao-ting fu-chih*, ch. 17. Only 3 out of 21 schools of the prefecture are selected as examples.

large increase in student numbers after 1575, the early Ming system of total cumulative quotas was retained, at least in theory. The prefectural history does not explain how the local cumulative quotas were fixed. We can only venture a guess. Since late in Ming times it gradually became customary for various localities to hold two *sheng-*

*yüan* examinations every three years and since by the statute of 1575 a prefectural school should admit 20 new students each examination year, the cumulative quota of the Pao-ting prefectural school of 400 represented exactly the aggregate of students admitted in twenty examinations over a period of thirty years—an average generation. But we do not know exactly why the cumulative quotas for Ch'ing-wan and An-su Counties, 226 and 197 respectively, were all lower than 300, a number which would have conformed to the principle laid down in 1575. On the other hand, in the densely populated, rich, and highly cultured Ch'ang-chou Prefecture in southern Kiangsu the cumulative quotas for the prefectural and five county schools as of 1618 were respectively 520, 435, 416, 413, 443, and 210.[23] With the exception of the small county Ching-chiang, which had a quota of 210, those of the rest were all considerably larger than those of Pao-ting. One possible explanation is the difference in population and cultural level. Second, comparatively small as the Pao-ting quotas were, the actual cumulative numbers were even smaller than the legal cumulative quotas, a phenomenon which was in contrast to many southern localities. Third, the mention of reinstated and expectant *ling-sheng and tseng-sheng, ling-sheng* deprived of stipend, and *fu-sheng* dismissed from school rosters

TABLE 20

MING STUDENT QUOTAS OF THREE LOWER-YANGTZE COUNTIES

| Nan-t'ung | | | Wu-hsi | | | P'ing-hu | | |
|---|---|---|---|---|---|---|---|---|
| Period | Total | Average per annum | Period | Total | Average per annum | Period | Total | Average per annum |
| 1371–1487 | 267 | 2.2 | | | | | | |
| 1488–1505 | 88 | 5.1 | | | | | | |
| 1506–1521 | 143 | 9.5 | | | | | | |
| 1522–1566 | 444 | 11.0 | | | | 1540–1566 | 311 | 12.0 |
| 1567–1572 | 35 | 7.0 | | | | 1567–1572 | 81 | 16.2 |
| 1573–1620 | 549 | 11.7 | 1602–1620 | 487 | 21.5 | 1573–1620 | 1,021 | 22.2 |
| 1621–1627 | 195 | 32.5 | 1621–1627 | 337 | 56.2 | 1621–1627 | 201 | 29.2 |
| 1628–1644 | 303 | 19.0 | 1618–1644 | 864 | 54.0 | 1618–1644 | 776 | 48.5 |

Sources: *T'ung-hsiang t'i-ming lu* (1933 ed.); *Hsi-chin yu-hsiang lu* (printed sometime after 1878); and *P'ing-hu ts'ai-ch'in lu* (1915 ed.).

shows that the routine periodic reviewing tests and regulations on promotion and demotion had been reasonably strictly observed.

By far the best sources for our study of the changes in the Ming *sheng-yüan* quota system are the three extant Ming *sheng-yüan* lists of Nan-t'ung and Wu-hsi Counties in southern Kiangsu and P'ing-hu County in northeastern coastal Chekiang. The latter two were densely settled and culturally and economically advanced countries.

The above table shows several things. First, we learn from the original breakdowns that for a greater part of the Ming period there were no fixed quotas for new *sheng-yüan* to be admitted in each examination. Until the Chia-ching period (1522–66) *sheng-yüan* were admitted on a piecemeal basis. Even during this period of more lenient policy toward *sheng-yüan* admission, we learn from the P'ing-hu list that in the six years between 1540 and 1546 two examinations were held and a total of only three degrees was granted. On the other hand, 51 degrees were granted in the year 1554 and as many as 81 granted in the year 1564. The sharp fluctuations indicate that the system was still very different from the comparatively stable and regular annual *sheng-yüan* quotas in Ch'ing times. Second, while the general tendency shows substantial increases in student numbers in the late Ming period, the extent to which student numbers were increased differed from one locality to another, depending much on local demands and the discretion of the educational commissioner, for the statutes of 1575 and 1583 set no upper ceiling for large counties. Third, a comparison with average annual Ch'ing figures given in table 21 below shows that the late Ming state actually adopted a laissez-faire policy toward *sheng-yüan* admission and seems to have lost its will to control the initial stage of socioacademic mobility. In fact, so hard pressed by the rising Manchus and so desperately in need of funds was the late Ming state that it allowed certain localities, such as Nan-t'ung, to sell *sheng-yüan* degrees outright between 1621 and 1627, a fact so far little known to students of Chinese institutional history. Fourth, the mounting increase in the numbers of *sheng-yüan* accumulated in an average generation in late Ming times accounted not only for the deterioration in student quality but also for an increasing glut of candidates at higher-level examinations.[24]

All this called for more regulation from the early Ch'ing state. To court popularity, the first Manchu emperor Shun-chih (1644–61) kept *sheng-yüan* quotas large for a number of years. But as the Manchu empire became more stable, his government decreed in 1661 that a large prefectural city should have a quota of 20, a large and cultured county a quota of 15, and a small backward county a quota of 4 or 5.[25] In other words, the minimal quotas set in 1575 now became maximal. For students of institutional history it is interesting to note that in fixing land tax, *corvée*, and *sheng-yüan* quotas, the early Ch'ing government invariably took those of the beginning of the Wan-li period (1573–1619) as a basis. Of the eight Ch'ing *sheng-yüan* lists available in North America, we choose three as a general illustration of the changing quotas which reflected Ch'ing government policy.

From the setting of new quotas in 1661 and from figures of the early K'ang-hsi era, which in our table is the period 1662–77, there can be little doubt that the new dynasty, somewhat reminiscent of the early Ming state, earnestly attempted to narrow the channel of initial socioacademic mobility in order better to regulate the later stages of mobility. The unusually low averages per annum during the period 1662–77 were accounted for by the reduction of the frequency of examinations and by adherence to the curtailed 1661 quotas. The government would have been able to maintain this restrictive policy much longer had it not been for the financial need caused by the war against the three rebellious southern feudatories. In the four years 1678–82, for a large county, only three or four *sheng-yüan* degrees were granted in each examination, but there was practically no ceiling for the number of *sheng-yüan* degrees sold to commoners for 120 taels apiece. After the pacification of the south and the consequent conquest of Formosa in 1683, *sheng-yüan* quotas became stabilized and remained considerably below the late Ming and pre-1661 levels. In all likelihood the fluctuations in the total cumulative number of *sheng-yüan* in an average lifetime during the first two centuries of the Ch'ing period were not very great.

## TABLE 21

## CH'ING STUDENT QUOTAS OF THREE LOWER-YANGTZE COUNTIES

| Period | Ch'ang-shu | | | Chia-shan | | | P'ing-hu | | |
|---|---|---|---|---|---|---|---|---|---|
| | Number | Average per annum | Percent above or below norm | Number | Average per annum | Percent above or below norm | Number | Average per annum | Percent above or below norm |
| 1644–1661 | 389 | 23.0 | 30.0 | 488 | 27.0 | 41.4 | 525 | 31.0 | 61.4 |
| 1662–1677 | 79 | 6.0 | −66.1 | 151 | 12.6 | −34.0 | 94 | 6.0 | −68.7 |
| 1678–1682 | 232 | 58.0 | 227.7 | 250 | 62.5 | 227.2 | 411 | 103.0 | 436.4 |
| 1683–1722 | 535 | 13.7 | −22.6 | 619 | 15.9 | −16.7 | 482 | 12.4 | −35.4 |
| 1723–1735 | 230 | 19.2 | 8.5 | 268 | 22.3 | 11.5 | 222 | 18.5 | −3.6 |
| 1736–1795 | 1,002 | 16.8 | −5.1 | 1,045 | 17.7 | −7.4 | 1,044 | 17.4 | −9.4 |
| 1796–1820 | 415 | 17.3 | −2.3 | 444 | 18.5 | −3.2 | 447 | 18.6 | −3.1 |
| 1821–1850 | 527 | 18.0 | 1.7 | 521 | 18.0 | −5.7 | 521 | 18.0 | −6.2 |
| 1851–1861 | 187 | 18.7 | 5.6 | 160 | 16.0 | −15.7 | 172 | 17.2 | −10.4 |
| 1862–1874 | 331 | 27.7 | 56.5 | 329 | 27.4 | 43.5 | 342 | 28.5 | 48.4 |
| 1875–1904 | 675 | 23.3 | 31.6 | 689 | 24.0 | 25.7 | 751 | 26.0 | 35.4 |
| Total | 4,602 | 17.7 (norm) | | 4,964 | 19.1 (norm) | | 5,011 | 19.2 (norm) | |

Sources: *Kuo-ch'ao yü-yang k'o-ming lu* (1905 ed.); *Chia-shan ju-p'an t'i-ming lu* (1908 ed.); and *P'ing-hu ts'ai-ch'in lu* (1915 ed.).

While it is true that at the beginning of the dynasty local quotas were considerably above norm, the Shun-chih period was one of short duration and the sharp contraction and expansion during the period 1662–82 largely offset each other. In addition, the number of schools was increasing along with the continual growth of population and the development of new areas. It is significant to note that the estimate on the cumulative number of *sheng-yüan* in an average generation's time made by the great scholar and traveler Ku Yen-wu in the third quarter of the seventeenth century coincides almost exactly with the one made by Father Jean J. M. Amiot in 1777, both being in the neighborhood of 500,000.[26]

The outbreak of the Taiping rebellion in 1851 forced the government to raise funds by every conceivable means. Various localities made monetary contributions to the government in return for a temporary or permanent increase in local *sheng-yüan* quotas. It ought to be pointed out that the figures for the period 1851–61 would have been larger but for the suspension of certain local examinations because of the war. The figures for the period 1862–74 should have been smaller because they included *sheng-yüan* of certain examinations of the preceding period belatedly held. By the time when the last edition of the *Cases of the Collected Statutes of the Ch'ing Empire* was compiled in 1886, the annual national *sheng-yüan* quota had increased from slightly over 25,000 in 1812 to a little over 30,000. Taking thirty years as the average career span of a *sheng-yüan*, during which twenty examinations were held, the cumulative number of *sheng-yüan* during the latter half of the nineteenth century was probably around 600,000, a figure which, though some 20 percent higher than that of the pre-1850 period, is not likely to be higher than that of the late Ming.

In retrospect it may be said that, although the Ming and Ch'ing states always realized the importance of controlling the size of the *sheng-yüan* body, actually this control was often difficult to exercise. The only exception was the early Ming state, whose policy of making the *sheng-yüan* body exclusive was fairly strictly based on the principle of individual merit and accompanied by constant vigilance and pruning. The continual growth of population and popular demand made it necessary for the later Ming government to adopt a more lenient policy toward *sheng-yüan* admission. From the last quarter of the sixteenth century on, it seems that the Ming government practically lost its will to control the initial stage of socio-academic mobility, as may be evidenced from the virtual absence of upper ceilings for large and culturally advanced counties. While the population increased from over 65,000,000 in the late fourteenth century to probably 150,000,000 in 1600, the national *sheng-yüan* total possibly increased twentyfold. The enhanced chances for commoners to acquire the first degree did not mean that it was easier for them to reach the final goal in social mobility. On the contrary, the inflated number of *sheng-yüan* resulted in a glut at higher-level examinations and engendered an increasing amount of social frustration, for the state could not afford to abandon its control over *chin-shih* quotas, which had a direct bearing on the size of the bureaucracy.

The Ch'ing state succeeded in the main in keeping a stable *sheng-yüan* quota system. The sharp fluctuations were over by 1683, and the subsequent increases in *sheng-yüan* quotas were gradual and modest. Even after the Taiping rebellion there was no runaway inflation in *sheng-yüan* numbers as had been the case in late Ming times. It would appear, prima facie, that the stabilized Ch'ing quota system failed to synchronize with the sustained and rapid multiplication of the population which increased from probably somewhat less than 150,000,000 in 1700 to about 300,000,000 in 1800 and further shot up to 430,000,000 in 1850.[28] That it was becoming increasingly difficult for commoners to make the initial socioacademic transition cannot be much doubted, although the situation was somewhat mitigated by the government's virtual laissez-faire policy toward the sale of Imperial Academy studentships, which conferred on commoners rights and status equal to those of *sheng-yüan*. While systematic data on the sale of *chien-sheng* titles for the entire Ch'ing period are lacking, we know that during the Chia-ch'ing (1796–1820) and Tao-kuang (1821–50) periods the total number of studentships sold probably exceeded 600,000.[29] All in all, therefore, while the arithmetical chances for commoners of above average economic means to acquire the first academic degree were reduced to only a modest extent, the chances for poor commoners of nonscholastic families to seek their first degree within the stabilized *sheng-yüan* quota seem to have been reduced greatly. The persistent downward trend in the percentage figures of *sheng-yüan* from non-scholastic commoner families in Ch'ang-shu, Nan-t'ung, and Hai-men during Ch'ing times, as shown in table 15, was probably representative of most parts, if not all, of China.

The attainment of *kung-sheng* or *chü-jen* status was vital from the standpoint of individual upward mobility because either of these degrees qualified the holder for minor office. To regulate their number and to devise their fair geographical, and sometimes social, representation was therefore one of the functions of the Ming and Ch'ing states. Unlike the fundamental change in the principle of *sheng-yüan* admission in Ming times, there was a remarkable continuity between the Ming and Ch'ing system of selecting these intermediate degree holders. Since the Ch'ing examination system at its various levels has been described elsewhere,[30] we need to recapitulate only a few aspects of a complex system which had an important bearing on social mobility.

*Kung-sheng* and *chü-jen* quotas should be reviewed briefly. *Kung-sheng* quotas were first set in 1383, when a statute provided that every prefectural or county school should annually "tribute" one student to the imperial capital for further apprenticeship and for eventual official appointment. Although at first the selection was apparently based on literary merit, it gradually became a routine matter based almost exclusively on seniority. The *kung-sheng* quotas became permanent after 1441, when a statute provided that a prefectural school should "tribute" one *kung-sheng* annually, a large county school two every three years, and an ordinary county school one every two years.[31] These quotas remained unchanged until the end of the examination system in 1905. In the course of time there came into being four other categories of regular *kung-sheng* periodically selected through fixed channels. From the late sixteenth century onward, if not earlier, senior *sheng-yüan* on government stipend could also acquire the graduate *kung-sheng* status through purchase. In Ch'ing times it became a common practice for junior *sheng-yüan* to purchase *kung-sheng* status as well, particularly after

1850. The total number of five categories of regular *kung-sheng* cumulated in an average generation has been estimated at between 32,000 and 40,000 during Ch'ing times.[32] The number would be several thousands less if those who eventually became *chü-jen, chin-shih,* and officials were deducted. The total in an average generation must have been somewhat smaller in late Ming and considerably smaller in early Ming times. There is no means of knowing accurately the number of irregular *kung-sheng* in late Ming and Ch'ing times, but even at its peak in the post-1850 period this number was not likely to be larger than that of regular *kung-sheng*. This was because the *kung-sheng* title could be bought only by those who had earned their first degree through examination, whereas the title of imperial student in Ch'ing times was open to commoners without any degree. The total increase in all categories of *kung-sheng* probably failed to keep pace with the rapid growth of population.

*Chü-jen* quotas were first set in 1370 for various provinces at a total of 470 with the provision that quotas should be flexible for large provinces.[33] Thus in the examination of 1384 as many as 229 *chü-jen* degrees were granted for the southern metropolitan province of Nan-Chihli, which comprised modern Kiangsu and Anhwei.[34] The total quota was successively increased to meet the growing population until it exceeded 1,100 in the 1450s and 1,200 in the 1570s. During the Ch'ing period the quota ranged from 1,200 to 1,800. The Taiping rebellion brought about moderate temporary and permanent increases. Deducting those who later became *chin-shih* and officials, the total cumulative number of *chü-jen* in an average generation was probably in the neighborhood of 10,000 in the greater part of the Ch'ing period. It is certain that after 1450 the stabilized *chü-jen* quota failed to synchronize with the continually growing population and the arithmetical chances for people to obtain this second degree became almost progressively less.

In addition to freezing or moderately increasing the *chü-jen* quota at long intervals, the Ming and Ch'ing states paid a great deal of attention to securing a fair geographic representation of provincial graduates. The first provincial quotas set in 1370 were roughly proportionate to population, land tax payment, and cultural tradition. The largest quotas were given to Nan-Chihli (Kiangsu and Anhwei together) and to Kiangsi because the former constituted the metropolitan area and the latter had been culturally most advanced since Sung times.[35] Chekiang and Fukien, with their fine cultural tradition and large literate population, were considered as "large" provinces with large quotas. Other Yangtze provinces and northern provinces were regarded as "medium," and southwestern provinces like Kwangsi, Yunnan, and Kweichow "small." After Peking became the national capital in 1421 the quota of the northern metropolitan province of Pei-Chihli was successively enlarged until it became the largest in the country. The provincial quotas of 1748, which did not differ much from those of the late Ming and were fairly representative of greater parts of the Ch'ing were as follows: metropolitan Chihli, 206; Chiang-nan (Kiangsu and Anhwei), 114; Chekiang and Kiangsi, 95 each; Fukien, 85; Kwangtung, 72; Honan, 71; Shantung, 69; Shensi, including Kansu, 61; Shansi and Szechwan, 60 each; Yunnan, 54; Hupei, 48; Hunan and Kwangsi, 45 each; Kweichow, 36.[36]

It should be noted that but for this fixed quota system the northern and peripheral provinces would have produced fewer and the culturally advanced southeastern provinces would have predominated even more. Owing to the fact that Kiangsu was traditionally grouped together with Anhwei to form the large province of Chiang-nan, its ability to produce *chü-jen* was particularly handicapped by this fixed quota system. Special consideration was given to areas with substantial minority races so that in spite of their cultural backwardness a certain number of *chü-jen* could still be regularly produced.

The early Ch'ing state had much less concern for the humble and poor because dynastic interests dictated that it would be wise to appease and win the support of the key social class of the conquered land, namely, the official class.[37] By the turn of the seventeenth century such a high proportion of members of influential official families had obtained their *chü-jen* and *chin-shih* degrees, sometimes through means not entirely legitimate, that frustrated candidates and conscientious officials protested vigorously. Upon discovering certain instances of scandal, the K'ang-hsi emperor was compelled in 1700 to improvise special quotas and a coding system for members of influential official families as a means of limiting their *chü-jen* productivity. Thenceforth direct descendants and brothers of central officials of the fourth rank and above, imperial tutorial and Han-lin Academy officials irrespective of rank, provincial officials of the third rank and above, and military officials of the second rank and above were required to take provincial examinations under special quotas set at ratios of one *chü-jen* every 20 candidates for a large province, one every 15 for a medium province, and one every 10 for a small province. After minor changes these quotas became permanent in 1758. The inclusion of imperial tutorial and Han-lin Academy officials irrespective of rank was based on the theory that being "literary" officials they had superior cultural advantages. Superficially and arithmetically these quotas appear to have been set at ratios very favorable to members of high and literary official families,[38] but in reality the competition within this select group was extremely keen and many of those who failed to obtain their *chü-jen* degrees within the "official" quotas would have been able to pass the provincial examination if they had been allowed to compete against ordinary commoners. These "official" quotas might change slightly at each examination, but the 1844 edition of the *Statutes of the Board of Rites* listed a total quota of only 59 for the entire country.[39] Figures are lacking for pre-1800 *chü-jen*, but from table 10 we learn that throughout the nineteenth century less than three percent of *chü-jen* came from high official families. Owing to this rather effective control of numbers of *chü-jen* from high official families, there was no similar restriction imposed in the metropolitan examination.

The Ming and Ch'ing states were most concerned with regulating the final stage of socioacademic mobility. Although the first metropolitan examination was held in 1371, the second did not take place until after a lapse of fourteen years in 1385. The numbers of doctoral degrees granted also fluctuated sharply. Whereas there were 119 degrees granted in 1371, the number suddenly jumped to 472 in 1385. This was because for several decades after the founding of the Ming dynasty the examination system, though revived and integrated with the school system, was not the only channel for the selection of officials, and its importance was less than that of *ad hoc* recommendations of men of talent by officials. Not until the second quarter of the fifteenth century did the examination system begin to assume an overwhelming importance. Although quotas for *chü-jen* and *kung-sheng* gradually become stabilized, the state theoretically always reserved its right to set *chin-shih* quotas according to its needs of the time.

Since the metropolitan and final palace examinations were national in character, there were at first no regional or provincial quotas. The steady southward shift in demographic, economic, and cultural centers of gravity after the middle of the T'ang period conferred on certain southern provinces, particularly Kiangsi, Chekiang, Kiangsu, and Fukien, an incomparable competitive advantage.[40] The predominance of southerners in the metropolitan examination of 1397 brought about widespread complaints by northerners and led to the Ming founder's investigation. Although no scandal was uncovered, Ming T'ai-tsu executed the chief examiner, Liu San-wu, partly because of his vindictiveness but largely for considerations of fairer regional representation.[41] For political reasons, too, the early Ming government had to buy the goodwill of the northerners, who had been under alien rule for more than two centuries and whose nationalistic feeling was much weaker than that of the southerners. After this episode broad regional quotas were set up in the ratio of 60 percent for the south and 40 percent for the north. Further to benefit certain peripheral and culturally backward provinces, a middle region was created in 1425, which comprised chiefly Szechwan, Kwangsi, Yunnan, and Kweichow.[42]

It must be pointed out, however, that while this system prevented any region from gaining complete domination, it could not prevent culturally advanced provinces from producing considerably more *chin-shih* than others within the same region, for a region was sufficiently large to allow provincial differences. Throughout Ming and early Ch'ing times, Chekiang, Kiangsu, and Kiangsi consistently produced larger numbers of successful candidates than other southern and northern provinces, and some backward provinces like Kansu failed in a number of consecutive examinations to produce any. This led to the institution in 1702 of a sliding scale of provincial quotas within each major region. The quota for each province was set shortly before the metropolitan examination in proportion to the sum total of the number of its participants in the three preceding examinations.[43]

Since the number of participants in the metropolitan examination bore a close relationship to a province's cumulative number of *chü-jen* and since the latter was roughly proportional to the fixed *chü-jen* quota for each provincial examination, provincial *chin-shih* quotas after 1702 became virtually frozen, with only minor readjustments during and after the Taiping rebellion. Thenceforth all peripheral and backward provinces substantially benefited and the culturally advanced southeastern coastal provinces actually suffered. It is necessary to point out that these more rigid post-1702 provincial *chin-shih* ratios were far from fair, because provincial *chü-jen* quotas were by no means entirely rational. For example, during a greater part of the Ming and Ch'ing periods, Chekiang, because of its large initial population and unusual academic success up to 1600, had a larger *chü-jen* quota than Kiangsu, although by late Ming times Kiangsu had a much larger population and had clearly shown its superiority in *chin-shih* productivity from roughly 1600 to 1702. Under the broad regional quota system Kiangsu produced 1,015 *chin-shih* between 1644 and 1702, as compared with Chekiang's 766 for the same period. Under the rigid provincial ratio system, however, Kiangsu produced only 1,466 *chin-shih* between 1703 and 1861 as against Chekiang's 1,621. Not until after 1862 was Kiangsu allotted a *chin-shih* ratio larger than Chekiang's. It was able to nose out Chekiang as the leading producer of *chin-shih* in the whole Ch'ing period largely because of its superiority built up under the pre-1702 regional quota system. Hunan, to mention another case, though culturally relatively backward in Ming and early Ch'ing times, was making rapid progress in the later Ch'ing period, especially after 1850. Yet, owing to its traditionally small *chü-jen* quota and its small post-1702 *chin-shih* ratio, it ranked a lowly fifteenth in *chin-shih* productivity during the entire Ch'ing period. Speaking of the general effect of the post-1702 system, there can be little doubt that a more even geographical representation was achieved at the expense of certain culturally advanced provinces.[44]

A far more important factor affecting mobility rates was the changing total *chin-shih* quotas, which are shown in the following table.

TABLE 22

MING-CH'ING *CHIN-SHIH* QUOTAS

| Period | Number of examinations | Total of chin-shih | Average per examination | Average per annum |
|---|---|---|---|---|
| (1) 1368–1450 | 19 | 3,636 | 227.2 | 44.3 |
| (2) 1451–1644 | 66 | 20,958 | 317.6 | 108.6 |
| Total (Ming) | 85 | 24,594 | 289.3 | 89.1 |
| (3) 1644–1661 | 8 | 2,964 | 370.5 | 174.8 |
| (4) 1662–1678 | 5 | 1,029 | 205.8 | 64.3 |
| (5) 1679–1699 | 7 | 1,115 | 159.3 | 55.7 |
| (6) 1700–1722 | 9 | 1,944 | 216.0 | 88.4 |
| (7) 1723–1735 | 5 | 1,499 | 300.0 | 125.0 |
| (8) 1736–1765 | 13 | 3,422 | 263.0 | 118.0 |
| (9) 1766–1795 | 14 | 1,963 | 142.1 | 67.7 |
| (10) 1796–1820 | 12 | 2,821 | 235.0 | 117.5 |
| (11) 1821–1850 | 15 | 3,269 | 218.0 | 112.8 |
| (12) 1851–1861 | 5 | 1,046 | 209.2 | 104.6 |
| (13) 1862–1874 | 6 | 1,588 | 264.3 | 132.3 |
| (14) 1875–1911[a] | 13 | 4,087 | 315.2 | 113.6 |
| Total (Ch'ing) | 112 | 26,747 | 238.8 | 100.2 |

Sources: Li Chou-wang, *Kuo-ch'ao li-k'o t'i-ming pei-lu ch'u-chi*, list of Ming *chin-shih*, amended in accordance with Shen Te-fu, *Yeh-huo pien pu-i*, which gives total numbers of candidates of the years 1385 and 1404. For the Ch'ing period, Fang Chao-ying and Tu Lien-che, *Tseng-chiao Ch'ing-ch'ao chin-shih t'i-ming pei-lu*.

[a] Actually the last examination was held in 1904, since the examination system was abolished in 1905.

Although the per annum *chin-shih* figure for the early Ming period up to 1450 was very small, there were channels other than examination, all of which recruited officials *en masse*. As will be discussed later in this chapter under wars and social upheavals, the opportunity-structure during early Ming times was actually broader than during any subsequent period. After the closure of other channels of bureaucratic recruitment, the Ming state kept the *chin-shih* quota large. The average per examination for the period 1451–1644 is 78.8 more than the average for the entire Ch'ing period. On a purely arithmetical basis, therefore, it was considerably easier for a scholar to attain the highest degree in Ming than in Ch'ing times. When the growth of population is taken into account, the chances of reaching the final mobility goal in Ming times seem to have been many times greater than during the Ch'ing, with the exception of certain peripheral backward provinces which actually improved their chances after the institution of the new *chin-shih* quota system in 1702.[45] From table 9 one striking statistical trend is noticeable, that the percentage of *chin-shih* from families without officials and degree holders began to drop sharply from the late sixteenth century onward. This decline was unavoidable because of the increasingly keen competition and the various advantages enjoyed by members of old scholarly and official families. But it was the sudden and drastic shrinkage of *chin-shih* quotas during the K'ang-hsi (periods 4, 5, 6) and later Ch'ien-lung (period 9) eras that hit the humble and relatively humble commoners particularly hard. Other things being equal, the smaller the quota, the higher the academic standard required for passing the metropolitan examination and the more difficult the chances for commoners without a family scholastic tradition to attain the degree. It does not seem entirely coincidental that the lowest percentages of Category A candidates in table 9 are found in 1692 and 1703, the quotas of which were 168 and 166, two of the smallest among our available lists. So far only one incomplete *chin-shih* list of 1703 and several miscellaneous eighteenth-century *chü-jen* and *kung-sheng* lists are known to be extant, and these show rather low percentages of candidates from nonofficial and nonscholarly families.

Before concluding this section a brief review of the impartiality and efficacy of the examination system as a major institutionalized channel for social mobility should be made. From as early as 992 the principle of a candidate's anonymity was established in order to prevent the operation of personal influence in the selection of *chin-shih*. The candidate's name was obliterated from his examination booklets and he was given a secret code number which was deciphered only after the final grading had been made. Further to guard against the possibility that examiners might recognize the candidate's handwriting, a bureau of examination copyists was established in 1015 to reproduce all examination booklets in another hand before they were read by the examiners. "Little more," says a modern historian of Sung civil service, "could be done to safeguard objectivity." [46] These and many other means of preventing collusion were adopted by the Ming and Ch'ing governments.

However, as the examination system became an increasingly important channel of bureaucratic recruitment, scandals at the various levels of the examination system were inevitable. Ming and Ch'ing literary works and miscellaneous notes are full of accounts of corrupt practices in examinations, but these must be carefully scrutinized. Occasionally during the Ming certain powerful political figures used their influence to secure larger temporary quotas for their provinces or high honors for their children or protégés. For example, in 1508 the eunuch Liu Chin, a native of Shensi, and his protégé Chiao Fang, a native of Honan, secured *chü-jen* quotas for their provinces which were larger than those of the culturally advanced southeastern provinces. In the metropolitan examination of the same year it was said that Liu Chin handed to the examiners a list of fifty names of persons whom he wished to be granted the *chin-shih* degree. According to the inquisitive and well-informed late Ming scholar Shen Te-fu, however, at the most only a few of Liu's protégés attained the degree through his influence, and the extent of the scandal was certainly exaggerated and probably based on hearsay. [47] The powerful prime minister Chang Chü-cheng, to give another example, secured for his son the highest honor in the palace examination of 1580, although otherwise there is no evidence showing the existence of collusion of any significant scale. [48] With the rapid decline of the Ming empire after 1600 it is possible that subornation in examinations became somewhat less uncommon.

In examination affairs the early Ch'ing was a period of relative administrative laxity. It was said that in the 1650s members of high official families had little difficulty in passing the provincial examination of Chihli. In the 1657 Chihli examination it was proved that some of the fourteen officials and examiners accepted bribes and connived with twenty-five go-betweens to tamper with the examination. Seven officials and higher degree holders were executed, their properties confiscated, and members of their families exiled. The chief and deputy examiners were demoted, and the twenty-five persons who served as go-betweens were exiled along with their families and their properties were confiscated. Altogether several hundred people were punished. A critical review of this unusually serious scandal, however, reveals that actually the candidates involved were limited to eight sons of high officials and a few rich men's sons of lower Yangtze, not all of whom passed the examination. By a special imperial edict all successful candidates were subjected to another written test, personally invigilated by a prince of the blood. The result was that of a total of 190 *chü-jen* granted in the scandal-ridden examination, 182 proved their literary proficiency and only 8 were disqualified on their poor showing.[49] Throughout the remainder of the seventeenth century, members of high official families continued to excel in examinations in general and in Chihli provincial examinations in particular. The persistency of this phenomenon is probably due more to their incomparably superior family scholastic training than to the exercise of illegitimate influence. The imperial court, however, was compelled by public opinion to proclaim that from 1700 onward members of high and literary official families should compete against each other within their respective provincial "official quotas," a system which proved to be an effective check on their otherwise disproportionate academic success.

Another serious scandal was also found in the administration of the Chihli provincial examination in 1858, as a result of which the chief examiner Po-chün, who was a grand secretary, and several other officials were executed or dismissed. The main evidence was that certain candidates passed paper slips to some examiners in order to help to identify their essays. Actually the case was purposely magnified by the powerful Su-shun, an archenemy of Po-chün at court. In fact, many contemporaries sympathized with the venerable, benign, if mediocre Manchu grand secretary and believed that the seriousness of the scandal was exaggerated beyond reason. The most detailed and popular account of this case contains obvious errors and probably was based partially on hearsay.[50] Most of the allegations and proven scandals in metropolitan examinations were related to relatively few candidates and sometimes to the selection of first-class honors men, which might not have significant bearing on the whole examination. Even favoritism limited to the choice of first-class honors men was not always feasible. For example, Weng T'ung-ho (1830–1904), the imperial tutor and associate grand secretary, had for years taken Chang Ch'ien (see Appendix, case 24) as his protégé. In the metropolitan examination of 1892 Weng, one of the examiners, believed that he had identified Chang's secretly coded and recopied examination books and given him high ranking, but was dismayed to learn later that Chang had failed. In 1894 Chang passed his metropolitan examination on his own merit. Weng was able to place him first in the final palace examination only because of the establishment of a new rule that for the palace final candidates' examination books were no longer reproduced by government copyists.[51]

It should also be briefly mentioned that frustrated candidates were naturally indignant, credulous, and eager to accept gossip as truth. To compensate for their failure, they frequently wrote satires and used every means to launch vicious attacks on examiners. Many times in the Ming-Ch'ing period examiners became innocent victims of irresponsible charges. Liu San-wu, the chief examiner of the metropolitan examination of 1397, was the first victim. Chiang Ch'en-ying (1628–99), a well-known scholar who became a *chin-shih* of first-class honors at the advanced age of sixty-nine, died in prison because of the smear of frustrated candidates. He was posthumously cleared by the reexamination of Chihli *chü-jen* of the class of 1699 whom he had selected. The result showed that all the candidates wrote essays and poems of sufficiently high quality to deserve the degree.[52] Li Fu, a deputy censor-general who served as deputy chief examiner in the metropolitan examination of 1721, lost his office and was sentenced to hard labor because he had passed members of several distinguished scholarly families of Kiangsu and Kiangsi. The subsequent investigation found no trace whatever of bribery or collusion.[53] All in all, therefore, while venality and favoritism on a limited scale were discovered at fairly long intervals, they seldom reached so serious a degree as to alter the fundamental character of the examination as a universal system of recruitment based on individual merit. In fact, the Ming and Ch'ing states never lost the will to stave off particularism and to ensure honest conduct in the examination system, which they regarded as an august and almost sanctified institution.

### COMMUNITY SCHOOLS AND PRIVATE ACADEMIES

County and prefectural schools, all financed by the state, were open only to those who had attained the *sheng-yüan* degree. They did not deal with elementary education. The logical need for elementary education was early realized by the Ming founder, who from 1375 onward issued a series of edicts exhorting village and urban communities throughout the country to establish *she-hsüeh*, or community schools.[54] As it turned out, although by imperial order such schools were to be established by the effort of the village and urban communities themselves, their success depended to a considerable extent on the initiative and guidance of local authorities. Wu Liang, for example, in addition to his duty of guarding the strategic post of Chiang-yin on the southern bank of the lower Yangtze, established many community schools and employed scholars of local renown as teachers.[55] Fang K'o-ch'in, an early Ming "model official," set up hundreds of such schools within his prefectural area of Chi-ning in Shantung.[56] While at the beginning a good deal of genuine interest in elementary education was found among conscientious local officials, instances of officials utilizing these opportunities to profit themselves were also known to the Ming founder. Hence a special imperial injunction was issued in 1383 that local authorities should not interfere in matters of local elementary education.[57] On the other hand, from the imperial injunctions we also learn that some eager local officials forced rustic boys into community schools against the wishes of their parents who could not afford to do without their sons' labor on the farm.[58] From our general knowledge of the Ming founder's high-handed ways in enforcing law and order and particularly from the local histories, it would be unfair to suspect that early Ming exhortations to create facilities for elementary education were a mere formality.

Throughout the fifteenth century, when the nation in general enjoyed a long period of recuperation and reduced fiscal burdens, the movement to set up community schools went on apace, often under the initiative of local officials. To save the cost of school buildings local officials sometimes transformed unlicensed temples and shrines into schools.[59] In some localities in Chekiang community schools utilized the surplus space of existing public buildings, such as public granaries.[60] The general reference in late Ming and Ch'ing local histories to the existence of community schools after 1375 seems to suggest their rather wide geographic distribution during at least the first half of the Ming period. Instances are known in which community schools were set up even in some aboriginal districts of the southwest.[61] Particularly noteworthy was the effort of the statesman, general, and philosopher Wang Yang-ming, who set up elementary and higher schools in Kwangsi in 1528 as a chief means of sinicizing the aborigines.[62]

The repeated imperial exhortations, such as those of 1436, 1465, and 1504, made it obligatory for provincial educational and local officials to expand facilities for elementary education.[63] In the Sung-chiang prefectural area, of which Shanghai was a constituent county, for example, the number of community schools greatly multiplied in the wake of these imperial orders. In Hua-t'ing County in 1462 a censor and the prefect hired a scholar of local renown to supervise the administration of the increasing number of community schools, with a view to recruiting candidates for *sheng-yüan*. In the next year another censor concurrently in charge of provincial education added 60 more community schools which had a combined enrollment of 1,152. "Thenceforth," as the prefectural history testified, "every village had its schools." In Shanghai as many as 96 new schools were created between 1472 and 1521, not including those 49 founded earlier which had altogether 50 teachers and 1,224 pupils.[64] In the mid-sixteenth century some elders of Li-yang County in Kiangsu testified that up to the early decades of the century official and private effort in maintaining community schools had never slackened and that such schools had served as an important channel of upward social climb by the poor.[65]

In the long run, however, many community schools became derelict owing either to chronic financial difficulties or to the decline of official and community zeal. The reigns of Ming shih-tsung (1522–66) and Ming Shen-tsung (1573–1619) are generally known for their administrative laxity and official peculation, but an over-all generalization for the state of elementary education in the whole country during later Ming times is impossible. For example, Hsiang-yang Prefecture in northern Hupei and Hsin-hui County near Canton witnessed great expansion in community schools during precisely these two periods of general laxity.[66] As many as twenty-one community schools originally founded in the Ming were still in operation in Shun-te County, near Canton, by the 1850s.[67] Wherever community schools had owned permanent landed property, as in a number of Shensi localities, they not only survived the general negligence of the late Ming period and the change of dynasty but have lasted until the twentieth century.[68] It ought also to be pointed out that although community schools are generally known to have been a typically early Ming institution, new ones were nevertheless established in many localities throughout the Ch'ing period.[69]

A few words should be said about the various types of *i-hsüeh*, or charitable schools. There were charitable schools set up by various clans exclusively for the education of their own members. These will be discussed later in this chapter, under The Clan System. There were charitable schools established by the well to do of various localities which were open to youths of the neighborhood who could not afford private education. Some depended on periodic donations and some had permanent endowments.[70] In addition, it was becoming increasingly common in Ch'ing times for merchant associations of various geographic origins to set up charitable schools in leading coastal and inland ports. For example, those in Chungking which were established by merchants of the lower Yangtze provinces offered not only free schooling to their own and their employees' children but also subsidies to their alumni who took the local, provincial, and metropolitan examinations.[71] It is interesting to note that two such charitable schools in Macao, which were set up in Ming times, still exist today. One is located in the temple of the patron saint of Chinese mariners, locally called Ma-ke (Maiden Saint Ma's Pavilion), from which the name Macao was first derived by the Portuguese. It has been maintained throughout the centuries

by merchants who originally came from two southern costal prefectures of Fukien and their descendants. Another is located in the
Buddhist temple where Caleb Cushing negotiated his famous Treaty
of Wanghia. This Wang-hsia charitable school has been maintained
by people of Amoy descent.[72]

To sum up, facilities for elementary education in a large historical society such as that of Ming-Ch'ing China cannot be compared
with those of modern industrialized societies where elementary
education is compulsory. But it is important to bear in mind that
centuries before universal education was tackled by the modern
West, the early Ming rulers had already realized its importance.
There can be little doubt that during at least the first half of the
Ming community schools were established extensively in the country
and they served an important educational purpose. While it is true
that never in Ming-Ch'ing times did the Confucian ideal of equal
educational opportunity for all fully materialize, it is likely that
education in the first 150 years of the Ming was more widely available than in most countries of contemporaneous Europe.

Just about the time when the decline of community schools began
to set in, the country witnessed the mushrooming growth of private
academies which, though often not serving the purpose of elementary education, nevertheless helped to make good the deficiencies of
state schools. The name *shu-yüan,* or academies, originated in T'ang
times when they were more in the nature of publicly established
libraries than schools. Not until Sung times did *shu-yüan* begin to
become both libraries and places where famous scholars lectured.
While such distinguished philosophers as Chu Hsi made *shu-yüan*
famous, less than fifty such academies are known to have existed
from the eleventh century to the end of the Southern Sung in 1279.[73]
Probably owing to the negligence of the Mongol Yüan government
in educational affairs, Chinese scholars and officials established
additional private academies in the Yüan period (1260–1368). From
various sources a modern student is able to list 390 old and new
academies that were maintained or created in fourteen provinces
during Yüan times.[74]

Although cases of early Ming officials who restored old academies or set up new ones are known,[75] private academies in general suffered a temporary setback. This may be accounted for partly by the much-expanded state school facilities and partly by the high-handed measures by which early Ming emperors exacted strict ideological conformity from officials. The intellectual atmosphere in early Ming times was hardly conducive to the free philosophical inquiry that had characterized Sung and Yüan academies. By the late fifteenth century many old academies had become dilapidated and requests for the establishment of new ones were often rejected by the imperial government.[76]

Shortly after 1500, however, a powerful movement toward intellectual emancipation was inaugurated by the statesman and general Wang Shou-jen, commonly known as Wang Yang-ming (1472–1529), the most creative philosopher since Chu Hsi (1130–1200), the synthesizer of traditional Chinese thought. Wang's emphasis on intuitive knowledge and on the unity of knowledge and conduct, in sharp contrast to Chu Hsi's stress on prolonged bookish study and social *status quo*, fired the nation with new intellectual enthusiasm.[77] While a systematic appraisal of the influence of Wang's teachings lies outside the sphere of the present study, it is necessary to point out briefly the revolutionary character of his philosophical battle cry and its social consequence.

Since the core of his philosophical system is his theory of intuitive knowledge which is latent within everbody, it implies, and was made much more explicit by some of his disciples, that potentially everybody could achieve enlightenment and reach sagehood. The historic significance of his doctrine is well pointed out by one of his second-academic-generation disciples:

In ancient times peasants, artisans, tradesmen, and merchants, though holding different occupations, all had the right to education. Among some three thousand disciples of Confucius those who mastered the six disciplines numbered only seventy-two; all the rest were but ignorant, vulgar people. After the proscription of learning by the Ch'in and the rise of the Han, the so-called learning was handed down from generation to generation by those who could memorize ancient classics and hence became the exclusive property of classicists and erudites. The true teachings of ancient sages, which originally could be understood and shared by all men, have thus fallen into complete oblivion. As if by Heaven's will our Master was born and arose from the eastern seashore. His largeness of mind led to his unique enlightenment, which follows straightly the teachings of Confucius and Mencius and which strikes directly at everybody's heart. Thenceforth even the untutored, common, illiterate people all know that from one's own nature and intelligence one can achieve intellectual self-sufficiency, which depends on neither oral nor visual instruction. The message that had failed to be transmitted for two thousand years has again been made comprehensible overnight.[78]

While like all traditional philosophers Wang and his disciples had to justify their central doctrine by harking back to the much-idealized antiquity and by attributing it to Confucius, actually Wang's message of the intrinsic equality of all men was truly revolutionary.

Since Wang insisted on the importance of the unity of knowledge and action, his numerous followers and admirers went on to establish private academies and to give public lectures which were open to high and low alike. Wang Ken (1483–1541), in particular, the son of a poor salt producer of T'ai-chou in Kiangsu, became the leader of the radical wing of the Wang Yang-ming school by sheer genius and force of character. He and his second son carried the intellectual torch to the masses. Here and there in Kiangsu and Anhwei, where this radical wing flourished, we find agricultural tenants, firewood gatherers, potters, brick burners, stone masons, and men from other humble walks of life attending public lectures and chanting classics. Not a few of these humble men eventually became famous.[79] Never before and never afterward, in traditional China, were so many people willing to accept their fellow men for their intrinsic worth or did they approach more closely the true Confucian ideal that "in education there should be no class distinctions." Whatever the evil consequence of the intensified Ming autocracy, the Ming period as a whole must be regarded as one of remarkable intellectual and social emancipation.

To be sure, the conservative officials and the court were not blind to the challenge to the traditional philosophy and social order implied or explicit in Wang's teaching. Private academies and public lectures were thrice proscribed, in 1537, 1579, and 1625.[80] An imperial decree of 1538, while avoiding the mention of Wang's name, condemned his teaching as highly heterodox and harmful.[81] Fortunately, so large and influential was Wang's following that private academies survived the first half-hearted prohibition and the more severe second ban, which resulted in the dissolution of sixty-four academies in the Kiangsu area. But the most daringly nonconformist of Wang's followers, Ho Hsin-yin (1517–79) and Li Chih, commonly known as Li Cho-wu (1527–1602), died in prison.[82] By the time of the third persecution some famous academies had become so deeply involved in government factional strife that they openly courted disaster. Although toward the end of the Ming period the intellectual and social forces unleashed by the doctrine of intuitive knowledge had spent themselves, private academies had already fulfilled their mission and left a permanent imprint on the nation's educational systems.

After a respite of more than half a century private academies once more flourished in Ch'ing times, but their goals and curricula underwent a drastic change. Whereas Ming academies were concerned primarily with philosophical discourses and only accidentally with preparation for examinations, those of the Ch'ing period took the latter as their engrossing aim. After the accession in 1723 of the Yung-cheng emperor, who worked ruthlessly for the strict ideological conformity of the scholar-official class, the so-called private academies became in fact almost supplementary state schools. From the standpoint of social mobility, however, although Ch'ing academies lost their ideological freedom and became little more than training grounds for examination candidates, they continued to improve earlier systems of endowments and scholarships.

A modern writer has culled some 300 names of academies from various Ch'ing biographical series.[83] This total number is too far from complete to be of any use. A sampling of Ch'ing local histories shows that nearly all prefectures and counties had at one time or another one or more academies. This impression is confirmed by an excellent monograph on academies in Kwangtung Province, based on extensive study of local histories.

Such a high density of academies in a newly rising province like Kwangtung would indicate a rather wide geographic distribution of academies in the country in general, with the exception of remote backward provinces. The breakdowns also reveal the official and semiofficial nature of the majority of academies, although

TABLE 23

KWANGTUNG ACADEMIES ESTABLISHED IN CH'ING TIMES

| Period | Academies set up under official initiative | Academies set up under private effort | Total |
|---|---|---|---|
| 1662–1722 | 69 | 12 | 81 |
| 1723–1735 | 20 | 0 | 20 |
| 1736–1795 | 82 | 21 | 103 |
| 1796–1820 | 31 | 20 | 51 |
| 1821–1850 | 24 | 22 | 46 |
| 1851–1861 | 4 | 24 | 28 |
| 1862–1874 | 14 | 17 | 31 |
| 1875–1908 | 14 | 37 | 51 |
| Total | 258 | 153 | 411 |

Source: Liu Po-chi, *Kuang-tung shu-yüan chih-tu yen-ke* (Shanghai, 1937), pp. 46–79.

after the outbreak of the Taiping rebellion in 1851 official initiative slackened and private effort increased.

The success and duration of academies depended on management and size of endowments. Generally speaking, the tendency was for endowments to grow through periodic donations by the local rich or by officials. Yü-lu Academy in the capital city Ch'ang-sha of Hunan, which dates back to the eleventh century, had a modest endowment of 1,824 *mu* of land up to 1539, which steadily expanded afterwards.[84] The famous Po-lu-tung Academy in the scenic Lu-shan in lakeside Kiangsi, where once the great master Chu Hsi served as director, had in 1673 an endowment of 3,851 *mu* in four neighboring counties.[85] Though substantial, these endowments were dwarfed by those of later institutions. Wei-ching Academy, for example, the largest in Shensi, after 1870 had an enlarged endowment of more than 17,000 taels which enabled it to build up a library of over 10,000 *chüan* and to offer bursaries to students ranging from one-half tael to two taels monthly.[86] Ming-tao Academy in the capital city of K'ai-feng of Honan, which also had a long history going back to the eleventh century, had laid down an ingenious rule for raising funds which provided that an alumnus who later became an official should on each appointment or promotion contribute between 40 and 1,000 taels. Although the sum total of its endowments is unknown, it must have been fairly large because the academy was able to give each student on the main roster four taels and each one on the supplementary roster two taels a month.[87] Ho-shuo Academy in Wu-chih in Honan, which served three prefectures, had in the second quarter of the nineteenth century an endowment as high as 24,700 taels.[88]

Academies which served strictly local purposes also varied greatly in resources. An-ting Academy of Yang-chou, a school exclusively for children of salt merchants, had an ample endowment of 7,400 taels after 1733 which enabled it to offer to each student a stipend of 3 taels a month.[89] Lung-hu Academy in K'un-yang in remote Yunnan, on the other hand, had an endowment of but 244 *mu* of paddies.[90] Library resources ranged from 60,000 *chüan* for Hsüeh-ku-t'ang Academy in Su-chou to a handful of basic classics, a few dynastic histories, and some scattered literary works for Yün-shan Academy of Ning-hsiang county in a relatively isolated part of Hunan.[91]

Scholarship provisions were no less varied. The majority offered monthly stipends ranging from 3 or 4 taels to one-half tael to *sheng-yüan* as well as to younger students who aspired to take the first examination. Some offered in addition monthly stipends to more advanced students, such as *kung-sheng* and *chü-jen*. Since the aims of Ch'ing academies were highly utilitarian, the admission of more advanced students became a more common practice in later Ch'ing times. The majority of the academies also offered subsidies to those students who took their provincial or metropolitan examinations. From the late eighteenth century onward, nineteen larger Kwangtung academies worked out elaborate subsidy systems to enable students to take higher examinations.[92] Academies located in cities where Bannermen were garrisoned usually set up a special scholarship quota for their children because most of the rank and file had been subjected to so long a process of economic leveling that they needed financial help for their children's schooling.[93]

The effect of Ch'ing academies on social mobility must have been considerable, although a systematic statistical statement is impossible because of the lack of student rosters and information as to the ancestry of students. Even granted that not all students of academies were actually poor, still there is little reason to doubt the important social and educational functions that the academies served. In a culturally advanced area like Chen-chiang in southern Kiangsu, for example, the well-endowed Pao-chin Academy was able to produce between 1767 and 1880 as many as 69 *chin-shih* and 262 *chü-jen*.[94] In the culturally relatively backward Shensi the Wei-ching Academy produced within the short span of twenty years, between 1874 and 1894, no less than 18 *chin-shih* and 76 *chü-jen*.[95] It would not be an exaggeration to say that, in a period in which county and prefectural schools were scholastically listless and became little more than distributors of government student stipends, academies did much to make up deficiencies in educational facilities. While the number of scholarships offered by a small academy may have been a mere 10, the number offered by the majority may have been 40 or more, which roughly equaled or somewhat exceeded the total *ling-sheng* quota of a state school. For the province of Kwangtung the number of scholarships offered by various academies ranged from 10 to 320 with a mathematical mean of 80,[96] which may have been somewhat higher than the national average.

It should be pointed out in passing that in spite of the strict ideological conformity required of the academies by the Ch'ing government some academies by avoiding philosophical studies became famous centers of scholarly research. The Ku-ching-ching-she at Hang-chou, for example, established by the great scholar and official Juan Yüan (1764–1849) in 1801, produced a galaxy of scholars of national renown. Its scholarly tradition was kept up under the thirty-one-year directorship of the famous scholar Yü Yüeh (1821–1907). As Juan Yüan moved south to serve as governor general of Kwangtung and Kwangsi, he set up in Canton in 1820 another academy called Hsüeh-hai-t'ang, which soon embarked upon large-scale printing. Up to the late nineteenth century it boasted of collected literary and scholarly works by its alumni in four series totaling 90 *chüan*. The new Kuang-ya Academy in Canton set up by Chang Chih-tung in 1887 rivaled the Hsüeh-hai-t'ang in scholarly reputation and printing zeal.[97]

### SUNDRY COMMUNITY AIDS FOR EXAMINATION CANDIDATES

Further to supplement the formal educational channels, various localities offered sundry financial aids to examination candidates.

The most noteworthy was the system of local community chests for the express purpose of subsidizing native sons who had to travel to the provincial or national capital to take higher examinations. It is difficult to say precisely when and where this community chest system made its earliest appearance. So far as Sung sources show, in 1184 a provincial official had initiated it in fourteen localities in Hupei. By the first half of the thirteenth century community chests were fairly common in such Yangtze provinces as Hupei, Hunan, Chekiang, Kiangsu, and especially Kiangsi.[98] In the collected works of the statesman and patriot-martyr Wen T'ien-hsiang (1232–82), a native of Chi-shui County in the culturally advanced Chi-chou (in Ming-Ch'ing times Chi-an) Prefecture in central Kiangsi, we find two fairly detailed accounts of the founding and management of community chests. In his native Chi-chou the community chest was first established under the leadership of Hu-Kuei, a prominent native son and president of a central board, in the early thirteenth century. The chest was called *kung-shih-chuang*, which literally means the "estate for candidates qualified for metropolitan examination." It began with a modest capital of 2,200 bushels of rice. When Yeh Meng-ting (d. 1278) served between 1151 and 1153 as commissioner in charge of public granaries and sundry economic matters of Kiangsi and concurrently as prefect of Chi-chou, he secured an additional 600 bushels of rice for the chest. Through successive donations and official efforts the chest was increased to 6,100 bushels by 1272. The administration of the chest was entrusted to the prefectural school of Chi-chou.[99]

Wen also described the existence of similar chests in the capital and county cities of the neighboring Chien-ch'ang military circuit (in Ming-Ch'ing times Chien-ch'ang Prefecture). Community chests in this area served a wider purpose in that they gave aid not only to those who were qualified for the metropolitan examination but also to those who sought such a qualification at the provincial examination. Donations were made in rice and cash, kept in abandoned temples. After several decades' experimentation these localities converted everything they received for the chests into land in the hope that funds might not be depleted. Chests in these localities were called more figuratively *ch'ing-yün-chuang,* that is, "estates" by which scholars might rise toward the clouds in the blue sky.[100]

After making an auspicious start during the late twelfth and early thirteenth centuries, however, the community chest system suffered a setback during the Mongol Yüan and Ming periods. Under the Mongols the competitive examinations were first suspended and then sporadically revived. Some officials of the Yangtze provinces repeatedly sent memorials to the throne suggesting that landed properties originally belonging to various local community chests be appropriated by the state. These proposals were eventually approved by the imperial Yüan government in 1288 and 1292. The subsequent Ming government was in general unsympathetic toward officials' requests that community chests be reinstituted in the south, because from 1384 onward the Ming government provided free transportation, board, and pocket money for all candidates qualified for the metropolitan examination. This provision made it unnecessary in theory for various southern localities to reestablish community chests.[101]

Despite all this, however, some Kiangsi localities reestablished community chests out of communal effort. For example, throughout Ming times the community chest, under the name *chin-shih-chuang,* was well maintained in Fu-liang County, which was internationally famous for its porcelain-making borough Ching-te-chen.[102] As will be further discussed in chapter VI, the existence of community chests in a number of Kiangsi localities may have been a minor but not insignificant reason for the province's exceptional academic success during the first half of the Ming period.

The comparative scarcity of Ming local histories in North America makes it difficult to trace systematically changes in the community chest system in Ming times. It may be surmised from Ch'ing accounts, however, that local chests depended on sustained interest and periodic donations and that they existed probably only in localities of above average resources and academic success. Wherever the available funds were limited, the locality paid primary attention to the struggling *sheng-yüan* who hoped to establish themselves by passing the provincial examination. In Shao-yang County in Hunan, for instance, the community chest dates back to 1639, when officials converted surplus public grain into land from which funds were drawn triennially to subsidize *sheng-yüan*'s participation in provincial examinations. In the 1730s the chest was entrusted to a local academy which annually deducted 11 taels as fee for management, while the rest of the proceeds went to subsidize the candidates. Owing to the academy's shortage of funds and poor management, the chest became gradually depleted. Then in the 1820s a magistrate, after studying early precedents, again converted surplus public grain into 1,000 taels to be invested in a local pawnshop. After paying the customary high interest rates for a number of years, the pawnshop dodged its contractual obligation and a long series of litigations ensued. The chest was not stabilized and expanded until after 1850. The case of the Shao-yang community chest may have been typical of those of many localities. But the editor of the 1875 edition of the county's history remarked that the enhanced chest was one of the factors contributing to the locality's increasing academic success in the past two decades.[103]

In wealthier areas community chests were more amply provided. Hsiu-ning and Chi-hsi Counties in the actively trading Hui-chou prefecture, for example, each had a chest permanently endowed with 5,000 taels for helping *sheng-yüan* to take provincial examinations, at least from the early nineteenth century onward.[104] Ho-fei County in northern Anhwei, Ch'ang-te Prefecture in northwestern Hunan, and Chi-mo County in eastern Shantung were other communities which were concerned exclusively with offering aid to the struggling *sheng-yüan*.[105] That many localities used their chests to help *sheng-yüan* to attain their second degree may probably be accounted for by the fact that the *chü-jen* degree was crucial in social stratification and that anybody who became an "established man" would have less difficulty in securing further financial aid for undertaking the metropolitan examination through means other than the community chest. Since after the founding of the Ming *chü-jen* had become a formal degree and qualification for minor office, it was natural for the majority of Ming-Ch'ing local community chests to shift their emphasis from helping to produce *chin-shih* to aiding native sons to attain their vital second degree.

In the course of time many localities worked out rather comprehensive community chest schemes. The rich city of Canton, for example, had ample funds to subsidize both *sheng-yüan* and *chü-jen*. Since the locality is very far from Peking, by far the greater part of the chest was allocated for *chü-jen,* the total endowment for which amounted to more than 20,000 taels in the third quarter of the nineteenth century.[106] From the late eighteenth century onward, Lan-hsi County, in the heart of Chekiang, worked out one of the most complete, though not really ample, systems of subsidies. In addition to giving aid to *sheng-yüan* who took their provincial examination at Hang-chou and to *chü-jen* who had to seek their third degree in Peking, a certain portion of the chest was permanently earmarked for subsidizing *sheng-yüan* taking their routine periodic tests at the prefectural city of Chin-hua. Candidates for the second and third military degrees were given smaller subsidies.[107] Sometimes a locality was so much more concerned with social justice than with social strategy that it spread its limited chest resources thin over various categories of degree holders.[108]

Perhaps the most elaborate chest provisions were worked out by Lu-ling County in Kiangsi in the nineteenth century. Although the locality's astounding academic success during Southern Sung and early Ming times was now but a memory, it provided separate community chests for *chü-jen, sheng-yüan,* and *ling-sheng,* and also for local literary societies which had been created in Ming times as an additional means of improving the *sheng-yüan's* skill in writing examination essays.[109] While it is true that even relatively late in the Ch'ing period not all localities had a community chest system, in a substantial number of localities where it existed and was well maintained it cannot have failed to have some effect on social mobility.

It should be mentioned in passing that while most places maintained a single chest, usually administered by the largest local academy, a number of localities had in addition small separate chests managed by charitable schools of certain villages or boroughs. Ch'eng-hsien in Shao-hsing Prefecture in Chekiang and Chi-chou in Hupei were examples.[110]

In addition to community chests, at least from the early sixteenth century on there gradually arose the custom for various provinces, large prefectures, sometimes even counties, to establish in the nation's capital *hui-kuan,* or hostels for native sons who came to Peking to take the metropolitan examination. Etymologically, therefore, the name *hui-kuan* is derived from *hui-shih* (metropolitan examination). From the richly documented history of Fukien hostels in Peking we learn that as early as the Cheng-te period (1506–21) the hostel of Fu-chou Prefecture accommodated not only candidates from home districts but also native officials in need of temporary lodging in the national capital.[111] Before the end of the Ming period all prefectures of Fukien except one had established their hostels in Peking. From the beginning of Ch'ing times to 1760 no fewer than eight Fukien counties maintained their own separate *hui-kuan* in the capital city.[112] There is reason to believe that Kiangsi, a pioneering province in community chests, cannot have set up its hostels in Peking later than did Fukien. As the statesman and prime minister Chu Shih (1665–1736) testified, the province and its various prefectures had established many such hostels in Peking in Ming times and even his native county Kao-an alone had two, which gradually became dilapidated and eventually were consolidated in 1723.[113] Shen Te-fu, a native of Chia-hsing in Chekiang, was impressed by the number of *hui-kuan* in Peking during the late sixteenth century.[114] Some northern provinces near Peking, however, may have established their *hui-kuan* somewhat later than the remote southern provinces. Shansi, for example, did not have a hostel for examination candidates until late in the seventeenth century, although its enterprising merchants had set up their guildhalls in Peking earlier.[115] It may be fairly safe to say, in the light of our knowledge of modern Peking, that all provinces, many large prefectures, and a certain number of large counties maintained their *hui-kuan* in Ch'ing times, although it is often difficult to ascertain the precise dates of their founding.

One interesting feature is that these hostels originally excluded native merchants who resided in Peking. Some late-established *hui-kuan,* like that of Pao-ch'ing Prefecture of Hunan, still abided by the early customs.[116] However, as interregional merchants were usually men of means, the hostel in Hui-chou, for one, allowed native merchants to utilize its facilities almost right from its inception in the sixteenth century. In Ch'ing times native merchants contributed funds for its maintenance periodically.[117] It is known that a rich tobacco merchant set up in 1772 single-handed a *hui-kuan* for his native Lung-yen County of southern inland Fukien.[118] While reestablishing the Kao-an *hui-kuan* in 1723 native merchants contributed so substantially that they were entitled to various hostel facilities including the right to set up a store there to display their goods.[119] It is common knowledge that with the passage of time most of the Peking hostels lost their social discrimination.[120] The fact that prefectures and counties maintained their hostels in provincial capitals to accommodate their *sheng-yüan* is too well known to need any elaboration.

To sum up, while neither the community chest system nor the *hui-kuan* was a major factor in promoting an area's social mobility, their very existence in Ming-Ch'ing times reflects the more important psychological fact that in securing academic success and social prominence local communities in general left almost no stone unturned.

THE CLAN SYSTEM

Unlike the family or extended family, which constituted a true unit of common consumption and which by virtue of division of inheritance tended in the long run to be an economic leveling factor, the clan or "common descent group" with its permanent common property and welfare provisions often turned out to be a not insignificant factor in promoting the upward social mobility of poor kin.[121] Thanks to the existence of some useful modern studies,[122] the organization of the traditional Chinese clan and its various functions need no detailed discussion.

As is well known, the clan system in its modern form was organized after certain famous Sung models, particularly after the one established by the statesman Fan Chung-yen (989–1052) in 1050, subsequently revised by his descendants and universally hailed by contemporaries and later rulers, officials, and scholars.[123] For our purpose a salient feature is that although Fan originally was concerned exclusively with the sustenance and relief of poor kin, one of his sons added in 1073 provisions dealing with common clan education and financial aid to kin who took examinations. In an age when examinations became the most effective avenue to prominence the importance of education in a clan's welfare program was widely appreciated. The Southern Sung writer on family affairs, Yüan Ts'ai, for example, went so far as to suggest the substitution for general clan welfare provisions of those dealing exclusively with education. The main reasons he gave were that while the former were likely to generate a sense of dependence on the part of laggards among kin, the latter would secure greater social reward for the clan as a whole.[124] After the late eleventh century and through the Southern Sung and Yüan periods, therefore, larger and more resourceful clans usually set aside certain portions of their land as permanent endowments for clan charitable schools or for subsidizing kinsmen's examination travels.[125] In the remote and still substantially aboriginal Yunnan province in the 1730s, for example, more than 30,000 clan charitable schools were formally registered with the provincial and local authorities.[126]

The utilization of a substantial number of Ch'ing genealogies makes it possible for a modern writer to make a quantitative statement as to the availability of educational awards and of assistance systems among clans. Of a total of seventy-five late Ch'ing and early Republican clan rules analyzed, most of which were probably a continuation of older ones, fifty contained such provisions. Speaking generally, "reward connected with clan prestige is valued considerably higher than relief of members in need."[127] Thus kinsmen who passed the first, second, or third examinations were usually given at least a token monetary reward. Those who had to travel to take their provincial or metropolitan examinations had their expenses partially or entirely paid out of common clan coffers. Young aspirants to the first degree were either allowed to study free within the existing clan institutional framework or given aid to study elsewhere. Some resourceful clan schools, like those of the rich silk-producing borough of Nan-hsün in Hu-chou in northwestern Chekiang, had permanent funds ranging from 25,000 to over 40,000 taels.[128]

This being the fairly common practice, an informant of a modern study had the expenses of his whole education paid out of funds of the ancestral hall instituted by his grandfather.[129] Professor Franklin L. Ho of Columbia University has kindly permitted me to cite his case as an example of clan aid to education. A native of Shao-yang in Hunan, he finished the elementary grades at the school established by his own branch of the clan. Then he studied for a while in the main charitable school of the entire clan. Between 1907 and 1909 he was given by the clan authorities an annual subsidy of fifty silver dollars so that he could study in the high school set up by people of Shao-yang in the provincial capital city Ch'ang-sha. Even his subsequent education at Yale in China in Ch'ang-sha and his travel to Pomona College in California were defrayed in part out of common clan funds.

In spite of these examples, the effect of the traditional clan system on upward social mobility should not be exaggerated. For one thing, the clan system was never uniformly well developed or evenly distributed geographically. It is well known that the clan system was most highly developed in the two southernmost coastal provinces of Fukien and Kwangtung, well organized and widely distributed in the lower and central Yangtze provinces, somewhat underdeveloped and thinly distributed in a number of northern provinces.[130] In areas where the clan system was underdeveloped or the clans were small in number the poor could have no access to education through such clan institutions as those described above. Second, educational facilities and examination subsidies instituted by clans were not always adequate but were likely to benefit those whose families' economic standing was above average.[131] On the other hand, the clan system as a channel for social mobility should not be minimized. In the first place, even in cases where a clan's educational facilities were limited, priority was usually given to orphans and poor members.[132] Moreover, the fact that a clan did not have permanent institutionalized schools does not necessarily indicate that financial assistance to poor kinsmen for educational purposes did not exist. Throughout the Sung and subsequent periods the influence of Neo-Confucian teaching which extolled the virtue of looking after poor kinsmen and relatives was very potent. With the decline of community schools from late Ming times onward families which could afford to hire private tutors often opened their family schools to poor, struggling, intelligent, and ambitious kinsmen. Not a few prominent Ming-Ch'ing people who did not have the benefit of institutionalized clan schools owed their early education to kinsmen's private schools. The example of Hsü Kuo (1527–96), who eventually became a prime minister, is given in the Appendix, case 5. In this connection it may be said that the role played by such personal factors as sympathetic relatives, friends, neighbors, and patrons in promoting the upward mobility of the poor who possessed intelligence and determination may have been no less significant than that of institutionalized clan educational facilities.

PRINTING

Block printing was first developed in the early half of the eighth century, chiefly in Buddhist monasteries.[133] But the technique of printing and the supply of books did not become significant until Sung times. While in terms of quality and aesthetic appeal Sung editions are unsurpassed, really large-scale printing had to await the mid-Ming period. As has been repeatedly mentioned, the Ming founder took a keen interest in education. As early as 1368 a statute provided that all books be exempt from taxes. He twice issued orders that basic Confucian classics be distributed freely by the government to northern provinces where books were not easily available. The Imperial Academy at Nanking, where the imperial Yüan library collection was deposited, was instructed to collate the missing pages and chapters in certain old works as a preparation for reproduction.[134] In 1417 the government gave every prefecture and county in the country sets of four basic Confucian texts, five classics, and some fundamental works on the Sung Rationalist school of philosophy, which was made the orthodox philosophy by the state. Emperors of the early fifteenth century expressed a sustained interest in building up the imperial collection. But printing facilities still remained limited, as may be evidenced by the fact that of some 20,000 titles totalling nearly 1,000,000 *chüan* in the imperial collection only three tenths were printed works, the rest being manuscripts.[135]

The general peace, government retrenchment, economic recovery, the gradual rise of bibliophiles, and especially the tremendous increase in state school enrollments and the ever-increasing importance of the examination system could not in the long run fail to stimulate the art of printing. By the Chia-ching period (1522–66) the Imperial Academy in Nanking undertook among other things the task of printing the *Thirteen Classics* and *Twenty-one Dynastic Histories* to meet the growing demand for basic texts and references. After the first printing blocks were destroyed by fire, new blocks were completed between 1586 and 1596. These large-scale reproductions of gigantic basic works did much to disseminate knowledge and made books available to many localities. Although the Imperial Academy in Peking was not nearly as important a center of printing as that in Nanking, it nevertheless paid primary attention to these basic voluminous works which were independently printed and widely distributed. The Ssu-li-chien or Supervisorate of Ceremonies, the Boards of Rites, War, and Public Works, the Censorate, the Imperial Bureau of Astronomy, the Imperial Bureau of Physicians, and not a few provincial authorities all embarked upon some printing, although most of the works they printed were of a more technical nature.[136]

The real initiative and progress in the technique of printing which made the mid-Ming period famous were due to private individuals. Hua Sui (1439–1513) and his descendants, of Wu-hsi in southern Kiangsu, were important pioneers in the use of copper movable type. Among the large number of titles they printed were some highly useful literary encyclopedias. If the very rich An Kuo (1481–1534) of the same district printed fewer titles than his close rivals, the books he printed were famous for their outstanding quality. It is interesting to note that the prime minister and bibliophile Wang Ao's eldest son, Wang Yen-che, was one of the pioneers in the art of reproducing earlier rare editions in facsimile. Mao Chin (1599–1659) of Ch'ang-shu in southern Kiangsu printed during his lifetime as many as 600 titles including the much demanded *Thirteen Classics* and *Seventeen Dynastic Histories*.[137]

The leading centers of printing in Ming times were Nanking, Hang-chou, Hui-chou, Peking, and Chien-yang in northern hilly

Fukien, where bamboo and other kinds of fiber abounded. Quantitatively speaking, Chien-yang played a particularly important role in the dissemination of inexpensive editions of fundamental works.[138] Characteristic of the time, the strictly utilitarian publications of successful examination essays began to find an insatiable market from about the middle of the sixteenth century onward.[139] By late Ming times not only were basic texts and references readily available to the nation but repeated reproductions of early rare and often voluminous works greatly broadened scholars' intellectual horizons.

After a respite of more than half a century, because of large-scale peasant rebellions and the Manchu wars of conquest, printing facilities once more expanded. While the Ch'ing period is not particularly noted for the quality of its printed books, there can be little doubt that books were more plentiful and more inexpensive than ever. Various government agencies, officials, great bibliophiles, and large private academies all undertook large-scale printing. It seems more than coincidental that the age of great bibliophiles and printers was concurrent with the age of great research scholars for which the mid-Ch'ing period is famous. Indeed, the zeal for printing and the multiplication of books in Ch'ing times are so well known that the generalization made by the late Professor Giles that up to about 1750 China had printed more books than probably the rest of the world put together has yet to be challenged.[140]

While it is obvious that the development of the Ming-Ch'ing printing presses helped immensely to disseminate knowledge among the relatively poor and humble, its precise effect on their social mobility cannot easily be gauged. On one hand, the early emphasis of government and private printing presses on reproducing large numbers of basic texts, classics, and reference books would seem to better the chances of men of humble circumstances to master minimal examination curricula and hence to help them to ascend socially. On the other hand, later reproductions of vast numbers of specialized and expensive works, which were beyond the reach of the poor, would seem rather to help the well to do to achieve higher scholastic standards. In the early sixteenth century when printing facilities began to expand, the unusually observant scholar and retired official Lu Yung already deplored that poor studious scholars and people outside large urban centers had little means of getting hold of more specialized and expensive works.[141] It is true that the successful upward mobility of the poor depended on a combination of factors of which the general cultural advancement brought about by the printing press was but one. But the coincidence that soon after the rise of great private libraries in the sixteenth century men of humble circumstances found it increasingly hard to compete successfully against members of official families in higher examinations is worth observing. Our available *chin-shih, chü-jen,* and *kung-sheng* lists of the eighteenth century would suggest that in this age of great bibliophiles the poor and humble had probably the lowest ratios of academic success. If the continued multiplication of books partially accounted for the increasing educational disparity between the rich and the poor, it probably facilitated the initial stages of social mobility of the latter and the eventual success of the unusually gifted and determined among them.

WARS AND SOCIAL UPHEAVALS

The more systematic data available for this study deal exclusively with social mobility under normal peaceful circumstances. Wars and social upheavals, though not frequent during the Ming-Ch'ing period, seem to have brought about more drastic social mobility. While the lack of systematic data of a cross-sectional nature makes it impossible to study the more drastic types of social mobility quantitatively, a few general observations should be made.

The widespread revolts against the Mongol Yüan dynasty and the prolonged turmoil during the third quarter of the fourteenth century could not fail to have an important bearing on social mobility. As is well known, the Ming founder Chu Yüan-chang himself was the son of a poor peasant. In his teens he was further impoverished by famine, epidemics, and deaths in the family. He was so poor that he had to seek survival by becoming a Buddhist novice. Continued famine forced him to join a group of rebels which consisted mostly of hungry peasants, bandits, vagabonds, and men of humble walks of life. There can be little doubt about the lowly social origins of his band which called itself the "Red Army."

It was his political genius and sagacity that enabled him later on to enlist the support of some minor Yüan officials, government clerks, scholars, and powerful landlords as well. By the time he enthroned himself in Nanking in 1368 the original "proletarian" character of his revolution had been transformed beyond recognition.[142] The extremely wide range of social statuses from which his officials and generals originated would seem to suggest that the amount and degree of social mobility represented among them were unprecedented since the founding of the Han dynasty in 206 B.C.[143]

So drastic was the change in the social order and so great the task of re-creating a ruling class that for several decades after the founding of the Ming dynasty both the amount and the degree of social mobility remained abnormally great. Our data on the social composition of early Ming *chin-shih* tell only a partial story. In fact, it is probable that a great amount of mobility was brought about through channels other than the examination system. From the very beginning the Ming founder repeatedly issued orders that men of merit be recommended by central and provincial officials for government service, with almost no consideration to be given the social status of the recommended. In 1380, for example, some 860 persons were recommended and invested with office, a number which was equivalent to the aggregate of several *chin-shih* examinations.[144] Although the number of recommended men never again reached this height, it is likely that during the early Ming period their total number exceeded that of those recruited by examination. These new officials were recommended for their learning, literary skill, or personal integrity, or were the rich men and highest tax-payers of certain localities, village elders, local-government clerks, filial sons, Taoist and Buddhist monks, apothecaries, geomancers, fortunetellers, carpenters, stonemasons, cooks, etc. Many of them eventually reached high office.[145] Strangest of all, even a poor young man who requested an office in order to support his mother was immediately rewarded with one.[146]

Even larger numbers of students of the Imperial Academy were recruited into the government without having to attain higher degrees. Although these students were probably socially more homogeneous than the specially recommended men, yet substantial numbers of them might well have originated from families of scholastic tradition but humble economic circumstances. From 1369 onward they were appointed to responsible provincial and local posts and as middle-ranking central officials. In 1368 and 1391, respectively, for example, over 1,000 and 639 students were given offices.[147] Smaller numbers of Imperial Academy students and specially recommended men continued to enter government service until the second quarter of the fifteenth century, when government offices were saturated and the examination system began to become the most important institutionalized channel for bureaucratic recruitment. Not until then did the most unusual chapter of social mobility come to an end. The effect of the great social upheaval that had resulted in the establishment of the Ming dynasty thus lingered for nearly three quarters of a century.

The change of dynasty in 1644 failed to bring about a chapter of social mobility similar to that of the early Ming period. For one thing, the large groups of rebellious peasants who overthrew the Ming dynasty were soon crushed by the invading Manchus. They left no permanent mark on Chinese society in general. Moreover, the early Manchu rulers realized that they were aliens whose prolonged and successful rule depended mainly on the support of the most influential of the Chinese social classes. Every effort therefore was made to secure the services of those Chinese who had established themselves officially, socially, and academically before the change of dynasty.[148] The old social order remained intact.

In spite of the continuity in the social order, the Manchu war of conquest and the campaigns against southern feudatories, Ming loyalists in Formosa, and soon afterwards the southwestern aborigines, enabled a number of men of humble birth to move up the social ladder. Several chapters in *Kuo-ch'ao chi-hsien lei-chang*, the largest collection of Ch'ing biographies and epitaphs, deal with early Ch'ing generals and officers. While the criteria for inclusion in its gigantic biographical series leave much to be desired, such chapters are full of instances of successful careers originating from obscurity. A few examples will suffice. Ma Wei-hsing, who eventually became a *tsung-ping* (brigade general, rank 2a), had been a bandit during his early manhood. He was so poor and illiterate that he did not even know his parents' names. Ch'en Eng and Lin Liang, who also reached high military posts, were originally poor orphans of coastal Ch'üan-chou in southern Fukien. After drifting aimlessly for years they joined the Manchu marine forces as privates. Scores of late-seventeenth century generals started their careers as army privates.[149]

In later internal campaigns similar cases occurred. One of the most famous was that of Lo Ssu-chü, a highwayman, repeated jail-breaker in his early manhood, and even a onetime cannibal, who rose to prominence during the campaigns against the rebellious White Lotus Sect between 1796 and 1802.[150] Indeed, it may be conjectured that even in peacetime the army was seldom shut against the poor, for military examinations stressed only physical prowess and the required written tests were a mere formality and sometimes nothing but a joke.[151]

More is known about the effect of the Taiping rebellion (1851–64) on social mobility. Excluding Tseng Kuo-fan, the commander in chief of the Hunan Braves, who were instrumental in putting down the rebellion, there are 182 persons associated with this army who have left biographical records. Of these 182, 2 reached the highest office of grand secretary and were ennobled as marquises; 25 became governors general and governors; 17 became financial and judicial commissioners; 5 attained the same ranks but were not invested with office; 37 became *t'i-tu* (commanding general of provincial forces, rank 1b) and *tsung-ping*; 10 attained the same ranks without actually holding such posts. Of the rest all except a handful reached middle ranks in civil and military service. Their statuses on the eve of their joining the government forces are given in the following table.

Thus 64 percent of the total did not even have the elementary degree. Of them Pao Ch'ao, for example, who eventually became a *t'i-tu*, had been so indigent while young that before joining the army he had attempted suicide to end his miserable life. Among scores of others who rose to prominence but were not associated with the Hunan Braves, Chang Chia-hsiang had been a bandit before he eventually became a *t'i-tu*, Huang I-sheng had been a

TABLE 24

INITIAL STATUSES OF PROMINENT
MEMBERS OF HUNAN BRAVES

| *Initial status* | *Number* |
|---|---|
| *Chin-shih* | 8 |
| Military *chin-shih* | 1 |
| *Chü-jen* | 10 |
| Military *chü-jen* | 3 |
| *Kung-sheng* | 7 |
| *Sheng-yüan* and *chien-sheng* | 31 |
| Minor military officer | 5 |
| Without any degree | 117 |
| Total | 182 |

Source: Lo Erh-kang, *Hsiang-chün hsin-chih* (Shanghai, 1939), table on pp. 55–62.

repairer of boilers and peddler of firecrackers before he finally became a provincial commanding general, and Liu Ming-ch'uan had been a salt smuggler before he became governor of Fukien and Formosa.[152]

DEMOGRAPHIC AND ECONOMIC FACTORS

The growth of population during Ming-Ch'ing times and the various factors which contributed to such a manifold growth have already been discussed in my recent book.[153] Brief mention of the correlation between population changes and mobility has been made earlier in this chapter and a more detailed analysis will be made in chapter VI. Only a very brief recapitulation is needed here.

Demographically, with the exception of the zigzags of the seventeenth century, which were accounted for by large-scale peasant rebellions, Manchu wars of conquest, and gradual recovery, the population of China was almost continually increasing from the late fourteenth century to 1850. The population was more than 65,000,000 at the beginning of the Ming period and probably more than doubled itself by about 1600. From the late seventeenth century onward population was growing at rates hitherto unknown. By 1800 it reached 300,000,000 and it shot up by 1850 to some 430,000,000. Other things being equal, the competition in higher examinations was bound to be progressively keener as the nation's population multiplied.

The generally ever-decreasing chances for men of humble birth to enter the ruling bureaucracy can be better understood if the demographic factor is broadly related to the changing economic factor. The Ming period as a whole was one of remarkable economic expansion. The extension of the frontier of rice culture, the commercialization of farming in many areas, the rise of cotton textiles as a nationwide rural industry, the growth of industries and crafts, the development of domestic and international trade, the continual influx of silver from Europeans and Japanese, and the increasing commutation of labor services, all helped to make the economy more variegated than ever before. In fact, mainland Chinese historians have recently coined the term "incipient capitalism" to describe the Ming and early Ch'ing economy. In addition, the population was relatively small by modern standards and plenty of land was available. Despite the burden of taxes and labor services, the chances for the small man to climb up the social ladder seem to have been considerably better than in modern China. With certain interruptions in the seventeenth century the economy continued to grow until its gains were nullified by a still more rapid growth of the population. From the late eighteenth century onward keen observers like Hung Liang-chi (1746–1809), the so-called Chinese Malthus, Kung Tzu-chen (1792–1841), and Wang Shih-to (1802–89) all testified to an unmistakable trend of rapidly falling living standards and mounting economic strains which culminated in the Taiping rebellion, 1851–64, the most massive civil war in world history and probably the most powerful manifestation of the operation of Malthus' positive checks in the annals of men.

The civil wars of the third quarter of the nineteenth century at best conferred upon the nation a brief breathing space and failed to restore the old population-land balance. While the growth of the lower Yangtze population was definitely halted by the Taiping wars, the population of the low plain provinces of north China seems to have been increasing even faster than it had been before 1850. We may surmise that in all likelihood China's total population surpassed the 1850 peak sometime in the last quarter of the nineteenth century. The opening up of Manchuria and overseas emigration, though having regional alleviating effects, failed to bring about a more favorable population-land ratio for the nation at large.

The absence of a major technological revolution in modern times has made it impossible for China to broaden the scope of her economy to any appreciable extent. It is true that, after the opening of China in the 1840s, a moderately expanding international commerce, the beginnings of modern money and banking, the coming of steamers and railways, the establishment by both Chinese and foreigners of a number of light and extractive industries have made the Chinese economy more variegated, but these new influences have been so far confined largely to the eastern seaboard and a few inland river ports. There has not been a significant change in the basic character of the national economy. In fact, for a century after the Opium War the influence of the West on the Chinese economy was as disruptive as it was constructive. Moreover, the financial straits of the late Ch'ing central and provincial governments made large increases in surtaxes and perquisites inevitable. The people's fiscal burden was made even heavier by nationwide official peculation. All in all, therefore, the combined economic and political conditions in post-1850 China were such that the nation seems to have barely managed to feed more mouths at the expense of further deterioration of its living standard. Thus the broad changing demographic and economic factors throughout the centuries are consistent in the main with our mobility trend.

# CHAPTER VI

# REGIONAL DIFFERENCES
# IN SOCIOACADEMIC
# SUCCESS AND MOBILITY

REGIONAL differences in socioacademic success and mobility depended on a combination of factors such as population, migration, economy, cultural tradition, available institutionalized and non-institutional channels, regional *chin-shih* and *chü-jen* quotas, and the degree of permeation of the social concepts and myths which stimulated social mobility. Even in studies of contemporary societies of a limited geographic extent not all these factors can be clearly known, much less in the present study of a large historical society which covers a span of five and a half centuries. The main purpose of this chapter is therefore to present statistics on the geographic distribution of *chin-shih* and regional variations in mobility rates, while any explanations of regional and local differences attempted herein are necessarily of a tentative nature.

## POPULATION OF THE PROVINCES

Provincial population figures are basic to the study of the geographic distribution of socioacademic success and regional variations in social mobility rates. Even provincial population figures confront modern researchers with an almost insurmountable difficulty. Although long series of national and not a few sets of provincial population figures are available for the Ming-Ch'ing period, most of them deal with fiscal rather than total population. As has been systematically discussed in another study of mine, the relatively useful figures are those of the very beginning of the Ming period and those of the mid-Ch'ing period between 1776 and 1850, which by definition and in practice covered the entire population, although serious regional errors are known.[1] These few relatively useful provincial figures, together with those of the 1953 census which have some reference value, are given in the following table.

TABLE 25

OFFICIAL PROVINCIAL POPULATION FIGURES
(*in millions*)

| Province | 1393 | 1787 | 1850 | 1953 |
|---|---|---|---|---|
| Hopei[a] | 1.9 | 23.0 | 23.4 | 38.7[b] |
| Shantung | 5.3 | 22.6 | 33.1 | 48.9 |
| Honan | 1.9 | 21.0 | 23.9 | 44.2 |
| Shansi | 4.1 | 13.2 | 15.1 | 14.3 |
| Shensi & Kansu | 2.3 | 23.6 | 27.5 | 28.8 |
| Kiangsu | 6.6 | 31.4 | 44.2 | 47.5 |
| Chekiang | 10.5 | 21.7 | 30.0 | 22.9 |
| Anhwei | 4.2 | 28.9 | 37.6 | 30.3 |
| Kiangsi | 9.0 | 19.2 | 24.5 | 16.8 |
| Fukien | 3.9 | 12.0 | —[c] | 13.1 |
| Hupei | 4.7 | 19.0 | 33.7 | 27.8 |
| Hunan | | 16.2 | 20.6 | 33.2 |
| Szechwan | 1.5 | 8.6 | 44.2 | 62.3 |
| Kwangtung | 3.0 | 16.0 | 28.2 | 34.8 |
| Kwangsi | 1.5 | 6.4 | 7.8 | 19.6 |
| Yunnan | .26 | 3.5 | 7.4 | 17.5 |
| Kweichow | — | 5.2 | 5.4 | 15.0 |
| Liaoning[d] | — | .8 | 2.6 | 18.6 |

Source: Ping-ti Ho, *Studies on the Population of China, 1368–1953*, tables on p. 258 and p. 283.

[a] For simplicity its historic names of Pei-Chihli and Chihli are not used.

[b] This figure does not include the population of Peking. None of the Ch'ing figures included Peking population.

[c] It has been proved that Fukien shortly after 1800 began to compile its population figures at random. The figure of 19 million for 1850 must therefore be rejected.

[d] For simplicity its historic names of Liaotung and Fengtien are not used. It included other parts of Manchuria in the greater part of the Ming-Ch'ing period.

Our chief difficulty is the absence of relatively useful figures for the four centuries between 1393 and 1787. We know that China's population was increasing at moderate rates from early Ming times to about 1600. The seventeenth century was one of sharp fluctuations because of large-scale peasant rebellions and wars in its second and third quarters, although the tempo for a much more rapid growth of population was set after the etsablishment of domestic peace and material prosperity in 1683. The eighteenth century was one of sustained and rapid growth of population. I have hazarded the speculation that the peak Ming total population was probably in the neighborhood of 150,000,000, reached shortly after 1600, which would seem to be about one half of the total of 1787. Since neither the provincial figures of 1393 nor the peak populations at the beginning of the seventeenth century were representative of the whole Ming period, we have to work out arbitrarily the "mean" populations for various provinces as base figures for further analysis and comparison. These mean provincial population figures are obtained by averaging the 1393 figures and one half of the 1787 figures.

In the light of serious under-registration of the populations of southwestern provinces throughout the Ming-Ch'ing period, we have to revise the official figures drastically. Szechwan, in particular, had most unusual population fluctuations because the population of the fertile Red Basin was nearly exterminated during the middle decades of the seventeenth century. By 1787 its large-scale repopulation had barely begun. Our suggested figures for Yunnan and Kweichow are no doubt much too low, but they are intended to serve as very rough indicators of the Chinese population in an overwhelmingly aboriginal region. Likewise, our figure for Liaoning is also highly arbitrary, as Manchuria did not begin to be systematically colonized until the 1860s. Our reconstructed mean provincial populations for the Ming period must not be regarded as even approximately accurate; they merely serve as very rough indices without which regional differences in socioacademic success and mobility rates cannot be demonstrated.

For the Ch'ing period more figures are available. Since 1787 is practically midway between 1644 and 1911 and since its figures are of comparatively good quality, they are used as our mean provincial populations for the Ch'ing period. We have to bear in mind, however, certain complicating factors. For one thing, the total national population in 1787, being over 292,000,000, is likely to be too high

TABLE 26

MEAN MING PROVINCIAL POPULATIONS

| Province | Population (in millions) | Province | Population (in millions) |
|---|---|---|---|
| Hopei | 6.7 | Fukien | 5.0 |
| Shantung | 8.4 | Hupei[a] | 5.9 |
| Honan | 6.2 | Hunan | 5.2 |
| Shansi | 5.3 | Szechwan | 8.0[b] |
| Shensi & Kansu | 6.8 | Kwangtung | 5.5 |
| Kiangsu | 11.2 | Kwangsi | 4.4 |
| Chekiang | 10.7 | Yunnan | 2.0[b] |
| Anhwei | 9.3 | Kweichow | 2.0[b] |
| Kiangsi | 9.3 | Liaoning | 1.0[b] |

[a] It is assumed that Hupei and Hunan each had one half of the combined 1393 population.

[b] Very rough guesses which, though they are intended to indicate the Chinese populations, are likely to be considerably below the truth.

as a mean for the entire Ch'ing period. The total national population of the last pre-Taiping year of 1850, being 430,000,000, probably represented the peak Ch'ing population. We do not know the total population at the beginning of the Ch'ing, around 1650, which must have been considerably smaller than my estimated peak Ming population of 150,000,000, owing to large-scale peasant rebellions, massacres, and the Manchu wars of conquest. It is my impression that the mean Ch'ing population was probably not too far from 250,000,000. Second, the Taiping rebellion of 1851–64 brought about a drastic reduction of the populations of five Yangtze provinces which is partially reflected even in the 1953 census. As mean populations of Chekiang, Kiangsu, Anhwei, Kiangsi, and Hupei for the whole Ch'ing period, the 1787 figures for these provinces are definitely too high, although the 1787 figures for the northern provinces are probably much nearer to the truth. Since the 1787 provincial figures are the first relatively accurate ones available, no attempt will be made to modify them, in order to simplify our task, to avoid minute arbitrary revision, and to prevent exaggeration of the academic success and mobility rates of the historically advanced southeastern provinces. Third, a far more drastic change in population has taken place in Szechwan in late Ch'ing and modern times. Although its 1787 figure of 8.6 million reflected the piecemeal migrations into the province since the late seventeenth century, large-scale immigration began only in the late eighteenth century. Its population shot up to 44.2 million by 1850 and further increased to 62.3 million by 1953. Its 1787 figure is therefore much too low as the mean for the Ch'ing period; a more realistic one, we suggest, might be 20,000,000. Fourthly, under-registration remained serious in the southwest, particularly in Yunnan, where the aboriginal population was large, up to at least 1787. We prefer its 1850 figure as the mean. Lastly, granted that Manchuria was not systematically colonized until after 1860, there can be little doubt that its population figures prior to the first systematic survey officially carried out in 1908 were the most under-registered in the entire country. We make a conservative guess of 2,000,000 as its mean during the Ch'ing period. For the rest of the provinces the 1787 figures are used as denominators.

DISTRIBUTION OF ACADEMIC SUCCESS BY PROVINCES

The following three tables will deal with the geographic distribution of *chin-shih* in Ming-Ch'ing times.

Since our study covers a period of five and a half centuries, significant changes in the geographic distribution of *chin-shih* during various subperiods should be briefly explained. So far as *chin-shih* productivity irrespective of provincial population was concerned, Kiangsi led the country during the early Ming period up to 1439. It was barely nosed out by Chekiang during the period 1440–72. In the first century of the Ming period Kiangsi, Chekiang, Kiangsu, and Fukien constituted the four leaders. There are various possible explanations for the remarkable headstart of the southeastern region.

Ever since the middle of the eighth century there had been a steady shift from the north to the southeast of the demographic, economic, and cultural centers of gravity. This shift became more noticeable after north China became a theater for prolonged wars during the Five Dynasties (907–60), particularly after the fall of north China to the Juchens in 1126. The large-scale southward migration of the educated northern Chinese, the unrivaled network

TABLE 27

GEOGRAPHIC DISTRIBUTION OF *CHIN-SHIH* IN MING TIMES

| Province | 1371–1439 | 1440–1472 | 1473–1505 | 1506–1538 | 1539–1571 | 1572–1604 | 1605–1644 | Provincial total | Ranking |
|---|---|---|---|---|---|---|---|---|---|
| Hopei | 72 | 251 | 339 | 335 | 348 | 251 | 302 | 1,898 | 5 |
| Shantung | 53 | 124 | 219 | 270 | 325 | 310 | 422 | 1,723 | 6 |
| Honan | 105 | 167 | 201 | 260 | 229 | 295 | 341 | 1,598 | 7 |
| Shansi | 49 | 88 | 154 | 190 | 207 | 180 | 241 | 1,109 | 8 |
| Shensi and Kansu | 39 | 83 | 153 | 184 | 139 | 146 | 237 | 981 | 10 |
| Kiangsu | 150 | 328 | 442 | 398 | 395 | 389 | 619 | 2,721 | 2 |
| Chekiang | 290 | 363 | 488 | 532 | 561 | 471 | 575 | 3,280 | 1 |
| Anhwei | 76 | 109 | 157 | 167 | 169 | 170 | 188 | 1,036 | 9 |
| Kiangsi | 345 | 361 | 354 | 357 | 367 | 266 | 350 | 2,400 | 3 |
| Fukien | 237 | 211 | 232 | 354 | 309 | 352 | 421 | 2,116 | 4 |
| Hupei | 40 | 59 | 113 | 154 | 165 | 191 | 246 | 968 | 11 |
| Hunan | 27 | 66 | 89 | 72 | 47 | 57 | 68 | 426 | 13 |
| Szechwan | 57 | 87 | 125 | 137 | 128 | 88 | 169 | 791 | 12 |
| Kwangsi | 10 | 16 | 30 | 35 | 36 | 19 | 27 | 173 | 15 |
| Yunnan | 4 | 13 | 27 | 45 | 35 | 39 | 78 | 241 | 14 |
| Kweichow | 0 | 7 | 4 | 10 | 17 | 20 | 27 | 85 | 16 |
| Liaoning | 0 | 10 | 13 | 13 | 10 | 4 | 7 | 57 | 17 |
| Total | 1,616 | 2,522 | 3,367 | 3,754 | 3,718 | 3,444 | 4,559 | 22,980 | |

Source: Li Chou-wang, *Kuo-ch'ao li-k'o t'i-ming pei-lu ch'u-chi*. It should be noted that certain years contain no information on candidates' geographic origin. The small numbers of Korean and Indochinese candidates are omitted. The grand total does not therefore agree with that of table 21.

of rivers, lakes, and canals in the Yangtze region, the almost incessant construction of irrigation projects, and the dissemination of early-ripening rice which greatly extended the frontier of rice culture all helped to make certain Yangtze provinces and Fukien economically and culturally more advanced.[2]

But not all the southern provinces benefited equally from these long-range, many-sided changes. Educated northerners generally trekked southward along easily accessible waterways. Kiangsi, thanks to its Po-yang Lake and Kan River and its relatively central location, had attracted northerners ever since the time of the Five Dynasties, if not earlier. By the eleventh century, descendants of northern immigrants of Kiangsi had already begun to ascend the academic-bureaucratic ladder.[3] It is worth mentioning that Wang

## TABLE 28

### GEOGRAPHIC DISTRIBUTION OF *CHIN-SHIH* IN CH'ING TIMES

| Province | 1644–1661 | 1662–1722 | 1723–1735 | 1736–1795 | 1796–1820 | 1821–1850 | 1851–1861 | 1862–1874 | 1875–1904 | Provincial total | Ranking |
|---|---|---|---|---|---|---|---|---|---|---|---|
| Hopei | 432 | 498 | 161 | 488 | 275 | 313 | 92 | 135 | 307 | 2,701 | 3 |
| Shantung | 419 | 429 | 105 | 259 | 210 | 268 | 79 | 118 | 273 | 2,260 | 4 |
| Honan | 297 | 311 | 81 | 282 | 133 | 169 | 95 | 108 | 217 | 1,693 | 6 |
| Shansi | 250 | 268 | 81 | 311 | 141 | 143 | 47 | 58 | 131 | 1,430 | 7 |
| Shensi and Kansu[a] | 169 | 190 | 60 | 228 | 121 | 138 | 94 | 95 | 280 | 1,385 | 9[a] |
| Kiangsu | 436 | 666 | 167 | 644 | 233 | 263 | 69 | 124 | 318 | 2,920 | 1 |
| Chekiang | 301 | 567 | 183 | 697 | 263 | 300 | 87 | 108 | 302 | 2,808 | 2 |
| Anhwei | 128 | 142 | 43 | 216 | 164 | 166 | 39 | 76 | 215 | 1,189 | 12 |
| Kiangsi | 83 | 200 | 115 | 540 | 223 | 265 | 74 | 122 | 273 | 1,895 | 5 |
| Fukien | 118 | 178 | 99 | 301 | 156 | 150 | 46 | 82 | 269 | 1,399 | 8 |
| Hupei | 189 | 191 | 69 | 212 | 126 | 135 | 43 | 72 | 184 | 1,221 | 11 |
| Hunan | 30 | 44 | 39 | 128 | 102 | 106 | 31 | 68 | 178 | 726 | 15 |
| Szechwan | 15 | 61 | 31 | 159 | 88 | 108 | 49 | 71 | 181 | 763 | 14 |
| Kwangtung | 34 | 91 | 69 | 252 | 106 | 139 | 36 | 79 | 206 | 1,012 | 13 |
| Kwangsi | 2 | 28 | 17 | 102 | 67 | 91 | 27 | 72 | 164 | 570 | 18 |
| Yunnan | 0 | 46 | 48 | 129 | 117 | 119 | 36 | 42 | 156 | 693 | 16 |
| Kweichow | 1 | 31 | 29 | 129 | 98 | 95 | 29 | 44 | 143 | 599 | 17 |
| Liaoning | 4 | 25 | 10 | 29 | 20 | 26 | 12 | 17 | 40 | 183 | 19 |
| Bannermen | 56 | 122 | 92 | 179 | 178 | 275 | 61 | 97 | 240 | 1,300 | 10 |
| Total | 2,964 | 4,088 | 1,499 | 5,385 | 2,821 | 3,269 | 1,046 | 1,588 | 4,087 | 26,747 | |

Source: Fang Chao-ying and Tu Lien-che, *Tseng-chiao Ch'ing-ch'ao chin-shih t'i-ming pei-lu.*

[a] The ranking is not exact because the number of candidates is the total of two provinces. Separately Shensi ranks 12th with a total of 1,130 and Kansu ranks barely above Liaoning with a total of 255. For comparison with Ming data these two provinces are grouped together.

TABLE 29

NUMBER OF *CHIN-SHIH* PER MILLION MEAN POPULATION
*(by provinces)*

| Province | Ming Period | | Ch'ing Period | |
|---|---|---|---|---|
| | Number | Ranking | Number | Ranking |
| Hopei | 283 | 3 | 117 | 3 |
| Shantung | 205 | 8 | 100 | 7 |
| Honan | 258 | 5 | 81 | 13 |
| Shansi | 209 | 7 | 108 | 6 |
| Shensi and Kansu | 144 | 11 | 59 | 16 |
| Kiangsu | 243 | 6 | 93 | 10 |
| Chekiang | 307 | 2 | 130 | 1 |
| Anhwei | 111 | 14 | 41 | 18 |
| Kiangsi | 260 | 4 | 99 | 8 |
| Fukien | 428 | 1 | 117 | 3 |
| Hupei | 164 | 10 | 64 | 14 |
| Hunan | 82 | 15 | 45 | 17 |
| Szechwan | 172 | 9 | 38 | 19 |
| Kwangtung | 144 | 11 | 63 | 15 |
| Kwangsi | 40 | 18 | 90 | 12 |
| Yunnan | 120 | 13 | 94 | 9 |
| Kweichow | 42 | 17 | 116 | 5 |
| Liaoning | 57 | 16 | 91 | 11 |
| Bannermen[a] | — | — | 130 | 1 |

[a] There was no formal registered figure for Manchu, Mongol, and Chinese Bannermen and their families in Ch'ing times. We arbitrarily estimate their total mean number for the Ch'ing period at 10,000,000.

Ch'in-jo, the first southerner to become a premier (at the beginning of the eleventh century), and such prominent statesmen as Ou-yang Hsiu (1007–72) and Wang An-shih (1021–86) were all from Kiangsi. Of the six Sung prose masters traditionally ranked foremost, three were natives of Kiangsi, namely, Ou-yang Hsiu, Wang An-shih, and Wang's contemporary Tseng Kung. It may indeed be said that Kiangsi enjoyed an unduly large share of literary prominence in the eleventh century because the other three great prose masters were of the same Su family of Szechwan, of which only Su Shih, commonly known as Su Tung-p'o (1036–1101), was a true literary giant. Only the choice of Hang-chou as the Southern Sung capital made it possible for Chekiang to surpass Kiangsi in academic-cultural prominence during the twelfth and thirteenth centuries.

In the Yangtze area much of Hupei, northern Anhwei, and northern Kiangsu became the scene of seesaw battles between the Chinese and Juchens and suffered a severe economic and cultural decline. For some time after the fall of north China in 1126 even southern Kiangsu was repeatedly harassed by the invading Juchens. In the southern Sung period therefore the more southerly provinces benefited from greater security and from steady economic and cultural expansion. In addition to Chekiang and Kiangsi, Fukien in the twelfth and thirteenth centuries forged ahead as a culturally advanced province, thanks to the dissemination of early-ripening rice, the prosperous maritime trade, and the influx of famous scholars and philosophers like Chu Hsi.[4]

The following multiple cultural indices for various provinces during the Mongol Yüan period may offer a partial explanation of the regional differences in academic success in early Ming times.

TABLE 30

NUMBERS OF PROMINENT SCHOLARS AND ACADEMIES
DURING THE YÜAN PERIOD
(*by provinces*)

| Province | Classicists | Historians | Philosophers | Men of Letters | Academies |
|---|---|---|---|---|---|
| Hopei | 23 | 18 | 18 | 40 | 20 |
| Shantung | 0 | 6 | 6 | 17 | 22 |
| Honan | 6 | 5 | 8 | 12 | 10 |
| Shansi | 3 | 7 | 7 | 16 | 12 |
| Shensi and Kansu | 3 | 4 | 2 | 8 | 7 |
| Kiangsu | 27 | 9 | 25 | 68 | 26 |
| Chekiang | 79 | 30 | 45 | 125 | 62 |
| Anhwei | 22 | 11 | 17 | 34 | 17 |
| Kiangsi | 90 | 24 | 34 | 86 | 73 |
| Fukien | 25 | 4 | 7 | 31 | 55 |
| Hupei | 2 | 0 | 0 | 2 | 19 |
| Hunan | 2 | 0 | 4 | 8 | 37 |
| Szechwan | 10 | 2 | 2 | 6 | 23 |
| Kwangtung | 1 | 1 | 0 | 2 | 24 |
| Yunnan | 0 | 0 | 0 | 1 | 0 |

Sources: Ho Yu-shen, "Yüan-tai hsüeh-shu chih ti-li fen-pu" [Geographic distribution of scholars during the Yüan period], *Hsin-ya hsüeh-pao*, I (no. 2, February, 1956); and "Yüan-tai shu-yüan chih ti-li fen-pu" [Geographic distribution of academies during the Yüan period], *Hsin-ya hsüeh-pao*, II (no. 1, August, 1956).

The combined indices show Chekiang's aggregate numerical superiority, followed by that of Kiangsi and Fukien. The exact reasons for Kiangsi's astounding academic success in early Ming times cannot be exactly known. Although Kiangsi was behind Chekiang in numbers of historians, philosophers, and men of letters during the Yüan period, it led the nation in numbers of classicists and private academies. As classics constituted the basic curriculum of examinations, and academies with their scholarship provisions had much to do with educational facilities, Kiangsi's cultural assets in the early decades of the Ming may not have been much less than those of Chekiang. We may speculate as to whether Kiangsi's unique record of academic success in early Ming times was in part due to its better community effort to maintain a number of community chests for subsidizing candidates, in which Kiangsi had been a pioneer. While it is always difficult to know the exact reasons for a region's unusual academic success, we do know that prior to Wang Yang-ming's (1472–1529) rise to political and philosophical prominence Kiangsi had been the nation's most important intellectual center.[5]

Chekiang, which boasted in the early Ming period the largest population and a long cultural tradition, soon overtook Kiangsi in academic success. The trend became clear during the latter half of the fifteenth century, but it was during the sixteenth that the province securely established its primacy over the rest of the country. Whether its unusual academic success in the sixteenth century was due in part to the impact of Wang Yang-ming's revolutionary theory of intuitive knowledge and the unity of knowledge and conduct cannot be definitely proved. Judging by the large numbers of *chin-shih* of humble families from Wang's native county Yü-yao and native prefecture Shao-hsing, there is reason to believe that concepts and myths conducive to social mobility may have been widely disseminated in the greater parts of that province. In any case, in the sixteenth century Chekiang definitely replaced Kiangsi as the intellectual center of gravity and our statistics show that the province's leadership in academic success was not taken over by its richer and more resourceful neighbor Kiangsu until the last five or four decades of the Ming period.

Kiangsu in the long run had various unequaled advantages. While the northern two thirds of the province did rather poorly in academic competition during a greater part of the Ming period, the prefectures south of the Yangtze underwent a remarkable economic and cultural development. Thanks to its geographic location, southern Kiangsu was definitely the country's leading trading area. Its increasingly variegated economy further stimulated crafts and industries, particularly the cotton textile industry of Sung-chiang and Su-chou Prefectures. The late Ming official and traveler Hsieh Chao-che was certainly right in saying that it was the gainful opportunities created by a many-sided economy that made southern Kiangsu by far the richest area in the country, despite a fiscal load so heavy as to have crushed any other region.[6] From the latter half of the fifteenth century onward, this area's unique wealth was partially reflected in the rise of some outstanding bibliophiles, printers, and connoisseurs. If southern Kiangsu was not the seat of intellectual dynamism, it was at least the home of the largest number of men of letters and artists.

Moreover, Kiangsu's unparalleled economic and cultural development in the greater part of the Ming period should be partially attributed to immigration and to the influx of wealth and talent. For Nanking was the original capital city of the Ming empire and remained the second capital after the court had moved to Peking in 1421. As the second capital, Nanking maintained a separate smaller central government and the larger and more important Imperial Academy. Many of the officials and officers were so much attracted by the region's wealth and comfort that they chose to settle here permanently. Their descendants benefited from family influence and often passed higher examinations under their official southern Kiangsu residential registrations. In addition, the reform in the salt administration around the turn of the fifteenth century further attracted many rich merchant groups to Yang-chou, the headquarters of the country's largest salt administration, although many of them chose to reside permanently in other southern Kiangsu cities. Unlike Chekiang, which on balance was a talent-exporting province, Kiangsu was one of the two largest recipients of both talents and wealth. By the last half century of the Ming dynasty there was every indication that Kiangsu had caught up with, and was destined to outdistance, Chekiang in the race for academic success.

Although Kiangsu continued its remarkable economic and cultural development in Ch'ing times, its academic success was severely handicapped by the change of the official *chin-shih* quota system in 1702. As has been explained at the beginning of chapter V, from early Ming times to 1702 the country was divided for the purpose of metropolitan examination into three broad regions within which the constituent provinces still varied considerably in the members of *chin-shih* they produced. From 1702 onward sliding provincial *chin-shih* quotas were fixed within each broad region, and these were set shortly before the metropolitan examination in rough proportion to the sum total of participants of the provinces in the three preceding examinations. Since the number of participants in the metropolitan examination bore a close relationship to a province's cumulative number of *chü-jen* and since the latter was roughly proportionate to a province's fixed *chü-jen* quota, new *chin-shih* quotas for various provinces became virtually frozen in the same proportions. Kiangsu thus suffered severely from its historically smaller *chü-jen* quota which had been justified at the beginning of the Ming period because of its smaller population and less advanced culture in comparison with Chekiang and Kiangsi. Owing to the post-1702 quota system, Chekiang was able to hold its lead in *chin-shih* productivity up to about 1860, after which Kiangsu went slightly ahead. Had it not been for its substantial numerical superiority built up between 1644 and 1702 Kiangsu would have been unable to nose out Chekiang in the aggregate *chin-shih* production during the whole Ch'ing period.

If Kiangsu was handicapped by the post-1702 *chin-shih* quota system, Anhwei suffered even more severely from it and from the Ming quota system. Since throughout the Ming-Ch'ing period, from the standpoint of administration and examinations, Anhwei was practically an appendage of Kiangsu, its small share of *chin-shih* in comparison with those of other southeastern provinces was by no means an indication of cultural backwardness. From mid-Ming times onward Anhwei was one of the leading talent-exporting provinces, a fact which was not reflected in its relatively modest share of *chin-shih.* Actually the province contributed considerably to the unusual academic prominence of southern Kiangsu and northern Chekiang, where rich and often highly cultured Hui-chou merchants of southern Anhwei congregated. The 1827 edition of the Hui-chou prefectural history lists for the area 142 *chin-shih* between 1647 and 1826 as against at least 377 native sons and their descendants who had obtained the degree under different residential registrations. During the same 180-year period the prefecture also contributed 14 of a total of 94 first-class honors men of Kiangsu and 5 of a total of 59 of Chekiang.[7] We have reason to believe that the list given in the prefectural history is not complete and that actually Hui-chou's contribution to the academic prominence of southern Kiangsu and northern Chekiang was greater. For example, Hung Liang-chi, who won the second highest honor in the palace examination of 1799, though officially registered as a resident of Yang-hu county in southern Kiangsu, was of Hui-chou descent, a circumstance over-looked by the editor.[8] Hua I-hsing of Wu-hsi in southern Kiangsu, who won similar honors in the palace examination of 1659 and whose original surname was Pao, was almost certainly of Hui-chou descent. In fact, most if not all of the Wangs, Paos, Ch'engs, and Chiangs, whatever their officially registered residence, are likely to have originated from the Hui-chou area.[9] When the effect of emigration and of its traditionally small quotas of higher degrees is taken into account, Anhwei by no means broke the general pattern of the southeastern region.

Fukien had an unusually large share of academic success in proportion to its population, especially in Ming times. Ever since the Southern Sung period Fukien had been one of the culturally advanced provinces. Down to late Ming times the port of Zayton, or Ch'üan-chou, had been one of the world's greatest trading centers, where many rich Persian and Arabian merchants had resided in Sung and Yüan times.[10] After their expulsion from Canton in 1522, the Portuguese developed an illegal but highly lucrative trade with Ch'üan-chou and the neighboring Chang-chou, from which an enormous amount of silver flowed into China.[11] From Ming accounts and from early Ch'ing Jesuit testimonials Fukien's economy, if not quite as advanced as that of southern Kiangsu, was much more diversified than that of most provinces.[12] It ought also to be mentioned that Chien-yang in northern Fukien was the greatest center of printing in Ming times and that the province as a whole and the two southern coastal prefectures of Ch'üan-chou and Chang-chou in particular had probably the most highly developed kinship organization, which helped the needy and ambitious.[13] Its long cultural tradition, wealth, and diversified economy, coupled with a moderately growing population which was partially the result of overseas emigration, gave the province a most favorable *chin-shin* ratio towards population in Ming times.

The other three Yangtze provinces of Hupei, Hunan, and Szechwan and the southernmost coastal province of Kwangtung all suffered indirectly from their small early-Ming *chü-jen* quotas, which were not revised in accordance with their growing population, and directly from the post-1702 provincial *chin-shih* quotas. Hupei and Hunan during the greater part of the Ming-Ch'ing period formed the single province of Hu-kuang. Moreover, up to 1702 all these four provinces had to compete against culturally advanced southeastern provinces within the so-called southern quota. They may not be regarded as culturally backward.

For centuries before the founding of the Ming dynasty the economic and cultural backwardness of the north had been apparent. Its landlocked and self-sustaining agricultural economy and its long rule under the alien Khitans, Juchens, and Mongols, not to mention its earlier barbarian conquerors, kept it hopelessly outdistanced by the south. Ever since Sung times the north's cultural plight had been testified to by contemporaries.[14] Northern provinces were so short of books that the Ming founder and his son Ming Ch'eng-tsu repeatedly ordered that basic classics be brought from the south and distributed to northern schools. Even in early Ch'ing times the great scholar Ku Yen-wu (1613–82), who traveled extensively and lived many years in various northern provinces, mentioned two kinds of general under-development in the north, namely, land utilization and human talents.[15] The famous novelist P'u Sung-ling (1640–1715), a native of Shantung, pointed out that the quality of teachers and the educational standards in his native province were deplorable.[16]

Yet there can be little doubt that the north was more than adequately protected from the advanced southeast by the Ming broad regional *chin-shih* quota and especially by the post-1702 provincial quota system. Prior to the setting up of regional quotas from 1397 onward, so few northerners had passed the metropolitan examinations that the Ming founder executed the chief examiner in that year in spite of lack of evidence of collusion and instituted the new system whereby northern provinces competed among themselves. The post-1702 provincial quota system brought about even greater advantages for some of the most backward northern provinces. To mention an extreme case, Kansu, which failed to place a single *chin-shih* between 1644 and 1702, produced a total of 255 after the quota reform.

Among northern provinces Hopei benefited the most from the quota systems and from the fact that Peking was the national capital. Being the metropolitan province, its *chü-jen* quota was successively enlarged until by late Ming times and for the entire Ch'ing period it well exceeded 200, as compared with less than 100 for such advanced provinces as Chekiang and Kiangsi. Its large *chü-jen* quota indirectly helped it to secure for itself a favorable provincial *chin-shih* ratio after 1702. In addition, many central officials from various provinces settled permanently in the metropolitan Peking area or at least had one or two sons registered as residents of Hopei. As will be shown below, under Academically Outstanding Localities, by far the greatest contributors to Hopei's better than average academic success were the two metropolitan counties of Wan-p'ing and Ta-hsing, where families of central officials, subofficials, and clerks of various central government organs congregated. While they were from practically everywhere in the empire, many of them came from the highly cultured and mobile area of Shao-hsing prefecture in Chekiang. Hopei therefore benefited even more from immigration than Kiangsu. It should also be pointed out that the imperial clansmen, Manchu, Mongol, and Chinese Bannermen had a higher than average ratio of academic success because their quota was a generous one relative to the size of their populations.

Since our mean population figures for the southwestern provinces of Szechwan, Kwangsi, Yunnan, and Kweichow are likely to be too low to represent their approximate Chinese populations, their ratios of *chin-shih* to population may be considerably exaggerated. Szechwan's disaster in the mid-seventeenth century and its slow recovery, which dragged into the late eighteenth century, brought about a drastic decline in its *chin-shih* productivity. When its population shot up rapidly from about 1800 onward, it failed to secure a substantial revision of its *chin-shih* quota. But the three other southwestern provinces all registered substantial gains in numbers of *chin-shih,* and Kweichow and Kwangsi even improved their *chin-shih* ratios in terms of population during the Ch'ing period.

In brief, during the rapid multiplication of population in Ch'ing times all provinces, except Kwangsi, Yunnan, Kweichow, and Liaoning, suffered a sharp decline in the number of *chin-shih* per million mean population.

REGIONAL DIFFERENCES IN MOBILITY RATES

Since none of the available Ming-Ch'ing *chin-shih* lists are arranged according to provinces, it would require much more time and effort than the author can afford to tabulate provincially the family backgrounds of all the 12,000 odd *chin-shih*. Ten Ming-Ch'ing *chin-shih* lists, selected to cover as many reign periods as possible, are tabulated as a general illustration. Owing to the fact that mobility rates began to drop drastically from the late sixteenth century onward, all three extant lists of the Wan-li period (1573–1619) are included. The eight extant lists of the Shun-chih (1644–61) and K'ang-hsi (1662–1722) periods are available only in microfilm which, coupled with the fact that the candidates officially registered residence is given in very small characters, makes tabulation extremely taxing. For the Ch'ing period therefore we are compelled to tabulate ten lists of the nineteenth century which cover every decade from the 1820s onward. As shown in table 9, the few available lists of the third quarter of the seventeenth century yield mobility rates which are quite in keeping with those of the last two Ming lists and somewhat higher than nineteenth century averages. But if the mobility rates computed from nineteenth-century lists are not entirely representative of the Ch'ing period as a whole, they should not be too far from the actual Ch'ing averages because of our lack of data for the eighteenth century, a period which is likely to yield rates even lower than the averages of the nineteenth century.

From table 9 we know that with the exception of the years 1553, 1586, and 1610 Category B *chin-shih,* that is, those originating from families which during the three preceding generations had produced only lowest degree holders, are either nil or very insignificant. Thus for the Ming period our concern is regional differences in the percentages of Category A *chin-shih,* that is, those who rose from obscurity in their own generation. Since Category A rates dropped drastically in Ch'ing times and since Category B candidates were in fact from relatively humble families, our tabulation for the Ch'ing period includes the latter category. Mobility rates of various provinces are shown in the following three tables.

Table 31 shows that in Ming times the percentages of Category A candidates of all provinces were very substantial. Despite the high average of 47.6 percent for ten lists analyzed, the most significant thing is that the percentages of Category A candidates of culturally advanced provinces such as Chekiang, Kiangsu, Kiangsi, and Fukien were above the national average. Although Anhwei had a smaller share in the total *chin-shih* production, it nevertheless achieved the highest Category A percentage. Even in terms of population Chekiang, Kiangsu, Kiangsi, and Fukien also occupied leading positions. Fukien's ratio of 262 *chin-shih* of humble non-degree-holding families per million mean population was the highest of all. From these very rough figures and ratios and from our knowledge of Ming history it can be said that much of the cultural and social dynamism of the Ming period originated in the southeast. Compared with the southeast, northern, upper-central Yangtze, and backward southwestern provinces had lower mobility rates.

Table 32 shows that by Ch'ing times Category A percentages of the majority of provinces had sharply declined, particularly in the culturally advanced southeastern provinces, a fact which testifies to the increasing disadvantage of the poor and humble in competing against their social superiors. The competition became most acute in Kiangsu, as its combined percentage of Categories A and B was 8.5 percent below the national average, which was itself much

TABLE 31

REGIONAL DIFFERENCES IN MOBILITY RATES
DURING MING TIMES

| | | | *Category A* chin-shih | |
| Province | Total number of chin-shih | Number | Percent of provincial total | Percent above or below national average |
|---|---|---|---|---|
| Hopei | 287 | 117 | 40.8 | −6.8 |
| Shantung | 219 | 78 | 35.6 | −12.0 |
| Honan | 206 | 79 | 38.3 | −9.3 |
| Shansi | 119 | 50 | 42.0 | −5.6 |
| Shensi and Kansu | 112 | 49 | 40.2 | −5.4 |
| Kiangsu | 356 | 186 | 52.2 | 4.6 |
| Chekiang | 370 | 177 | 47.8 | 0.2 |
| Anhwei | 116 | 71 | 63.8 | 16.2 |
| Kiangsi | 301 | 170 | 56.5 | 8.9 |
| Fukien | 255 | 156 | 61.2 | 13.6 |
| Hupei | 122 | 52 | 42.6 | −5.0 |
| Hunan | 55 | 23 | 41.8 | −5.8 |
| Szechwan | 188 | 82 | 43.6 | −4.0 |
| Kwangtung | 91 | 49 | 53.0 | 6.3 |
| Kwangsi | 27 | 9 | 33.3 | −14.3 |
| Yunnan | 29 | 12 | 41.4 | −6.2 |
| Kweichow | 9 | 5 | 55.5 | 7.9 |
| Liaoning | 10 | 5 | 50.0 | 2.4 |
| Total | 2,882 | 1,373 | 47.6 (national average) | |

Sources: Based on *chin-shih* lists of 1412, 1457, 1472, 1496, 1521, 1544, 1568, 1580, 1586, 1610. For titles of these lists, see Bibliography, *chin-shih* lists under Main Statistical Data.

less than the national Category A average of the Ming period. Chekiang did somewhat better in that, although its Ch'ing Category A percentage was almost as low as Kiangsu's, it achieved a much higher Category B percentage. This would suggest that even in this most mobile province commoners usually required more than a single generation to ascend the social ladder. Tables 32 and 33 reveal a very drastic decline in mobility rates in Kiangsi, Fukien, and Anhwei as well. While in terms of absolute numbers of *chin-shih* produced in Ch'ing times the southeastern provinces still re-

TABLE 32

REGIONAL DIFFERENCES IN MOBILITY RATES
DURING CH'ING TIMES

| Province | Total number of chin-shih | Category A | | Category B | | Combined percent of A and B | Combined percent of A and B above or below national average |
|---|---|---|---|---|---|---|---|
| | | Number | Percent of provincial total | Number | Percent of provincial total | | |
| Hopei | 188 | 24 | 12.8 | 37 | 20.0 | 32.8 | −5.7 |
| Shantung | 164 | 23 | 14.0 | 35 | 21.3 | 35.3 | −3.2 |
| Honan | 109 | 24 | 22.0 | 24 | 22.0 | 44.0 | 5.5 |
| Shansi | 76 | 14 | 18.4 | 18 | 23.7 | 42.1 | 3.6 |
| Shensi and Kansu | 108 | 38 | 35.1 | 20 | 18.5 | 53.6 | 15.1 |
| Kiangsu | 183 | 21 | 11.4 | 34 | 18.6 | 30.0 | −8.5 |
| Chekiang | 190 | 22 | 11.6 | 56 | 29.5 | 42.1 | 3.6 |
| Anhwei | 127 | 20 | 15.8 | 30 | 23.6 | 39.4 | 0.9 |
| Kiangsi | 161 | 21 | 13.0 | 34 | 21.2 | 34.1 | −4.4 |
| Fukien | 118 | 19 | 16.1 | 23 | 19.7 | 35.8 | −2.7 |
| Hupei | 105 | 20 | 19.0 | 31 | 29.5 | 48.5 | 10.0 |
| Hunan | 94 | 23 | 24.4 | 29 | 30.8 | 55.2 | 16.7 |
| Szechwan | 98 | 26 | 26.5 | 15 | 15.3 | 41.8 | 3.3 |
| Kwangtung | 99 | 21 | 21.2 | 18 | 18.2 | 39.4 | 0.9 |
| Kwangsi | 83 | 15 | 18.1 | 15 | 18.1 | 36.2 | −2.3 |
| Yunnan | 74 | 16 | 21.6 | 16 | 21.6 | 43.2 | 4.7 |
| Kweichow | 66 | 16 | 24.2 | 14 | 21.2 | 45.4 | 6.9 |
| Liaoning | 17 | 4 | 23.5 | 6 | 35.3 | 58.8 | 20.3 |
| Bannermen | 121 | 17 | 14.0 | 2 | 1.6 | 15.6 | −22.9 |
| Total | 2,181 | 384 | 17.6 (national average) | 457 | 20.9 (national average) | 38.5 (national average) | |

Sources: Based on *chin-shih* lists of 1822, 1829, 1833, 1844, 1859, 1868, 1876, 1886, 1895, 1904. For titles of sources, see Bibliography, *chin-shih* lists under Main Statistical Data.

mained national leaders, the drastic change in the regional mobility pattern must have generated a great deal of social frustration among the humble and relatively humble.

In the rest of the country, on the other hand, the decline in mobility rates in Ch'ing times was considerably less drastic than in the southeast. The only exceptions were the metropolitan province of Hopei, where academic competition was always keener because

TABLE 33

NUMBER OF *CHIN-SHIH* PER MILLION MEAN POPULATION
*(of commoner origin only, by provinces)*

| Province | Ming period (Category A only) | Ch'ing period | | |
|---|---|---|---|---|
| | | Category A | Category B | Total of A and B |
| Hopei | 115 | 15 | 23 | 38 |
| Shantung | 73 | 14 | 21 | 35 |
| Honan | 99 | 18 | 18 | 36 |
| Shansi | 88 | 12 | 16 | 28 |
| Shensi and Kansu | 58 | 20 | 11 | 31 |
| Kiangsu | 127 | 10 | 14 | 24 |
| Chekiang | 147 | 15 | 38 | 53 |
| Anhwei | 71 | 7 | 9 | 16 |
| Kiangsi | 147 | 8 | 21 | 29 |
| Fukien | 262 | 11 | 23 | 34 |
| Hupei | 70 | 7 | 13 | 20 |
| Hunan | 34 | 11 | 14 | 25 |
| Szechwan | 75 | 10 | 6 | 16 |
| Kwangtung | 76 | 13 | 12 | 25 |
| Kwangsi | 13 | 15 | 15 | 30 |
| Yunnan | 50 | 30 | 30 | 60 |
| Kweichow | 33 | 28 | 25 | 53 |
| Liaoning | 28 | 21 | 32 | 53 |
| Bannermen | — | 18 | 1 | 19 |

Sources: Table 26 and 1787 population figures of various provinces, some of which are revised; tables 27, 28, 29, and 30.

of the constant influx of officials and educated people from various places, and Shantung, which was traditionally a conservative and less mobile province. Because of their modest share of academic success in Ming times and especially because of the stabilizing effect of the post-1702 provincial quota system, northern provinces in general suffered a relatively mild decline in mobility rates in terms of their mean population. In fact, the post-1702 quota system, the cultural backwardness, and the obviously lower regional standards required for passing the metropolitan examination made it possible for Shensi and Kansu to achieve one of the highest Category A percentages in Ch-ing times.

Owing to their relatively small Chinese population and especially to the reform of the quota system in 1702, the southwestern provinces of Kwangsi, Yunnan, and Kweichow and Liaoning in Manchuria achieved virtually greater mobility rates in Ch'ing times, even in terms of their mean populations. Although the majority of Bannermen *chin-shih* originated from official families, their Category A ratio per million of mean population was above average. This was because scholarships for Bannermen's sons were relatively amply provided in Peking, Mukden, and provincial cities where Bannermen were garrisoned.[17] What is more, in 1727 the Yung-cheng emperor, who legally manumitted scattered small groups of "declassed" Chinese, also made it a fundamental principle that in making scholarship awards to Bannermen's sons there should be no consideration of students' family status and that descendants of *booi,* bond servants in the Eight Banners, should also be selected according to personal merit. This policy was observed and educational facilities for *booi* descendants were expanded by the Ch'ien-lung emperor.[18]

In short, the smaller population and unusual circumstances of the Ming period brought about substantial mobility rates for the whole country, most of all for the southeast, which was culturally ready to take full advantage of opportunities. The greatly increased population of Ch'ing times sharply reduced the mobility rates of the majority of the provinces, particularly those of the southeast. Under the post-1702 provincial quota system the northern provinces suffered a less drastic shrinkage in mobility rates and backward peripheral provinces achieved mobility rates even higher than those of Ming times. Thus while mobility rates for the country as a whole were declining, a more even geographic distribution of academic success and a somewhat broader opportunity structure for the backward areas were brought about at the expense of the advanced southeast.

Some available *chü-jen* and *kung-sheng* data should also be analyzed. For two reasons, however, they cannot be analyzed as minutely as *chin-shih* data. First, for the Ch'ing period the total numbers of these intermediate degree holders for the nation and for various provinces can be only roughly estimated and the numbers for the Ming period cannot be even roughly estimated. It is impossible therefore to compute regional differences in productivity of these intermediate degree holders or their family background in terms

TABLE 34

PERCENTAGES OF INTERMEDIATE DEGREE HOLDERS FROM COMMONER FAMILIES

*(nineteenth century only, by provinces)*

| Province | Provincial total of candidates of all categories | Category A | | Category B | | Combined percent of A and B |
|---|---|---|---|---|---|---|
| | | Number | Percent | Number | Percent | |
| Hopei | 3,561 | 530 | 14.9(−5.1)[a] | 698 | 19.6(−5.6)[a] | 34.5(−10.7)[a] |
| Shantung | 1,503 | 227 | 15.0(−5.0) | 386 | 25.6 (0.4) | 40.6 (−4.6) |
| Honan | 1,446 | 331 | 23.4 (3.4) | 411 | 28.4 (3.2) | 51.8 (6.6) |
| Shansi | 1,129 | 235 | 20.8 (0.8) | 292 | 25.9 (0.7) | 46.7 (1.5) |
| Shensi and Kansu | 1,372 | 364 | 26.5 (6.5) | 259 | 26.2 (1.0) | 52.7 (7.2) |
| Kiangsu and Anhwei | 2,119 | 271 | 12.8(−7.2) | 605 | 28.6 (3.4) | 41.4 (−3.8) |
| Chekiang | 1,570 | 170 | 10.8(−9.2) | 484 | 30.8 (5.6) | 41.6 (−3.6) |
| Kiangsi | 1,532 | 211 | 13.8(−6.2) | 453 | 29.5 (4.3) | 43.3 (−1.9) |
| Fukien | 1,183 | 287 | 24.3 (4.3) | 279 | 23.6(−1.6) | 47.9 (2.7) |
| Hupei | 966 | 190 | 19.6(−0.4) | 252 | 26.1 (0.9) | 45.7 (0.5) |
| Hunan | 799 | 227 | 28.4 (8.4) | 250 | 31.2 (7.0) | 60.6 (15.4) |
| Szechwan | 1,409 | 472 | 33.5 (13.5) | 300 | 21.2(−4.0) | 54.7 (9.5) |
| Kwangtung | 1,291 | 332 | 25.7 (5.7) | 302 | 23.4(−1.8) | 49.1 (3.9) |
| Kwangsi | 851 | 175 | 20.6 (0.6) | 202 | 23.7(−1.5) | 44.3 (−0.9) |
| Yunnan | 1,179 | 282 | 24.0 (4.0) | 327 | 27.8 (2.6) | 51.8 (6.6) |
| Kweichow | 581 | 175 | 30.0 (10.0) | 101 | 17.4(−7.8) | 47.4 (2.2) |
| Total | 22,491 | 4,479 | 20.0 (national average) | 5,701 | 25.2 (national average) | 45.2 (national average) |

Sources: Based on national *chü-jen* lists of the years 1804, 1807, 1808, 1816, 1821, 1828, 1831, 1832, 1834, 1835, 1844, 1855, 1870, 1879; national *pa-kung-sheng* lists of the years 1849, 1885, 1897; 1 *yu-kung-sheng* list of 1906; and 1 list of *chü-jen* and *kung-sheng* who passed a special court examination in 1910. For complete titles, see Bibliography. The numbers include only those who give information on ancestry.

[a] The figures within parentheses indicate the percentages above or below the national averages of Category A, Category B, and Categories A and B combined.

of mean provincial populations. Second, since all the known extant national lists of *chü-jen* and special categories of *kung-sheng* are confined to the nineteenth century, there is no basis of comparison with earlier periods. Within these limitations the above tabulation of *chü-jen* and *kung-sheng* merely serves as a supplement to our previous tables on Ming-Ch'ing *chin-shih*. But it is interesting to observe that the broad regional patterns shown in the previous table by and large conform to those indicated in table 32.

### ACADEMICALLY OUTSTANDING LOCALITIES

No discussion of the geographic distribution of academic success is complete without mention of certain localities which had a high concentration of *chin-shih*. While for the Ming and Ch'ing periods special compilations of *chin-shih* names and their geographic origins are available,[19] to tabulate the 50,000 odd candidates according to their officially registered counties of residence would require endless labor, for the total of each of the more than 1,800 counties necessitates a separate sorting of the combined Ming-Ch'ing list. We have to rely on local histories and a few special local lists of degree holders. For the Ming period the task is simpler because Ch'ing editions of local histories invariably contain lists of local *chin-shih* of the previous Ming period, although the listing is not absolutely correct. This is because, on one hand, information is lacking for certain early Ming examinations and, on the other hand, the figures almost certainly include *chin-shih* of local origin registered under different residences. Since most Ch'ing local histories were compiled before the abolition of the examination system in 1905, the listing of *chin-shih* of the Ch'ing period is as a rule incomplete. Whenever the listing is incomplete, we have to amend it with *Tseng-chiao Ch'ing-ch'ao chin-shih t'i-ming pei-lu*, compiled with meticulous care by Fang Chao-ying and Tu Lien-che. For three reasons our local *chin-shih* totals so arrived at may still contain a certain margin of error. First, the sorting of candidates by their prefectural or county origins being so tedious and laborious, small numbers of omissions are likely to be unavoidable. Second, accurate as the Fang-Tu compilation is, it may not entirely agree with totals given in local histories. It has been discovered that on several occasions after passing the metropolitan examination a candidate was unable to take the ensuing palace examination. He may have died before he was entitled to take the next palace examination three years later. Or ill health or the death of one or both of his parents may have prevented his taking further examinations. For any of these reasons, his name is therefore missing from the Fang-Tu list. While it is true that without taking the palace examination one was not technically granted the *chin-shih* degree, yet he was invariably considered by all but the government as a *chin-shih* and so listed in the local history. Third, by far the most serious complication is that whenever information was available editors of local histories included native sons who had obtained their degrees under other officially registered residences. For instance, editors of Hui-chou local and prefectural histories took special pains to differentiate between native sons who obtained the degree under formal Hui-chou residence and those who became *chin-shih* under extra-prefectural residential registration. This was because Hui-chou was an exceptionally heavy emigrating area. But many other local histories did not make this important technical differentiation. Through sampling checks on a few localities which were academically outstanding, it has been discovered that local history totals are usually higher than those of the Fang-Tu list. All in all, therefore, our data on the most academically successful localities should merely serve as rough samples, while exhaustive tabulation for all localities must await future research.

It should be noted that the northern Ming metropolitan prefecture of Shun-t'ien produced 936 *chin-shih* in Ming times, thus ranking fourth among the prefectures.[20] But since it consisted of as many as twenty-three counties and *wei* (military garrison posts) in Ming times and twenty-four counties in the Ch'ing period, it should not be regarded as an ordinary prefecture but should be treated as a subprovince. Since our purpose is to study the concentration of *chin-shih* within a reasonably small area, any prefecture of fifteen or more counties is excluded. In addition to the following thirteen prefectures which produced over 400 *chin-shih,* we should mention Hui-chou Prefecture in southern Anhwei, which claimed 445, including native sons and their descendants who obtained the degree

TABLE 35

PREFECTURES OF UNUSUAL ACADEMIC
SUCCESS IN MING TIMES

| Prefecture | Total number of chin-shih |
|---|---|
| Chi-an, Kiangsi | 1,020 |
| Shao-hsing, Chekiang | 977 |
| Su-chou, Kiangsu | 970 |
| Nan-ch'ang, Kiangsi | 713 |
| Ch'ang-chou, Kiangsu | 661 |
| Fu-chou, Fukien | 654 |
| Ch'üan-chou, Fukien | 627 |
| Ning-po, Chekiang | 598 |
| Chia-hsing, Chekiang | 528 |
| Hsing-hua, Fukien | 524 |
| Hang-chou, Chekiang | 520 |
| Sung-chiang, Kiangsu | 466 |
| Kuang-chou, Kwangtung | 437 |

Sources: *Chi-an fu-chih* (1876 ed.); *Shao-hsing fu-chih* (1792 ed.); *Su-chou fu-chih* (1862 ed.); *Nan-ch'ang fu-chih* (1873 ed.); *Ch'ang-chou fu-chih* (1794 ed., 1887 reprint); *Fu-chou fu-chih* (1754 ed.); *Ch'üan-chou fu-chih* (1763 ed.); *Ning-po fu-chih* (1730 ed., rev. in 1741, 1846 reprint); *Chia-hsing fu-chih* (1878 ed.); *Fu-chien t'ung-chih* (1922 ed.), from which data on Hsing-hua prefecture are derived; *Hang-chou fu-chih* (compiled between 1879 and 1919, printed in 1923); *Sung-chiang fu-chih* (1819 ed.); *Kuang-chou fu-chih* (1879 ed.). All of them have special chapters on Ming chin-shih.

under extra-prefectural residential registration.[21] Some prefectures, like Hu-chou in northwestern Chekiang and Chang-chou on the southern Fukien coast, actually achieved a high density of *chin-shih,* but their unusually small areas prevented them from taking a place among the national leaders.[22]

It should be noted that in Ch'ing times the metropolitan prefecture of Shun-t'ien actually led the nation with 1,038 *chin-shih.*[23] Between 1644 and 1826 Hui-chou Prefecture boasted 519 *chin-shih,* of whom only 142 were under prefectural residential registration.[24] If all its native-son candidates are included, it would of course rank among the top five or six. But when those candidates under extra-prefectural registration are excluded, it lags far behind the national leaders. It ought to be pointed out that the above ranking is not exact because the numbers given for those prefectures which compiled their histories late in the Ch'ing period are likely to be

## TABLE 36

### PREFECTURES OF UNUSUAL ACADEMIC
### SUCCESS IN CH'ING TIMES

| Prefecture | Total number of chin-shih |
|---|---|
| Hang-chou, Chekiang | 1,004 |
| Su-chou, Kiangsu | 785 |
| Fu-chou, Fukien | 723 |
| Ch'ang-chou, Kiangsu | 618 |
| Kuang-chou, Kwangtung | 597 |
| Shao-hsing, Chekiang | 505 |
| Chia-hsing, Chekiang | 476 |
| Hu-chou, Chekiang | 421 |
| Nan-ch'ang, Kiangsi | 413 |

Sources: *Hang-chou fu-chih* (1923 ed.); *Su-chou fu-chih* (1862 ed.), amended with Fang-Tu list; *Fu-chou fu-chih* (1754 ed.), amended; *Kuang-chou fu-chih* (1879 ed.), amended; for Hu-chou the data are derived from *Kuo-ch'ao Hu-chou-fu k'o-ti piao* (printed some time after 1905).
Figures for the remaining prefectures are all based on the Fang-Tu list.

exaggerated as compared with data which are derived partially from early-Ch'ing prefectural histories or entirely from the Fang-Tu national list. Whatever the limitations of our data, they still serve as interesting material for our historical study of cultural geography.

While failing to produce 400 *chin-shih,* Yang-chou Prefecture north of the Yangtze in Kiangsu where the wealth of the Liang-huai salt merchants created a high culture deserves a brief mention. Its total of 348 *chin-shih* derived from the Fang-Tu list and its total of 11 first-class honors men should place it among the nation's leading cultural areas. Chen-chiang Prefecture, between Ch'ang-chou Prefecture and Chiang-ning Prefecture, of which Nanking was the leading city, was very small in size and consisted of only four counties. Yet it managed to produce 266 *chin-shih* and 12 first-class honors men. In terms of density of academic success it ranked very high.

Tables 35 and 36 show continuity as well as changes which should be briefly discussed. Chi-an Prefecture in central Kiangsi, owing to its long cultural tradition and facilities for study and examination, led the prefectures by a substantial margin during the first century of the Ming period. Up to 1464 it produced 449 *chin-shih* as compared with 248 for Fu-chou, 184 for Shao-hsing, and 146 for Su-chou. What was even more remarkable, the prefecture monopolized first-class honors in 1400 and 1404, a record which stands unchallenged. Its astounding head start enabled it to secure the highest *chin-shih* total for a prefecture for any single dynastic period, excluding the metropolitan prefecture of Shun-t'ien in Ch'ing times. Academic success in Kiangsi in Ming times was so concentrated that the two prefectures of Chi-an and Nan-ch'ang accounted for 72.2 percent of the provincial total. In the long run, however, Kiangsi as a whole and Chi-an in particular were bound to be overshadowed by the more resourceful and fortunately situated southern Kiangsu and northern and east-central Chekiang. By Ch'ing times Chi-an's record had diminished to a mere shadow of its old glory and only Nan-ch'ang Prefecture, the provincial capital area, barely squeezed into the front rank. During the period of general decline in academic success *chin-shih* in Kiangsi in Ch'ing times became more evenly distributed.

In Ming times a similar concentration was found in the three southern Kiangsu prefectures of Su-chou, Ch'ang-chou, and Sung-chiang, and the three coastal Fukien prefectures of Fu-chou, Hsing-hua, and Ch'üan-chou. The former three accounted for 77 percent of the Kiangsu provincial total and the latter three for nearly 85 percent of the Fukien provincial total. Granted that these percentages are somewhat exaggerated because of our reliance on local history figures, there can be little doubt about the high degree of concentration.

The unique economic and cultural opportunities of the eastern half of southern Kiangsu have been explained above, under Distribution of Academic Success by Provinces. The relative backwardness of two thirds of Kiangsu north of the Yangtze also helped to make possible the concentration of academic success in the south. With prolonged peace, material prosperity, and dissemination of culture during the Ch'ing up to 1850, many other areas in Kiangsu forged ahead economically and culturally. The Liang-huai Salt Administration, with its headquarters in Yang-chou and its large salt factories along the northern and central Kiangsu coast, spread wealth and culture far and wide in the once backward northern two thirds of the province. The importance of the Grand Canal as inland transportation and a commercial artery made many a northern Kiangsu locality prosperous. While in Ch'ing times Su-chou and Ch'ang-chou remained national leaders, academic success was much more evenly shared by the rest of the province except the poor Hai-chou department county in the extreme northeast. It seems that the rest of the province registered gains in Ch'ing times mainly at the expense of Su-chou and Sung-chiang. Although Su-chou with a total of 785, which being based largely on local history is likely to have been somewhat exaggerated, ranked second in the country, it suffered a loss of 185 as compared with the Ming total. The reasons for the drastic decline in academic success of Sung-chiang Prefecture, which produced 229 *chin-shih* as compared with 466 for the Ming period, cannot be exactly known.[25] It was definitely due in part to the increasing competition from other parts of the province and also to the probability that much of its human resources was diverted to the economic sphere, especially after the rise of Shanghai as the nation's leading port.

Whatever the explanation for the significant change in geographic distribution of academic success in Kiangsu in Ch'ing times, our figures show that the three historically prominent prefectures of Su-chou, Ch'ang-chou, and Sung-chiang accounted for a reduced share of 57.6 percent of the provincial total. The remarkably wide dissemination of academic success in this province during the Ch'ing period may be partially evidenced by the prefectural distribution of first-class honors men who depended as much on personal genius as on local cultural milieu. This will be shown in table 37.

The striking inter-dynastic change in the distribution of academic success in Fukien was that whereas the three coastal prefectures of Fu-chou, Hsing-hua, and Ch'üan-chou had dominated in Ming times, Fu-chou alone achieved an astounding degree of concentration under the Ch'ing at the expense of the rest of the province. The concentration of academic success along the central and southern Fukien coast in Ming times was apparently accounted for by its long cultural tradition and particularly by the unusual opportunities provided by a flourishing international trade. Ch'üan-chou, a leading international port of call in Eastern Asia through-

TABLE 37

PREFECTURAL DISTRIBUTION OF FIRST-CLASS
HONORS MEN IN KIANGSU
(*Ch'ing period*)

| Prefecture | Number |
|---|---|
| Su-chou | 42 |
| Ch'ang-chou | 20 |
| Sung-chiang | 7 |
| Chen-chiang | 12 |
| Yang-chou | 11 |
| Chiang-ning | 7 |
| Hsü-chou | 1 |
| T'ai-ts'ang[a] | 9 |
| T'ung-chou[a] | 4 |
| Hai-chou | 0 |

Source: Fang-Tu list.
  [a] Department counties which were smaller than ordinary prefectures.

out the Ming, created huge fortunes for the comparatively few and ample opportunities of gainful employment for the poor. It was not only an area of high academic success but also one of very high mobility rates for the poor and humble. The 1621–25 edition of its prefectural history testified: "Almost every household, down to the poorest, considers classical studies an honor and a necessity, with the result that high degree holders and officials often arise from the very humble."[26] The 1763 edition of its prefectural history, based apparently on old local impressions, said that it was common for "the poor who did not even have enough to eat to come back as new officials but with hardly any cash in their pockets."[27] To a lesser extent this was true for other parts of Fukien in Ming times, as may be evidenced by the fact revealed in table 33 that Fukien led all provinces in Ming times in the ratio of Category A candidates per million mean population, which is 262 as compared with the next highest average of 147, shared by Chekiang and Kiangsi.

The historically flourishing international trade along much of the Fukien coast was disrupted by the struggle between the Ming loyalist Cheng Ch'eng-kung, commonly known to western scholars as Koxinga, and the Dutch, and later between him and the conquering Manchus, the subsequent closure of all southeastern ports, and the compulsory evacuation of southeastern coastal inhabitants. After the completion of the Manchu conquest most of the foreign trade gravitated to Canton. It seems to be more than coincidental that the permanent decline of coastal trade in this over-congested and mountainous province was accompanied by a drastic fall of mobility rates in Ch'ing times. Thanks to the post-1702 provincial quota system, Fukien was able to maintain a more or less fixed portion of *chin-shih*. But it was the provincial capital area, Fu-chou Prefecture, that gained at the expense of Ch'üan-chou, Hsing-hua, and Chang-chou. As shown in table 36, Fu-chou increased its number of *chin-shih* from 654 to 723 and its percentage in the provincial total from 39 to 51.7. From late Ming times onward Fu-chou has been known as an area of prominent clans and families.[28]

Significant changes in the geographic distribution of academic success took place in Chekiang as well. Our statistics show that in Ming times four prefectures of Chekiang produced over 500 *chin-shih*, a record which remained unsurpassed in the Ch'ing period. The two prefectures Shao-hsing and Ning-po south of the Hang-chou Bay produced more *chin-shih* than the three richer northern prefectures of Hang-chou, Chia-hsing, and Hu-chou. The precise reasons for this unusual phenomenon cannot be known, but the 1586 edition of the history of Shao-hsing Prefecture yields some valuable clues:

The number of local students has been increasing ever since the beginning of the Southern Sung period. . . . Nowadays even the very poor would be ashamed if they did not instruct their sons in the classics. From tradesmen to local-government runners there are very few who cannot read or punctuate. . . . Our local people are generally arrogant and the distinction between officials and commoners is rather blurred. When one has got barely enough to live one is reluctant to accept others as his social superiors. Nor is he willing to pay respect to the wealthy and powerful. . . . [Our locality] does not have the very rich but it is also free from the indigent. . . . Compared with neighboring areas, our locality has always placed more emphasis on culture. It is fairly common for students to be proficient in literature or to set up literary societies. Lately people have been influenced by Wang Yang-ming and interested in philosophy as well. Both in literature and in philosophical discussions there has been considerable achievement.[29]

It goes on to testify to the fact that in Wang Yang-ming's native county of Yü-yao the poorer one was the more arrogant one became, and that scholars and officials were usually men of moral fiber.[30]

Although there may have been many other factors we do not know, this description of local customs and traits corroborates the known fact that Shao-hsing had been an area of high mobility rates before and after Wang Yang-ming. It may indeed be said that Wang, with all his emphasis on intuitive knowledge and belief in the intrinsic equality of men, was a product of the typically Shao-hsing milieu which he in turn profoundly influenced. Throughout the sixteenth century the prefecture held the national leadership in academic success, which was not taken over by Su-chou until after 1600.

In the Ming period Shao-hsing and Ning-po produced 1,575 *chin-shih* as against an aggregate of 1,351 for the three rich northern prefectures of the province. Other relatively poor Chekiang prefectures were by no means insignificant in *chin-shih* production. In fact, Chekiang in Ming times was much like Kiangsu during the Ch'ing period, characterized by a remarkably wide dissemination of academic success, despite the astounding records of certain prefectures. One indication of this was that of the eleven prefectures of Chekiang only the two poorest mountainous areas, Ch'ü-chou and Ch'u-chou, failed to produce at least two first-class honors men. This record is surpassed only by that of Kiangsu in Ch'ing times.

The most significant change in Chekiang in Ch'ing times was the heavy concentration of academic success in the three northern prefectures, particularly Hang-chou. Their share in provincial *chin-shih* rose from 41.2 percent to 70 percent after the change of dynasty. Hang-chou, with a total of 1,004, led the prefectures of the country by a wide margin, if the subprovince of Shun-t'ien is excluded. One obvious reason was that the delta along the Hang-chou Bay and the T'ai-hu Lake was among the country's most advanced areas of rice, tea, and silk production and that this area's great economic and human resources could not in the long run fail to be translated into academic success. But there were other more specific reasons too. The continual influx of wealth, talent, and culture after the reform of the Liang-che Salt Administration in the late Ming period made

Hang-chou one of the greatest cultural centers of the country. The metropolitan Hang-chou area in Ch'ing times boasted, among other things, of more nationally famous libraries than any other large urban center.[31] The contribution of Hui-chou salt merchants and their descendants to Hang-chou's academic preeminence was known even to the Ch'ien-lung emperor.[32] Moreover, while Hang-chou benefited greatly from immigration and Chia-hsing and Hu-chou either maintained or improved their academic success, the once dynamic area of Shao-hsing and Ning-po suffered from considerable emigration and hence contributed significantly to the success of Hang-chou and especially other provinces.[33] Over-congestion and limited resources had forced many Shao-hsing and Ning-po people to earn their livings elsewhere, a phenomenon which deeply struck a scholar-official of Shanghai in the sixteenth century.[34] In fact, emigration was not confined to these two prefectures but was fairly common in the rest of the province south of the Hang-chou Bay, which is traditionally called Che-tung.[35] By late Ming and Ch'ing times so many Shao-hsing people had gone out that Shao-hsing *shih-yeh,* subofficials, or members of officials' private staffs who had an expert knowledge of fiscal and legal matters, were to be met almost everywhere in the country. Those who served in various central government agencies often chose to settle permanently in the metropolitan counties of Wan-p'ing and Ta-hsing near Peking in order that their profession could be handed on from one generation to another. A sampling of Ming-Ch'ing *chin-shih* lists reveals that dozens of *chin-shih* of these two metropolitan counties were of Shao-hsing descent. It was indeed remarkable for Shao-hsing to be able to produce 505 *chin-shih* in Ch'ing times who were strictly under Shao-hsing residential registration. Ning-po's decline in academic success in Ch'ing times was much more drastic, and is comparable to that of the Sung-chiang area. With its total reduced from 598 to 219, Ning-po lagged far behind the Ch'ing prefectural leaders, although it still compared favorably with ordinary and many larger prefectures. Whether there was any causal relationship between its declining academic success and the rise of Ning-po merchants, shippers, industrialists, and financiers, which is common in modern China, we can only surmise. As academic competition became ever more acute in Ch'ing times, the advantages of large urban centers with great cultural resources became more obvious. The other six Chekiang prefectures were hopelessly outdistanced by the northern three.

The fact that in the course of time academic success tended to become concentrated in a few large urban centers can be partially illustrated with figures. Since many large counties in Ming-Ch'ing times were split into two or three counties but in modern times are consolidated into one, we treat them as one unit. Wan-p'ing and Ta-hsing, though always two counties, were in fact inseparable. Likewise, we treat Chiang-tu, the capital city of Yang-chou Prefecture, and its virtual appendage I-cheng, and the twin cities of P'an-yü and Nan-hai, which make up metropolitan Canton, as one unit.

TABLE 38

### LOCALITIES OF OUTSTANDING ACADEMIC SUCCESS IN CH'ING TIMES

| County | Prefecture and province to which the county belonged | Modern name of the county | Total number of chin-shih |
|---|---|---|---|
| Jen-ho and Ch'ien-t'ang | Hang-chou, Chekiang | Hang-hsien | 756 |
| Wan-p'ing and Ta-hsing | Shun-t'ien, Hopei | Same | 691 |
| Min-hsien and Hou-kuan | Fu-chou, Fukien | Min-hou | 557 |
| Ch'ang-chou, Yüan-ho and Wu-hsien | Su-chou, Kiangsu | Wu-hsien | 504 |
| Wu-ch'eng and Kuei-an | Hu-chou, Chekiang | Wu-hsing | 325 |
| Shan-yin and K'uei-chi | Shao-hsing, Chekiang | Shao-hsing | 277 |
| Wu-chin and Yang-hu | Ch'ang-chou, Kiangsu | Wu-chin | 265 |
| P'an-yü and Nan-hai | Kuang-chou, Kwangtung | Same | 248 |
| Shang-yüan and Chiang-ning | Chiang-ning, Kiangsu | Nanking | 184 |
| Chiang-tu and I-cheng | Yang-chou, Kiangsu | Same | 175 |
| Chia-hsing and Hsiu-shui | Chia-hsing, Chekiang | Chia-hsing | 168 |
| Wu-hsi and Chin-k'uei | Ch'ang-chou, Kiangsu | Wu-hsi | 163 |

Sources: For Jen-ho and Ch'ien-t'ang, *Hang-chou fu-chih* (1923 ed.); for Wan-p'ing and Ta-hsing, *Shun-t'ien fu-chih* (1885 ed.), amended by Fang-Tu list; for Min-hsien and Hou-kuan, *Fu-chou fu-chih* (1754 ed.), amended; for Ch'ang-chou, Yuan-ho and Wu-hsien, *Kuo-ch'ao Su-chou-fu ch'ang-yüan-wu san-i k'o-ti p'u* (1906 ed.); for Wu-ch'eng and Kuei-an, *Kuo-ch'ao Hu-chou-fu k'o-ti piao* (printed some time after 1905); for P'an-yü and Nan-hai, *Kuang-chou fu-chih* (1879 ed.), amended. All the rest are based on the Fang-Tu list. It should be noted that *Wu-hsi chin-k'uei hsien-chih* (1883 ed.) and *Wu-chin-yang-hu-hsien ho-chih* (1879 ed.) yield totals much larger than those obtained from the Fang-Tu list and are therefore rejected.

# CHAPTER VII

# RECAPITULATION AND CONCLUSION

THE major ancient Chinese schools of thought, being products of the feudal age, all advocated the maintenance of a hierarchical society with a sharp demarcation in rights and obligations between the ruling and the ruled and justified such a social system by the principle that ruling-class membership should be based on individual merit. While all the major schools eventually resolved this antithesis in social ideology, the Confucian school alone offered a concrete solution—equal educational opportunity for all. The solution so offered was remote from social realities, but Confucius himself had already laid down an example by accepting students from the high and the low alike and Mencius never ceased harking back to the idealized antiquity when schools at various levels were alleged to have existed as a channel for the recruitment of men of merit for public service. With the triumph of Confucianism in the latter half of the second century B.C., the Imperial Academy was established and an *ad hoc* system of recommending men of talents for state service was introduced. This marked the first step toward the implementation of the Confucian social ideology. By the seventh century a further stride was made in this direction, as the T'ang empire made competitive civil-service examination a permanent system by which men of talents were selected as officials. From the eleventh century onward, more schools and private academies were established until, after the founding of the Ming empire, China began to have a rudimentary but nationwide state school and scholarship system. The repeated early Ming imperial exhortations for setting up community schools further tackled the problem of elementary education. While it is true that in no period of Chinese history did the Confucian ideal fully materialize, the institutionalization of a competitive examination system as the main avenue of socio-bureaucratic mobility and the existence of a large number of state and private schools are probably without parallel in major societies prior to the coming of the Industrial Revolution and national compulsory education.

Social stratification in traditional China was based in general on the Mencian principle that those who labor with their mind rule and those who labor with their physical strength are ruled. But this was only a broad principle which did not coincide exactly with the actual stratificational practice. We have found that throughout the past two thousand years not all those who labored with their mind were members of the ruling class, nor was traditional Chinese society a two-class society. While it is partially true that social stratification in Ming-Ch'ing society differs somewhat from that in the modern West because high statuses were determined primarily by higher academic degrees and position in the bureaucracy, yet the power of money was increasingly felt. Before 1450 money could indirectly help its possessor to attain higher academic degrees and statuses; after 1451 money could be directly translated into higher statuses through the purchase of studentships, offices, and official titles. This is partially shown by statistics on the initial qualifications of Ch'ing officials (tables 2 and 3) and the high ratios of academic success of salt-merchant families (table 6 and commentaries). In the light of our knowledge of late Ch'ing institutional history it may indeed be said that money, after 1850 at the latest, had overshadowed higher academic degrees as a determinant of higher statuses. Since education has become increasingly important as a determinant of social status in the advanced industrial societies of the modern West, we find that between late Ch'ing times and the rise of Communism in China in 1949 social stratification in China and in the West became increasingly similar.

Although the Ming-Ch'ing society, like the Chinese society of earlier periods, was a regulated society, we have found that the discrepancy between the social ideals embodied in legal texts and social realities was a very great one. Legally, the early Ming state prescribed that certain special-service statuses be hereditary; in fact, the complex social and economic forces, together with the lack of strong will on the part of the imperial government strictly to enforce the stringent law, made the maintenance of such special statuses impossible. In the Ming-Ch'ing period as a whole, the status system was fluid and flexible and there were no effective legal and social barriers which prevented the movement of individuals and families from one status to another.

The fluidity of the status system is partially shown by Ming statistics presented in table 4 but mainly by various types of non-quantifiable evidence ranging from biographies and genealogies to social novels and the comments of contemporary observers on clan and family affairs. So common was the fact that trade and other productive occupations either alternated or were synchronized with studies that many Ming-Ch'ing social observers were of the impression that the status distinction among the four major occupational categories (scholars, peasants, artisans, and merchants) was blurred. What is more, all types of literature agree that the most striking characteristic of the post-T'ang society was that, on one hand, social success depended more on individual merit than on family status, and that, on the other hand, high-status families had little means of perpetuating their success if their descendants were inept. Hence the long series of social observers from Sung times onward who formulated the theory of human environment as the most important factor in social success and propagated the typically post-T'ang pessimistic social view that wealth and glory were inconstant.[1] In the light of the evidence presented in chapters IV and V, these impressions and views are by and large justified. For during the Ming-Ch'ing period there were various institutionalized and noninstitutional channels which promoted the upward mobility of the humble and obscure but there were few institutionalized means to prevent the long-range downward mobility of successful families. In this sense, the Ming-Ch'ing society was highly competitive in its peculiar ways.

By far the most systematic statistics at our disposal deal with the social composition of Ming-Ch'ing *chin-shih*, the most important national elite group. From statistics presented in chapter III, the examination system does seem to have served an important political and social purpose. The early Ming Category A figures constitute a record that is probably hard for modern Western elite mobility data to surpass.[2]

Wang Ting-pao, a late T'ang *chin-shih* and the author of interesting anecdotes on the T'ang examination system, told the story that the great T'ang emperor T'ai-tsung (reigned 627–49), after seeing the theatrical and august procession of the newly graduated *chin-shih*, remarked with gratification: "The world's men of unusual ambitions have thus been trapped in my bag!" [3] Whether T'ang T'ai-tsung, from whose reign onward the examination system was regularly held, had indeed made this remark cannot easily be proved, because Wang lived nearly three centuries later. But this anecdote is indicative of what late T'ang Chinese, after having observed the political and social effect of the examination for more than two centuries, believed to have been the real purpose of the early T'ang state in making it a permanent system. In any case, subsequent rulers, especially the Ming founder, well understood that a certain degree of constant social circulation was vital to the stability of the dynasty. In fact, the examination system's long history of thirteen centuries is a most eloquent testimonial to its usefulness as a main channel of mobility and as a politically and socially stabilizing factor. It is inconceivable for a nation as large and pragmatic as China to have perpetuated an institution if it were truly a sham as some modern scholars, to whom systematic statistical data and complex institutionalized and noninstitutional factors relevant to social mobility are little or unknown, would have us believe.

It should be mentioned in passing, however, that the examination system was not without harmful effects on the state, economy, and society. As pointed out at the beginning of chapter V, ever since the eleventh century the question as to whether the examination system could meet the needs of the state had been debated. Yet within the ingenuity of the traditional Chinese it still remained by far the most objective method of talent selection. At its best the examination system, with its curricula centering on classics, literature, history, and administrative problems, produced men of sound common sense and judgment, even statesmen. At its worst it produced parrotlike scholar-officials without imagination and originality and fostered ideological conformity. (An important exception was the greater part of the sixteenth century, when Wang Yangming's doctrine of intuitive knowledge and the unity of knowledge and conduct brought about an intellectual emancipation seldom paralleled in Chinese history.) Furthermore, by rewarding one particular kind of accomplishment, the examination system accentuated the already monolithic Confucian value system. Success in trade, industry, finance, science, and technology, which has for centuries been socially esteemed in the west, was viewed in traditional China as secondary achievement. The social and cultural milieu in Ming-Ch'ing China was therefore hardly conducive to scientific and technological inventions. Socially, since the examination system was highly competitive at all its three levels, it entailed a wastage of human effort and talent on a scale vaster than can be found in most societies. The detailed records of ancestry given in late-Ch'ing *chin-shih* lists make rather sad reading, for it was not uncommon for a scholar to have failed a dozen or more times in higher-level examinations which were usually held at a three-year interval. The whole life of such luckless scholars was thus wasted in their studies and examination halls. But in terms of its effect on social mobility and social changes in post-T'ang China, few factors can compare with the examination system.

Although this study deals with the last two dynasties in Chinese history, it may be useful in the final consideration to make some observations on the important changes in Chinese society and social mobility over a longer period. In retrospect, the T'ang period was an important transition during which the monopoly of political power by the early-medieval hereditary aristocracy was gradually broken up under the impact of the competitive examination system. The fact that there was more social circulation during the T'ang than during the previous three centuries cannot be much doubted, although it is difficult to say whether the truly humble and poor had much chance of social success. Very little is known of the precise family background of prominent T'ang Chinese who owed their success to the examination. Even when T'ang literature and biographies refer to an individual's social origin as humble or lowly, the adjective must be interpreted in the T'ang social context. It is probable that such adjectives as humble and lowly were used by contemporaries only in comparison with the hereditary aristocratic clans which, if they were no longer able to monopolize political power from the mid-seventh century onward, remained the dominant political factor and enjoyed unrivaled social prestige down to the very end of the T'ang period.[4]

After the great T'ang clans finally declined amidst the incessant wars of the Five Dynasties (907–60) and the perpetuation of the examination system under the Sung (960–1279), Chinese society definitely became more mobile and the social composition of the ruling bureaucracy more broadened. An excellent recent study shows that of the early Sung (960–1126) officials with biographical entries in the *History of the Sung Dynasty* 46.1 percent may be regarded as coming from *han-tsu* (literally "humble" clans or families); whereas officials of similar social origin constitute a mere 13.8 percent of the late T'ang (756–906) officials with biographical entries in the two *Histories of the T'ang Dynasty*.[5] While within the limitations of dynastic histories the descriptions of the social origin of late T'ang and early Sung officials in the above study are as specific as can be expected, the key word "humble" must be interpreted in the T'ang context. For the Southern Sung period (1127–1279) two *chin-shih* lists with ancestral information are extant, which reveal that successful candidates from nonofficial families constituted 56.3 percent of the total of the class of 1148 and 57.9 percent of the total of the class of 1256.[6]

It should be noted that these Southern Sung figures, while highly significant, are not strictly comparable to our Ming-Ch'ing Category A *chin-shih* figures. The main reason is that in Sung times the passing of the provincial examination was merely a requisite for taking the *chin-shih* examination, not a formal degree or qualification for minor office, as it was in Ming-Ch'ing times. Perhaps a not inconsiderable portion of Sung *chin-shih* classified as coming from non-official families may well fall into our Category B and the lower stratum of Category C.

There is reason to believe that the extant Sung data, if they could be classified by the same criteria used in this study on the Ming-Ch'ing period, would yield considerably smaller Category A figures, at least in comparison with the early Ming period. As has been discussed in detail in chapter V, the number of prefectural and county schools and private academies in Sung times was much smaller than that during the Ming, and printing and other channels such as clans and community chests, which had a bearing on social mobility, were still in a stage of dormancy toward the end of the Southern Sung period.

The trend of increasing mobility continued after the founding of the Ming, when the examination and academic degree system became more elaborate and the school system truly nationwide. All this, together with the most unusual political and social circumstances in which the Ming dynasty was inaugurated, created a chapter of social mobility probably unparalleled in Chinese history. One of the important findings of this study is that Category A *chin-shih* figures were highest at the beginning of Ming times gradually became stabilized at a high level during the fifteenth and the greater part of the sixteenth centuries, began to decline drastically in the late sixteenth century, and further dropped to a stabilized low level of below 20 percent after the late seventeenth century. Other things being equal, members of successful families naturally had various competitive advantages and must in the long run prevail over the humble and poor in the competitive examination. It would appear that the chances of successful mobility for ordinary commoners would have begun to decline drastically earlier had it not been for the combined effect of the early stage of large-scale reproduction of basic classics and reference tools, the teachings of Wang Yang-ming, and the subsequent mushrooming growth of private academies. The rise of a large number of private academies, with their usual scholarship provisions, occurred just about the time that community schools had begun to decline.

The early Manchu rulers, unlike the Ming founder who came

from a poor peasant family, were mainly concerned with winning the support of the key social class in their conquered land, namely, the scholar-official class. With the exception of the Shun-chih period (1644–61), when the unusually large *chin-shih* quotas helped to maintain the Category A figures at the late Ming level, the chances of social success for ordinary commoners were continually being reduced because of the restrictive *chin-shih* quotas and the rapid multiplication of the national population, with its eventual grave economic consequences. Although the average Ch'ing Category A recruitment ratio was still not insubstantial, the consequence of this much curtailed opportunity-structure for the humble and obscure must be assessed in the Chinese social context of the time. For a nation which in the light of Ming experience had come to believe in a sort of academic Horatio Alger myth, the facts and factors reflected in the persistent downward trend in Category A series must have engendered a widespread sense of social frustra·tion. It seems pertinent to speculate whether this has had anything to do with the increasing social unrest and revolutions that have characterized nineteenth- and twentieth-century China. It was perhaps more than coincidental that the Taiping rebellion, the most massive civil war in world history, was precipitated by Hung Hsiuch'üan (1813–64), a member of a small landowning peasant family who had repeatedly failed to obtain his first degree. It ought to be pointed out, however, that while during the greater part of the Ch'ing period the rulers' "bag" had obviously failed to trap sufficient numbers of the socially ambitious, the rebellion engineered by one of the frustrated made possible a brief chapter of increased social mobility which is not shown in the statistics of chapter III but is partially reflected in table 24.

In concluding this study an attempt should be made to integrate the main statistical data with various types of qualitative evidence. Our more systematic data deal with one particular kind of social mobility, namely, entry into officialdom. Concerning occupational and other broader aspects of social mobility our available evidence, though not inconsiderable, is impressionistic and non-quantifiable. Up to the present, elite mobility and general social mobility have been separate studies and the methodological problem as to whether the former has any inferential value to the study of the later has yet to be systematically discussed. So far as the present study is concerned, fortunately, in addition to the extensive *chin-shih* series there are some useful data on *chü-jen, kung-sheng,* and *sheng-yüan.* While the attainment of the *chin-shih* degree represented almost the highest goal in social mobility, the entry into the vast body of *sheng-yüan* was very near to social mobility at the grass-roots level. The statistical data on socioacademic mobility at the local, provincial, and national levels are marked by their consistency. The bulky nineteenth-century *chü-jen* and *kung-sheng* data, for example, yield a slightly higher Category A percentage and considerably higher combined Categories A and B percentages than those of the *chin-shih* series of the corresponding period. The *Sheng-yüan* data of Nan-t'ung County show the same long-range downward trend during the whole Ming-Ch'ing period as the *chin-shih* series; the *sheng-yüan* data of Ch'ang-shu County and Hai-men Sub-county show the same trend during the entire Ch'ing period. Even during the Ch'ing period of much reduced mobility rates students from nonscholastic commoner families accounted for 48.1 percent of the total of Hai-men Sub-county and more than 50 percent of the totals of Nan-t'ung and Ch'ang-shu Counties (table 15). All the national, provincial, and local series of figures must be set against the fact that the three stages of socioacademic mobility were by nature highly competitive. Thus by implication there should have been considerable mobility at or near the broad baseline of the social pyramid before there could be a reasonably broad social representation in three categories of degree holders.

What is more, our study does not have to rely on implication alone. In arriving at a major conclusion, the historian must rely on the aggregate evidence at his disposal. Systematic statistics are the most valuable, but he must not overlook the importance of various types of qualitative evidence, such as, for the present study, biographies, genealogies, social novels, comments of contemporary observers on social, clan, and family affairs, the existence of various institutionalized and noninstitutional channels which promoted mobility, the almost complete lack of institutionalized means to prevent the long-range downward mobility of high-status families, the custom of equal inheritance which probably more than anything else functioned as a powerful leveling factor, the absence of effective legal and social barriers to status mobility, and the reasonably deep permeation into the masses, not infrequently including women and juveniles, of certain social concepts and myths conducive to mobility. In a study of this nature and scope, statistics pertaining to a specific type of mobility can have fuller meaning only when they are interpreted and assessed against the aforementioned facts, facets, and impressions, some of which are illustrated in the concrete cases of social mobility given in the Appendix. Unless the Confucian moralist authors of these types of non-quantifiable literature who unanimously testified to the common social phenomenon of inter-generation fluctuations in family fortune and the generally mobile character of the Ming-Ch'ing society were all wrong, our aggregate qualitative evidence, when integrated with statistics on socioacademic mobility, would suggest the existence of substantial mobility at all levels.

If we hazard a speculation, we find that Chinese socioacademic mobility data do seem to have certain inferential value to an understanding of general social mobility. The trend in socioacademic mobility appears to concur in the main with what we conjecture to have been the trend in general social mobility in Ming-Ch'ing times, although not without lags. It is true that no statistical data on general social mobility for the Ming-Ch'ing period exist, but we do have a considerable amount of evidence on such changing factors as economic and social conditions, fiscal burden, standard of living, and population growth, factors which must have had some bearing on social mobility in general. Much of the evidence of this type has been analyzed in detail in my study of Ming-Ch'ing population and need not be repeated here.[7]

Suffice it here to say that the early Ming period up to 1500 was one of peace, prosperity, government retrenchment, reduced fiscal burden, and steady agricultural and commercial expansion which, together with the government's unusually sympathetic attitude toward the upward mobility of the humble and the vast expansion of educational facilities, cannot have failed to have a beneficent effect on both types of mobility. Indeed, unless the combined economic, social, and institutional factors were unusually favorable to the upward mobility of the majority of the nation, it would be extremely hard for modern students to explain how the early Ming Chinese were able to achieve Category A *chin-shih* figures at such a sustained high level. The beginning of the first drastic decline in Category A figures in the late sixteenth century coincided almost exactly with the beginning of a period in which the consequence of misgovernment and the mounting fiscal burden of the people seems to have more than offset the effect of an increasingly variegated economy.

The only significant period of lag between our conjectured general mobility trend and that of socioacademic mobility is the one falling roughly between 1683 and 1775 (or possibly ending slightly earlier). During this period the power and prestige of the Ch'ing empire reached its apogee and the nation enjoyed prolonged peace, material prosperity, a lenient fiscal burden, an improved living standard, and an unprecedented population growth. The only factor that may have had some adverse effect on general social mobility during this period of contentment was the increasing concentration of landownership in the Yangtze region. The combined economic and institutional factors were so favorable that even the rapid and sustained population growth was viewed by contemporaries, up to about 1775, as an almost unqualified blessing. Yet, owing to the government's restrictive *chin-shih* quotas, the Category A figures show a further decline from the late Ming level.

After 1775 the conjectured general mobility trend and the trend of socioacademic mobility again seem to concur. From 1775 onward the momentum of population growth and technological stagnation created various economic difficulties which were further aggravated by deterioration in government administration. The economic and social effect of overpopulation was observed by a number of scholars of the late eighteenth and early nineteenth centuries. The gifted scholar Kung Tzu-chen, for example, observed in 1820: "Since the late Ch'ien-lung period [roughly 1775–1795] the officials and commoners have been very distressed and slipping fast. Those who are neither scholars and farmers nor artisans and merchants constitute nearly one half of the population. . . . In general, the rich households have become poor and the poor hungry. The educated rush here and there but to no avail, for all are impoverished." [8] It ought to be noted that in the post-1775 period the decline in Category A figures appears to be milder than the rapid and drastic deterioration in economic and social conditions. But our *chin-shih* data do not deal with the entry into officialdom by purchase; if the latter factor is taken into account, the actual chances of successful upward mobility of the humble and obscure would have been much less. The trends in socioacademic and general social mobility seem therefore by and large compatible.

What appears to be the fundamental difference between social mobility in Ming-Ch'ing China and social mobility in the modern West is the long-range changing trends. Whereas in industrial societies the continual technological revolution and economic dynamism, on balance, brought about a steady upward mobility trend in terms of income and occupation,[9] in Ming-Ch'ing China the multiplication of population and technological and institutional stagnation made a long-range downward mobility trend inevitable.[10]

# SELECTED CASES
# OF SOCIAL MOBILITY

THIS appendix illustrates the different patterns and processes of social mobility with twenty-seven cases selected from Ming-Ch'ing biographical literature. While the aggregate quantity of Ming-Ch'ing biographical literature is impressive, the amount useful for social mobility studies is limited. Dynastic histories and standard biographical series, being highly formalistic in style and in content, offer little more than a chronological summary of a man's public service or other types of achievements. His family background and early life are in most cases unrecorded or given a cursory mention. Biographical sketches in local histories, though useful for checking the lives of local notables who failed to achieve national prominence, are so brief that they are risky sources for the study of inter-generation social mobility. Biographies in the modern sense, therefore, simply did not exist in traditional China. There is, however, a fair amount of better quality *nien-p'u* (biographical sketches arranged chronologically), *tzu-ting nien-p'u* (autobiographical sketches arranged chronologically), collected works of prominent men which sometimes contain materials on their family background and early life, and obituary articles and commemorative albums either by descendants of the deceased or by well-known scholars. All these types of literature, if unsatisfactory as biographies, throw more light on social mobility than do standard biographical series.

In presenting these cases my guiding principle has been to summarize those based on two or more sources and to paraphrase or translate the shorter ones based on one source with as little alteration as possible. When the original literature contains information about a family over a number of generations, the early history of the family prior to the crucial stage of mobility is briefly summarized, because this kind of information helps us to understand better the vicissitudes of family fortune which, though taken by contemporaries as normal social phenomena, cannot be shown by the statistics of chapter III. When broad information on the family or ancestry is lacking in the original literature, we have to deal with the individual rather than with the family. It is impossible therefore to give all cases uniform treatment. There were certain values, deeds, and sentiments which the traditional Chinese Confucian moralists chose to emphasize. Unless such elements in a biographical article are proved to be apocryphal, no attempt is made to exclude them from the summary of life or family histories. This is not entirely unjustifiable because, however historically minded the modern historian may be, he cannot be expected to comprehend to the full the experiences and emotions of men of bygone times. Only by preserving the original literary flavor and by sampling it in the light of our knowledge of Ming-Ch'ing social circumstances can we gain a certain degree of insight into the hopes, fears, aspirations, and frustrations which, though they are remote to modern students, once shaped the lives and destinies of men.

The criteria of selection should be briefly explained. The cases are selected partly because of the quality of the literature, the nature and interest of the individual case, or useful side lights on mobility, partly because of superior chronological coverage. Even though the predominant characteristics of two cases may be essentially similar, the very fact that they are a century or more apart merits the inclusion of both. For the period covered by our study is long and we want to know whether certain types of mobility were possible in different subperiods. The inclusion of similar cases occurring at different times therefore seems justified because the combined institutional, economic, and demographic factors were constantly changing. However, in terms of early career patterns and the processes of early mobility many good cases of the same broad pattern have to be excluded in order for us to illustrate as many different types of mobility as possible.[1] The numbers of cases which fall into certain broad categories, if indeed broad categorization of the mobility pattern is possible, do not indicate even roughly the actual proportions of types of mobility in Ming-Ch'ing society. For example, cases of "ploughing with the writing brush," which means earning a living by teaching with meager pay, may well have been numerically the most important in successful upward mobility. But for the reasons given above, we select only five cases which are fairly well spaced between the end of the fifteenth century and the end of the nineteenth century.

All in all, therefore, these twenty-seven selected cases are intended to be little more than raw materials for social mobility studies. The best of the selected cases specify the social and economic standing of the individual or the family at every major stage of the mobility process. At the very least, the cases so selected, being more detailed and precise than the briefer examples given in chapter II and elsewhere in the main text, provide some information on the patterns and processes of mobility, and many of them reveal the complex interplay of social and psychological factors which the statistics in chapter III, in their necessary simplification, cannot adequately describe. It is also hoped that these cases will demonstrate more concretely the social contexts of each of the broadly defined status categories used in chapter III and further illustrate the fact that the mobility rates shown in that chapter are minimized.

The twenty-seven cases are arranged chronologically. Notes at the end of each case point out certain facts and factors which appear to me to be of special interest.

CASE 1: T'ang Kuei, *chin-shih* of 1490[2]

T'ang Kuei, who eventually became a *chin-shih* in 1490, was born in a poor family of Wu-chin in southern Kiangsu. His father, being an invalid, could not earn a living. Owing to the family's scholarly tradition, T'ang Kuei never had the inclination to be anything but a scholar, although the family had not produced any degree holder. In the latter half of the fifteenth century essays by successful candidates were not yet systematically compiled and printed for sale. T'ang Kuei, however, saw the possibility of making a living by carefully selecting and editing them for sale to students of government and private schools. Whenever he came across such essays he borrowed and copied them. In order to support his parents, younger brothers, and sisters, he sometimes went to neighboring counties to sell his anthologies of winning examination essays. In the beginning he not infrequently traveled without sufficient food. Once he sighed: "If I cannot achieve success, my parents will someday be buried in a ditch [as the poor and humble]." He therefore redoubled his scholastic effort. Neither hunger nor cold could stop him.

When he was sixteen years old [3] he passed the local examination and acquired his *sheng-yüan* degree. To increase his chances of employment he prematurely capped himself.[4] He was therefore hired by a local family as teacher for beginners. After placing first in subsequent reviewing tests supervised by the provincial educational commissioner, he became better known and offers came from well-to-do local or even distant families. His salary was increased from a mere pittance to 100 taels a year. Not until then could he provide proper food and basic necessities for his parents and pay for his brothers' and sisters' weddings. After some twenty years he had accumulated sufficient savings to buy some 300 *mu* of rice paddies. Then he decided to quit teaching and to concentrate on advanced studies.

He passed the provincial examination in 1489. In 1490 he placed third in the metropolitan examination. Later he was appointed a supervisory censor of the Board of Revenue. While in Peking he often wrote home advising his younger brothers not to seek office or profit with too much eagerness, for what he had earned would be shared with all of them. He was later transferred to Hainan Island, where he died in active service as a prefect. At time of his death the family property remained the same 300 odd *mu*.

His son T'ang Pao, after becoming a *chü-jen* in 1510, failed six times to obtain the *chin-shih* degree. He was appointed magistrate of Hsin-yang department county in Honan and eventually promoted to the position of prefect of Yung-chou in Hunan. The third generation produced the most famous of the T'angs, T'ang Shun-chih (1507–60), who placed first in the metropolitan examination of 1529. He reached the office of deputy censor-general (rank 3a) and was an essayist and historian of national renown. The most successful of the fourth generation was T'ang Ho-cheng, son of T'ang Shun-chih, also a *chin-shih,* who compiled the 1618 edition of the prefectural history of his ancestral Ch'ang-chou, which is rich in institutional and fiscal matters.

*Note:* This is a case of "ploughing with the writing brush" *par excellence.* One important social and cultural fact to be noted is that the editing and sale of winning examination essays as supplementary reading for aspirants to academic degrees did not begin to become common until the second quarter of the sixteenth century. It is doubtful whether in a later period struggling scholars of a social and economic status comparable to T'ang Kuei's could acquire the same amount of property by the same profession.

CASE 2: Ch'i Hsien, *chin-shih* of 1526[5]

Ch'i Hsien was a native of Ch'üan-chiao, Anhwei. His great-grandfather, Ch'i T'ung, was a tall, handsome, and ambitious man. When a young man Ch'i T'ung once performed *corvée* duties in the national capital and became envious of the high officials who rode in sedan chairs and horse carriages, followed by large retinues. He stamped his feet and sighed: "Alas! With my seven-foot body, why should I serve others! How I wish that someday my sons and grandsons may become high officials to wash away my shame!" But his sons and grandsons remained farmers and did not study. When he was dying at the age of ninety-two he clapped his hips and sobbed, saying: "Is it not Heaven that my family should have failed to produce a single degree holder, let alone high officials!"

When he was buried, a tatterdemalion Taoist monk pointed at the grave and said to Ch'i Ssu-an, one of the old man's grandsons: "Ten years after this burial a man destined for high position will be born to you and will change your commoner's attire; how regrettable that the old man could not see that day!" Ten years afterwards Ch'i Hsien was born in the eighth lunar month of 1492.

Ch'i Ssu-an had four sons; all except Ch'i Hsien were engaged in farming. Ch'i Hsien, being young and feeble, could not stand heavy field work, but he was intelligent and fond of studies. As a little boy he heard from his elders what his great-grandfather had said on his deathbed. He was saddened and humiliated, and vowed to become established. His father, however, disliked study and often ordered him to carry a heavy load. He entreated that he be exempted from strenuous physical labor but to no avail. His mother often sobbed together with him. A neighboring elder found this out and offered Ch'i Hsien room and board so that he could study.

Shortly after the turn of the fifteenth century Ch'üan-chiao county was short of people who could be enlisted for clerical work at the magistrate's office. Some local-government underlings tried to draft Ch'i Hsien. He entreated his father once more that he be allowed to take the *sheng-yüan* examination in order to avoid lowly clerical work. His father at last gave in and stopped interfering with his studies. In two years Ch'i Hsien obtained his *sheng-yüan* degree.

Because of the number of people to be fed, the family was now poor. Ch'i Hsien contracted tuberculosis, a result of prolonged malnutrition. His mother's death dealt him a further blow. He lay in bed for several years before he finally recovered and was married at the age of twenty-nine. He was one of the two *sheng-yüan* of the locality chosen to supervise famine relief in 1522. The next year for the first time he came across the recent writings of the great statesman-philosopher Wang Yang-ming, which opened up a new intellectual vista for him. Thereafter he acquired an unusual fluency of thought which greatly helped his literary compositions. In 1525 he passed the provincial examination held in Nanking and in the following year he became a *chin-shih*. He eventually reached the office of supervisory censor of the Board of Punishments (ranks 5a).

*Note:* This case is interesting for several reasons. First, in spite of the monolithic value system in traditional China, many small landowning peasant families like the Ch'i family were more concerned with practical living than with the upward social climb. The reason may well have been the need for all available hands for farm work. Second, at a crucial stage in Ch'i Hsien's upward mobility aid came from a sympathetic neighbor, a fact which was fairly common in traditional Chinese society. Third, Ch'i Hsien represents many cases in which psychological challenge played an important role in eventual success. Fourth, Ch'i Hsien was one of the many humble men of the early sixteenth century intellectually emancipated by Wang Yang-ming's teaching of the intrinsic equality of all men and the importance of intuitive knowledge. It should be mentioned that three or four decades after Wang's theories became an intellectual vogue topics for examination essays were often philosophical in nature, based more on Wang's theories than on the state-sponsored classical commentaries by the Sung philosopher Chu Hsi.

CASE 3: Chang Feng (*fl.* mid-sixteenth century)[6]

The family of Chang Feng in T'ai-ts'ang County in Kiangsu had for generations been engaged in farming and studies. The family holding being small, it did not enable him to concentrate on his studies without material worries. His devotion to studies interfered with his farm work. Thus farm work and studies hampered each other. His father was deaf and invalid so that the burden of supporting the family fell upon him when he was young. When he grew a little older he sometimes went out to seek better teachers but he could not afford the tuition. Some teachers pitied him and taught him without charge. He disliked farming so much that he decided at the age of fifteen to become a village teacher. Although short and unattractive, he was dignified and took to teaching very seriously. He soon passed his *sheng-yüan* examination and ranked high in subsequent reviewing tests and hence later received government stipends. Being confident of his mastery of literature, he thought that higher degrees were within his grasp. However, it was his fate that after having been a *ling-sheng* for some thirty years he had still not been promoted to *kung-sheng* by the time he died at the age of seventy-two.

The family was so poor that not until seven years after his death did his son, also a *sheng-yüan,* muster enough money to bury him properly. It was then that his son requested the most famous man of letters of his native T'ai-ts'ang, Wang Shih-chen, one of the foremost poets, prose masters, and historians of the sixteenth century, to write this biographical essay for his luckless father.

*Note:* This case is interesting in reflecting the permeation of the Confucian value system into the minds of economically hard-pressed small landowning peasants, a case which is in contrast to case 2. Also, it represents a large number of cases of arrested social mobility, for which written records have been preserved only by accident. Furthermore, it shows that a poor struggling *sheng-yüan*'s social status was far from a high one: hence the dubious status concept of Chang Chung-li that *sheng-yüan* constituted what he calls "lower gentry."

CASE 4: Sun I-ch'ing (*fl.* mid-sixteenth century)[7]

Sun I-ch'ing was a native of Hsiu-ning County in Hui-chou. Even when young he despised people of his ancestral area who were money-minded. His father, a small tradesman, once took him on a business tour of the lower Yangtze. One day he said to his father: "What is better, to study Confucian Classics or to follow the Hui-chou people in trade? Sir, since I am your only son, why should you ruin my future by forcing me to learn trade?" His father was impressed by his ambition and agreed to let him study. Sun thereupon concentrated on his studies and soon became a *sheng-yüan*. His high ranking in reviewing tests entitled him to enter a leading local private academy where he had better facilities and intellectual associations. However, he repeatedly failed the provincial examinations.

The fact that his father was aging and that he had never helped to manage the business put the family in a difficult economic position. Some tradesmen of the area asked his father whether he regretted that he had let his son quit trade and take up studies. His father, still hoping for his son's eventual success, said that he was pleased and had no regret. In fact, the reward never came. For when Sun I-ch'ing died at the age of over seventy neither he nor his son was established. It was many years after his death that his son finally went to Peking to take a special *kung-sheng* examination in the hope of receiving a minor office. He met Wang Shih-chen in Peking and in tears pleaded with the great writer that, since he had fallen far short of his late father's expectations, only through Wang's biographical essay could his late father's memory be salvaged from complete oblivion.

*Note:* This is essentially similar to the preceding case except that the family background was different and that eventually the biographee's son acquired the minimum qualification for a minor office.

CASE 5: Hsü Kuo (1527–96), Prime Minister, 1583–90[8]

The Hsü family of She-hsien, the capital city of Hui-chou Prefecture, had been engaged in trade for generations. Some branches were comparatively well to do, but Hsu Kuo's own branch was poor. As far as he could recall, none of his direct ancestors was a degree holder. His maternal ancestors were likewise obscure and humble commoners. Before she was married, his mother used to listen to neighboring school lectures so that she could grasp the general meaning of basic Confucian texts, a quality which later on helped her son to begin his studies at home at a time when the family could not afford a formal tutor.

Like many another small Hui-chou tradesmen, Hsü Kuo's father had a certain degree of literacy but very little working capital. The initial trading capital was derived from his wife's small dowry. Being an assistant to his tradesman uncle in southern Kiangsu most of the time, he returned home once every three or four years, sometimes once every eight or nine years. Family reunions were usually of short duration, lasting only three or four months. The burden of supporting the family fell mostly on Hsü Kuo's mother, who made a living by doing embroidery. The income being small, she was forced to wear thin clothes the year round and not infrequently stretched one day's food over two. Because of the brief reunions at long intervals with her husband her children were widely spaced. Hsü Kuo was fifteen years younger than his brother. Not until he was six years old did he see his father for the first time.

An intelligent and studious child, Hsü Kuo won the sympathy of one of his father's paternal cousins who could afford to hire a family tutor. He was admitted to the family school and given a certain amount of financial aid in times of dire need. When he was nine his tradesman granduncle died and his father brought the family to Ch'ang-shu, in southern Kiangsu, where the whole family lived together for six years. The opportunities for associating with the scholars of a highly cultured city proved to be of great help to Hsü Kuo scholastically. Two years after the family returned to She-hsien, Hsü Kuo obtained his *sheng-yüan* degree, at the age of seventeen. But what little savings his father had accumulated through the years were wiped out by a series of misfortunes such as famine, epidemic, deaths in Hsü Kuo's mother's family and costs of burial, as well as extortion and blackmailing by neighboring scoundrels. His father was rapidly losing his eyesight. Fortunately, by this time the family was able to keep going on Hsü Kuo's small income as a teacher of the deputy magistrate's family school.

In 1562 Hsü Kuo obtained his *chü-jen* degree in his fifth trial. His father died the same year and his mother passed away in the following year. In 1565 he placed seventh in the palace examination and was selected as a bachelor of the Han-lin Academy. The opportunities to further his advanced studies in this highly respected institution and later to serve as a tutor to the heir apparent accounted for his rapid official advancement.

Hsü Kuo's prolonged hardships as a child and young man made him extremely mild-mannered and compassionate. His daily almsgiving to the beggars of Peking was widely known and occasionally ridiculed.[9] In spite of his successful career, none of his descendants became prominent. Among his four sons, the eldest was a *sheng-yüan* and the second entered government service through the *yin* privilege as a secretary of the Imperial Patent Office (rank 7a). Both died before Hsü Kuo. The two other sons were still young at time of his death. Of his four daughters, two married students of Imperial Academy, one married an ordinary commoner, and only one married the son of a minor official. The second of his brother's sons became a minor official, probably owing to Hsü Kuo's help. His unusual personal success does not seem to have brought about any change in the pattern of life of the Hsü clan—that of trade in combination or alternation with studies.

*Note:* In spite of the clan's pattern of life, Hsü Kuo never deviated from his studies; hence this is a modified case of "ploughing with the writing brush." The two most crucial factors in his life seem to have been his mother's literacy and aid from a sympathetic kinsman. It should be pointed out that the latter half of the sixteenth century was in general a period in which *she-hsüeh,* or community schools, declined and that Hsü Kuo's was one of the fairly numerous cases in which a man's success was due in part to noninstitutional, personal help from kin or friends.

CASE 6: The Hsü Family of Hsüan-cheng[10]

The father of Hsü Yüan-t'ai, *chin-shih* of 1565, was originally a jail warden of a Chekiang county. Once he offended a circuit censor and was severely humiliated and punished. He was so ashamed that he resigned and retired to his native Hsüan-ch'eng in southern Anhwei. Up to this time his two sons had not been able to make rapid progress in their studies, due partly to his low emolument and partly to the lack of proper supervision. The ex-warden had been so deeply hurt that he sometimes sobbed. One day his two sons knelt before him and asked the reason for his sadness. After telling them his humiliating experience, he said: "If you brothers do not redouble your scholastic effort, I would better regard myself as having no sons." The brothers swore that they would work hard and wash away his shame.

Consequently, the elder brother Hsü Yüan-ch'i[11] became a *chin-shih* in 1562 and was later promoted to the position of governor of Yunnan and commissioner of the Office of Transmission. One of his grandsons became a prefect and one of his great-grandsons was a *kung-sheng*. The younger brother Hsü Yüan-t'ai became a *chin-shih* in 1565 and eventually reached the high office of president of the Board of Punishments. Of his three sons, the eldest was a *chü-jen* of 1582 but died young. The second son, though receiving the *yin* privilege, did not enter government service. The third son became a first-class secretary of the Board of Punishments (rank 5a).

*Note:* This is another example showing how psychological challenge was a factor in social success. To be noted, too, is the fact that the *yin* privilege had no effect on the subsequent mobility of the family.

CASE 7: The Ancestry of Hsü Kuang-ch'i (1562–1633) [12]

The ancestry of Hsü Kuang-ch'i, the famous Christian prime minister, scientist, and cotranslator with Matteo di Ricci and other Jesuits of several European scientific, technological, geographic, and theological treatises, offers an excellent case of the zigzag course that a family might take before it was socially elevated through academic success.

The Hsü family first migrated from Lo-yang, Honan, to Su-chou in southern Kiangsi in the 1120s, when North China fell to the invading Juchens. By the time of Hsü Kuang-ch'i's great-great-grand-father the family had moved to Shanghai. Little is known about this great-great-grandfather because the family genealogy was lost during the frequent pillaging raids of Japanese pirates. What is known

is that he was referred to by Hsü as *kuang-wen,* an epistolary designation for a director or subdirector of a county school. He was
obviously a *kung-sheng,* possibly a *chü-jen.*

Hsü's great-grandfather could not carry on the family scholastic
tradition because of the crushingly heavy local incidence of *corvée.*
He was forced to till the family land and the family fortunes sank.
The younger of his two sons was Hsü Kuang-ch'i's grandfather,
who gave up farming and took up trade. Consequently the family
fortunes improved considerably. However, he died in the prime of
life, leaving Hsü Kuang-ch'i's father an orphan of six. On his
deathbed he entrusted the management of his property to his
father-in-law, who, in addition to offering his widowed daughter
and her only son protection, wisely chose a husband for Hsü
Kuang-ch'i's aunt, whose son later became a *chin-shih.* Thanks to
joint management by maternal relatives during a crucial period
in the family's history, the family property further expanded. To
repay the kindness of these relatives, Hsü Kuang-ch'i's grandmother
offered a tripartite division of her property.

Hsü Kuang-ch'i's father grew up a filial son and a generous man.
He donated heavily to local and clan charities. After engaging in
trade for a while he retired early to the family farm. Being the head
of a well-to-do family, he was required by the local government to
contribute to the cost of local defense against Japanese pirates. The
repeated contributions, together with his habitual generosity, his
negligence of family management, and his interest in astrology,
medicine, and the Taoist and Buddhist religions, drained most of
his once substantial resources. When Hsü Kuang-ch'i was young the
family suffered a further blow from robbers and became poor. After
obtaining his *sheng-yüan* degree in 1581, therefore, Kuang-ch'i had
to earn a living by teaching.

Between 1581 and 1597 he drifted from one place to another, first
to Shao-kuan in northern Kwangtung, where he met the Jesuits for
the first time, then to Kwangsi and Peking, "ploughing with the
writing brush." In 1597 he obtained his *chü-jen* degree in Peking
and finally, in 1604, he became a *chin-shih* and was selected as a
bachelor of the Han-lin Academy. Not until the family had gone
through a zigzag course of four generations, from scholarly pursuits

to farming, to trade, back to farming and leisured life, and then back to studies, did Hsü Kuang-ch'i finally become successful at the age of forty-two.

*Note:* This case tends to confirm the impression of many post-Sung social observers that it was fairly common for a family to witness sharp fluctuations in fortune within a limited number of generations. It also illustrates how changing fiscal burdens could affect a family's economic status.

CASE 8: The Ancestry of Li Yin-tu (1631–92)[13]

The Li family had for generations lived in Fu-p'ing County in Shansi. Li Yin-tu, the famous scholar who was called to Peking to take a special imperial examination and appointed preceptor of the Han-lin Academy in 1679, recalled that his family had begun to become rich ten generations earlier. His great-great-grandfather was a frontier merchant who regularly supplied grain to northern garrisons along the Great Wall and then sold salt in the Liang-huai area. The volume of business was large because he was responsible for the grain supply for several tens of thousands of garrison soldiers. Evidently he purchased an official title, because he was referred to by Li Yin-tu as *shang-kuan* (merchant-official). He was treated with courtesy by all officials below the rank of circuit censors. But his wealth made him the target of an unnamed powerful figure whose plots resulted in his death.

Li Yin-tu's great-grandfather spent much of his life seeking to right the wrong and eventually succeeded but wrecked the family fortune in doing so. This made it necessary for Li Yin-tu's grandfather, a military *chü-jen* and an army officer, to concentrate once more on the frontier trade. The family property was restored and its landed property expanded from some 200 *mu* to over 900 *mu,* contrary to the usual custom of Shansi merchants, who felt that silver and other forms of property constituted real wealth. The greater part of his wealth lay outside his ancestral county. At the peak of his success he had estates near the northern Shansi frontier posts as well as in the Yang-chou area, the center of the Liang-huai salt trade. For over a century the Li family was rich and allied itself through marriage with three prominent local clans.

But in 1634, when Li Yin-tu was only three years old, both his grandfather and his father died. In the same year the bandits, led by Li Tzu-ch'eng, overran the area, and eighty-one members and servants of the clan perished. The survivors were mostly women and children. The family property in and near Yang-chou was all gone. As a consequence of war and banditry Fu-p'ing was struck by serious famine which in turn further reduced the family's income. Li's mother now could not afford to pay the land tax. Moreover, the absence of adult males made it impossible for her to defend herself and her two young sons. Therefore she brought her sons to her father's house, and Li Yin-tu began to study with his maternal grandfather in 1635. At the age of ten Li placed first in the county qualifying examination and became a *sheng-yüan*.

In 1644 Li Tzu-ch'eng's forces again sacked Fu-p'ing and captured Li Yin-tu's maternal uncle, who was killed the next year. By this time even his maternal relatives had to live on borrowed money. After the restoration of peace three of the local officials who admired Li's literary talents occasionally helped him financially. Not until 1659, at the age of twenty-nine, was Li employed by an intendant as a family tutor. From this time on "the family property was gradually restored and the family could afford two dishes at each meal."

His literary fame gradually spread far and wide until he was specially recommended to the court in 1697. But he chose to remain a Ming loyalist and to retire to his ancestral district. His only son was a *ling-sheng* who bought the title of student of Imperial Academy. Of his four grandsons, the eldest became a *chü-jen* and the second a *sheng-yüan*.

*Note:* The Li family fortune took a zigzag course which is similar to that of Hsü Kuang-ch'i's. This case illustrates more clearly than the preceding one how various accidents, which were by no means uncommon in traditional China, could bring about the downfall of a sizable family fortune. Not the least of these accidents was the frequent encroachment upon the property of a widow by family employees or rapacious kinsmen.

CASE 9: Li Yung (1627–1705)[14]

Li Yung was a native of Chou-chih County in Shensi. His family had been humble for so long that he did not know the name of any ancestor except his father. The family had no land whatever and was supported by his father, an army private. Li Yung entered a village school at eight and learned from a maternal uncle to read basic classics. In 1642 his father was killed by the bandit army of Li Tzu-ch'eng. Devoid of any property, Li Yung and his mother drifted from one place to another until in the fall of 1643 they found a hut for shelter. In the next few years they were often on the verge of starvation but Li Yung, with the full approval of his mother, resolutely resisted the temptation to earn a living as a local-government runner. He once had the chance to learn geomancy and astrology free of tuition in order to make a living, but when he passed a village school the sound of boys chanting the classics convinced him that he should stand firm and resume his studies at all costs. Because of his abject poverty he was refused by several village teachers. The best he could do was constantly to review the *Analects* and the *Book of Mencius* and to ask to be enlightened whenever there was an opportunity.

Since Shensi was a cotton-producing province and cotton spinning and weaving was a common rural industry, his mother was hired as a spinner. The meager income from her spinning was not enough to buy adequate food and they often mixed grain with bran for cooking. Daily he gathered firewood, wild vegetables, and edible herbs but never forsook his studies. In 1644 a friend gave him two dictionaries which greatly helped to enlarge his vocabulary. As a youth he was so undernourished that his complexion was greenish; villagers therefore gave him the nickname of Li Ts'ai (Li, the vegetable-complexioned man).

Precisely because of his determination to become a scholar against all odds, he gradually became known to local officials. From 1646 onwards some of them occasionally gave him presents, but the family remained destitute. His mother was sick and could not spin. It is not clearly stated when Li Yung took a wife, but his mother's sickness and the family shortage of labor made it necessary that he marry. In 1648 he was asked by the magistrate to help with secretarial work. In 1650 he was already so well known to people of the locality as a poor scholar of unusual perseverance that the rich and cultured offered him the facilities of their private libraries. Thenceforth he began to read extensively and to make rapid progress in the classics, history, and literature.

There was no change in the pattern of his life during the 1650s except that he was forced to rent a small plot of land to raise food, often without success, and his growing scholarly stature and fortitude of mind won him more admirers among officials and degree holders. Some officials even called at his shabby hut and subsidized him out of their emoluments. His reputation began to spread far and wide, so far indeed that the great Kiangsu scholar Ku Yen-wu took a long trip to visit him in the tenth month of 1663. When his mother died late in 1655 many officials, degree holders, and commoners of the locality and neighboring counties came to her funeral, the expenses of which were defrayed by his admiring patrons. After the funeral was over the magistrate bought ten *mu* of land which he forced Li Yung to accept so that his sons could cultivate it.

When his patron magistrate left his post for a higher position in 1667, Li at long last went beyond the county boundaries to bid him farewell. This marked the beginning of his long tours of the country which took him to the highly cultured lower Yangtze area in the early 1670s. Everywhere he went he was requested by local officials and scholars to give public lectures. Although he had never obtained any academic degree, he was hard pressed by provincial authorities in 1679, when the K'ang-hsi emperor held a special examination for scholars of national renown. He resolutely refused to participate because he was at heart a Ming loyalist. A great honor nevertheless befell him when in 1703 the emperor toured Shansi Province and insisted on seeing him. Li Yung was then seventy-six years old and preferred death to prostrating himself before an alien conqueror. Hence his elder son went to Shansi in his stead and submitted to the emperor his father's literary and philosophical works which had been printed by his admiring friends and patrons. The emperor later bestowed on him a tablet inscribed with four characters "ts'ao-chih kao-chieh," stating that his "discipline and purpose are lofty and pure."

*Note:* While Li Yung's determination was very unusual, this case shows the permeation of Confucian values among people of abject poverty. It is interesting that Li's family moved up the social ladder despite his reluctance to acquire any degree. His two sons and one nephew were all degree holders. The elder son was a *pa-kung-sheng,* a qualification which entitled him to a minor office. Several other Ming loyalists, like Li Yung, also refused to serve the Manchus during their own lives, but they were realistic enough not to insist that their descendants follow their own examples.

CASE 10: The Fan Family of Chieh-hsiu, Shansi[15]

The Fan family had lived in Chieh-hsiu County in Shansi since the beginning of Ming times. After seven generations the family began to engage in frontier trade and became very rich. Fan Hsiao-shan, the able merchant, was called to Peking by the Shun-chih emperor (r. 1644–61), who entrusted him with trading with the Mongols of Inner and Outer Mongolia and gave him property in Kalgan, the chief trading center of Chahar. He thus became a designated merchant of the Imperial Household Department, one of his various duties being to buy furs for the department. Owing to the poor health of his son, the business passed to the eldest of his three grandsons, Fan Yü-pin.

Inheriting his grandfather's wealth and knowledge of the Mongol tribes, Fan Yü-pin became well known north of the Great Wall. When the Ch'ing empire was at war with Galdan, chieftain of the Eleuths in Chinese Turkestan, who invaded Outer Mongolia, Fan Yü-pin was charged with the task of transporting grain to the extreme northwest. His expert knowledge and careful preparation reduced the transportation cost by some two thirds. Between 1721 and 1732 he supervised the shipment of more than 1,000,000 bushels of grain. In 1729 his services were rewarded by the title of director of the Imperial Stud (rank 3a), with the additional privilege of wearing the robe and cap of an official of the second rank.

Typical of the rich merchants who enjoyed a business monopoly, Fan had to take the risks of his trade. In 1731 the war situation in the northwest was temporarily out of control and there was a heavy loss of grain and of camels and other draft animals. But within a few months the war was concluded in the government's favor, so that the bulk of grain destined for remote Turkestan was ordered to be shipped to nearer places. The total transportation cost had therefore to be reduced. Since the coolie carriers had already been paid in advance, he could not avoid taking the whole loss of 2,620,-000 taels himself. In 1738 the Ch'ien-lung emperor ordered him to purchase ginseng in the Ussuri region and copper from Japan for the government, while paying his debt to the government in installments. Despite the lenient discounts allowed for his debt, in that year he still owed the government 1,140,000 taels. But this marked the revival of the copper trade in which the family had engaged in 1699 as a side line.

While the family now concentrated on the copper trade and was no doubt able to recoup a part of the heavy loss incurred in 1731–32, there is an indication that the family fortunes never fully recovered. For in 1797 the Fan family, or rather the descendants of Fan Yü-pin, could no longer retain the right to deal in salt in the metropolitan Shun-t'ien Prefecture.

As to the pattern of social mobility of this rich merchant family, it should be said that Fan Yü-pin's two brothers became officials, one by purchase, one by obtaining a military *chü-jen* degree. The latter, Fan Yü-ch'i, though listing his military degree as his initial qualification for a junior officer post, possibly facilitated his entrance into the service by purchase. But in any case during the campaigns against the Eleuths in 1718 he did not distinguish himself on the battlefield but helped in shipping military supplies. In 1722 his promotion to *ts'an-chiang* (lieutenant colonel) was due to his monetary contribution. Although he eventually reached the position of *tsung-ping* (brigade general, rank 2a), his repeated offers to replenish draft animals and military supplies out of his own purse were refused by the court and his lack of ability was known to and despised by the Ch'ien-lung emperor. He was forced to retire in 1746 and died in 1751.

Fan Yü-pin, the merchant and pillar of the family, had four sons. Two of them obtained their *chü-jen* degrees in 1738, one was a *fu-pang* (probational *chü-jen*) in 1746, and the youngest became a *chin-shih* in 1748. With the exception of the last, who became a compiler of the Han-lin Academy on the strength of his advanced degree, the other three sons seem to have used purchase at least in part to enter government service and to facilitate their promotions. Fan Yü-pin's second brother, Fan Yü-t'an, the least known of the brothers, definitely purchased a middle-ranking office, as is evidenced by the honorary title bestowed on his father and grandfather. One of Fan Yü-t'an's sons purchased the office of a subprefect (rank 5a), and together with his intendant first cousin received a government contract for military supplies in 1757 from the governor general of Shensi and Kansu. Another of his sons was engaged in the copper trade. Fan Yü-ch'i, the brigade general, had six sons. The eldest entered government service through *yin* and eventually became a prefect. The other five were either active or expectant officials through purchase.

It should be noted that the history of Chieh-hsiu County, the ancestral district of the Fan family, lists three more members of the family in its tables of higher degree holders, a *chü-jen* of 1774, a *chü-jen* of 1777 who later became a county magistrate, and a *chin-shih* of 1834 who later became a magistrate of the department county. They can be identified as descendants of Fan Yü-pin or his brothers by the unmistakable fact that all of them, as in earlier cases in the family's history, passed their provincial examinations in Peking. This was because ever since the time of Fan Yü-pin's grandfather the family had been given property in Kalgan, designated as merchants of the Imperial Household Department, and therefore registered as residents of the metropolitan Chihli Province. The few other higher degree holders by the surname Fan in the history of Chieh-hsiu County may not have been related.

In Fan Yü-pin's prime, as testified by Wang Yu-tun, the prime minister and author of his biographical essay, the Fan family had business establishments or connections in Chihli, Hupei, Canton, and Indochina, in addition to its activities in Inner and Outer Mongolia, Manchuria, and Japan. While the element of officials and higher degree holders in the family became more and more predominant, the wealth from which much of its social success was derived was progressively diluted. It seems more than coincidental that after the Fan family had lost its right to the salt trade in Chihli in 1797 it produced few officials and higher degree holders who can be found and identified in the Chieh-hsiu County history.

*Note:* The pattern of social mobility of this very rich family of government contractors conforms in the main to those of other groups of merchant princes, such as Liang-huai salt merchants (cases 12 and 13 and Canton Co-hong merchants (case 18).

CASE 11: The Chu Family of Kao-an, Kiangsi[16]

The most prominent member of the Chu family of Kao-an in central Kiangsi was Chu Shih (1665–1736), prime minister (grand secretary) between 1725 and 1736. For centuries the Chu family had been well to do. Chu Shih's tenth generation ancestor was a *chin-shih* of 1415 who served as a first-class secretary of the Board of Punishments in Nanking. In three more generations the family reached the peak of success and prosperity, being described as "full of degree holders." But Chu Shih's seventh-generation ancestor, a typically prudent Confucian scholar, moved his own branch of the family to the countryside in the hope that his descendants would not be exposed to the corrupting influence of rich and successful kinsmen. Three generations later Chu Shih's great-grandfather, tired of taking examinations, studied Neo-Confucianism with a philosopher of prefectural renown and contributed generously to local famine relief in the early seventeenth century. Up to this time the Chu family had been wealthy.

Chu Shih's grandfather, the younger of two brothers, was a *sheng-yüan* who had hard luck in provincial examinations. Repeated failures damaged his none too robust health and he died relatively young. This left Chu Shih's grandmother and her two young sons utterly defenseless against certain rapacious kinsmen who had set their eyes on her property.

Sensing that her two sons' lives would be endangered, she chose the lesser of two evils and decided to let her property go. Although the landed property was gone, the burden of land tax remained because of her greedy kinsmen's clever contrivances. After paying taxes, her family was impoverished. Thus Chu Shih's uncle and father grew up in very difficult circumstances. His father was a *sheng-yüan* who earned a meager living by teaching. The family was now so poor that Chu Shih's mother could not afford a wet nurse during the years when his three younger brothers were born in quick succession. After Chu Shih became a *sheng-yüan* in 1687 he had to "plough in the inkslab" to help his father support the family. During the serious crop failure of 1691, when one tenth of a bushel of rice cost a hundred cash, the family did not eat for three consecutive days and nearly starved. It was with the utmost difficulty that Chu Shih's father mustered enough money to enable him to take the provincial examination in 1691, in which he placed first.

Chu Shih had much less difficulty in going to Peking to take his metropolitan examination the following year, because as a *chü-jen* he was entitled to adequate travel expenses paid out of the local community chest. After passing the metropolitan and palace examinations he was appointed a bachelor of the Han-lin Academy. The path of his official career was smooth, and he became a prime minister on the strength of his ability and personal integrity.

*Note:* Four things deserve our attention. First, the reason behind the decision made by Chu Shih's seventh-generation ancestor to move away from successful and rich kinsmen supports one of the themes presented in chapter IV: that human environment was a significant factor in the long-range downward mobility of a successful family. Second, this case is one of the many in which a widow and her young sons were victimized by rapacious kinsmen. While some, like Chu-Shih, eventually achieved success by strengthening their determination to excel scholastically, many could not recover from such a severe economic blow. Third, even a *sheng-yüan* from an old official family, like Chu Shih and his father, might actually live under very difficult circumstances. Fourth, it is abundantly clear that the *sheng-yüan* status, though necessary as a stepladder in the long process of social ascent, was far less crucial than the status of *chü-jen*.

CASE 12: The Chiang Family of Yang-chou[17]

The first known ancestor of the Chiang clan was Chiang Kuo-mao, a native of She-hsien, Hui-chou, and a *sheng-yüan* of the late Ming period. He gave up his precarious scholarly career and took up the salt trade in Yang-chou because he anticipated that the change of dynasty would offer him golden opportunities to become rich. He died without fully realizing his ambition. The family did become rich, however, during the lifetime of his son, Chiang Yen, who became a head salt merchant. One of Chiang Yen's sons succeeded him as head merchant, another became a prefect, owing to the recommendation of an imperial prince, whose favor the family must have curried through lavish entertainment. The fourth generation produced a long galaxy of men of letters, artists, connoisseurs, and officials, the most famous of whom was Chiang Ch'un,

a poet and the most colorful head salt merchant of the second half
of the eighteenth century.

Chiang Ch'un raised several monetary contributions which helped
to finance the military campaigns of the Ch'ien-lung era. For his
efforts he was awarded the title of financial commissioner (rank 2b),
the highest honor ever bestowed on a merchant. Although he was
a merchant, his poetry was highly rated by contemporaries. His
other hobbies were archery and fighting crickets, which he raised
in urns designed after an expensive Sung model. He built a villa,
called K'ang-shan-yüan, with a garden which was visited by the
Ch'ien-lung emperor in 1780. "He loved literary associations. Men
of letters from all over the country were invited to his house. He
had a hall which could accommodate a hundred guests, and that hall
was often filled." He entertained the Ch'ien-lung emperor six times
and twice represented the Liang-huai merchant body in presenting
congratulations to the empress dowager on her birthday. Finally he
participated in the imperial banquet for a thousand elders. But by
1771 he had spent and contributed so heavily that he was short of
working capital. The emperor, remembering his past service, lent
him 300,000 taels out of the treasury of the Imperial Household
Department, the profit from which, after deducting a ten percent
interest for the government, was to provide for his maintenance.
Being an old man without a male heir, he finally managed to live
on an annual income of 16,000 taels, which must have been small
in comparison with his former income. After his death in 1793, his
once famous garden was sold, upon the suggestion of the emperor,
to the whole Liang-huai merchant body as a clubhouse for 50,000
taels, a sum which was to be used by his poetry-loving adopted son
as working capital.

Although the exact size of the Chiang clan is not known, fifteen
of Chiang Ch'un's cousins and their sons were mentioned in a
famous guidebook of Yang-chou as poets, artists, and connoisseurs.
Chiang Fang, his gifted cousin, was a poet and painter of distinction.
Chiang Lan, also his cousin, entered government service through
purchase after obtaining his *kung-sheng* degree. He once served
as governor of Honan and was fined 50,000 taels for an administrative blunder. Hoping that he might regain imperial favor, he twice

contributed 30,000 taels for flood relief and public construction and died in 1809. In 1798 his son Chiang Ning, at the age of sixteen, became an expectant second-class secretary of a central Board through *yin* and purchase.[18] One of Chiang Lan's nephews also purchased a similar position, probably later than his son.[19] Chiang Hsün, also Chiang Ch'un's cousin, became an intendant; and since he did not have an advanced degree, it seems fairly certain that he entered government service through purchase. His collection of bronzes, stone rubbings, paintings, and calligraphic specimens was said to be the best south of the Yangtze. His son Chiang Te-liang (1751 or 1752–93) won the second highest honors in the palace examination of 1779 and later became a censor. Thanks to his family collection, he was a calligrapher of national renown, particularly famous for his Han style of calligraphy. The rest of the Chiang clan listed in the famous guidebook of Yang-chou were either poets or connoisseurs.

It is worth noting that Chiang Ch'un's branch was not the only one of the clan that eventually lost its wealth. However rich a family might be, the contribution in a single lifetime of a sum of 110,000 taels by one branch, as in the case of Governor Chiang Lan, must have adversely affected its economic resources, which further suffered from purchases of office by descendants, the cultivation of various expensive hobbies, and extravagant living. Ch'ien Yung, the painter of lower Yantze and a friend of Chiang Lan's nephew, recalled that Chiang Lan's garden at its prime could almost vie with Chiang Ch'un's K'ang-shan-yüan in beauty and luxury. Ch'ien had feasted and wined with Chiang Lan's nephew in the garden while listening to golden orioles. "In less than thirty years," as Ch'ien sadly testified, "the uncle and nephew have passed away and the garden has been sold to others; whenever I passed its gate I could not help feeling haunted." [20]

*Note:* It is suggested that this classic case be read in connection with the general discussions on downward mobility given in chapter IV.

CASE 13: The Ts'ao Family of She-hsien, Anhwei[21]

The grandfather of the first prominent official of the family, Ts'ao Wen-chih, was Ts'ao Shih-ch'ang, who was engaged in the salt trade in Honan. When his elder son Ts'ao Ching-t'ing obtained his first degree, his younger son Ts'ao Ching-ch'en, father of Ts'ao Wen-chih, decided that he should be a full-time salt merchant in order that, as he said, "a scholar and a merchant should each assume his distinct responsibility [to the family]."

Realizing that Honan was an area of limited business opportunity, Ts'ao Ching-ch'en switched his business to Yang-chou, the headquarters of the Liang-huai salt administration at the junction of the Yangtze and the Grand Canal. Owing to his shrewd management he built up a sizable fortune in a few years, so that his father was able to retire comfortably to She-hsien. Although he was well to do during his prime, he firmly believed in the policy of family division of function. He apprenticed his eldest son to the salt trade in Yang-chou, entrusted his second son with managing the family property in ancestral She-hsien, and gave full opportunity for serious studies to his brilliant youngest son, Ts'ao Wen-chih. Thanks to this policy of family division of labor, Ts'ao Wen-chih became a *chin-shih* and placed forth in the palace examination of 1760 at the age of twenty-five, after years of association with famous scholars of the lower Yangtze area. At fifty he reached the high office of president of the Board of Revenue.

Like his prudent father, Ts'ao Wen-chih, even during his highly successful official career, apprenticed his elder son to a salt-merchant cousin at Yang-chou, while taking with him his younger son, Ts'ao Chen-yung. The excellent opportunity for literary studies in Peking and the lower Yangtze enabled Ts'ao Chen-yung to obtain his *chin-shih* degree in 1781, at the age of twenty-six. He eventually climbed to the top of the officialdom in 1831. For approximately a quarter of a century he was in fact one of the most trusted and powerful of ministers, conservative in political outlook but incorruptible in character.

The male members of the family in 1776, when Ts'ao Wen-chih wrote his father's obituary, are given in the chart.

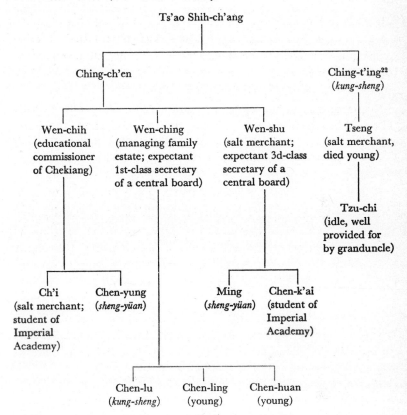

*Note:* The Ts'ao family of She-hsien, Hui-chou, which produced a president of the Board of Revenue, Ts'ao Wen-chih (1735–98), a powerful prime minister, Ts'ao Chen-yung (1755–1835), and a commissioner of the Office of Transmission (rank 3a), Ts'ao En-ying (1798–1854), in three consecutive generations, may be regarded as a classic case of success based on a realistic family strategy of division of function.

Actually the policy of family division of function was fairly common in Ming-Ch'ing times.[23] The records of the Ts'ao family also shed an interesting side light on the rather common fact that, after the family had become well to do, those of its members who could not achieve academic success purchased studentships and official titles to enhance their individual prestige. Very little is known of the Ts'ao family after Ts'ao Chen-yung's death except that one of his sons, Ts'ao En-ying, was granted the *chü-jen* degree by special imperial favor, entered government service through *yin*, and eventually rose to rank 3a.[24] Ts'ao Chen-yung's elder brother, Ts'ao Ch'i, though a salt merchant, later compiled the descriptive catalogue of the family holdings of famous paintings and calligraphic specimens, entitled *Shih-ku-yen-chai so-ts'ang shu-hua lu,* a fact which indicates the inter-generation pursuance of an expensive hobby. The Ts'ao family's lack of academic success in the nineteenth century may perhaps be partially attributed to the fact that it was no longer able to derive its wealth from the Liang-huai salt trade, which was thoroughly reformed in 1831.

CASE 14: Wang Hui-tsu (1730–1807)[25]

Wang Hui-tsu was a native of Hsiao-shan County in Shao-hsing Prefecture, Chekiang. Although this area was agriculturally and culturally advanced, the pressure of population often forced people to seek their living elsewhere as merchants, or, more often, as members of officials' private staffs. For generations Wang's ancestors were traders; some died in the remote provinces of Kweichow and Yunnan. His father, after accumulating savings from trade by which he added some 100 *mu* to the family's original modest holdings, purchased the lowly office of county jail warden (unranked) in 1730, the very year in which Wang Hui-tsu was born. The bulk of the family land was soon mortgaged because Wang Hui-tsu's uncle was addicted to gambling and the family property was not yet divided.

An early episode left a permanent imprint on Wang Hui-tsu's mind. One day in 1741 when the family was traveling to Kwangtung, his father asked him: "Son, do you know why we are going to such a remote place?" Wang Hui-tsu could not answer. His father said: "It is all for your sake; for if I were not going to work there you would have nothing to live on." Wang Hui-tsu wept; so did his father. His father immediately picked up a classic and told him to read and recite. After a while his father turned to him again, asking: "What do you think to be the purpose of studying?" Wang replied: "To hope to become an official." His father thereupon told him that he was wrong, for although with a touch of luck hard scholastic work could lead to an office, the real purpose of studying was to be a good man. Honesty, integrity, and compassion for the poor thus became the principles which guided Wang Hui-tsu's thirty-four-year career as private secretary to sixteen local officials of Kiangsu and Chekiang.

His father's death in 1741 left Wang Hui-tsu, his mother, and his father's concubine, whom the boy also called mother out of gratitude and affection, in grave financial straits.[26] When the three returned to ancestral Hsiao-shan from Kwangtung, they had less than 20 *mu* left. His mothers supported him by weaving and by resorting to extremely frugal living. All year round they wore the same thin clothes. Fortunately, the six years during which Wang had lived with his father in Honan and Kwangtung had enabled him to learn the rudiments of classics. The neighboring village teacher pitied him and his widowed mothers and hence accepted him without tuition. Another elderly teacher often urged him by reminding him that should he fail to establish himself through hard work his mothers would be doomed for life. In 1746, at the age of sixteen, Wang Hui-tsu became a *sheng-yüan*. The next year he began to teach village boys at a salary of twelve strings of cash a year, out of which he spent three strings as a token present to a locally known scholar whom he had asked to correct his prose compositions. After failing for the third time to pass the provincial examination in 1752, Wang joined the private secretarial staff of his remote maternal uncle, an acting magistrate of Chin-shan County, near Shanghai, at a monthly salary of three taels.

At first he did routine secretarial work which was poorly paid. From 1755 onwards he became a specialist in legal matters, particularly criminal cases. His salary gradually increased with his growing reputation as a legal expert until in 1768 he was offered by the intendant of Taiwan a fabulous annual salary of 1,600 taels, as against 300 or 400 which was usually regarded as good pay for the profession. He had to decline it upon his mothers' order but in the same year he obtained his *chü-jen* degree after years of associating with scholars and studying in his spare time. Even after he passed the *chin-shih* examination in 1775 there was no immediate breach in the pattern of his career. Only between 1787 and 1791 did he act on his own as magistrate of Ning-yüan County in Hunan, a post in which he served with distinction. One secret of his success and fame in his long career as a *shih-yeh* (official's private staff member) was that he always insisted on being treated with dignity by his employer and always abode by what he believed to be an upright principle. For this reason he never associated himself with any official for very long and always preferred to work for local rather than high provincial officials. Among his sixteen employers the highest ranking official was an intendant.

In 1793 he retired permanently to his ancestral home, where he managed family affairs, compiled an index to biographies of dynastic histories, and wrote his memoirs, instructions for his descendants, and two famout guides for local officials entitled *Hsüeh-chih i-shuo* and *Tso-chih yüeh-yen,* which were immediately hailed as the best works of their kind and were reissued in many editions during the last years of his life and after his death.

He had five sons by his wife and a concubine. His wife's three sons lived in the walled city of Hsiao-shan and were engaged in studies. His concubine's two sons lived in the country cultivating the family farmland. He paid off the mortgage of some 20 *mu* of land originally owned by his grandfather and purchased another 70 odd *mu* out of his savings, of which 40 *mu* was to remain perpetual sacrificial land. Consequently each of his five sons received just about 10 *mu.* Two of his wife's sons became higher degree holders and officials. One, a *chü-jen* of 1786, later became a magistrate of a department county. One was a *chin-shih* of 1805 and served as third-class secretary in the Board of Civil Appointments.

*Note:* This is a variation from orthodox pattern of "ploughing with the writing brush" in that Wang was realistic enough to earn his living by secretarial work while he pursued his goal. Here, again, early psychological challenge played a significant role in eventual success. From Wang's father and from the father of the Hsü brothers in case 6, we know that *tso-tsa* (lowly ranking and unranked "auxiliary and miscellaneous" officials) were actually men of rather humble circumstances. It is important to bear in mind that a significant portion of Category C *chin-shih* in our main statistical tables in chapter III originated from *tso-tsa* families.

CASE 15: Chang Ch'üan (1739–1821)[27]

The Chang family of Nan-hsün borough of Hu-chou in Chekiang had for generations been humble. It did not even have a genealogy. Chang Hsün, the first successful member of the family, began to study at seven when his father served on the private secretarial staff of a local official in remote Yunnan. His father soon returned home because of the advanced age and poor health of Chang Ch'üan's grandmother. However, it was Chang Ch'üan's mother who was to die unexpectedly when he was only ten. In her last rally she called Chang Ch'üan, her only son, to the bed, held his hand, and said tearfully: "I have nothing to say except that you must study hard to get established." From this time on Chang Ch'üan was determined to fulfill his mother's expectations.

At ten he could already learn and memorize more than a hundred lines of basic classics a day. He took no time out whether it was bitterly cold or oppressively hot. He was so studious and intelligent that he was admitted to the local An-ting Academy at the age of twelve. Owing to his family's poverty, he could afford neither a private tutor nor books. He studied at night and went to local bookstores to read in the daytime. Sometimes he borrowed books from friends and neighbors and copied them for further study. When lectures were going on in neighboring private schools, he asked to sit in. Some local people suggested that since the family was poor he should quit studies and earn a practical living. But he stood firm and redoubled his efforts.

He obtained his *sheng-yüan* degree at eighteen and received a government stipend at twenty-four. At twenty-seven he passed a special examination and became a *pa-kung-sheng*. Upon hearing this, his grandmother, who was already eighty years old, held his hand and said proudly: "You have now compensated for your grandfather's vain toil of thirty years for a *sheng-yüan* degree." In 1770 he passed the provincial examination and in 1771 obtained his *chin-shih* degree and was selected as a bachelor of the Han-lin Academy.

After staying in Peking for six years and being appointed a third-class secretary of the Board of Revenue, he brought his family to the capital. Upon arrival, his father said with deep emotion: "After our family has declined for over a hundred years, you are the first to climb up from anonymity; your privilege of receiving an advanced apprenticeship in the Han-lin Academy and the honors you have brought to the two elder generations are beyond my dreams." Chang Ch'üan eventually reached the office of grain intendant in Kwangtung and was at one time acting financial commissioner.

*Note:* This is another case in which psychological challenge was an important factor in success and it also shows the permeation of Confucian values among womenfolk.

CASE 16: Liu Ch'eng-hsü (*fl.* late eighteenth and early nineteenth centuries)[28]

Liu Ch'eng-hsü was a Chinese Bannerman belonging to the Bordered White Banner, stationed in Canton. He lost his father when he was a small boy and was reared by his widowed grandmother and mother who made a living by embroidering. When he grew up he could read basic Chinese and Manchu and was proficient in horse riding and archery. In 1787 he served as a private first class in the expedition to Taiwan. After pacifying the rebellion he had to retire from service because of injured feet. The commanding general pitied him and enlisted his younger brother in the army so that the Liu family could survive.

In a few years his injured feet healed. Some advised him to reenter the army but he declined on the ground that his quota had already been filled by his brother. He started to trade in a small way, buying and selling from one place to another. After putting by a little he began to hire poor kinsmen and friends and to expand his business. In about ten years he became rich.

Once well to do, he purchased paintings and calligraphic masterpieces and began to associate with men of letters. He once accompanied his sons to Peking, where the latter took their *chü-jen* examination. During his northern tour he frequented many famous sites and ancient remains. In his old age he particularly loved to sing Yüan drama with literary friends.

He had seven sons, all of whom became *sheng-yüan*. The elder two successively managed family affairs so that the younger ones could concentrate on their studies. Among his more than twenty grandsons four became *chü-jen*.

*Note:* This case is interesting in showing not only the unusually zigzag pattern of initial mobility but also the permeation of Confucian values among the humble Bannermen.

CASE 17: The T'ao Family of An-hua, Hunan[29]

The most prominent member of the T'ao clan of An-hua, Hunan, was T'ao Chu (1779–1839), who rose to the position of governor general of Kiangsu and Anhwei and was famous for his reform of the Liang-huai salt administration.

For generations the T'ao clan had lived in the village called T'ao-chia-hsi (T'ao-Family-Stream), where it owned large tracts of land. T'ao Chu's great-great-grandfather owned more than ten estates within and without the T'ao village and contributed generously to local charities, including a donation of eight ferry boats. "He loved to study, established clan schools, and hired good teachers whom he respected and whom he showered with extra gifts." Of his two sons neither obtained the *sheng-yüan* degree. The younger of the two was T'ao Chu's great-grandfather, who managed the family estates. When inspecting tenants he was followed by four or five grandsons and more than ten servants. The size of his retinue, all mounted on horses, was an impressive rural sight. He also donated generously to local philanthropy, took good care of poor kinsmen, and treated servants and tenants kindly. Of his five sons the third was T'ao Chu's grandfather.

T'ao Chu's grandfather was by nature taciturn, stern, and dignified. His extensive properties made him a major target of unscrupulous neighbors and scheming kinsmen. For protection, he carried weapons or took along a retinue of robust servants whenever he went. He occasionally traded tea between his native tea-producing Hunan and Hankow, the main port of central Yangtze. His frequent donations to local charities and his pursuit of various side interests such as history, astrology, and astronomy were a drain on his financial resources. He died before he reached fifty. His widow was also by nature generous and hospitable—so generous and hospitable that she was often taken advantage of by clever younger kinsmen. By the time of her death at the age of eighty-six, she had six sons, nineteen grandsons, thirty-six great-grandsons, and twenty-two great-great-grandsons.

Soon after the old lady's death the family property was divided among the various branches. Generations of overspending and the large number of descendants meant that the share received by each branch and subbranch was relatively small. The successive crop failures in the late 1790s further drained the resources of the various branches. By this time T'ao Chu's father, who had obtained his *sheng-yüan* degree in 1777, was forced to earn his living by teaching. In the famine year 1797 he and his family had no food for several days and lived on wild herbs and roots which his wife and elder son, T'ao Chu, gathered from the hills. Although respected locally as a scholar, he never passed the provincial examination. All his life he remained a teacher, wandering from one county to another. But everywhere he went he took T'ao Chu with him, while leaving his younger son, T'ao Chin, at home working on the farm.

Thanks to the constant supervision of his father, T'ao Chu obtained his *chü-jen* degree in 1800. Two years later he passed the *chin-shih* examination and became a bachelor of the Han-lin Academy. When his father learned of this success, he clapped the side of his bed and said: "Now my wishes are fulfilled." He did not live to see his son become a high official and statesman.

T'ao Chin was less fortunate than his elder brother. The much reduced family circumstances forced him, along with most of his impoverished cousins, to take up the plough. By the time he was seventeen he decided that he should quit farming and study. Not until T'ao Chu had passed his provincial examination in 1800 did he have an opportunity to study under his father. Although he obtained his *sheng-yüan* degree in 1809, his late scholastic start precluded any further advance. On learning that his brother had passed the county examination, T'ao Chu wrote him a letter from Peking together with a poem, the last two lines of which read: "For your self-sacrifice in sustaining the family we all owe you a debt, but [the *Book of*] *Odes* and [the *Book of*] *Documents* will never mislead you." T'ao Chin, in his reply, also composed a poem:

> Who of us does not miss his brother?
> Though widely separated we share our hearts together.
> *Odes* and *Documents* shall never mislead me,
> So let us wait for the time of joyful reunion.

But the time of "joyful reunion" never occurred, for T'ao Chin died three years later at the age of thirty-one. As T'ao Chu recalled, T'ao Chin was always simple, quiet, hard-working, frugal, but often took to hard drinking as if he had some unexplainable sorrow.

*Note:* The main characteristics of the mobility pattern of the T'ao family are essentially the same as those of a few other cases except that this case shows more clearly how the custom of equal inheritance, coupled with rapid multiplication of family members, was a very potent economic leveler. While T'ao Chu was a success, his brother was a victim of the policy of family division of function.

CASE 18: The Liang Family of Canton[30]

The founder of the Liang family fortune derived from the T'ien-pao-hang, one of the famous thirteen Canton Co-hongs, was Liang Ching-kuo (1761–1837), commonly known to Western traders as Kingqua of Tienpow. His father was a teacher in the village of Huang-p'u (Whampoa) near Canton. The family being poor and the number of pupils large, his father could not carefully supervise his work. In 1767 his father died, leaving him an orphan at the age of six in a destitute family of four. Even at such a tender age he had to go back and forth between Huang-p'u and Canton to peddle so that he could help his mother, who constantly spun and wove, to sustain the family. Sometimes he even helped in weaving at night. When he grew older he went out to earn a living as a hired worker. Because of his total lack of property and his ability to survive despite all odds, he gave himself a nickname "T'ien-pao" (literally "Blessed by Heaven"). The name was later adopted as his firm name except that the "Pao" which means "Blessed" was changed into its homonym "Pao" which means "Treasure." [31]

Not much is known of his early struggling years. Typical of many rich Chinese merchants in their early difficult times, Liang Ching-kuo was hard-working, honest, loyal, and trustworthy. He worked for many years, first as as apprentice and then as manager of a Co-hong owned by the Feng family. During the owner's long absence overseas he accumulated considerable working capital as a managing partner and consequently established his T'ien-pao-hang in 1808. After becoming rich he made successive monetary contributions to the state and eventually purchased the title of intendant (rank 4a), the highest rank money could buy. Because of the failure of the Liang clan to produce any degree holder in the past, he donated generously to the common clan property and clan school and often assisted poor kinsmen and local people.

It seems that three of his four sons grew to maturity, as evidenced by the listing of their names in his obituary essays printed in 1841. Liang Lun-shu (1790–1877), his second son, became a *sheng-yüan* in 1809. Between 1810 and 1837 he competed fourteen times in provincial examinations without success. He purchased the title of expectant subdirector of a county school in 1827, but his father's advanced age made it necessary for him to take over the Hang management. He also was widely known to Westerners as Kingqua. He contributed 95,000 taels to the government in 1828 and another 20,000 taels in 1832 and was consequently awarded the title of salt comptroller (rank 3a). Although before his death at the age of eighty-seven he had seen the birth of his great-great-grandson, most of his descendants are unknown.

His youngest brother, Liang T'ung-hsien (1800–60), had a successful academic career. At eighteen he obtained his *chü-jen* degree. After failing several times in the metropolitan examinations, he purchased the title of secretary of the Grand Secretariat (rank 7a). At the tenth trial he obtained his *chin-shih* degree in 1846 and was selected as a bachelor of the Han-lin Academy. He was later appointed a compiler in the same office and a deputy director of the State Historiographer's Office. After serving as provincial examiner and educational commissioner, he was promoted to the post of governor of the metropolitan Shun-t'ien prefecture (rank 3a) but was eventually demoted to the fourth rank because of a blunder.

Owing to Liang T'ung-hsin's academic success and also to the fact that his children lived with him, away from the rest of the clan, his descendants have provided the largest number of officials, higher degree holders, and scholars among branches of the Liang clan. The most successful of his sons, Liang Chao-huang (1827–86), was a *chin-shih* of 1853 who later reached the high office of financial commissioner of Kiangsu. Liang T'ung-hsin's eldest son, Liang Chao-ching, purchased the rank of assistant salt comptroller (rank 4b). His third and youngest son, Liang Chao-chin, was a *chin-shih* of 1874 but died young while serving as a third-class secretary of the Board of Rites.

Information about later generations is comparatively full only with regard to Liang Chao-huang's descendants, although other branches produced two *chü-jen*. Of his eleven sons four died young. Of the remaining seven who grew to maturity, only one failed to go beyond *sheng-yüan*. There were two *chü-jen*, one of whom became an assistant reader of the Grand Secretariat (rank 6a) and the other an expectant subprefect rank 5a). The other four all purchased official titles. The youngest studied at Columbia University and received his B.A. The three of Liang Chao-huang's grandsons who had grown to manhood at the time when his biographical essay was posthumously compiled all purchased official ranks. Of his three great-grandsons listed in the biographical essay the second is Liang Fang-chung, originally named Liang Chia-kuan, a graduate of Tsing Hua University, the mainstay of the former Institute of Social Sciences of Academia Sinica, a recognized authority on Ming fiscal history, and now professor at National Sun Yat-sen University in Canton. The third is Liang Chia-pin, also a Tsing Hua graduate, holder of the certificate of the graduate History Department of Imperial Tokyo University, author of the well-known monograph on the thirteen Co-hongs, and now professor of history at Tung-hai University in Taiwan.

*Note:* In the six generations, and more than a century, since the founding of the family fortune, members of even the most successful branch of the Liang clan have had to live on their special skills and knowledge. The pattern of mobility conforms to those of other rich merchant families. The case of Liang Ching-kuo is one of "from rags to riches."

CASE 19: Peng Yü-lin (1816–90) and His Father[32]

The most prominent member of the P'eng family of Heng-yang in southern Hunan was P'eng Yü-lin, the famous admiral who crashed the Taiping fleet, one of the most upright high officials of late Ch'ing times. His ancestors had for generations been agricultural tenants. His father, P'eng Ho-kao, studied for some time when young but never acquired any degree. Because of P'eng Ho-kao's scholastic inclination the uncles and cousins all complained loudly, for the family needed every available hand to make ends meet. His failure at the county and prefectural examinations further strengthened the opposition. His father, though sympathizing with him, was afraid of incurring the family wrath and hence ordered him to quit his studies.

After the New Year's Eve dinner the eldest member of the family handed P'eng Ho-kao a plough, saying: "Tomorrow, New Year's Day, is a lucky day; everybody should turn up the soil." He had to comply. In the spring and summer of this year he daily worked in the fields, toiling in muddy rice paddies without complaint or lassitude. After the autumn harvest was reaped, he asked for permission to repair to Heng-shan, the famous mountain resort, to pray. Since Heng-yang was only thirty miles from the mountain and since many peasants annually made their pilgrimage in the fall, he was allowed to go, carrying 300 copper coins. After a few days a letter arrived home in which he said that he had complied, against his wishes, with his father's and elders' order to do a year's farm work. Farm work was beyond his physical endurance and he would leave home permanently unless he could become established. He returned the unspent 200 coins and begged his parents to forget him, an unfilial son by ordinary standards.

He drifted to Chen-chiang, Kiangsu, where he made a living by selling scrolls which he wrote. Some local scholars were impressed by his calligraphy, pitied him after finding out his story, and sent him to a private academy. After a few years he was appointed to teach young boys on a government tribute grain boat which later took him to Peking. By passing an examination he became a *kung-shih* (unclassed clerk). After accumulating merit he was eventually promoted to the position of *hsün-chien* (submagistrate, rank 9b) of an Anhwei county. Not until then did he marry. His wife was the thirty-five-year-old daughter of one of the magistrate's private secretaries. P'eng Yü-lin and his younger brother were born in Anhwei. When P'eng Yü-lin was sixteen the family returned to Heng-yang, where his father died the next year.

Thanks to his father's lifetime savings, P'eng Yü-lin's branch of the family owned land which yielded 40 bushels of rent grain a year. Some rapacious kinsmen envied this property and tried to harm the young brothers. Once when the younger brother went to the market to buy salt, he was thrown into a river by an uncle. Although the boy was saved by neighbors, P'eng's mother knew that it was time to send off her sons in order to avoid further plots against their lives. P'eng Yü-lin was sent to a private academy and his younger brother was apprenticed to trades.

P'eng Yü-lin's mother could not defend herself against her voracious kinsmen and consequently lost much of her property. This made it necessary for the brothers to earn their living as best they could. By chance P'eng Yü-lin's calligraphy attracted the notice of an official who took him under his temporary tutelage and in a few years P'eng obtained his *sheng-yüan* degree. In the early 1850s he was forced by circumstances to become a bookkeeper at a pawnshop. After the rebel Taiping forces became a serious menace in 1853, he joined a marine unit newly organized by Tseng Kuo-fan, the chief architect of the anti-Taiping war. He later became a famous admiral, an incorruptible official, and eventually president of the Board of War.

His younger brother, who had left home very young and whose whereabouts had not been known for some two decades, finally turned up when P'eng Yü-lin became famous. Drifting first to Chekiang and later to Szechwan, he eventually became a wealthy salt merchant.

*Note:* P'eng's was one of dozens of cases in which a person rose from obscurity to prominence during and after the Taiping wars. All these cases of nonacademic success, partially shown in table 24, are not reflected in our *chin-shih* statistics in chapter III. The fact that P'eng Yü-lin's father was an agricultural tenant deserves special attention.

CASE 20: T'ao Mo (1835–1902)[33]

The T'ao family of Hsiu-shui, a part of modern Chia-hsing County, Chekiang, had for generations failed to produce a single degree holder. Although T'ao Mo eventually became governor general of Shensi and Kansu, his family was a typical small, poor family without property. The premature death of his grandfather forced his father and only uncle to quit their elementary studies and to take up trade. On their return visits from northern Kiangsu they sometimes brought home some basic classics. His father died of sunstroke in northern Kiangsu when T'ao Mo was only five years old. Since his uncle was childless and too poor to have a concubine, T'ao Mo, in accordance with local custom, became the male heir of both his father and his uncle. Supported by his uncle, he began to study at eight. Being poor, he early in life was accustomed to manual work. His uncle wished him to concentrate on his studies but could not afford tuition. Friends and relatives all urged his uncle to apprentice him to a trade, but T'ao Mo refused. He studied all the harder and did his best to help the family. Every morning he went to the market place to sell silk fabrics woven by his mother and brought home rice, salt, and daily necessaries. He studied in the afternoon and at night, sharing the light with his mother, who constantly wove. In 1865, at the age of twenty-one, he obtained his *sheng-yüan* degree. Not until then did he have a chance to associate with local scholars and to improve his style of essay writing.

The Taiping rebels sacked Chia-hsing in 1860. Both T'ao Mo and his uncle were taken prisoner by the rebels. Their small, run-down house was burned. For four months T'ao Mo was forced to do coolie work. By the time he and his uncle managed to escape and get home, T'ao Mo's mother and wife had both died. After the partial restoration of local order he taught in a village school and also looked after his two young sons himself. He was remarried in 1863 but still had to do various kinds of manual work at home. As his eldest son recalled, until T'ao Mo became a *chü-jen* in 1867 he went to market almost every morning to sell silk piece goods and to carry a tubful of river water home. After all these daily chores were done he still had to take his elder sons to the village school where he taught. In 1868 he became a *chin-shih*. Not until 1869 did he have sufficient means to rebury his more than ten ancestors properly.

Starting as a local official in the remote northwest, which was devastated by the wars of Moslem rebellion, he attracted by his ability and integrity the attention of the famous soldier-statesman Tso Tsung-t'ang. By stages he was promoted to the post of governor general of Shensi and Kansu.

*Note:* This account is representative of the lives of many who in the early stage of their struggle had to combine studies with various types of menial work to survive. That T'ao Mo still had to do menial work after obtaining his first degree deserves special attention.

CASE 21: Hu Ch'uan (1841–95)[34]

Hu Ch'uan was the father of Dr. Hu Shih. The Hu family of Chi-hsi, the poorest of six Hui-chou counties, had for generations been in the tea trade. The family first got into the tea business when Hu Ch'uan's great-grandfather set up a tea store in Ch'uan-sha-t'ing near Shanghai. His business apparently prospered because he acquired, among other things, the title of student of the Imperial Academy, as was customary with small substantial tradesmen of Hui-chou. The family seems to have suffered a setback when Hu Ch'uan's grandfather died young, only fourteen days after the birth of his second son, Hu Ch'uan's father. This forced Hu Ch'uan's great-grandfather to entrust the business to others in his old age and consequently the business drastically declined.

When Hu Ch'uan's father reached his late teens he took over the management. Through his hard work and frugal living the business gradually recovered. He returned home every spring to buy tender-leaved tea for sale in Kiangsu. His elder brother was engaged in his studies most of the time, although he had to help with business management and bookkeeping occasionally. He was busy making his own living and did not have sufficient time to teach his nephew Hu Ch'uan and the other boys of the family. For this reason Hu Ch'uan learned only the short Confucian primer *Classic on Filial Piety* and a short anthology of 300-odd T'ang poems in two years in the Hu clan school. When he was ten he still had not tackled the four basic Confucian Classics.

Hu Ch'uan was physically well developed. At thirteen he looked like an adult and could do various kinds of manual work. His father wanted him to go into business but his scholarly uncle suggested that since he was by far the most promising of the boys he should be allowed to pursue his studies. When Hu Ch'uan was asked to state his own wishes, he was honest enough to say that although studies were good he had an obligation to help the family. He feared that frequent calls to do menial work might interrupt his studies. However, in 1857, at sixteen, he accompanied his father to Ch'uan-sha-t'ing, where he studied in a school operated by a local scholar. There he came into contact with his teacher's several poet friends, including two cloth merchants and a salt-police sergeant, an association which fully reflected the fluidity of social status. In the course of the next few years, while preparing for the first examination, he several times accompanied his father back to the southern Anhwei mountains to buy tea and transport it to the family store.

The years 1861 and 1862 were times of great crisis and distress, when the Taiping rebels more than once sacked Chi-hsi. While the large Hu clan suffered greatly during the turmoil, Hu Ch'uan's own branch, which consisted of more than twenty members, mostly women and children, survived. The only war casualty was his first wife. Owing to the Taiping invasion of northwestern Chekiang and southern Anhwei, trade routes were disrupted and new ones had to be found. The Hus soon discovered that T'un-hsi in southern Anhwei had become a temporary center of distribution. Thus Hu Ch'uan's scholarly uncle, a paternal cousin, and two maternal cousins each contributed 50 taels to a common pool with which to set up a shack store near T'un-hsi, selling various daily necessaries. Hu Ch'uan took charge of purchase and shipping, while a younger brother helped the three cousins in sale. (Note: This was typical of the shrewd and hardy Hui-chou tradesmen who, owing to the pressure of living, left no stone unturned in the world of business.)

In 1865, a year after the pacification of the Taiping rebellion, Hu Ch'uan obtained his *sheng-yüan* degree. In the next eleven years he spent much time and energy in helping with local rehabilitation, enumerating surviving kinsmen, and reconstructing the clan ancestral hall. Only between 1868 and 1871 had he opportunities of broadening his intellectual horizon by enrolling in the Lung-men Academy in Shanghai. There he was deeply influenced by Sung rationalism, a philosophical school which taught him the cultivation of fortitude and an inquisitive mind. In the 1870s he became intensely interested in the geography of China's frontier regions.

After devoting so many years to clan affairs he eventually borrowed 100 silver dollars from a tradesman cousin and set off for Manchuria, armed with a letter of introduction to Wu Ta-ch'eng (1835–1902), then a third-ranking official charged with strengthening frontier defense. Wu was a native of Hui-chou and a descendant of salt merchants, and was later famous as an archaeologist and calligrapher. Hu Ch'uan made it clear that he had come to ask not for an office but for an opportunity to study and survey the northern Manchurian frontier. His geographic knowledge and his conscientiousness so impressed Wu that he made him a member of his private secretarial staff in 1882. Meanwhile, thanks to Wu's special recommendation to the throne and to the sudden need for men of Hu Ch'uan's specialty, he successively served in Manchuria, Honan, Hainan Island, and Taiwan, where he became a magistrate of a department county (rank 5a), concurrently in charge of the local army and salt administration. He died, probably of beri-beri, in Shanghai, a few days after the last Chinese defense in Taiwan collapsed before the advancing Japanese forces in 1895.

Very little is known of Hu Ch'uan's four younger brothers except that the second youngest eventually became a deputy director of studies in Fu-yang County, northern Anhwei. The rest probably remained tradesmen all their lives.

*Note:* In the Taiping and post-Taiping period, a significant number of *sheng-yüan* eventually became officials either by joining the army or by serving on officials' private staffs. In both cases they qualified for minor office not on the strength of their degrees but on recommendations by their official employers. See also case 24, Chang Ch'ien.

CASE 22: Tsou T'ao (*fl.* latter half of nineteenth century)[35]

The following are Tsou T'ao's reminiscences: "My family used to be engaged in farming. My grandfather was the first to study, but was compelled by poverty to take up trade later. My father took several trials at the county examination before he finally gave up. During the Taiping wars my family further suffered but my elders encouraged me to carry on my studies in the hope that I might one day become established. When I was fifteen I almost quit studies because of poverty, but my grandfather insisted that I should continue. At eighteen I went to Su-chou. . . . Two years later I was about to take the prefectural examination. My family at that time did not have a surplus bushel of rice nor know where to borrow. My grandfather had only seven coins but walked with me to the city [to borrow from his friend]. Next year in the fifth lunar month

I took the examination. . . . My grandmother was then sick. When the news that I had passed the [*sheng-yüan*] examination arrived, she felt better. . . . My younger brother was filial and very considerate of me. From an early age he knew life's difficulties so that he took up trade in Su-chou. . . . He once said to my mother: 'I hope to earn more some day in order to support you more adequately and to take the load off my elder brother.' Because of hard work and self-abnegation, he died young."

*Note:* This was another case of arrested mobility. Tsou T'ao in the 1870s wrote a series of miscellaneous notes from which the above passage is selected. From his two prefaces dated 1871 and 1875 we know that he was a family tutor in Shanghai.

CASE 23: Yeh Ch'eng-chung (1840–99)[36]

The Yeh family had for generations been poor peasants of Chenhai, near Ning-po. Yeh Cheng-chung, who eventually became a rich merchant and industrialist of Shanghai, was only five years old when his father died. His two brothers and two sisters were all young. All his mother had was a run-down hut which barely provided shelter and sacrificial land of 8 *mu* (a little over an acre). In the daytime she led the children to work in the field and at night spun and wove. Only by the utmost physical exertion could the family survive. Yeh Ch'eng-chung went to a village school for less than six months when he was eight. Poverty forced him to join his mother and elder brother in farm work. At ten he was employed in a small neighboring vegetable-oil workshop, at a nominal pay of one string of copper coins and one bundle of firewood a year, because his mother's main purpose was to save family food consumption. Still he frequently had to endure abusive treatment from the owner's wife. After three years he quit. The family could hardly feed another mouth. An old family friend pitied him and consented to take him to Shanghai. Since the family was indigent and could not muster the necessary 2,000 cash for the overnight trip, his mother had to mortgage the rice crop that was still in the fields. Yeh was then thirteen years old.

The old family friend made him an apprentice at a grocery in the French Concession. In the 1850s Shanghai was already outstripping Canton as the leading treaty port. Every dawn Yeh rowed the owner's sampan to the Huang-p'u River, where foreign vessels congregated, and sold groceries. He had to do additional manual work in the afternoon and at night, including the chore of cleaning the toilet. The owner being lazy, the store did not promise any future. In three years Yeh left but continued to trade with Westerners on his own account. Gradually he picked up Western ways of commercial dealing and also pidgin English. Soon he was able to set up a small store of his own in Hung-k'ou, which was later moved further towards the river.

Though starting in a small way, he became more and more prosperous because of his diligence, agreeable personality, and business acumen. As early as the 1860s he hired an English teacher to teach his employees English at night. He and his employees also studied commercial law and customs regulations. His business expanded so quickly that before his death he had six stores in Shanghai, two in Hankow, and one each in Chiu-chiang, Wu-hu, Chen-chiang, Chefoo, Tientsin, Ying-k'ou, Ning-po, and Wen-chou, which were engaged in imports and exports, dealing in machines and machine parts and iron and steel products. Although his commemorative album never describes in detail his business ramifications, it does mention that his firms had contracts with the Hanyang steel plant, the North and South China fleets, and the machine bureaus of several provinces. In the 1890s he moved on from commerce to industry by establishing silk-reeling and match factories in Shanghai and Hankow and ranked among the leading Chinese industrialists of the time. The ramified business was entrusted to employees of tested integrity.

Being rich, he donated generously to famine relief, local charities, and philanthropy. Since the Yeh clan in Chekiang was poor, he built its first ancestral hall and donated more than 400 *mu* as common sacrificial land. Shortly before his death he further contributed 20,000 silver dollars as a common clan fund for the sustenance of the aged and destitute. He also set up a clan school to teach its youths. In his many philanthropic activities in Shanghai perhaps the most important was the establishment of a school which cost him over 100,000 silver dollars. A sum of 20,000 dollars was also set aside to provide pensions for the families of his old employees.

He first bought the title of student of the Imperial Academy and then in successive stages the titles of subprefect and intendant. He has seven sons and seven daughters. Except for the two sons who were still young at the time of his death in 1899, the other five had all purchased the ranks of expectant subprefect or first-class assistant department magistrate. From the short biographical sketch of his eldest son appended to his commemorative album, there is reason to believe that the family fortune was not likely to last very long. This eldest son, who died two years after his father at the age of thirty-three, was depicted as a good-natured young man, who had just begun to atone for his indulgence in "music, women, dogs, and horses" by implementing his father's philanthropic projects shortly before his own premature death.

*Note:* This case provides more detail than case 18 on the processes through which an indigent young man eventually made his fortune. Although Yeh's early poverty may have been unusual, he is fairly representative of many other enterprising merchants, industrialists, and financiers of the Ning-po area who, after the opening of China in the 1840s, have overshadowed the Hui-chou group in the business world.

CASE 24: Chang Ch'ien (1853–1927)[37]

Chang Ch'ien was a native of Nan-t'ung, a Kiangsu county just north of the Yangtze which in modern times is a cotton-growing and textile district. For generations the Changs were the Chinese counterpart of the English yeomen, owning a modest amount of land and working in the field, with the occasional help of farm hands. The family's middling economic status in traditional rural china is indicated by Chang Ch'ien's statement that it had "no worry for food and clothing."

Upon the death of Chang Ch'ien's great-grandfather in 1796, the family property was divided among three sons, of whom the youngest, aged only seven, was Chang Ch'ien's grandfather. The two elder sons moved out. The second later became a playboy who squandered his money and never returned home. Chang Ch'ien's grandfather as a young boy lived with his widowed mother. He studied in a village school until he was fifteen, when his mother suddenly died. Misled by scheming kinsmen, he took up gambling and soon lost all his property. A small local pottery dealer, who later also did part-time farming, pitied him and took him as son-in-law. The lesson which he had learned in his teens was never forgotten, for he grew up a diligent, prudent, and frugal man who moved out of his father-in-law's home after acquiring some property of his own.

Although in his later years he recovered much of his previous loss, he was reluctant to let the second of his three sons, Chang Ch'ien's father, study. Only after the latter's repeated entreaties, supported by one of the village teachers, did he allow his second son to study half a day, working the remainder of the day in the fields. For this reason Chang Ch'ien's father barely managed to finish his studies of the elementary Confucian classics and remained a landowning peasant his whole life.

Chang Ch'ien had three brothers. Although his father sent all four boys to school when they were young, there is evidence that only Chang Ch'ien, the youngest, who had shown early intelligence and promise, was allowed to study full-time. He began to study at the age of four, under his mother's supervision. In spite of his tender age, Chang Ch'ien had to do his studies at night in an unheated house during the winter months. As he recalled, so great were his mother's hopes for him that during her supervision of his night work she sometimes sobbed. The family could afford to send him to the village school when he grew a little older. In the summer of 1864, when he was eleven, he and his brothers were ordered by their father to work in the cotton fields. His dislike of physical toil convinced him that he had to study doubly hard to justify his escape from it. Five years later he obtained his *sheng-yüan* degree.

It ought to be pointed out in passing that for a boy of a family which for generations had not produced a single degree holder, local and legal customs sometimes required a written pledge from at least one *ling-sheng* before he could take the county examination. Chang Ch'ien, with the approval of his inexperienced father, was tricked by a scheming village teacher into falsifying his ancestry and taking the examination in a neighboring county. This exposed him to three years of blackmail by the pledger and his accomplice. To bribe them and local-government runners, the Chang family spent altogether over 1,000 taels and went heavily into debt. It was finally decided that Chang Ch'ien should confess his misdeed to the provincial educational commissioner. Thanks to the latter's sympathy, Chang Ch'ien's degree was not rescinded. This episode, together with the division of family property consequent upon the passing of Chang Ch'ien's grandfather, made it necessary for him to take a job as member of an official's private staff. He studied in his spare time and passed the examination for entrance into a private academy. His small salary was sent home in order to help to pay the family debt. Early in 1875 he was married to the daughter of a substantial land-owning peasant.

Chang Ch'ien repeatedly failed his provincial examinations. In 1876 he was introduced by his Nanking employer, an official in charge of river conservancy supplies, to General Wu Ch'ang-ch'ing, his first important patron. Chang served on Wu's private secretarial staff at a monthly salary of twenty taels. Sustained scholastic work in his spare time enabled him to pass a special examination in 1879 and consequently to obtain the degree of *yu-kung-sheng* (*kung-sheng* of special literary merit). Following General Wu first to North China and then to Korea, he played a useful role in putting down a palace mutiny in Seoul in 1882. For his service the general awarded him 1,000 taels. When he obtained his *chü-jen* degree in Peking in 1885, he was already widely known as a man of considerable ability and a Korean expert. Thenceforth he became the protégé of Weng T'ung-ho, the imperial tutor and later prime minister. In the nine years following his successful provincial examination he moved on from one secretarial job to another, while qualifying himself as an expectant director of a county school.

Finally, in 1894, he became nationally famous for placing first in the palace examination. Later he became a pioneering industrialist in his native Nan-t'ung and continued to advise high-ranking officials on vital policies. He served briefly in the early Republican cabinet. Among his kinsmen only a son of his uncle became a local official. His only son, also his biographer, studied briefly in the United States but died in his prime.

*Note:* The value of this case lies in its precise description of the family's social and economic status, that of landowning peasants, before the combined career of "ploughing with the writing brush" and secretarial work paid off.

CASE 25: The Wang Family of Chi-hsi, Anhwei[38]

Wang Wei-ch'eng, the compiler of his clan genealogy, which is of unusual interest to social historians, was the first member of a humble clan who became an official, his position being that of secretary of the Department of Economic Reconstruction of the Provincial Government of Anhwei.

For generations the Wang clan had lived in the village of Miao-tzu-shan in Chi-hsi, Dr. Hu Shih's ancestral county, as agricultural tenants. Most if not all of the farmland of the village before the Taiping rebellion belonged to the Ts'ao clan, which boasted, among other things, of at least one *chü-jen*.

At the age of eleven Wang Wei-ch'eng's father, Wang Pang-ch'ing (1843–1929), had to leave home for Hsüan-ch'eng county as an apprentice in a bamboo-craft shop because his extended family of some thirty souls, mostly agricultural tenants, seldom had enough to eat. In the catastrophe of the Taiping invasion in 1861–62 all the other members of his family perished. The extensive devastation wrought by wars and the drastic reduction of the local population created a serious shortage of labor and brought about a sensational decline in land values. In the late 1860s and early 1870s wages were high but a *mu* of farmland cost less than 1,000 copper coins, as compared with 8, 9, or over 10 taels per *mu* in pre-Taiping times. Wang Pang-ch'ing was able to save a little and get married. His fortune further improved when his elder sons reached their teens and could help him in the fields.

The eldest of his five sons, who was born in 1867, was an especially good farmer who usually tilled one *mu* of land before the sun rose. Though he had studied for only four years, he could do all the family bookkeeping. In the latter half of the Kuang-hsü period (1875–

1908) the Wangs were cheated by an unscrupulous villager in a land deal and lost over 80 taels. This incident convinced the eldest son that his youngest brother had to be given an opportunity to study, for without an educated man the family could not defend itself against local sharpers in the future.

The third brother (1878–1927) went to Shanghai as an apprentice in a tea store owned by a relative. He gradually rose to the position of manager and eventually set up his own store. At the peak of his prosperity the store's volume of annual business reached 10,000 silver dollars. It was owing chiefly to his financial support that his youngest brother, Wang Wei-ch'eng, was able to study, to obtain his *sheng-yüan* degree, and, after the abolition of the civil service examination system in 1905, to graduate from the Anhwei provincial Kao-teng-hsüeh-t'ang, probably equivalent to a modern junior college. He eventually served in the Anhwei provincial government.

The family's modest success was due primarily to its policy of division of function. The elder brothers remained farmers, the third took up trade, and every opportunity was given to the fifth to study. (The fourth brother had died young.) In the annals of the Wang clan one of the most significant events was the day when Wang Wei-ch'eng obtained his *sheng-yüan* degree. That very night his eldest brother hurriedly ran a three-mile stretch without pause to his married sister, to whom he announced the happy tidings interrupted by coughs and stutters: "Wei-Wei-Wei-ch'eng has placed first in the county examination!" He and his sister thereupon immediately wrote to their tea-merchant brother in Shanghai passing on this news. Next morning the eldest brother returned home and on his way encountered the man who years before had cheated him and his father in a land deal. When the scoundrel bowed low and offered his congratulations, Wang Wei-ch'eng's eldest brother stared at him for several minutes before replying with pride and sarcasm: "Thank you, sir!"

*Note:* This case is by far the most detailed and specific account of the upward social mobility of a family of agricultural tenants known to me. In the light of the peculiar circumstances of war-torn post-Taiping lower Yangtze which enabled tenants to become landowning peasants and small landlords,[39] this case may well have been representative of many. Since it usually took a considerable time for a family's improved economic status to be expressed in its improved socioacademic status, many similar cases may not have been recorded because of their relatively recent occurrence and the decline of the customs of periodic recompilation of clan genealogy in the Republican era. It seems that the post-Taiping lower Yangtze area may have been an exception to the general economic pattern of continual deterioriation in the nation's standards of living and of increasing pressure of population.

It should also be mentioned that, in spite of the relatively lowly and humble circumstances of many Ming-Ch'ing *sheng-yüan,* such as have been concretely illustrated in a number of the above cases, this degree did have an elevating effect on the truly humble and poor. The social realities behind *sheng-yüan* as a status group are therefore so complex as to make any abstract generalization, such as their belonging to the "lower gentry," impossible and untenable.

CASE 26: Chou Fan (*fl.* late nineteenth and early twentieth centuries)[40]

The following are reminiscences of Chou Fan, member of the last class of *sheng-yüan* of Wu-hsi, Kiangsu: "My family first built its own house and acquired some landed property in my great-great-grandfather's time. . . . My great-grandfather managed the family's property carefully, but after division none of his six sons got enough for sustenance. Still every one of them studied and prepared for examinations in which they repeatedly failed. For this reason the male members of my grandfather's generation warned each other that they should never encourage themselves or their descendants to study for examinations. Consequently all eleven brothers and cousins went out as apprentices to trade in their early teens; none cared to study for examinations.

In my generation there are also eleven members, ten being my cousins. All except me went to trade and never bothered with an academic degree. The reason why my father let me study was because of the persuasion of my late uncle [husband of Chou Fan's maternal aunt]. . . . Unfortunately, I spent more than ten years preparing for the examinations but the best I could get was a *sheng-yüan* degree and *ling-sheng*'s stipend. In four trials at the provincial examination I was thrice recommended for further consideration but flanked all the same. . . . The prolonged preparation for examinations cost us a great deal. My family did not have a library, but I loved books. Every time I took the provincial examination I brought some books home. My father, then aged over sixty, still operated his cotton piece-goods store. Since I was his only son, he did his utmost to support me. . . . I was born relatively late in his life, and he only hoped that I would become a *sheng-yüan*. He was satisfied with my degree and therefore insisted on my staying home to teach neighborhood pupils."

*Note:* After the abolition of the examination system in 1905 Chou Fan studied Japanese. In the last years of the Ch'ing dynasty and during the early Republican period he was employed by the army as a translator. This is another of the very few available cases showing arrested social mobility.

### CASE 27: Ch'i Po-shih (1863–1957)[41]

The paternal and maternal ancestors of Ch'i Po-shih, the world-famous painter, were all humble folks of rural Hsiang-t'an, Hunan, who for generations had failed to produce any degree holder. The men cultivated the limited acreage and the women spun, wove, and occasionally helped in the fields. As a boy Ch'i Po-shih was delicate in health but showed unusual intelligence. In winter the family could afford to heat only a single room with pine needles collected from the woods. When he was a little boy of three his grandfather, a semiliterate peasant, made simple Chinese characters with fire tongs in the ashes and taught him to read. By the age of seven he was able to learn several tens of characters a day in this way. His grandmother was saddened by the family's inability to send him to school. She thereupon sold four bushels of grain and bought a few books and necessary stationery in order to send her grandson to a nearby school, the teacher of which accepted him without tuition. His early schooling lasted only a year, partly because of his poor health but largely due to the family's need for manual help. At seven Ch'i Po-shih had to collect firewood every day so that the family could cook. He hung the *Analects* on the water buffalo's horn and managed to carry on his studies while gathering wood and pasturing the animal. His grandmother once said to him: "What a pity that you have been born to the wrong family!"

In 1874 his grandmother died, leaving a property worth only 60,000 copper coins, which was all spent on her funeral. By this time Ch'i Po-shih already had two brothers and his family was expanding. This made it necessary for him to go out to learn carpentry at the age of eleven. Being by nature fond of painting, he learned his craft by day and painted by night. The only model for painting he could afford to buy was a cheaply reproduced painting primer, *The Mustard-Seed Garden Album*. At fifteen Ch'i advanced to skillful and fanciful woodwork. At nineteen he was wed to a girl who had come to live with the family as a child bride seven years earlier, in order that the family might have extra manual help.

Since in the next few years Ch'i's skillful woodwork was demanded by prominent local clans, he came to know the local elite for the first time. He began to have access to local libraries and better painting models. In 1889 he was admitted into the local elite circle which included members of two great clans, scholars, poets, and artists of local renown. This new association broadened his intellectual and artistic horizon and led him further to the art of seal carving, for which he was equally famous. Ten years later he was accepted as a disciple by the famous Hunan scholar Wang K'ai-yün, himself son of a small tradesman. Ch'i was by no means the only disciple of Wang's who came from a humble family; among Wang's other disciples were a Buddhist monk, a blacksmith, a maker of bamboo baskets, and a buffalo boy.

In his reminiscences Ch'i seldom mentions his economic status during these years. There is reason to believe that it was improving, for in 1900 he moved his family to a new house built on a piece of land near a foothill. From 1902 onwards he traveled extensively in the country. The newly acquired leisure further enabled him to plunge more deeply into classics, particularly poetry, in which he sometimes displayed considerable unconventionality, humor, and sarcasm. But the foundation was laid in his early days when he read T'ang poetry by the pine-needle fire. In 1911, at the age of forty-eight, he was invited to feast and versify with his teacher Wang K'ai-yün and Ch'ü Hung-chi (1850–1918), onetime grand secretary and grand councillor. To escape from the civil wars he took up permanent residence in Peking in 1917. His later career as a painter needs no elaboration.

*Note:* The fact that Ch'i was invited in 1911 to feast and versify with one of the foremost Hunan scholars and an ex-prime minister is not surprising because he was already a painter of rising stature. What is surprising is the fact that while he was still a carpenter he was admitted into the local elite. Ch'i's early life and the social origins of some of Wang K'ai-yün's disciples provide us with an excellent example of the flexibility of status concepts and the fluidity of the status system.

# *NOTES*

CP        Commercial Press     SPPY *Ssu-pu pei-yao* 四部備要
CLHP    *Chi-lu hui-pien* 紀錄彙編   SPTK *Ssu-pu ts'ung-k'an* 四部叢刊
CTPCTK*Ch'ing-tai pi-chi ts'ung-k'an* TSCC*Ts'ung-shu chi-ch'eng* 叢書集成
        清代筆記叢刊

## *I: SOCIAL IDEOLOGY AND SOCIAL STRATIFICATION*

1. *Meng-tzu chu-shu,* 5B.3a; also James Legge, tr., *The Chinese Classics,* vol. 2, *The Works of Mencius,* p. 132.

2. Sun I-jang, *Mo-tzu chien-ku,* pp. 164–65; trans. by Mei Yi-pao, *The Ethical and Political Works of Motse,* p. 179.

3. For Mo-tzu's social and political thought, see Feng Yu-lan, *A History of Chinese Philosophy,* vol. 1, ch. 5, esp. pp. 100–3.

4. For an authoritative summary of the textual problems and political thought of this school, see Hsiao Kung-ch'üan, *Chung-kuo cheng-chih ssu-hsiang shih,* vol. 1, ch. 6.

5. The translation is taken from L. A. Maverick, ed., *Economic Dialogues in Ancient China, Selections from the Kuan-tzu,* p. 39.

6. *Ibid.,* pp. 46, 51.

7. *Kuan-tzu,* 8.5b–6b. The reason that we say this concept of society was probably Kuan-chung's own is because with only minor differences in wording the long passage appears in the Ch'i annals in *Kuo-yü* (SPTK ed.), 6.3a–5a.

8. *Shang-tzu,* 5.4a–4b; trans. by J. J. L. Duyvendak, *The Book of Lord Shang, a Classic of the Chinese School of Law,* p. 306.

9. *Han Fei Tzu,* 2.2b; trans. by W. K. Liao, *The Complete Works of Han Fei Tzu, a Classic of Chinese Legalism,* p. 41.

10. Feng Yu-lan, *A History of Chinese Philosophy,* vol. 1, chs. 8 and 10; vol. 2, ch. 6.

11. It should be noted that the Buddhist thinkers of medieval China also had their theory of equality, but this, too, is metaphysical rather than social and political. See Ting Fu-pao, *Fo-hsüeh ta-tz'u-tien,* pp. 854–56. Similarly, the Taoist philosophers are concerned with "absolute freedom" in a purely metaphysical sense. The absence of the freedom concept in its

modern Western sense in traditional China is also observed by E. G. Pulleyblank, "The Origins and Nature of Chattel Slavery in China," *Journal of Economic and Social History of the Orient,* I (part 2, April, 1958), 209.

12. An excellent study of the concept of *chün-tzu* is that of Lei Haitsung, "Ch'un-ch'iu shih-tai cheng-chih yü she-hui" [Political and social developments in the Ch'un-ch'iu period], *She-hui k'o-hsüeh,* IV (no. 1, October, 1947). An authoritative discussion of the etymology of the term *chün-tzu* is made in Hsiao Kung-ch'üan, *Chung-kuo cheng-chih ssu-hsiang shih,* ch. 2, sec. 5.

13. *Lun-yü chu-shu,* 15.6a.

14. Legge, *Works of Mencius,* p. 118.

15. Mei, *Works of Motse,* pp. 32–33.

16. Duyvendak, *Book of Lord Shang,* p. 48.

17. Homer H. Dubs, tr., *The Works of Hsüntze,* p. 121.

18. The passage is taken from *ibid.,* pp. 65–66, except that the italicized words are mine and different from Dubs's "Great Equableness." T. T. Ch'ü, in his "Chinese Class Structure and its Ideology," in J. K. Fairbank, ed., *Chinese Thought and Institutions* (Chicago, 1957), p. 237, has rendered the key expression "chih-p'ing" as "ultimate equality." From *Hsün-tzu's* whole passage and from our discussion of the major social ideologies of ancient China, it is obvious that the idea of social equality is absent and that the best that ancient thinkers could do was to hope to bring about a maximum equity in a non-egalitarian society. The Chinese version used here for reference is *Hsün-tzu* (SPTK ed.), 2.22a–22b.

19. Lao Kan, "Han-tai ch'a-chü chih-tu" [The recommendatory system of the Han period], *Chung-yang yen-chiu-yüan li-shih yü-yen yen-chiu-so chi-k'an,* hereafter referred to as *Bulletin of the Institute of History and Philology, Academia Sinica,* XVII (1948), 79–131.

20. Liu Shao, *Jen-wu chih* (SPPY ed.), *passim.,* esp. 3A.6a–10b. Liu was entrusted with the task of laying rules for judging and recruiting talents for government service by the usurping Wei kingdom in the Ching-ch'u (237–39) period. See Lü Ssu-mien, *Ch'in-Han shih,* p. 659.

21. Shen Te-fu, *Yeh-huo-pien pu-i* (preface dated 1607, 1870 reprint), 2.47b–51a.

22. Chao I, *Nien-erh-shih tsa-chi,* p. 27. Lao Kan, "Recommendatory System," presents exhaustive biographical evidence on men recommended.

23. Yang Yün-ju, *Chiu-p'in chung-cheng yü liu-ch'ao men-fa, passim.*

24. T'ang Chang-ju, *Wei-Chin-Nan-Pei-Ch'ao-shih lun-ts'ung,* 6th essay, pp. 127–92.

25. Wang I-t'ung, *Wu-ch'ao men-ti, passim.*

26. Chao I, *Nien-erh-shih tsa-chi,* pp. 106–7, "Southern Dynasties often entrusted confidential administration to the humble," and pp. 157–58, "Meritorious generals of the Southern Dynasties were seldom members of the aristocracy"; Wang I-t'ung, *Wu-ch'ao men-ti,* ch. 4, sec. 3; T'ang Chang-ju, *Wei-Chin-Nan-Pei-Ch'ao-shih lun-ts'ung hsü-pien,* pp. 93–123, 128–31.

27. Space does not allow a full discussion of the long and complex history of the examination system. Suffice it to say that in Han times for certain categories of recommended men a written or oral examination was sometimes given. During the latter half of the period of political division examinations were held for a limited number of recommended men. The Sui and early T'ang system was a continuation, expansion, and rationalization of earlier *ad hoc* practices. For examples of examinations in Han times, see Homer H. Dubs, tr., *History of the Former Han Dynasty*, II, 20. For the sporadic examinations of the Later Han period and the Northern and Southern dynasties, see Tu Yu, *T'ung-tien*, chs. 13 and 14, and Ma Tuan-lin, *Wen-hsien t'ung-k'ao*, ch. 28. An informative brief study of the antecedents that led to the Sui-T'ang examination system is in T'ang Chang-ju, *Wei-Chin-Nan-Pei-Ch'ao-shih lun-ts'ung hsü-pien*, pp. 124–31.

28. Ts'en Chung-mien, *Sui-T'ang shih* (Shanghai, 1957), pp 183–84.

29. Tu Yu, *T'ung-tien*, p. 83.

30. Ts'en, *Sui-T'ang shih*, pp. 181–90.

31. For detailed annual quotas of various degrees conferred in T'ang times, see Ma Tuan-lin, *Wen-hsien t'ung-k'ao*, ch. 29.

32. Wang Ting-pao, *T'ang chih-yen*, p. 4.

33. Ch'en Yin-k'o, *T'ang-tai cheng-chih-shih lüeh-lun kao*, p. 63.

34. See below, ch. V, under Wars and Social Upheavals.

35. For a summary of the rejoinders on educational theories and methods of recruiting officials in the latter half of the eleventh century, see Fang Hao, *Sung-shih*, I, 66–70.

36. Professor Ch'en Yin-k'o's once brilliant thesis that the *chin-shih* examination was largely a result of Empress Wu's purposeful policy of breaking up the political monopoly of northwestern aristocracy of Early T'ang seems to have been effectively amended recently by E. G. Pulleyblank, *The Background of the Rebellion of An Lu-shan*, Vol. I, and especially by Ts'en Chung-mien, *Sui-T'ang shih*, pp. 181–90.

37. *Wen-hsien t'ung-k'ao*, chs. 40 and 41.

38. This will be discussed in detail in ch. V, pp. 212–15.

39. *Meng-tzu chu-shu*, 5B.1b–2a; Legge, *Works of Mencius*, pp. 125–26.

40. For an excellent study of the inequality in legal status in traditional China, see Ch'ü T'ung-tsu, *Chung-kuo fa-lü yü Chung-kuo she-hui*, chs. 3 and 4.

41. *Kuan-tzu*, 8.5b–6b.

42. *Ch'ing-ch'ao wen-hsien t'ung-k'ao*, pp. 5026–27.

43. This was because of the traditional Chinese concept of "good" and "base," which is so different from the traditional European concept of "free" and "unfree." Cf. Pulleyblank, "The Origins and Nature of Chattel Slavery in China," *Journal of Economic and Social History of the Orient*, I (part 2, April 1958), 207–9.

44. *Ch'ing-ch'ao wen-hsien t'ung-k'ao*, pp. 5026–27.

45. *Hsüeh-cheng ch'üan-shu* (1812 ed.), ch. 18.

46. Sylvia L. Thrupp, "Hierarchy, Illusion and Social Mobility: A Comment on Ping-ti Ho, 'Aspects of Social Mobility in China, 1368–1911,'" *Comparative Studies in Society and History*, II (no. 1, October, 1959), 126–28.

47. That their true status was still that of commoners is well testified by some Ming local histories and *chin-shih* lists. For example, see *T'ai-yüan fu-chih*, 20.75a, and *Jui-chou fu-chih*, 20.38b–39a. The grandfather of Chou Wen-chin was officially listed as *ching-piao i-min* (officially extolled philanthropic commoner) in *Cheng-te shih-lu-nien chin-shih teng-k'o-lu* (*chin-shih* list of 1521). But sixty-five years later Hsü Ju-k'uei listed his grandfather as *i-min-kuan* (philanthropic commoner-official) in *Wan-li shih-ssu-nien ping-hsü hui-shih lu* (*chin-shih* list of 1586). Later, in the well-known early-seventeenth-century novel *Chin-p'ing-mei,* some of the friends of Hsi-men Ch'ing (the hero of the novel), who contributed grain to the state, dropped the key appellation *min* and adopted the title *kuan.*

48. The fact that these honored "guests" in the semiannual ritualistic banquet were not necessarily degree holders is shown by fairly numerous cases in various Ming-Ch'ing *chin-shih* lists. Those "guests" who had an academic degree invariably mentioned their degrees.

49. Wang Shih-chen, *Yen-chou shih-liao*, 2d series, 37.6a–6b. The important sources on the Ming imperial clansmen are Huang-fu Ch'ung, *Huang-Ming fan-fu cheng-ling* (late Ming manuscript); Chang Huang, *T'u-shu pien*, (1621–25 ed.), ch. 80, which contains a chart showing the progressive descending scale of the imperial noble ranks; and Chang Hsüan, *Hsi-yüan wen-chien lu*, chs. 46 and 47, which contain valuable Ming discussions on the subject.

50. *Ming hui-yao* (Shanghai, 1956 reprint), p. 877.

51. Wang Shih-chen, *Yen-chou shih-liao*, 1st series, chs. 19 and 20, *passim.* A summary of the histories of various Ming nonimperial noble houses is given in 2d series, 38.1a–1b.

52. *Tsung-jen-fu tse-li* (1812 ed.), chs. 4 and 5.

53. This paragraph is based on *ibid.,* ch. 11, *passim.; Tsung-jen-fu tse-li* (1840 ed.), ch. 10, *passim.;* and Wang Chia-hsiang, *Ch'ing-mi shu-wen hsü* (1889 ed.), appendix.

54. *Tsung-jen-fu tse-li* (1840 ed.), 12.14a.

55. *Ta-Ch'ing hui-tien shih-li* (1818 ed.), ch. 118, *passim.*

56. *Li-pu tse-li* (1844 ed.), 93.4a.

57. For example, the statesman, general, and prime minister Yang I-ch'ing testified in 1526 that high-ranking military officers were frequently insulted and bullied by provincial and local officials. See Hsü Hsüeh-mo, *Shih-miao chih-yü lu*, 3.12b–13a.

58. This point is very well made by the great scholar Ku Yen-wu in his *Jih-chih-lu chi-shih*, ch. 17, p. 39a.

59. Ho Liang-chün, *Ssu-yu-chai ts'ung-shuo*, p. 318.

60. Kuo P'an, *Huang-Ming t'ai-hsüeh chih*, ch. 1, pp. 70b–73a.

61. Wang Ch'i, *Wang-shih-yü lei-kao*, ch. 11, "Life of Mr. Chang Chin-sung, posthumously honored with the title of lieutenant governor of Kwangtung."

62. Our general account of *kung-sheng* is based on *Ta-Ming hui-tien* (1587 ed.), ch. 77, which, however, lacks information on certain vital technicalities. The precise dating of the beginning of *en-kung-sheng*, for example, is not mentioned and is explained by some of the better-quality local histories, especially *Hang-chou fu-chih*, ch. 109.

63. The dating of the beginning of *pa-kung-sheng* and *yu-kung-sheng* is based on various local histories, especially *Shao-hsing fu-chih* (1792 ed.), ch. 34. For comment on the literary attainments of *yu-kung-sheng*, see Ch'en K'ang-ch'i, *Lang-ch'ien chi-wen*, ch. 14, pp. 5a–5b. The *kung-sheng* system of Ch'ing times is systematically described in *Ta-Ch'ing hui-tien shih-li* (1899 ed.), ch. 385.

64. *Hang-chou fu-chih* (1923 ed.), ch. 109.

65. Wang Shih-chen, *Yen-chou shih-liao*, 2d series, ch. 39, pp. 21a–21b; also Shen Te-fu, *Wan-li yeh-huo pien*, p. 427.

66. Shen Te-fu, *Wan-li yeh-huo pien*, p. 427.

67. To give one of several examples, *Shun-chih shih-erh-nien i-wei-k'o chin-shih san-tai lü-li* (*chin-shih* list of 1655) contains the case of Ch'ang Yün-hsiu, whose great-grandfather was a *ling-kung-sheng*. Taking the average generation as twenty-five years, it is quite possible that during the last quarter of the sixteenth century *ling-sheng* had already begun to buy *kung-sheng* titles.

68. Yeh T'ing-kuan, *Ou-p'o yü-hua*, ch. 3, pp. 3b–4b.

69. Chang, Chung-li, *The Chinese Gentry, Studies in Their Roles in Nineteenth-Century Chinese Society*, pp. 132–34.

70. *Hsüeh-cheng ch'üan-shu* (1793 ed.), 26. 7b–9a.

71. *Ta-Ch'ing hui-tien shih-li* (1899 ed.), ch. 385. This edition is unpaged.

72. *Ibid.*

73. See table 2 and table 3.

74. *Kuo-ch'ao yü-yang k'o-ming lu* (last edition printed some time after 1904), preface, p. 1b.

75. Kuo P'an, *Huang-Ming t'ai-hsüeh chih*, ch. 12, *passim*.

76. Ku Yen-wu, *Jih-chih-lu chi-shih*, 17.39a.

77. *Ming hui-yao* (1887 reprint), 25.8b.

78. Chang Hsüan, *Hsi-yüan wen-chien-lu*, 31.1a–2a.

79. Wang Shu, *Wang-tuan-i-kung tsou-i*, 7.17a–18a.

80. Kuo P'an, *Huang-Ming t'ai-hsüeh chih*, ch. 12, *passim*.

81. Shen Te-fu, *Yeh-huo pien*, 15.35a–35b.

82. *Kuo-tzu-chien tse-li,* 8.1a.

83. T'ang Hsiang-lung, "Tao-kuang-ch'ao chüan-chien t'ung-chi" [Statistics on the sale of *Chien-sheng* tiles during the Tao-kuang period], *She-hui k'o-hsüeh tsa-chih,* II (no. 4, December, 1931).

84. *Hui-chou fu-chih,* ch. 12, parts 4 and 5.

85. Ch'ü T'ung-tsu, *Chung-kuo feng-chien she-hui,* pp. 193–96.

86. Huan K'uan, *Yen-t'ieh lun,* ch. 5, pp. 16a–16b; Wang Ch'ung, *Lun-heng,* ch. 12; also Alfred Forke, tr., *Lun-heng,* II, 56–66.

87. Wu Ching-tzu, *Ju-lin wai-shih.* For example, Fan Chin was called "Mister" when he was a *sheng-yüan* but the address was changed to "Your Honor" after he obtained the *chü-jen* degree. See also Hsü K'o, ed., *Ch'ing-pai lei-ch'ao,* 16th *ts'e,* p. 11. In the late nineteenth century, however, the addresses were much inflated.

88. Yeh T'ing-kuan, *Ou-p'o yü-hua,* 2.19b.

89. *Hsüeh-cheng ch'üan-shu* (1793 ed.), ch. 34, and 1812 ed., ch. 43, *passim.*

90. *Ta-Ch'ing hui-tien shih-li* (1899 ed.), ch. 385.

91. The evidence is so plentiful that only a part of it will be presented in ch. II.

92. *Ju-lin wai-shih,* ch. 47.

93. For example, in ch. 2 Wu Ching-tzu makes it emphatically clear that he is describing the Ming custom by which *sheng-yüan* called each other "old friends," while local students without the *sheng-yüan* degree called themselves "little friends," whatever might be their actual ages.

94. Wang Shou-jen, *Yang-ming ch'üan-shu,* 30.30b.

95. P'u Sung-ling, *Hsing-shih yin-yüan,* chs. 79–83.

96. R. H. Tawney, "The Rise of the Gentry, 1558–1640," *Economic History Review,* 1st series, XI (no. 1, 1941); also David Mathew, *The Social Structure of Caroline England,* ch. 4, "The Stratification of the Gentry."

97. *Kuan-tzu,* 8.5b–6b; *Kuo-yü,* 6.5a.

98. *Shih-chi,* ch. 129, *passim;* Burton Watson, tr., *Records of the Grand Historian of China,* II, 476–99. See also Nancy Lee Swann, *Food and Money in Ancient China,* in which this famous chapter of the *Shih-chi* is translated.

99. *T'ang hui-yao,* 31.15a–15b.

100. Huang Tsung-hsi, *Sung-Yüan hsüeh-an,* 1.20a–20b, has a record of a debauched son of a very rich Canton merchant who eventually became a *chin-shih.* See also Ch'üan Han-sheng, "Pei-Sung Pien-liang ti shu-ch'u-ju mao-i" [Export and import trade of the east capital during the Northern Sung period], *Bulletin of the Institute of History and Philology,* VIII (part 2, 1939); and his "Sung-tai kuan-li chih ssu-ying shang-yeh" [Government officials and private trade during the Sung period], *ibid.,* VII (part 2, 1936); and Sung Hsi, "Sung-tai fu-shang ju-shih ti t'u-ching" [Avenues through

which rich merchants of Sung times entered the officialdom], *Ta-lu tsa-chih*, IV (no. 11, 1952).

101. Meng Ssu-ming, *Yüan-tai she-hui chieh-chi chih-tu*.
102. Wu Ching-tzu, *Ju-lin wai-shih*, ch. 3.
103. P'u Sung-ling, *Hsing-shih yin-yüan*, ch. 1.
104. Hsieh Chao-che, *Wu-tsa-tsu*, 4.25b.
105. *Hui-chou fu-chih*, 12.4a; *Ming Hsi-tsung shih-lu* (Kiangsu Sinological Library photostat ed.), 68.8b–9a, 75.2b.
106. Wu Ching-tzu, *Ju-lin wai-shih*, ch. 47.
107. Cited in Li Shao-wen, *Huang-Ming shih-shuo hsin-yü*, 2.31b.
108. Wang Ch'i, *Wang-shih-yü lei-kao*, 8.33a–33b.
109. *Kuan-ch'ang hsien-hsing chi*, preface.
110. Elinor G. Barber, *The Bourgeoisie in 18th-Century France*.
111. Yang shih-ts'ung, *Yü-t'ang k'uei-chi*, ch. 3.
112. Yeh T'ing-kuan, *Ou-p'o yü-hua*, 3.3b–4b; also *Kuo-ch'ao yü-yang k'o-ming-lu*.
113. Hsü Ta-ling, *Ch'ing-tai chüan-na chih-tu, passim*.
114. *Man-Han wen-wu kuan-sheng ming-tz'u lu* (1798).
115. Shen Yao, *Lo-fan-lou wen-chi*, 24.11b–13b, 10.15b–20b.
116. Many recent findings are summarized in Bernard Barber's *Social Stratification, a Comparative Analysis of Structure and Process*, from which I have drawn generalizations on Western societies for occasional comparison with traditional Chinese society.

## II: THE FLUIDITY OF THE STATUS SYSTEM

1. Robert M. Marsh, Mandarin and Executive: Elite Mobility in Chinese and American Societies.

2. Meng Ssu-ming, *Yüan-tai she-hui chieh-chi chih-tu* [Social classes in China during the Yüan period], *Yenching Journal of Chinese Studies*, Monograph series, no. 16, 1938, pp. 149–206.

3. *Yüan-t'ung yüan-nien chin-shih teng-k'o lu, passim*.

4. *Ming-shih*, ch. 77; *Ming T'ai-tsu shih-lu*, ch. 54.

5. Unless otherwise stated in footnotes, these few paragraphs on the artisan status are based on *Ta-Ming hui-tien* (1587 ed.), chs. 188–91 inclusive.

6. Liang Fang-chung, "Ming-tai kuo-chi mao-i yü yin ti shu-ch'u-ju," [International trade and silver movements during the Ming period], *Chung-kuo she-hui ching-chi-shih chi-k'an* [Chinese social and economic history review], VI (no. 2, 1939).

7. Interesting but scattered evidence is found in *Ta-Ming hui-tien*, chs. 190–201; for an excellent recent study, see Ch'en Shih-ch'i, "The artisan system of the Ming period," in *Chung-kuo tzu-pen-chu-i meng-ya*

*wen-ti t'ao-lun chi* [Symposium on the question of incipient capitalism in Chinese history], I, 436–66.

8. *Lung-chiang ch'uan-ch'ang chih* (original preface dated 1553), chs. 3 and 6.

9. *Ch'ing-ch'ao wen-hsien t'ung-k'ao,* ch. 21, p. 5044.

10. Chiao Hung, *Kuo-ch'ao hsien-cheng lu,* ch. 18; Chu Yün-ming, *Yeh-chi,* p. 105, mentions specifically that Wu K'uan's ancestors were hereditary weavers.

11. *T'ung-ch'eng Chang-shih tsung-p'u,* ch. 26; *Lung-ch'ing erh-nien chin-shih teng-k'o lu,* third class, no. 152.

12. The convenient source for a brief study of the changes in the military status is the four well-documented chapters, 89–92, in *Ming-shih.* The best modern study of the changes in the Ming army system is Wu Han, "Ming-tai ti chün-ping" [The hereditary and hired army of the Ming period], *Chinese Social and Economic History,* V (no. 2, 1937).

13. Wang Yü-ch'üan, "Ming-tai ti chün-hu" [The military households of the Ming period], *Li-shih yen-chiu* [Historical research] (1959, no. 8). It is to be noted that this article leans too heavily on the legal texts with the result that its conclusions are sometimes at variance with Wu Han's article, "The Hereditary and Hired Army of the Ming Period," which deals more with historical realities. In fact, for a greater part of the past two thousand years after the downfall of the Former Han empire the Chinese could seldom revive the system of universal conscription and the army usually bore a social stigma. A highly illuminating if somewhat sweeping discussion of the inability of the post-Han Chinese to solve the army problem is that of Lei Hai-tsung, "A Soldierless Civilization," in his collected historical essays entitled *Chung-kuo wen-hua yü Chung-kuo ti ping* [Chinese civilization and Chinese army].

14. A sixteenth-century scholar-official's essay on *chün-chi* people, cited in *Chiang-ning hsien-chih,* ch. 3, pp. 28b–29b.

15. *Hsü-wen-hsien t'ung-k'ao,* ch. 13, p. 2893.

16. Chao Kuan, *Hou-hu chih* (the manual of the Board of Revenue first compiled in 1513; rev. and expanded ed., 1621), ch. 4, pp. 9a–10b; also *Ta-Ming hui-tien* (1502 ed.), ch. 20, 15a–15b.

17. Ch'en Mao-heng, *Ming-tai wo-k'o k'ao-lüeh* [The invasion of China by Japanese pirates during the Ming dynasty], *Yenching Journal of Chinese Studies,* Monograph series, no. 6, 1934, pp. 34–36.

18. Liang Fang-chung, "Ming-tai ti min-ping" [The civilian corps and the hired soldiery of the Ming period], *Chinese Social and Economic History Review,* V (no. 2); also Li Kuang-ming, *Chia-ching yü-wo chiang-che chu-k'o-chün k'ao* [The repulse of Japanese pirates by provincial and extra-provincial armies of Kiangsu and Chekiang, 1551–1561], *Yenching Journal of Chinese Studies,* Monograph series, no. 4, 1933, *passim.*

19. Chiao Hung, *Kuo-ch'ao hsien-cheng lu,* ch. 14.

20. The best general study of salt producers of Ming times is that of Ho Wei-ning, "Ming-tai ti yen-hu" [The salt-producing households of the Ming period], *Chinese Social and Economic History Review,* VII (no. 2). It is based on Ming sources not easily available.

21. Ming salt administration documents, cited in *Liang-huai yen-fa chih* (1748 ed.), ch. 17, pp. 5a–7a.

22. Ho Wei-ning, "Ming-tai ti yen-hu," p. 143.

23. Ping-ti Ho, "The Salt Merchants of Yang-chou: a study of Commercial Capitalism in Eighteenth-Century China," *Harvard Journal of Asiatic Studies,* XVII (no. 1–2, June, 1954), esp. pp. 132–35.

24. Chiao Hung, *Kuo-ch'ao hsien-cheng lu,* ch. 113, pp. 10a–10b.

25. *Ibid.,* ch. 114, p. 48a; also Huang Tsung-hsi, *Ming-ju hsüeh-an,* ch. 32, pp. 6a–8a.

26. A more systematic discussion of the social and intellectual consequences of Wang Yang-ming's teachings will be given in ch. V, under Community Schools and Private Academies.

27. Li Huan, *Kuo-ch'ao ch'i-hsien lei-cheng,* ch. 258, pp. 18a–19a; Ch'ien Yung, *Lü-yüan ts'ung-hua,* ch 6., pp. 9a–9b.

28. Feng Ying-ching, *Huang-Ming ching-shih shih-yung pien,* ch. 12, pp. 4a–4b.

29. Hsü Hsüeh-chü, *Kuo-ch'ao tien-hui,* ch. 40, p. 9b.

30. *Ming-shih,* ch. 148.

31. Huang Tsung-hsi, *Ming-ju hsüeh-an,* ch. 7, p. 12a.

32. Liu Feng, *Hsü-wu-hsien-hsien tsan,* ch. 3, pp. 7a–8b, 11a–12a, 12a–12b.

33. *Ming-shih,* ch. 286.

34. Ho Liang-chün, *Ssu-yu-chai ts'ung-shuo,* p. 148.

35. This will be discussed in more detail in ch. V, under Wars and Social Upheavals.

36. See below, ch. V, under Community Schools and Private Academies.

37. By far the most precise definition of *kuan-chi* is found in *I-chen hsien-chih,* ch. 6, pp. 1a–1b.

38. *Liang-che yen-fa chih,* ch. 24, p. 2a.

39. *Li-pu tse-li* (1784 ed.), ch. 77; *K'o-ch'ang t'iao-li,* ch. 36.

40. *Ssu-ch'uan yen-fa chih,* ch. 25. pp. 9b–12a.

41. Wang Ch'ung-wu, "Ming-tai shang-t'un tsu-chih" [The organization of commercial colonization in Ming times], *Yü-kung,* V (no. 12, August, 1936).

42. Fujii Hiroshi, "A Study of Salt Merchants of Ming Times," *Shigaku zasshi,* LIV (no. 5–6, 1943).

43. This was the impression of the famous early-fifteenth-century offi-

cial Chou Chen, cited in *Ming-shih,* ch. 77, p. 3a and in *Hsü-wen-hsien t'ung-k'ao,* ch. 13, p. 2896.

44. Ch'u Jen-huo, *Chien-hu chi,* ch. 5, p. 9b. Biographies of several of these men may be found in *Ming-shih.*

45. Hsü Hsüeh-chü, *Kuo-ch'ao tien-hui,* ch. 40, p. 9b; Ch'u Jen-huo, *Chien-hu chi,* supplementary series, ch. 4, pp. 1b–2a.

46. Sun Ch'eng-tse, *Ch'un-ming meng-yü lu,* ch. 41, pp. 10a–11a.

47. Cha Chi-tso, *Tsui-wei lu,* ch. 18, p. 13a; Ch'u Jen-huo, *Chien-hu chi,* ch. 4, pp. 1a–1b.

48. Huang Yü, *Shuang-huai sui-ch'ao,* ch. 5, pp. 13b–14a; also Chang Hung-tao and Chang Ning-tao, *Huang-Ming san-yüan k'ao,* ch. 4, p. 17b.

49. *Chen-ch'uan hsien-sheng chi,* ch. 13, pp. 2a–2b.

50. *Tai-han chi,* ch. 52, pp. 10b–15a.

51. *Yüan-shih shih-fan,* ch. 2, pp. 23b–24a.

52. Ch. 4, p. 4a.

53. *Hu-shih tsung-p'u,* "Clan Instructions"; also *Ti-hsi Chang-shih chia-sheng,* "Family Instructions." The wisdom of engaging in agriculture and investing in land is systematically expounded by the prime minister Chang Ying (1638–1708) in the famous essay "Heng-ch'an so-yen" [Desultory notes on real estate] in his *Tu-su-t'ang wen-chi,* ch. 14.

54. *Lu-chiang-chün Ho-shih ta-t'ung tsung-p'u,* "Clan Instructions."

55. *Chin-hua hsien-cheng lu,* ch. 9, pp. 18b–19a.

56. Yang Chi-sheng, *Yang-chung-min-kung chi,* ch. 4 (biography of Yang by Wang Shih-chen).

57. Huang Tsung-hsi, *Ming-ju hsüeh-an,* ch. 1.

58. Li Shao-wen, *Huang-Ming shih-shuo hsin-yü,* ch. 1, p. 4b.

59. Huang Tsung-hsi, *Ming-ju hsüeh-an,* ch. 45, pp. 4b–5a.

60. Ho Ch'iao-yüan, *Min-shu,* ch. 90, p. 6b.

61. *Hui-chou fu-chih,* ch. 12, pt. 4, p. 47b.

62. Wu Te-hsüan, *Ch'u-yüeh-lou wen-chien lu,* ch. 2, pp. 2b–3a.

63. Chang Han, *Sung-ch'uang meng-yü* (*Wu-lin hsien-che i-shu* ed.), ch. 4, p. 27a and ch. 6, pp. 11a–11b.

64. Yang I, *Ming-liang chi,* p. 13.

65. Juan K'uei-sheng, *Ch'a-yü k'o-hua,* ch. 2, p. 5b. Hsü Ch'ao's father, however, had already made the initial change in status when he eventually earned his *sheng-yüan* degree. See the account of Hsü Ch'ao's ancestry in *K'ang-hsi shih-erh-nien kuei-ch'ou-k'o hui-shih chin-shih san-tai lü-li pien-lan,* no. 116.

66. For the more prominent members of the Hsü clan, see Li Huan, *Kuo-ch'ao ch'i-hsien lei-cheng,* ch. 57, p. 31a; ch. 19, p. 1a; ch. 57, p. 42a; ch. 57, p. 44b; *Ch'ing hua-chia shih-shih,* ch. 11, p. 23a; and Hsü K'o, ed., *Ch'ing-pai lei-ch'ao, ts'e* 16, "Prominent Clans."

67. So far the most extensive study of Ming and Ch'ing merchants and

commercial capital is that of Fu I-ling, *Ming-Ch'ing shih-tai shang-jen chi shang-yeh tzu-pen* [Merchants and commercial capital of Ming-Ch'ing times], which deals with various important regional merchant groups of Hui-chou, Tung-t'ing, southern coastal Fukien, and Shensi. It also deals with the copper-importing merchants of Ming and early Ch'ing times. The most solid study of Hui-chou merchants is that of Fujii Hiroshi, "A study of Hui-chou merchants" (five installments), *Tōyō gakuhō*, XXXVI-VII. *Kuang-tung shih-san-hang k'ao*, by Liang Chia-pin, remains the standard work on the rich Co-hong merchants of nineteenth-century Canton. A vast amount of useful if sometimes scattered information on commerce and capital accumulation is found in *Chung-kuo tzu-pen chu-i meng-ya wen-t'i t'ao-lun chi*, the various articles of which however, differ greatly in quality. "The Salt Merchants of Yang-chou," by Ping-ti Ho, deals with the leading merchant princes of the eighteenth century and ventures certain analyses of the factors which made impossible the development of a full-fledged capitalist system and continual capital accumulation.

68. Ping-ti Ho, "Salt Merchants," sec. 3.

69. T'ien Ju-ch'eng, *chin-shih* of 1526 and a native of Hang-chou, "Biography of Ah Chi," in *Shuo-fu*, vol. 165. The major details of the Ah Chi story given in Ming novels *Chin-ku ch'i-kuan*, ch. 25, and *Hsing-shih heng-yen*, ch. 35, agree with T'ien's biography.

70. *Ming-shih*, ch. 152, pp. 4a–5a.

71. A. W. Hummel, *Eminent Chinese of the Ch'ing Period*, II, 814–15.

72. *Ibid.*, pp. 834–35.

73. *Hui-chou fu-chih*, ch. 12, *passim*.

74. Wen Ch'un, *Wen-kung-i-kung wen-chi*, ch. 10, pp. 5a–7a; ch. 10, pp. 27a–29b; ch. 10, pp. 35a–36b; ch. 11, pp. 4b–6a; ch. 11, pp. 10b–12b; ch. 11, pp. 12b–14a; ch. 11, pp. 14b–16a; ch. 11, pp. 16a–17b. See also Fu I-ling, *Merchants and Commercial Capital in Ming-Ch'ing Times*, pp. 161–75.

75. Wu Te-hsüan, *Ch'u-yüeh-lou wen-chien lu*, *passim*.

76. Cheng Fang-k'un, *Pen-ch'ao ming-chia shih-ch'ao hsiao-chuan*, ch. 1, pp. 13b–14a.

77. Li Tou, *Yang-chou hua-fang lu* (Peking, 1959 reprint), pp. 91–92, 184.

78. See Appendix, case 27.

79. *Yen-cheng chih* (1529 ed.), ch. 5, p. 11b.

80. *Ming-shih*, ch. 150, pp. 2b–3a.

81. *Yen-cheng chih*, ch. 5, pp. 13a–14a.

82. Huang Hsing-tseng, *Wu-feng lu*, pp. 5a–5b.

83. Ho Liang-chün, *Ssu-yu-chai ts'ung-shuo ti-ch'ao* (TSCC ed.), pp. 353–55.

84. *Ch'ang-lu yen-fa chih* (1805 ed.), ch. 17, p. 12b.

85. Hummel, *Eminent Chinese of the Ch'ing Period,* I, 11–13.

86. The size of the fortunes of Liang-huai and Co-hong merchants, their monetary contributions to various agencies, and the relations between the Ch'ien-lung emperor and the salt merchants are all discussed in Ping-ti Ho's "The Salt Merchants of Yang-chou," *Harvard Journal of Asiatic Studies,* XVII (no. 1–2, June, 1954).

87. Ping-ti Ho, "The Salt Merchants," *Harvard Journal of Asiatic Studies,* XVII, sec. 1.

88. *Ibid.*

89. *Shan-tung yen-fa chih* (1806 ed.), ch. 9, pp. 5a–5b.

90. *Ho-tung yen-fa pei-lan,* chs. 5 and 6, *passim.*

91. *Ho-tung yen-fa chih,* ch. 3.

92. The size of the average household of fourteen provinces in 1812 was 5.33 persons and the total national population at the beginning of Ch'ing was probably considerably under 150,000,000. The national population shot up to 300,000,000 by 1800. See Ping-ti Ho, *Studies on the Population of China, 1368–1953,* chs. 4 and 11.

93. For details, see below, ch. VI.

94. P'an Shih-en, though generally known as a native of Su-chou, was the son of P'an I-chi, who was first registered as a *shang-chi* student of Hang-chou. See P'an Shih-en, *Ssu-pu-lao-jen shou-ting nien-p'u,* p. 1a. For other prominent members of the P'an clan who lived in Su-chou but were registered originally as *shang-chi* students of Chekiang, see *Liang-che yen-fa chih,* ch. 24.

95. *Liang-che yen-fa chih,* ch. 24; *Liang-huai yen-fa chih* (1806 ed.), ch. 48; *Shan-tung yen-fa chih* (1725 ed.), ch. 13.

96. *Hui-chou fu-chih* (1827 ed.), ch. 9, pts. 2 and 3.

97. Shen Yao, *Lo-fan-lou wen-chi,* ch. 24, pp. 11b–13a.

98. *Liang-huai yen-fa chih* (1806 ed.), ch. 25, pp. 2b–3a.

99. Chu Kuo-chen, *Huang-Ming k'ai-kuo-ch'en chuan,* ch. 10, pp. 1a–2b.

100. *Ming-shih,* ch. 209, pp. 5a–7a; ch. 216, pp. 10b–11b; ch. 261, pp. 5a–6a.

101. See Appendix, case 9.

102. *Wu-hsien chih,* ch. 43, pp. 18a–18b.

103. *Ibid.,* ch. 44, pp. 41b–42a.

104. *Ku-su chih,* ch. 52, pp. 34b–35a; *Ming-shih,* ch. 285, pp. 12b–13a; *Ku-su chih,* ch. 52, p. 49a; Li Tsung-fang, *Ch'ien-chi,* ch. 1, p. 3.

105. The tradesman father-in-law of Hsü Hsien, a native of Chekiang and an official in the first half of the sixteenth century, is an example. See Hsü Hsien, *Hsi-yüan tsa-chi,* Book A, p. 86.

106. Wu Huai-ch'ing, *Kuan-chung san-Li-hsien-sheng nien-p'u,* ch. 5.

107. Ping-ti Ho, "The Salt Merchants," *Harvard Journal of Asiatic Studies,* XVII, p. 162.

108. Yen Ch'en, *T'ung-hsi ta-sou tzu-ting nien-p'u,* p. 5a.

109. Chang Han, *Sung-ch'uang meng-yü,* ch. 6, pp. 13b–14a; also his *Hsi-nang tu-yü,* ch. 16, pp. 5a–7a.

110. See below, ch. IV, under Dilution of Wealth.

111. Ping-ti Ho, "The Salt Merchants," *Harvard Journal of Asiatic Studies,* XVII, pp. 159–168.

112. Wu Ching-tzu, *Ju-lin wai-shih,* ch. 13.

113. *Ibid.,* ch. 15.

114. Lu Yung, *Shu-yüan tsa-chi ti-ch'ao,* ch. 6, pp. 3a–3b.

115. A most elaborate system is found in *Ssu-hui hsien-chih,* Book IIA, pp. 90b–91b.


## *III: UPWARD MOBILITY: ENTRY INTO OFFICIALDOM*

1. Since 1949 more than 1,000 formerly unknown editions of Chinese local histories have been discovered, bringing the known total up to over 7,000. See Chu Shih-chia, *Chung-kuo ti-fang-chih tsung-lu.*

2. Chang, Chung-li, *The Chinese Gentry,* Part IV.

3. Ho Liang-chün, *Ssu-yu-chai ts'ung-shuo,* p. 124.

4. Kuo T'ing-hsün, *Kuo-ch'ao ching-sheng fen-chün jen-wu k'ao,* *passim.*

5. In this connection we may doubt the value of the mobility data and some sweeping generalizations on social mobility and the fundamental character of traditional Chinese society in Karl A. Wittfogel's works: (1) *New Light on Chinese Society,* (2) "Public Office in the Liao Dynasty and the Chinese Examination System," *Harvard Journal of Asiatic Studies,* X (June, 1947), (3) *Oriental Despotism,* and (4) with Feng Chia-sheng, *History of Chinese Society—Liao, 907–1125.* It goes without saying that the regional Khitan kingdom of Liao, which was comparatively little sinicized, is among the least representative of China's long history.

6. Shang Yen-liu, *Ch'ing-tai k'o-chü k'ao-shih shu-lu,* ch. 2.

7. A good study based on these examination booklets is P'an Kuang-tan and Fei Hsiao-t'ung, "K'o-chü yü she-hui liu-tung" [Examination system and social mobility], in *She-hui k'o-hsüeh,* IV (no. 1, October, 1947). This study relies on 917 booklets, most of which are of Chihli, Kiangsu, Chekiang, and Shantung of the late nineteenth century. Columbia University's East Asiatic Library has over 300 such booklets. For reasons here explained they have been consulted but rejected.

8. Textually, the available Ming *chin-shih* lists are of high quality. The total number of successful candidates of the 17 classes between 1371 and 1610, according to Li Chou-wang, *Kuo-ch'ao li-k'o t'i-ming pei-lu ch'u-chi,* is 4,963. In our 17 Ming lists the total of *chin-shih* for whom ancestral information is given is 4,790, or 96.1 percent of the Li total. If we

exclude two incomplete lists of 1371 and 1610, the remaining 15 lists are textually almost 100 percent complete. Except for those of the first Ch'ing reign period of Shun-chih (1644–61), our Ch'ing *chin-shih* lists usually contain a number of successful candidates without ancestral information. But the total of the useful cases of the 31 Ch'ing lists, being 7,436, still amounts to 85.1 percent of the total of 8,739 for the same 31 classes. The latter total is derived from Fang Chao-ying and Tu Lien-che, *Tseng-chiao Ch'ing-ch'ao chin-shih t'i-ming pei-lu.* Altogether, our 48 Ming-Ch'ing *chin-shih* lists give a total of 12,226 useful cases, which amounts to nearly 90 percent of the aggregate number of successful candidates of the same 48 examinations, which, according to the Li and Fang-Tu lists, is 13,702.

9. The exactitude with which honorific titles were conferred won the admiration of the great historian Chao I. For his opinion, see his *Hai-yü ts'ung-k'ao,* ch. 27, pp. 4b–5a.

10. A further discussion of the family and clan system will be given in ch. V, under The Clan System.

11. Ping-ti Ho, *Studies on the Population of China, 1368–1953,* pp. 10, 56.

12. Notably, for American business elite, Seymour M. Lipset and Reinhard Bendix, *Social Mobility in Industrial Society,* p. 122, table 4.2; for higher American civil service, Reinhard Bendix, *Higher Civil Servants in American Society, a study of the Social Origins, the Careers, and the Power-Position of Higher Federal Administration,* p. 26, table V; for higher British civil service, R. K. Kelsall, "The Social Origin of Higher Civil Servants in Great Britain, Now and in the Past," *Transactions of the Second World Congress of Sociology;* and his *Higher Civil Servants in Britain, from 1871 to the Present Day,* p. 153, table 25; for higher French civil service, Thomas B. Bottomore, "La Mobilité Sociale dans la Haute Administration Française," *Cahiers Internationaux Sociologie,* XIII (September, 1952); for Cambridge University students, Mrs. Hester Jenkins and D. Caradog Jones, "Social Class of Cambridge University Alumni of the 18th and 19th Centuries," *British Journal of Sociology,* I (No. 2, June, 1950). In addition to information on elite members' fathers' occupations, sometimes information is available for the occupations of elite members' fathers-in-law. See John Porter, "The Economic Elite and the Social Structure in Canada," *Canadian Journal of Economics and Political Science,* XXIII (No. 3, August, 1957); and his "Higher Public Servants and the Bureaucratic Elite in Canada," *ibid.,* XXIV (No. 4, November, 1958).

13. In searching for the rare *chin-shih* lists containing ancestry information, I used the following catalogues as the main guidance: (1) *Kuo-li pei-p'ing t'u-shu-kuan shan-pen shu-mu,* (2) *Kuo-li pei-p'ing t'u-shu-kuan shan-pen shu-mu i-pien,* (3) *Chung-kuo yin-pen shu-chi chan-lan mu-lu,* (4) *Kuo-li chung-yang t'u-shu-kuan shan-pen shu-mu,* (5) *Kuo-hui t'u-shu-kuan*

*ts'ang Chung-kuo shan-pen shu-lu*. Most of the rare *chin-shih* lists mentioned in the first two catalogues are available in microfilm at the Library of Congress. When I asked the National Library of Peking to reproduce in microfilm certain rare Ming and early Ch'ing lists, one item listed in (1), entitled *Chien-wen erh-nien chin-shih teng-k'o lu* (1400), was not requested. This was because I had been misled by the title of the list of successful candidates at the palace final examination of the same class, entitled *Chien-wen erh-nien tien-shih teng-k'o lu* (available at the Library of Congress in microfilm), into believing that the latter list contains information on *chin-shih* ancestry. But it turned out that my guess was wrong and, by the time the latter reached me, it was too late to include the former in my request to Peking. Very probably, therefore, data for *chin-shih* of the class of 1400 are extant but have been unavailable to this study due to my oversight. There is one more *chin-shih* list, that of the year 1675, which is listed in catalogue (2) and which was requested but was not reproduced. It remains to be confirmed whether this list is extant in Peking. Although a dozen or so Chinese and Japanese catalogues of rare Chinese works were consulted, only one rare item unavailable in North America has been located at the Jimbun Kagaku Kenkyūjo in Kyoto. This is not a *chin-shih* list but one of *yin* recipients in the year 1862. It thus fills up a gap in our knowledge as to the aggregate number of *yin* holders of the entire nineteenth century.

14. *Tao-kuang i-wei-k'o hui-shih t'ung-nien ch'ih-lu* (*chin-shih* list of 1835).

15. *Kuang-hsü keng-yin en-k'o hui-shih t'ung-nien ch'ih-lu* (*chin-shih* list of 1890).

16. *Wan-li shih-ssu-nien ping-hsü hui-shih lu* (*chin-shih* list of 1586).

17. Ch'en K'ang-ch'i. *Lang-ch'ien chi-wen*, ch. 14, pp. 5a–5b.

18. *Ching-hsiang t'i-ming lu*, introduction.

## IV: DOWNWARD MOBILITY

1. S. M. Lipset and R. Bendix, *Social Mobility in Industrial Society*, ch. 6.

2. Wang Shih-chen, *Ch'ih-pei ou-t'an*, ch. 10, p. 1a. It is to be noted that in *Ta-huai Wang-shih nien-tsu yüeh-yen shih-chi*, compiled by Wang Chih-yüan (Wang Shih-chen's great-grandfather) and Wang Hsiang-chin, no mention is made of Wang Kuei's having been a tenant before he acquired property of his own. It seems that in Wang Chih-yüan's sketchy and anecdotal history of his ancestry only good deeds and wise sayings are given as an inspiration to descendants, while the clan's humble origin is not specifically mentioned. Since Wang Kuei was forced to migrate to Hsinch'eng, it is unlikely that he could have owned property right from the

very beginning. Wang Shih-chen's testimonial, which is probably based on family oral tradition, may be more reliable.

3. *Ch'ih-pei ou-t'an,* ch. 5, pp. 8b–9a.

4. *Ta-huai Wang-shih nien-tsu yüeh-yen shih-chi,* Book A, p. 9a.

5. *Ibid.,* Book B, pp. 24a–24b. Book B was compiled by Wang Hsiang-chin.

6. Niu Hsiu, *Hu-sheng,* 2d series, ch. 3, p. 1a.

7. The list is compiled from *Hsin-ch'eng Wang-shih chia-sheng; Hsin-ch'eng hsien-chih,* both the 1693 and 1933 eds., chs. on degree holders and biographies; and *Shantung t'ung-chih,* chs. on degree holders and biographies. The main method used here is to trace the generation names through occasional cross-reference to kinship in local histories. For this reason, if some of the later-generation members of the Wang clan did not adopt common generation names, the list may not be complete. However, the omissions, if any, would be very few.

8. *Ch'ih-pei ou-t'an,* ch. 6, pp. 11a–11b.

9. Concerning the nature of the Tung-lin party, see Charles O. Hucker, "The Tung-lin Movement of the Late-Ming Period," in J. K. Fairbank, ed., *Chinese Thought and Institutions,* pp. 132–62.

10. Wang Wan, *Shuo-ling,* pp. 2b–3a.

11. Li Tou, *Yang-chou hua-fang lu* (Peking, 1959 reprint), pp. 220–21, gives a vivid account of Wang Shih-chen's early unusually wide literary and artistic associations.

12. *Hsin-ch'eng hsien-chih* (1933 ed.), ch. 15, pp. 12a–12b.

13. Hsü K'o, *Ch'ing-pai lei-ch'ao,* XVI, 15.

14. *Yün-tzu-tsai-k'an sui-pi,* p. 70.

15. Chang Ying, *Ts'ung-hsün-chai yü,* B, p. 3b.

16. Ch'en Ch'i-yüan, *Yung-hsien-chai pi-chi,* ch. 1. The author was a member of the Ch'en clan.

17. Hsü Hsi-lin, *Hsi-ch'ao hsin-yü,* ch. 2, pp. 9a–9b.

18. *T'ung-ch'eng Chang-shih tsung-p'u,* ch. 1; *Hai-ning Po-hai Ch'en-shih tsung-p'u,* ch. 1; Ch'en Ch'i-yüan, *Yung-hsien-chai pi-chi,* ch. 1.

19. For the long tradition of investment in land and serious studies of the T'ung-ch'eng area, see Ma Ch'i-ch-ang, *T'ung-ch'eng ch'i-chiu chuan,* *passim.* For the same tradition of the Chang clan, see Chang T'ing-yü's preface to the biographical chapters of the 9th generation in *T'ung-ch'eng Chang-shih tsung-p'u.*

20. Chang Ying, "Heng-ch'an so-yen" [Desultory notes on real estate], *Tu-su-t'ang wen-chi,* ch. 14.

21. *Chi-shih tsung-p'u* (1907 ed.), ch. 8, p. 26b.

22. Traditional Chinese calendrical year names are formed by one of the ten heavenly stems and one of the twelve earthly branches. Beginning with the first stem and the first branch there are altogether 60 combina-

tions, thus forming a large cycle of 60 years and a small rotation of heavenly stems once every 10 years.

23. *Yüan-shih shih-fan,* ch. 2, pp. 2b–3a.

24. *Ts'ao-mu-tzu,* ch. 4, p. 12b.

25. Cited in Ch'en Ch'i-yüan, *Yung-hsien-chai pi-chi,* ch. 1, pp. 5a–5b. The official's name is Wang Ch'i. There are at least six persons in Ming-Ch'ing times by the same name. The most famous is the compiler of *Hsü wen-hsien t'ung-k'ao, chin-shih* of 1565, a native of Shanghai. However, the account of family background given in the cited passage does not agree with that in Wang Ch'i's *Wang shih-yü lei-kao* (1585 ed.), ch. 5, pp. 39a–40a. The other Wang Ch'is are all of the Ch'ing period. *Fen-yang hsien-chih,* ch. 7, p. 33b, mentions a Wang Ch'i, who was a *chin-shih* of 1805 and later became a magistrate of a department county in Szechwan. The lack of further detail makes it impossible to identify him. The other four persons of this name were all painters.

26. *Ming-shih,* ch. 148.

27. Shen Te-fu, *Wan-li yeh-huo pien,* p. 458, "Descendants of the Three Yangs."

28. *Ibid.,* pp. 461–62.

29. Chao I, *Nien-erh-shih tsa-chi,* pp. 495–96.

30. Li Shao-wen, *Huang-Ming shih-shuo hsin-yü,* "Extravagance," p. 11b.

31. Yeh Ch'ang-chih, *Ts'ang-shu chi-shih shih,* pp. 86–87.

32. Wu Te-hsüan, *Ch'u-yüeh-lou wen-chien lu,* ch. 7, p. 8b.

33. A. W. Hummel, "Hsü ch'ien-hsüeh," *Eminent Chinese of the Ch'ing Period;* Yeh Ch'ang-chih, *Ts'ang-shu chi-shih shih,* pp. 220–21; Hsü Hsi-lin, *Hsi-ch'ao hsin-yü,* ch. 16, pp. 3b–4a, "Hsü, the Filial Son."

34. Huang Huai's biography is in *Ming-shih,* ch. 147; an account of his descendants is given in Hsü Hsien, *Hsi-yüan tsa-chi,* pp. 133–34.

35. Wang Shih-chen, *Hsiang-tsu pi-chi,* ch. 2, pp. 7b–8a.

36. Ch'en Mao-jen, *Ch'üan-nan tsa-chih,* Book A, p. 11.

37. *Yen-chou shan-jen ssu-pu kao,* ch. 84, pp. 12a–14a.

38. Lipset and Bendix, *Social Mobility in Industrial Society,* chs. 6 and 7.

39. *Ta-Ming hui-tien* (1587 ed.), ch. 6.

40. *Ming hui-yao,* ch. 48.

41. All the information about the working of the *yin* system in the Chang family is based on various biographies, arranged by generations, in *T'ung-ch'eng Chang-shih tsung-p'u.*

42. The above discussion is based on *Chi-shih tsung-p'u.*

43. P'eng Yün-chang, *P'eng-wen-ching-kung ch'üan-chi* (last preface dated 1868), ch. 8, pp. 13b–14b.

44. Chao I, *Yen-p'u tsa-chi,* ch. 2, pp. 4a–5a.

45. Yeh Ch'ang-chih, *Ts'ang-shu chi-shih shih, passim.* There are 427 persons of the Ming period and 497 of the Ch'ing period. These are, however, only bibliophiles of national renown.

46. For the advance in the technique of printing, see below, ch. V, under Printing.

47. Hummel, *Eminent Chinese;* see "Hsüan-yeh," "Mingju," "Singde," and "Songgotu." See also Yeh Ch'ang-chih, *Ts'ang-shu chi-shih shih,* pp. 192–93, "Prince I" and "Prince Kuo."

48. *Shih-ch'ü pao-chi, Shih-ch'ü pao-chi hsü-pien, Shih-ch'ü san-pien,* all printed in 1918.

49. Yeh Ch'ang-chih, *Ts'ang-shu chi-shih shih,* pp. 75, 89, 100, 113, 123, 157, 158, 160, 161, 163, 164, 171, 176, 177, 194, 203, etc. The information is necessarily fragmentary and incomplete.

50. Lu Yung, *Yü-t'ang man-pi ti-ch'ao,* p. 10b.

51. Hummel, "An Ch'i," *Eminent Chinese.*

52. *Nan-hai hsien-chih,* ch. 13, pp. 57b–59a.

53. K'ung Kuang-t'ao, *Yü-hsüeh-lou shu-hua lu,* postcript.

54. Wu Te-hsüan, *Ch'u-yüeh-lou wen-chien lu,* ch. 8, p. 1a.

55. Wang Shih-chen, *Chü-i lu,* cited in Yeh Ch'ang-chih, *T'sang-shu chi-shih shih,* pp. 216–17. The TSCC edition of Wang's work, however, does not contain this passage.

56. *Lü-yüan ts'ung-hua,* ch. 7, p. 7b.

57. *Ch'eng-huai-yüan yü,* ch. 1, pp. 14a–14b.

58. *Wu-tsa-tsu,* ch. 4, p. 25b, and ch. 7, pp. 26a–27a.

59. Li Tou, *Yang-chou hua-fang lu,* ch. 6, pp. 9b–10b.

60. Ping-ti Ho, "The Salt Merchants of Yang-chou: a Study of Commercial Capitalism in Eighteenth-Century China," *Harvard Journal of Asiatic Studies,* XVII (No. 1–2, June, 1954), 156–57.

61. The Wu family's better-known members were Wu Ch'o (1676–1733) and his sons Wu Ch'eng (1703–73) and Wu Yü-ch'ih, *chü-jen* of 1770. The first Wang family's better-known members were Wang Hsien (1721–70) and his eldest son Wang Ju-li. The second Wang family was known chiefly for the collecting zeal of the brothers Wang Jih-chang and Wang Jih-kuei (died in 1799). For a general description of their activities, see Nancy Lee Swann, "Seven Intimate Library Owners," *Harvard Journal of Asiatic Studies,* I (1936), 363–90. See also Hummel, *Eminent Chinese,* under "Wang Hsien." They are identified as descendants of Hui-chou merchants in *Liang-che yen-fa chih* (1806 ed.), chs. on biographies.

62. Hummel, *Eminent Chinese,* under "Pao T'ing-po" and "Wang Ch'i-shu."

63. Hummel, *Eminent Chinese,* under "Wu Ch'ung-yüeh" and "P'an shih-ch'eng."

64. This broad analysis is based on my "Salt Merchants" and *Studies on the Population of China, 1368–1953*, pp. 204–6.

65. Li Tou, *Yang-chou hua-fang lu, passim.*

66. Ch'ien Yung, *Lü-yüan ts'ung-hua*, ch. 6, pp. 7a–7b, 14b; ch. 20, p. 7b.

67. Li Huan, *Kuo-ch'ao ch'i-hsien lei-cheng*, ch. 435, the last essay on the life of Ma Yüeh-kuan.

68. Ping-ti Ho, "Salt Merchants," p. 159.

69. H. C. Hu, *The Common Descent Group in China and its Functions*, introduction and ch. 1.

70. Ssu-ma Ch'ien, *Shih-chi*, ch. 112, "Chu-fu Yen" (tr. by Burton Watson, in *Records of the Grand Historian of China*, II, 225–38); also Pan Ku, *Han-shu*, ch. 6, annals of reign of Wu-ti.

71. Ch'ü T'ung-tsu, *Chung-kuo fa-lü yü Chung-kuo she-hui*, pp. 3–4.

72. Hui-chen Wang Liu, *The Traditional Chinese Clan Rules*, p. 70.

73. Hu, *Common Descent Group*, p. 27.

74. *Ibid.*, p. 28.

75. Liu, *Traditional Chinese Clan Rules*, p. 69.

76. *Chi-shih tsung-p'u*, ch. 8, pp. 9a–9b, p. 26a.

77. P'eng Yün-chang, *Kuei-p'u-an ts'ung-kao*, ch. 8, p. 6a, p. 11b, in *P'eng-wen-ching-kung ch'üan-chi*.

78. Wang K'ai-yün, *Wang Hsiang-i hsien-sheng ch'üan-chi*, introduction by his son.

79. See Appendix, case 14.

80. Liu, *Traditional Chinese Clan Rules*, pp. 62–63.

81. See Appendix, cases 11 and 19.

82. Cited with many later similar writings in *Ku-chin t'u-shu chi-ch'eng*, "Chia-fan-tien," *ts'e* 321, p. 11b; *ts'e* 326, p. 10a and pp. 16b–17a.

83. R. H. Tawney, "The Rise of the Gentry, 1558–1640," *Economic History Review*, XI (no. 1, 1941).

84. Ke Shou-li, *Ke-tuan-su-kung chi*, ch. 7, pp. 17b–19b. It is to be noted that some Sung Neo-Confucian philosophers had said much the same thing, but Ke phrased it better.

85. Sir Lewis B. Namier, *The Structure of Politics at the Accession of George III*, ch. 1.

86. Wang Shih-chen, *Yen-chou shih-liao*, supplementary series, ch. 42.

87. P'an Kuang-tan, *Ming-Ch'ing liang-tai chia-hsing ti wang-tsu*.

88. Wu Ching-ch'ao, "Hsi-Han she-hui chieh-chi chih-tu" [The class system of the Former Han period], *Ch'ing-hua hsüeh-pao*, IX (no. 1, October, 1935).

89. *T'ung-hsiang t'i-ming lu*, introduction; *Ching-hsiang t'i-ming lu*, introduction.

90. Cited in *Ching-hsiang t'i-ming lu*, introduction.

## V: FACTORS AFFECTING SOCIAL MOBILITY

1. This statement is based on my own impression gathered from sampling Sung biographies. It must await further specialized studies by Sung experts to be confirmed or rejected.

2. Fang Hao, *Sung-shih,* p. 70.

3. Cf. ch. I, n. 37.

4. Fang Hao, *Sung-shih,* pp. 66–68. See also James T. C. Liu, "An Early Sung Reformer: Fan Chung-yen," in J. K. Fairbank, ed., *Chinese Thought and Institutions.*

5. Chao T'ieh-han, "Sung-tai ti chou-hsüeh," [The prefectural schools of the Sung period], *Ta-lu tsa-chih,* VII (nos. 10–11, 1953).

6. Chao T'ieh-han, "Sung-tai ti t'ai-hsüeh" [The imperial academy of the Sung period], *Ta-lu tsa-chih,* VII (nos. 4–5, 1953).

7. This is based on my count of the numbers of local and perfectural schools established during the Hung-wu period (1368–98) given in the gigantic geographical treatise *Ta-Ming i-t'ung-chih, passim.* Because of a few missing pages I prefer the round number 1,200.

8. The well-informed Lu Yung, in his much cited *Shu-yüan tsa-chi ti-ch'ao,* ch. 3, p. 22b, stated that at the beginning of Ming there were no schools for military garrison headquarters. It should be noted that a number of them were already established during the Hung-wu period, although more were set up in the Yung-lo (1403–24), the Hsüan-te (1426–35), and particularly the Cheng-t'ung (1436–49) periods. The dates are all given in *Ta-Ming i-t'ung-chih.*

9. *Hsüeh-cheng ch'üan-shu* (1812 ed.), chs. 66–68, and *Ta-Ch'ing hui-tien shih-li* (1899 ed.), chs. 370–81. The provincial breakdowns are tabulated in Chang Chung-li, *The Chinese Gentry,* tables 15 and 16.

10. Chang Huang, *T'u-shu pien,* ch. 107; Hsü Hsüeh-chü, *Kuo-ch'ao tien-hui,* ch. 129, p. 1b.

11. Hsü Hsüeh-chü, *Kuo-ch'ao tien-hui,* ch. 129, p. 3b.

12. Unless otherwise stated, the discussion of general Ming regulations on *sheng-yüan* is based on *Ta-Ming hui-tien* (1502 and 1587 eds.), chs. 76–77.

13. Ping-ti Ho, *Studies on the Population of China, 1368–1953,* chs. 1 and 11.

14. *Ming Ying-tsung shih-lu,* ch. 151, pp. 2b–3a, in *Ming-shih-lu.* Also *Ming hui-yao,* p. 410.

15. Yü Ju-chi, *Li-pu-chih kao,* ch. 24; also Ku Yen-wu, *Jih-chih-lu chi-shih,* ch. 17, pp. 1a–3a.

16. *Ming Hsüan-tsung shih-lu,* ch. 96, pp. 5a–5b; Ku Yen-wu, *T'ing-lin wen-chi,* ch. 1.

17. Huang Fu, *Hsien-chung chin-ku-lu ti-ch'ao,* pp. 5a–5b.

18. *Ming Shih-tsung shih-lu,* ch. 133, pp. 10a–10b.
19. Yü Ju-chi, *Li-pu-chih kao,* ch. 24, pp. 2b–3a.
20. *Hsi-chin yu-hsiang lu,* ch. 1.
21. *Ming hui-yao,* p. 718; *Hsü-wen-hsien t'ung-k'ao,* ch. 50, p. 3245. Wang Shih-chen, *Feng-chou tsa-pien,* ch. 5, pp. 4b–5a, gives by far the most detailed information, but he wrongly dated the establishment of provincial educational officials in the Hsüan-te period (1426–35).
22. Yü Ju-chi, *Li-pu-chih kao,* ch. 24, pp. 21a–25a.
23. *Ch'ang-chou fu-chih* (1618 ed.), ch. 11A, pp. 10a–10b.
24. Ku Yen-wu, *T'ing-lin wen-chi,* ch. 1.
25. *Ta-Ch'ing hui-tien shih-li* (1899 ed.), ch. 370.
26. Chang Chung-li, *The Chinese Gentry,* pp. 98–99.
27. Ping-ti Ho, *Studies on the Population of China,* ch. 1.
28. *Ibid.,* ch. 11.
29. Cf. above, ch. I, n. 83.
30. The most systematic study is Shang Yen-liu, *Ch'ing-tai k'o-chü k'ao-shih shu-lu.*
31. *Ta-Ming hui-tien* (1587 ed.), ch. 77, p. 2a.
32. Chang Chung-li, *The Chinese Gentry,* pp. 127–32.
33. *Ta-Ming hui-tien* (1587 ed.), ch. 77.
34. Shen Te-fu, *Wan-li yeh-huo-pien,* p. 857.
35. This will be discussed in detail in ch. VI.
36. Shang Yen-liu, *Ch'ing-tai k'o-chü k'ao-shih shu-lu,* pp. 76–78.
37. See the illuminating discussion of early Ch'ing policy toward the Chinese official class by Meng Shen, "Chi-wei tz'u-k'o-lu wai-lu," in *Chang Chü-sheng hsien-sheng ch'i-shih sheng-jih chi-nien lun-wen chi.*
38. Chang Chung-li, *The Chinese Gentry,* pp. 185–86, for example, completely fails to understand the original aim and real effect of the "official quota" system.
39. *Li-pu tse-li* (1844 ed.), ch. 93.
40. This will be further discussed in ch. VI.
41. Shang Yen-liu, *Ch'ing-tai k'o-chü k'ao-shih shu-lu,* pp. 290–91.
42. *Ta-Ming hui-tien* (1587 ed.), ch. 77.
43. *Li-pu tse-li* (1844 ed.), ch. 93.
44. For a further discussion, see below, ch. VI.
45. See below, ch. VI.
46. Edward A. Kracke, Jr., *Civil Service in Early Sung China,* p. 67.
47. Shen Te-fu, *Wan-li yeh-huo-pien,* pp. 862–63.
48. *Ibid.,* pp. 306–9.
49. Shang Yen-liu, *Ch'ing-tai k'o-chü k'ao-shih shu-lu,* pp. 299–303.
50. By far the most elaborate account of this 1858 scandal is given in Hsüeh Fu-ch'eng, *Yung-an pi-chi,* ch. 3, pp. 14b–16a. For a fair-minded appraisal of the true extent of the scandal, see Shang Yen-liu, pp. 312–17.

51. Shang Yen-liu, *Ch'ing-tai k'o-chü k'ao-shih shu-lu*, ch. 8, *passim*. For the Chang Ch'ien episode, see Chia Ching-te, *Hsiu-ts'ai chü-jen chin-shih*, appendix.

52. Shang Yen-liu, *Ch'ing-tai k'o-chü k'ao-shih shu-lu*, pp. 306–9.

53. *Ibid.*, pp. 310–11.

54. *Ta-Ming hui-tien* (1587 ed.), ch. 78, pp. 22b–23a.

55. *Ming-shih*, ch. 180.

56. *Ibid.*, ch. 181.

57. *Ta-Ming hui-tien* (1587 ed.), ch. 78, p. 23b.

58. *Ta-kao*, injunction no. 44.

59. *Ming hui-yao*, p. 412.

60. *Chia-hsing fu-chih* (1610 ed.), ch. 2; *Shao-hsing fu-chih* (1792 ed.), ch. 20.

61. *Ming hui-yao*, p. 410.

62. Wang Shou-jen, *Yang-ming ch'üan-shu*, chs. 32–37, Wang's chronological biography compiled by his disciples.

63. *Ta-Ming hui-tien* (1587 ed.), ch. 78.

64. *Sung-chiang fu-chih* (1819 ed.), ch. 31, pp. 19a–19b; ch. 32, pp. 17a–17b.

65. Ho Ch'iao-yüan, *Ming-shan ts'ang*, "Huo-ch'ih chi," p. 10a.

66. *Hupei t'ung-chih*, ch. 59, p. 1548; *Hsin-hui hsien-chih* (1840 ed.), ch. 3, pp. 41a–43b.

67. *Shun-te hsien-chih*, ch. 5, pp. 5a–6b.

68. *Shensi t'ung-chih kao* (1934 ed.), *passim*.

69. *Hupei t'ung-chih*, ch. 59; *Shensi t'ung-chih*, ch. 27; *Shensi t'ung-chih-kao*, chs. 37, 38, 39.

70. See *Ssu-hui hsien-chih*, Book 2A, p. 93b; *Hsin-hui hsien-chih*, ch. 3, p. 39b.

71. *T'ung-hsiang tsu-chih chih yen-chiu*, pp. 72–73.

72. This information was gathered during my trip to Hong Kong and Macao in December, 1958.

73. Fang Hao, *Sung-shih*, pp. 78–80.

74. Ho Yu-shen, "Yüan-tai shu-yüan chih ti-li fen-pu" [The geographical distribution of private academies in Yüan times), *Hsin-ya hsüeh-pao*, II (no. 1, August, 1956), pp. 361–408.

75. *Ming hui-yao*, pp. 415–16.

76. Lu Yung, *Chin-t'ai chi-wen ti-ch'ao*, pp. 8b–9a; Yü Chi-teng, *Tien-ku chi-wen*, ch. 16, p. 260.

77. For Wang Yang-ming's philosophical system, see Feng Yu-lan, *A History of Chinese Philosophy*, vol. II, ch. 14.

78. Cited in Huang Tsung-hsi, *Ming-ju hsüeh-an*, ch. 32, pp. 24a–24b.

79. *Ibid.*, ch. 32, *passim*.

80. *Ming hui-yao*, pp. 416–17.

81. Yü Chi-teng, *Tien-ku chi-wen*, ch. 17, p. 287.

82. Yung Chao-tsu, *Li Chih nien-p'u*, *passim*. For the causes of Ho Hsin-yin's death, see p. 54.

83. Sheng Lang-hsi, *Chung-kuo shu-yüan chih-tu*. See esp. p. 139.

84. *Yü-lu shu-yüan chih*, ch. 1, p. 23a.

85. *Po-lu-tung shu-yüan chih* (1673 ed.), ch. 16, p. 32b. The 1525 edition of the same work gives in ch. 2 detailed breakdowns on donated land, without totals. The amount seems to have been somewhat smaller than that in 1673.

86. *Shan-kan wei-ching shu-yüan chih.*

87. *Ming-tao shu-yüan chih*, ch. 6.

88. *Ho-shuo shu-yüan chih.*

89. *Liang-huai yen-fa chih* (1806 ed.), ch. 53.

90. *Lung-hu shu-yüan chih*, Book A, pp. 38a–43a.

91. *Ning-hsiang Yün-shan shu-yüan chih;* and Hsieh Kuo-chen, "Ch'ing-tai shu-yüan hsüeh-hsiao chih-tu pien-ch'ien k'ao" [A study of the changes in the Ch'ing academy and school systems], in *Chang Chü-sheng hsien-sheng ch'i-shih sheng-jih chi-nien lun-wen-chi.*

92. Liu Po-chi, *Kuang-tung shu-yüan chih-tu yen-ke*, pp. 332–33.

93. *Chin-chiang shu-yüan chi-lüeh.* This academy was located in Ch'eng-tu, the capital city of Szechwan, where Manchu Bannermen were garrisoned.

94. *Pao-chin shu-yüan chih*, ch. 3. The scarcity on this continent of Ming works on private academies makes it difficult to make a quantitative statement. However, the only available useful Ming work which contains information on a school's alumni seems to suggest that private academies had considerable effect on social mobility. Po-ch'ün Academy, which was established in the late fifteenth century in a Honan county with a modest endowment of 625 *mu*, produced 10 *chin-shih* between 1490 and 1529 and 29 *chü-jen* between 1479 and 1531. See *Po-ch'üan shu-yüan chih* (1533 ed.), chs. 1 and 4.

95. *Shan-kan wei-ching shu-yüan chih.*

96. Liu Po-chi, *Kuang-tung shu-yüan chih-tu yen-ke*, pp. 311–16.

97. A. W. Hummel, *Eminent Chinese of the Ch'ing Period*. See under "Juan Yüan" and "Chang Chih-tung." For a partial listing of other Ch'ing academies famous for scholarly research, see Hsieh Kuo-chen, "Ch'ing-tai shu-yüan hsüeh-hsiao chih-tu pien-ch'ien k'ao."

98. Sudō Yoshiyuki, *Chūgoku tochi seido-shi kenkyū* [A study of the history of land systems in China] (Tokyo, 1954), pp. 204–7; in more detail in Lien-sheng Yang, "K'o-chü shih-tai ti fu-k'ao lü-fei wen-t'i" [The travel expense problem of candidates for degrees in the examination system in imperial China], *Ch'ing-hua hsüeh-pao* (new series, II [No. 2, June, 1961]).

I regret that the late discovery of these two studies makes it impossible to include them in the Bibliography.

99. Wen T'ien-hsiang, *Wen-shan hsien-sheng ch'üan-chi,* ch. 9, pp. 1a–2b. It should be mentioned that Wen did not state the exact date of the founding of the community chest in Chi-chou. But we know that Hu Kuei was the grandson of Hu Ch'üan, who obtained his *chin-shih* degree in 1128 and died in the office of vice president of a central board in 1171. During his more than forty years' government service after attaining his degree, Hu Ch'üan very probably saw the birth of his grandson late in his life. Supposing that it took Hu Kuei equally long to reach a high office, the time for the setting up of the community chest in Chi-chou should be in the 1220s or 1230s. The biographical information on Hu Ch'üan, Hu Kuei, and Yeh Meng-ting is culled from *Sung-shih,* chs. 374 and 414, and *Chi-an fu-chih* (1776 ed.), ch. 24, p. 10a.

100. Wen T'ien-hsiang, *Wen-shan hsien-sheng ch'üan-chi,* ch. 9, pp. 14a–16a.

101. Lien-sheng Yang, "The Travel Expense Problem."

102. *Ku-chin t'u-shu chi-ch'eng,* "Chih-fang tien," ch. 857, p. 39a.

103. *Shao-yang hsien-chih,* ch. 4, pp. 12a–12b.

104. *Hui-chou fu-chih,* ch. 3A, p. 59b, pp. 95b–96a.

105. *Ho-fei hsien-chih,* ch. 10, pp. 23b–24b; *Ch'ang-te fu-chih,* ch. 15, pp. 11b–12a; *Chi-mo hsien-chih* (1873 ed.), ch. 3, pp. 27a–27b.

106. *P'an-yü hsien-chih,* ch. 16, p. 30b, pp. 41a–41b.

107. *Lan-hsi hsien-chih,* ch. 3, pp. 44b–47a.

108. *Shang-ch'eng hsien-chih,* ch. 5, pp. 43a–43b.

109. *Lu-ling hsien-chih,* ch. 14, pp. 16a–24a.

110. *Shao-hsing fu-chih* (1792 ed.), ch. 20, pp. 32a–32b; *Hupei t'ung-chih,* ch. 59, p. 1583.

111. *Min-chung hui-kuan chih,* Book on Fu-chou *hui-kuan,* pp. 28a–28b. *Chi-shui hsien-chih,* "Schools and Academies," records the establishment of the locality's *hui-kuan* in the 1510s under the influence of Wang Yang-ming.

112. *Min-chung hui-kuan chih, passim.*

113. Chu Shih, *Chu-wen-tuan-kung chi,* ch. 1, pp. 54a–55a.

114. Shen Te-fu, *Wan-li yeh-huo pien,* p. 608.

115. Ch'en T'ing-ching, *Wu-ch'iao wen-pien,* ch. 38, pp. 11a–12a.

116. *Pao-ch'ing hui-kuan chih,* Book A, p. 24b.

117. *She-hsien hui-kuan lu,* Book A, p. 1a, and detailed donors' lists in Book B.

118. *Min-chung hui-kuan chih,* Book on Lung-yen *hui-kuan.*

119. Chu Shih, *Chu-wen-tuan-kung chi,* ch. 1, pp. 54a–55b.

120. The well-known legal historian Ch'eng Shu-te's preface to *Min-chung hui-kuan chih* explains the change very clearly: "*Hui-kuan* in Peking were first established in Ming times with the original aim of accommodat-

ing candidates who came to take the metropolitan examination. This was why they were called *hui-kuan*. Since the abolition of the examination system they have become residences for all kinds of people from their native areas. The custom has therefore become different from that of old." But our evidence shows that the change had occurred long before the abolition of the examination system in 1905. For different kinds of merchants' guild-halls, which were also called *hui-kuan,* see Kato Shigeshi, *Shina keizaishi kōshō,* pp. 557–84.

121. It is true that even the large clan system might still be some sort of a financial drag on its most successful members who under Neo-Confucian teachings felt obligated to donate money or property to their clans. But such donations were usually modest as compared with property which they shared with their families. Throughout the Ming-Ch'ing period cases like that of the Sung pioneer clan organizer Fan Chung-yen, who contributed nearly all the land he owned to his clan, are almost unknown.

122. Notably, Hu Hsien-chin, *The Common Descent Group in China and its Functions;* Shimizu Morimitsu, *Chūgoku zokusan seido kō;* and Hui-chen Wang Liu, *The Traditional Chinese Clan Rules.*

123. Denis C. Twichett, "The Fan Clan's Charitable Estate, 1050–1760," in D. S. Nivison and A. F. Wright, eds., *Confucianism in Action,* takes pains to use the Fan clan as a case study of the historical evolution of the Chinese clan system.

124. Yüan Ts'ai, *Yüan-shih shih-fan,* ch. 1.

125. Shimizu, *Chūgoku zokusan seido kō,* ch. 1.

126. Ch'en Hung-mou, *Ch'üan-tien i-hsüeh hui-chi,* preface.

127. Liu, *Chinese Clan Rules,* p. 126.

128. *Nan-hsün chih,* ch. 35, pp. 4b–6a.

129. Hu, *Common Descent Group,* p. 88.

130. *Ibid.,* pp. 14–15; Liu, *Chinese Clan Rules,* Appendix, table 1. It must be pointed out, however, that the numbers of genealogies of various provinces available at Columbia University which supply the data for Liu's monograph may not be an accurate indication of the geographic distribution of traditional clans. The small number of Fukien and Kwangtung genealogies at Columbia or in any other significant American collection may well be due to the fact that they seldom reached the Peking book market, from which American libraries bought most of their old Chinese works.

131. Hu, *Common Descent Group,* p. 88. The same has been true of Professor Franklin Ho, whose father was a *chien-sheng* and a merchant of substantial means.

132. Liu, *Chinese Clan Rules,* p. 128.

133. Thomas F. Carter, *The Invention of Printing in China and Its Spread Westward,* ch. 6 and chronological chart. Also Li Shu-hua, "Yin-

shua fa-ming ti shih-ch'i wen-t'i" [The problem of dating the invention of printing], *Ta-lu tsa-chih*, XII (nos. 5–6, 1958).

134. *Ming-shih*, ch. 1, "reign of T'ai-tsu," *passim*.

135. *Ming hui-yao*, pp. 419–20.

136. K. T. Wu, "Ming Printing and Printers," *Harvard Journal of Asiatic Studies*, VII (1942–43), 225–29.

137. *Ibid.*, pp. 215–24, 244–45.

138. *Ibid.*, pp. 232–33.

139. Li Hsü, *Chieh-an man-pi*, ch. 8, pp. 15a–15b. See also Ku Yen-wu's comments, in his *Jih-chih-lu chi-shih*, ch. 16, pp. 9b–10b.

140. L. C. Goodrich, "The World's Greatest Book," *Pacific Affairs*, March, 1934.

141. Lu Yung, *Shu-yüan tsa-chi ti-ch'ao*, ch. 5, pp. 19b–20a.

142. Wu Han, *Chu Yüan-chang chuan*.

143. This generalization is derived from sampling Chu Kuo-chen, *Huang-Ming k'ai-kuo-ch'en chuan, passim*.

144. Hsü Hsüeh-chü, *Kuo-ch'ao tien-hui*, ch. 40.

145. Feng Ying-ching, *Huang-Ming ching-shih shih-yung pien*, ch. 12; also Ch'u Jen-huo, *Chien-hu chi*, ch. 5, p. 9b.

146. Huang Yü, *Shuang-huai sui-ch'ao*, ch. 4, pp. 7a–7b.

147. Kuo P'an, *Huang-Ming t'ai-hsüeh chih*, ch. 12, pp. 33a–34a.

148. For example, all the persons recommended by the educational commissioner of the metropolitan Shun-t'ien Prefecture in 1644 for appointment were ex-Ming officials and higher degree holders. *Kuo-ch'ao shih-liao shih-ling*, ch. 2, pp. 35a–36a. For the general policy of appeasing the Chinese official class, see Meng Shen, "Chi-wei tz'u-k'o-lu wai-lu."

149. Li Huan, *Kuo-ch'ao ch'i-hsien lei-cheng*, ch. 269, p. 51a; ch. 273, p. 28a; ch. 281, p. 46a; also chs. 265–81, *passim*.

150. Lo Ssu-chü, *Lo-chuang-yung-kung nien-p'u, passim*.

151. Chao I, *Yen-p'u tsa-chi*, ch. 2, p. 9b.

152. Chu K'ung-chang, *Chung-hsing chiang-shuai pieh-chuan*, ch. 11B, p. 1a; ch. 13A, p. 3b; ch. 24A, p. 4a; ch. 28B, p. 1a.

153. This entire section is based on various chapters of my *Studies on the Population of China*.

## VI: REGIONAL DIFFERENCES IN SOCIOACADEMIC SUCCESS AND MOBILITY

1. See Ping-ti Ho, *Studies on the Population of China, 1368–1953*, chs. 1–5.

2. For the southward shift of the economic, cultural, and demographic centers of gravity, see Ping-ti Ho, "Early-Ripening Rice in Chinese History," *Economic History Review*, 2d series, IX (no. 2, December, 1956),

esp. pp. 205–6, 215–18; Ch'üan Han-sheng, *T'ang-Sung ti-kuo yü yün-ho,* *passim.;* and Ch'ien Mu, *Kuo-shih ta-kang,* chs. 38–40.

3. Aoyama Sadao, "Godai-Sō ni okeru Kōsei no shinkō kanryō" [The rise of the new bureaucractic class in Kiangsi during the Five Dynasties and the Sung period], in *Wada Hakase Kanreki Kinen Tōyōshi Ronsō* [Oriental studies presented to Dr. Wada Sei on his sixtieth birthday], pp. 19–37.

4. For a systematic study of cultural regions in Sung times, see Ho Yu-shen, "Liang-Sung hsüeh-feng chih ti-li fen-pu" [The geographic distribution of scholars and thinkers of the Sung period], *Hsin-ya hsüeh-pao,* I (no. 1, August, 1955).

5. This becomes clear when one samples the early chapters of Huang Tsung-hsi, *Ming-ju hsüeh-an.*

6. Cited in Ping-ti Ho, *Studies on the Population of China,* pp. 263–64.

7. *Hui-chou fu-chih,* ch. 9B, *passim.*

8. *Ibid.,* ch. 12B, pp. 56a–57a.

9. This generalization is based on my own study of Hui-chou merchants and also on the intimate knowledge of Dr. Hu Shih, a native of Hui-chou.

10. Kuwabara Jitsuzō, *P'u Shou-ken k'ao;* and also Fang Hao, *Chung-hsi chiao-t'ung shih,* vol. III, chs. 4–5.

11. Liang Fang-chung, "Ming-tai kuo-chi mao-i yü yin ti shu-ch'u-ju" [The international trade and silver movements during the Ming period], *Chinese Social and Economic History Review,* vol. 7, no. 2, December, 1939.

12. Ping-ti Ho, *Studies on the Population of China,* ch. 9, sec. 1.

13. Ku Yen-wu, *T'ien-hsia chün-kuo li-ping shu,* part on Fukien, particularly on Ch'üan-chou and Chang-chou.

14. Ku Yen-wu, *Jih-chih-lu chi-shih,* ch. 17, pp. 16a–17a.

15. *Ibid.*

16. P'u Sung-ling, *Hsing-shih yin-yüan.*

17. *Pa-ch'i t'ung-chih,* ch. 46.

18. *Kuo-tzu-chien chih,* ch. 11, pp. 18a–23a.

19. Li Chou-wang, *Kuo-ch'ao li-k'o t'i-ming pei-lu ch'u-chi* (first compiled in 1720, revised to include Ming *chin-shih* list in 1746); Fang Chao-ying and Tu Lien-che, *Tseng-chiao Ch'ing-ch'ao chin-shih t'i-ming pei-lu,* to be referred to hereafter as Fang-Tu list.

20. *Shun-t'ien fu-chih,* ch. 115.

21. *Hui-chou fu-chih,* ch. 9B.

22. *Hu-chou fu-chih,* ch. on Ming *chin-shih.*

23. *Shun-t'ien fu-chih,* ch. 116.

24. *Hui-chou fu-chih,* ch. 9B.

25. The total is derived from *Sung-chiang fu-chih* (1883 ed.), amended by Fang-Tu list.

26. Cited in *Fukien t'ung-chih* (1849 ed., rev. and printed in 1867), ch. 56, pp. 1b–2a.

27. *Ibid.*, ch. 56, p. 2b.

28. *Fu-chou fu-chih* (1613 ed.), ch. on social custom.

29. *Shao-hsing fu-chih* (1586 ed.), ch. 12, pp. 2a–4b.

30. *Ibid.*

31. Cf. above, ch. IV, under Sample Genealogical Records.

32. *K'o-ch'ang t'iao-li,* ch. 25, pp. 15a–18a.

33. Between 1644 and 1784 Shao-hsing prefecture claimed in all 266 *chin-shih*, of whom 13 were registered under other Chekiang counties, especially those of Hang-chou, 57 under Ta-hsing and Wan-p'ing counties, 16 under other Hopei counties, and 16 under other provinces. *Shao-hsing fu-chih* (1792 ed.), ch. 31, *passim.*

34. Lu Chi, *Chien-chia-t'ang tsa-chu ti-ch'ao,* p. 3.

35. *Ibid.*

## VII: RECAPITULATION AND CONCLUSION

1. For example, even one of the most realistic social strategists, Ts'ao Ching-ch'en (Appendix, case 13), at the height of his business success, instructed his family: "Filial piety and fraternal love are the root. When the root is not cultivated, how are we to expect the luxuriant branches and leaves? . . . Wealth and glory are inconstant. If among the offshoots of our common ancestor there are those who are more successful than we, our whole family fortune will not decline. Others' success is in fact our success." Ts'ao Wen-chih, *Shih-ku-yen-chai wen-ch'ao,* ch. 19, p. 10a.

2. Vernon K. Dibble and Ping-ti Ho, "The Comparative Study of Social Mobility" (Debate), in *Comparative Studies in Society and History,* III (no. 3, April, 1961), especially Ho's reply, pp. 320–27.

3. Wang Ting-pao, *T'ang chih-yen,* p. 3.

4. Since dynastic histories seldom give precise information on relatively humble men's ancestry and since such words as humble and lowly were used in historical contexts peculiar to each period of Chinese history, I believe that one of the fruitful ways to speculate on aspects of social mobility of pre-Ming periods is to study the main avenues and opportunity-structure for social mobility. A recent study shows that in T'ang times one significant factor which may have helped the upward mobility of the humble was the rise of Buddhist monasteries as centers of learning, which were as a rule open to the poor and struggling. See Yen Keng-wang, "T'ang-jen tu-shu shan-lin ssu-yüan chih feng-shang," *Bulletin of Institute of History and Philology, Academia Sinica,* XXX (1960). It is fairly safe,

however, to say that there were many fewer educational facilities and other institutionalized and noninstitutional channels which had a bearing on social mobility in the T'ang than in the Sung and Ming-Ch'ing periods.

5. Sun Kuo-tung, "T'ang-Sung chih-chi she-hui men-ti chih hsiao-yung," *Hsin-ya hsüeh-pao*, IV (no. 1, August, 1959).

6. Kracke, Edward A., "Family vs. Merit in Chinese Civil Service Examinations under the Empire," *Harvard Journal of Asiatic Studies*, X (no. 2, September, 1947).

7. Ping-ti Ho, *Studies on the Population of China, 1368–1953*, Part II, "Factors Affecting Population," *passim*, and "Conclusion," *passim*.

8. Kung Tzu-chen, *Ting-an wen-chi*, Prose Works, ch. 2, p. 9b.

9. The general mobility pattern in the United States has been, on balance, upward in terms of the shift from manual and semiskilled to skilled and "tertiary" occupations. See S. M. Lipset and B. Reinhard, "Ideological Equalitarianism and Social Mobility in the United States," *Transactions of the Second World Congress of Sociology*, 1954. For a similar tendency in other industrial societies, see the same authors' *Social Mobility in Industrial Society*.

10. The decline and disappearance of traditional schools, academies, scholarship systems, clan organizations, etc., the relatively high cost of modern education, and the chaotic political, economic, and social conditions would seem to suggest that the Republican period (1911–49) probably continued the long-range downward mobility trend revealed in the present study. The energetic nationwide educational campaign and the earnest effort of the Government of the People's Republic of China to broaden the social base of education at all levels during the past eleven years, however, will definitely change the historical mobility trend. Possibly the Chinese nation is beginning to go through a chapter of social mobility which will eventually compare with or even overshadow that of early Ming times.

## APPENDIX: SELECTED CASES OF SOCIAL MOBILITY

1. Mobility through purchase of office is partially dealt with in four cases of rich merchant families. There are many known cases of mobility through purchase, but generally the literature yields little or no information on the individual's ancestry or his early life. Mobility through recommendation and military service has been briefly illustrated in ch. V, under Wars and Social upheavals. Some of the selected cases throw light on downward mobility as well, but no attempt is made in the Appendix to illustrate exclusively downward mobility, which has been systematically discussed in ch. IV.

2. *Ch'ang-chou fu-chih* (1618 ed.), part 3 of ch. 15, "The T'ang Family History."

3. The ages of people mentioned in the Appendix are a year less than the *sui* age (traditional Chinese counting) in order to avoid the repetition of the word *sui*.

4. By ancient custom a boy attained his majority at twenty *sui*, when he was properly capped.

5. Chang Hsüan, *Hsi-yüan wen-chien lu*, ch. 9, pp. 23b–24a. It should be noted that the original account makes the mistake of treating Ch'i T'ung as Ch'i Hsien's great-great-grandfather. Since this biographical essay mentions only four generations, Ch'i T'ung should be Ch'i Hsien's great-grandfather.

6. Wang Shih-chen, *Yen-chou-shan-jen ssu-pu kao*, ch. 85, pp. 7a–9a.

7. *Ibid.*, ch. 84, pp. 20a–21b.

8. Hsü Kuo, *Hsü-wen-mu-kung chi*, ch. 13. It contains six biographical sketches of his family members and kinsmen. See also Chiao Hung, *Kuo-ch'ao hsien-cheng lu*, ch. 17.

9. Shen Te-fu, *Wan-li yeh-huo-pien*, p. 847.

10. Wang Shih-chen, *Ch'ih-pei ou-t'an*, ch. 8, pp. 9a–9b; *Hsüan-ch'eng hsien-chih*, ch. 15, pp. 12a–13a; *Chiang-nan t'ung-chih*, ch. 148, pp. 10b–11a.

11. Wang Shih-chen mistakes Hsü Yüan-ch'i for the younger brother. My correction is based on *Chiang-nan t'ung-chih*.

12. Hsü Kuang-ch'i, *Hsü-wen-ting-kung chi*; Fang Hao, *Hsü Kuang-ch'i*.

13. Li Yin-tu, *Shou-ch'i-t'ang wen-chi*, ch. 4, biographical accounts of his father and mother. Also Wu Huai-ch'ing, *Kuan-chung san-Li-hsien-sheng nien-p'u*, chs. 6–8.

14. *Ibid.*, chs. 1–4.

15. This complex case is based on Wang Yu-tun, *Sung-ch'üan shih-wen chi*, "Prose Works," ch. 22, pp. 5a–9a; *Chieh-hsiu hsien-chih*, ch. 5, "Tables of Higher Degree holders"; Li Huan, *Kuo-ch'ao ch'i-hsien lei-cheng*, ch. 284, pp. 35a–37b, biographical essay on Fan Yü-ch'i; and Fu I-ling, *Ming-Ch'ing shih-tai shang-jen chi shang-yeh tzu-pen*, ch. 6.

16. Chu Shih, *Chu-wen-tuan-kung chi*, Appendix, his chronological biography compiled by his descendants but based on his own reminiscences.

17. Taken from Ho, "The Salt Merchants of Yang-chou: a Study of Commercial Capitalism in Eighteenth-Century China," *Harvard Journal of Asiatic Studies*, XVII (no. 1–2, June, 1954) with additional information from *Man-Han wen-wu kuan-sheng ming-tz'u lu* (1798) and Ch'ien Yung, *Lü-yüan ts'ung-hua*.

18. *Man-Han wen-wu kuan-sheng ming-tz'u lu*, under "yüan-wai-lang" or second-class secretaries of central boards.

19. Ch'ien Yung, *Lü-yüan ts'ung-hua*, ch. 20, p. 7b.

20. *Ibid.*

21. Since this is a classic case, I have taken it from my previous article on the salt merchants. Since further reading has uncovered new information on this family, I take this opportunity to fill some gaps in the history of the Ts'ao family.

22. The name and academic status of Ts'ao Ching-ch'en's elder brother, which are missing or incomplete in my article on the salt merchants, are given in *Hui-chou fu-chih*, part 5 of ch. 12, p. 24b.

23. Many similar cases can be found in Wang Tao-k'un, *T'ai-han chi* and *T'ai-han fu-mo*. Wang was a native of Hui-chou and a descendant of tradesmen. That family division of function was fairly common may also be evidenced by the fact that the Cheng clan of P'u-chiang in the heart of Chekiang, nationally famous since at least the beginning of the Ming dynasty for its communal living and repeatedly extolled by the Ming founder, laid down in its clan instructions the principle that all male members who had not shown scholastic promise by the age of twenty-one had to take up some productive occupation, in order to enable the intellectually alert to concentrate on their studies. *Cheng-shih chia-kuei*, section on "Learning."

24. See above, ch. IV, n. 39.

25. Based on three works by Wang Hui-tsu: *Ping-t'a meng-hen lu*, *Meng-hen yü-lu*, and *Shuang-chieh-t'ang yung-hsün*, all printed in his collected works entitled *Wang Lung-chuang hsien-sheng i-shu*.

26. Actually Wang Hui-tsu's father had both a wife and a concubine. But since the two women worked and lived together under great hardships during their widowhood, Wang Hui-tsu had equal respect and affection for them and called both of them "mother," a thing which was not uncommon in traditional China. His ancestral hall name "Shuang-chieh-t'ang" literally means "Hall of Two Chaste Women."

27. *Chang-fu-chün hsing-shu*, by Chang Ch'üan's son.

28. *Chu-yüeh pa-ch'i chih*, ch. 22, pp. 13b–15b.

29. T'ao Chu, *T'ao-wen-i-kung ch'üan-chi*, ch. 47. This chapter of his works is entirely devoted to his family history in the form of various biographical essays and epitaphs. It is to be noted that some late-Ch'ing accounts of T'ao Chu's early life exaggerated the poverty of his family. For example, Huang Chün-tsai, *Chin-hu ch'i-mo*, ch. 5, p. 9a.

30. This case is culled from the following sources: *Yüan-jen shun-t'ien fu fu-yin hou-pu ssu-p'in ching-t'ang Liang-kung chia-chuan*; and *Yüan-jen shun-t'ien-fu fu-yin Liang-kung mu-piao* by the famous Cantonese scholar Ch'en Li (both of these rare obituary albums are available at Columbia University); for the history of the Liang clan after Liang Ching-kuo, see Liang Ch'ing-kuei, *Shih-hung-t'ang i-kao* (with a postscript by his

grandson Professor Liang Fang-chung, dated 1931), which was kindly lent to me by Professor Liang Chia-pin; and Liang Chia-pin, *Kuang-tung shih-san-hang k'ao*.

31. The origin of the name T'ien-pao-hang was given me by Professor Liang Chia-pin.

32. Yü Yüeh, *Ch'un-tsai-t'ang sui-pi*, ch. 2, p. 3b, ch. 6, pp. 7b–8b; also Wang K'ai-yün, *Hsiang-i-lou wen-chi*, chs. 7–8.

33. *T'ao-ch'in-su-kung hsing-shu*, a sketch of T'ao Mo's life written by his son immediately after his death.

34. Hu Ch'uan, *Tun-fu nien-p'u* (unpublished manuscript of his chronological autobiography), kindly lent me by his son Dr. Hu Shih. Also Hu Shih, Oral Autobiography (uncompleted manuscript at the Oral History Project, Columbia University).

35. Tsou T'ao, *San-chieh-lu pi-t'an*, ch. 11, pp. 2a–3a.

36. Yeh's commemorative album entitled *Yeh-kung Ch'eng-chung ai-yung lu*, which, along with dozens of similar albums and obituary articles, is in the possession of Columbia University's East Asiatic Library.

37. Chang Ch'ien, *Se-weng tzu-ting nien-p'u, passim;* also Chang Hsiao-jo, *Nan-t'ung Chang Chi-chih hsien-sheng chuan-chi, passim.*

38. *Chi-hsi Miao-tzu-shan Wang-shih p'u*, compiled by Wang Wei-ch'eng. This genealogy of unusual interest is in possession of the Harvard-Yenching Institute Library.

39. For a detailed discussion of the economic forces at work in the post-Taiping lower Yangtze and their effect on tenancy and ownership, see my *Studies on the Population of China, 1368–1953*, pp. 221–22, 238–46, 275–76.

40. *Hsi-chin yu-hsiang t'ung-jen tzu-shu hui-k'an*, under "Chou Fan."

41. Hu Shih, Li Chin-hsi, and Teng Kuang-ming, *Ch'i Po-shih nien-p'u*. This chronological biography is based on the famous painter's own memoirs and various other writings. Dr. Hu Shih's inquisitiveness and Professor Li's own diary and personal reminiscences on Ch'i, an old friend of the prominent Li clan of Hsiang-t'an, make this biography unusually interesting reading.

# GLOSSARY

| | | | |
|---|---|---|---|
| Ah Chi | 阿寄 | Ch'ao Ssu-hsiao | 晁思孝 |
| An Ch'i | 安岐 | Ch'en Chi | 陳濟 |
| An Kuo | 安國 | Ch'en Chih-lin | 陳之遴 |
| An Shang-i | 安尚義 | Ch'en Eng | 陳昂 |
| An-ting | 安定 | Ch'en Mao-jen | 陳懋仁 |
| bithesi | 筆帖式 | Ch'en Shih-kuan | 陳世倌 |
| chan-chi | 站籍 | Ch'en Sung | 陳嵩 |
| Chang Chia-hsiang | 張嘉祥 | Ch'en Yü-hsiang | 陳輿相 |
| Chang Ch'ien | 張騫 | Ch'en Yüan-lung | 陳元龍 |
| Chang Chih-tung | 張之洞 | Cheng | 鄭 |
| Chang Chü-cheng | 張居正 | Cheng An | 鄭安 |
| Chang Ch'üan | 章銓 | Cheng Ch'eng-kung | 鄭成功 |
| Chang Ch'un | 張淳 | Cheng Ho | 鄭和 |
| Chang Feng | 張俸 | Cheng Ning | 鄭寧 |
| Chang Han | 張瀚 | Cheng Ping-t'ien | 鄭秉恬 |
| Chang Hsün | 張恂 | Cheng Te-shu | 鄭得書 |
| Chang Huan | 張桓 | Ch'eng | 程 |
| Chang Jo-ai | 張若靄 | Ch'eng Chin-fang | 程晉芳 |
| Chang Jo-ch'eng | 張若澄 | Ch'eng I | 程頤 |
| Chang Jo-shu | 張若淑 | Ch'eng Shu-te | 程樹德 |
| Chang Jo-t'ing | 張若淳 | Chi Chin | 嵇璡 |
| Chang Lin | 張霖 | Chi Huang | 嵇璜 |
| Chang Mao | 章懋 | Chi Tseng-yun | 嵇曾筠 |
| Chang Shih-i (Chin-sung) | | Chi Wen-fu | 嵇文甫 |
| | 張士毅(近松) | Chiang | 江 |
| Chang T'ing-yü | 張廷玉 | Chiang Ch'en-ying | 姜宸英 |
| Chang Tseng-i | 張曾誼 | Chiang-chi | 匠籍 |
| Chang Ying | 張英 | Chiang Ch'un | 江春 |
| ch'ang | 場 | Chiang Fang | 江昉 |
| Chao I | 趙翼 | Chiang Hsün | 江恂 |

| | | | |
|---|---|---|---|
| Chiang Kuo-mao | 江國茂 | Fan Chin | 范進 |
| Chiang Lan | 江蘭 | Fan Chung-yen | 范仲淹 |
| Chiang Ning | 江寧 | Fan Hsiao-shan | 范肖山 |
| Chiang Te-liang | 江德量 | Fan Yü-ch'i | 范毓馡 |
| Chiang Yen | 江演 | Fan Yü-pin | 范毓馪 |
| Chiao Fang | 焦芳 | Fan Yü-t'an | 范毓覃 |
| chien-sheng | 監生 | Fang K'o-ch'in | 方克勤 |
| Ch'ien Ch'ien-i | 錢謙益 | Fei-hung-t'ang yin-p'u | 飛鴻堂印譜 |
| Ch'ien Chin-jen | 錢近仁 | fu | 賦 |
| Ch'ien Lu-ssu | 錢魯斯 | Fu Heng | 傅恒 |
| Ch'ien Lü-t'an | 錢履垣 | fu-hsüeh-sheng-yüan | 附學生員 |
| Ch'ien Yung | 錢泳 | fu-hu | 富戶 |
| chih-p'ing | 至平 | fu-kung-sheng | 副貢生 |
| chin | 衿 | fu-pang | 副榜 |
| chin-shen | 縉紳 | Hai-shan-hsien-kuan ts'ung-shu | |
| Chin-shen ch'üan-shu | 縉紳全書 | | 海山仙館叢書 |
| chin-shih | 進士 | han-tsu | 寒族 |
| chin-shih-chuang | 進士莊 | Ho Hsin-yin | 何心隱 |
| Ch'in-t'ien-chien | 欽天監 | Ho Liang-chün | 何良俊 |
| Ching Lan-chiang | 景蘭江 | Ho-shuo | 河朔 |
| ching-piao i-min | 旌表義民 | hsiang-kung | 相公 |
| ch'ing-chü-tu-wei | 輕車都尉 | Hsiang Yüan-pien | 項元汴 |
| Ch'ing-shih lieh-chuan | 清史列傳 | Hsiao-ching | 孝經 |
| ch'ing-yün-chuang | 青雲莊 | hsiao-jen | 小人 |
| Chou Fan | 周藩 | hsiao-lien | 孝廉 |
| Chou Hui | 周蕙 | hsiao-t'i li-t'ien | 孝悌(弟)力田 |
| Chou Wen-chin | 周文燦 | Hsieh Chao-che | 謝肇淛 |
| Chu-fu Yen | 主父偃 | hsien-liang fang-cheng | 賢良方正 |
| Chu Shih | 朱軾 | hsing-hsien-chuang | 興賢莊 |
| chu-tso-jen-chiang | 住坐人匠 | hsiu-ts'ai | 秀才 |
| Chu Yüan-chang | 朱元璋 | Hsü | 徐 |
| chü-jen | 舉人 | Hsü Ch'ao | 徐潮 |
| Ch'ü Hung-chi | 瞿鴻機 | Hsü Ch'ien-hsüeh | 徐乾學 |
| Ch'ü Yu | 瞿祐 | Hsü Kuang-ch'i | 徐光啓 |
| ch'uan-lu | 傳臚 | Hsü Kuo | 許國 |
| chün-chi | 軍籍 | Hsü Pen | 徐本 |
| chün-tzu | 君子 | Hsü Ping-i | 徐秉義 |
| chung-cheng | 中正 | Hsü Tsan | 許讚 |
| ê-wei-chu-shih | 額外主事 | Hsü Yüan-ch'i | 徐元氣 |
| en-kung-sheng | 恩貢生 | Hsü Yüan-shan | 徐元善 |
| en-yin-sheng | 恩廕生 | Hsü Yüan-t'ai | 徐元太 |
| Erh-ya | 爾雅 | Hsü Yüan-wen | 徐元文 |

| | | | |
|---|---|---|---|
| hsüan-kung | 選貢 | lao-hu-pan | 老虎班 |
| Hsüeh-hai-t'ang | 學海堂 | lao-yeh | 老爺 |
| Hsüeh-ku-t'ang | 學古堂 | Li Chen-chu | 李楨苧 |
| Hu Ch'uan | 胡傳 | Li-chi | 禮記 |
| Hu Ch'üan | 胡銓 | Li Ch'i | 李齊 |
| Hu Kuang | 胡廣 | Li Chih (Cho-wu) | 李贄(卓吾) |
| Hu Kuei | 胡槻 | Li Chih-fang | 李之芳 |
| Hu Lin-i | 胡林翼 | Li Ch'ing | 李慶 |
| Hua Sui | 華燧 | Li Fu | 李紱 |
| Huang Hsing-tseng | 黃省曾 | li-hsien-wu-fang | 立賢無方 |
| Huang Huai | 黃淮 | Li Po | 李柏 |
| Huang I-sheng | 黃翼生 | Li Tao-nan | 李道南 |
| hui-kuan | 會館 | Li Tou | 李斗 |
| Hung | 洪 | Li Yin-tu | 李因篤 |
| Hung Liang-chi | 洪亮吉 | Li Yung | 李顒 |
| i-chi | 醫籍 | Liang Chao-chin | 梁肇晋 |
| i-hsüeh | 義學 | Liang Chao-ching | 梁肇燝 |
| ju-chi | 儒籍 | Liang Chao-huang | 梁肇煌 |
| Juan Yüan | 阮元 | Liang Chia-pin | 梁嘉彬 |
| kai-hu | 丐戶 | Liang Ching-kuo | 梁經國 |
| Kao Hung-t'u | 高弘圖 | Liang Ch'ing-piao | 梁清標 |
| Ke Shou-li | 葛守禮 | Liang Ch'u | 梁儲 |
| keng-tu | 耕讀 | Liang Fang-chung (Chia-kuan) | |
| Keng-tsu hsiao-hsia lu | 庚子消夏錄 | | 梁方仲(嘉官) |
| Ku-ching ching-she | 詁經精舍 | Liang Lun-shu | 梁綸樞 |
| kuan-chi | 官籍 | Liang T'ung-hsin | 梁同新 |
| Kuan Chung | 管仲 | Lin | 林 |
| kuan-shang | 官商 | Lin Liang | 林亮 |
| Kuang-lu-ssu ch'u | 光禄寺厨 | ling-sheng | 廩生 |
| kuang-wen | 廣文 | ling-kung-sheng | 廩貢生 |
| Kuang-ya | 廣雅 | Ling T'ing-k'an | 凌廷堪 |
| K'uang Ch'ao-jen | 匡超人 | Liu | 劉 |
| k'uang-chi | 礦籍 | Liu Ch'eng-hsü | 劉承緒 |
| Kuei Yu-kuang | 歸有光 | Liu Chih-lun | 劉之綸 |
| kung | 工 | Liu Chin | 劉瑾 |
| Kung I-ch'ing | 龔一清 | Liu Ming-ch'uan | 劉銘傳 |
| kung-sheng | 貢生 | Liu San-wu | 劉三吾 |
| kung-shih | 供事 | Liu Ta-hsia | 劉大夏 |
| kung-shih-chuang | 貢士莊 | Liu T'ung-hsun | 劉統勳 |
| Kung Tzu-chen | 龔自珍 | Liu Yü | 劉鈺 |
| K'ung Kuang-t'ao | 孔廣陶 | Lo Ssu-chü | 羅思舉 |
| lang-chung | 郎中 | Lo Wen-chün | 羅文俊 |

| | | | |
|---|---|---|---|
| Lu Chien-ying | 陸建瀛 | pien-t'i | 駢體 |
| Lu Chung | 盧忠 | Pien Yung-yü | 卞永譽 |
| Lu Shen | 陸深 | Po-chün | 柏浚 |
| Lu Shu-sheng | 陸樹聲 | Po-lu-tung | 白鹿洞 |
| Lung-hu | 龍湖 | p'u-hu | 捕戶 |
| Lung-men | 龍門 | P'u Sung-ling | 蒲松齡 |
| Ma (hsiu-ts'ai) | 馬 | se-mu | 色目 |
| Ma Ch'un-shang | 馬純上 | Shan Fu | 單輔 |
| Ma-ke | 馬閣 | shang | 商 |
| Ma Wei-hsing | 馬惟興 | shang-chi | 商籍 |
| Ma Yüeh-kuan | 馬曰琯 | shang-kuan | 商官 |
| Ma Yüeh-lu | 馬曰璐 | Shang Lo | 商輅 |
| Mao Chin | 毛晋 | she-hsüeh | 社學 |
| mao-ts'ai | 茂才 | shen | 紳 |
| min | 民 | shen-chin | 紳衿 |
| min-hu | 民戶 | shen-shang | 紳商 |
| ming-ching | 明經 | shen-shih | 紳士 |
| ming-suan | 明算 | Shen Te-fu | 沈德符 |
| Mingju | 明珠 | Shih | 士 |
| Ming-tao | 明道 | Shin Ching | 史經 |
| mo-chüan | 墨卷 | shih-min | 士民 |
| mu-so-chi | 牧所籍 | Shih P'an | 施槃 |
| nan-yin-sheng | 難蔭生 | shih-p'u | 世僕 |
| Nei-wu-fu | 內務府 | Shu-hsüeh | 述學 |
| nung | 農 | shu-yüan | 書院 |
| Ou-yang Hsiu | 歐陽修 | so | 所 |
| pa-kung-sheng | 拔貢生 | Ssu-k'u ch'üan-shu | 四庫全書 |
| pan-chiang | 班匠 | Ssu-li-chien | 司禮監 |
| P'an Kuang-tan | 潘光旦 | ssu-min | 四民 |
| P'an Shih-ch'eng | 潘仕成 | su-feng | 素封 |
| P'an Shih-en | 潘世恩 | Su Shih (Tung-p'o) | 蘇軾(東坡) |
| Pao | 鮑 | Su-shun | 蕭順 |
| Pao-chin | 寶晋 | sui-kung-sheng | 歲貢生 |
| Pao T'ing-po | 鮑廷博 | Sun I-ch'ing | 孫義卿 |
| P'eng Ch'i-feng | 彭啓豐 | T'ai-i | 太醫 |
| P'eng Ho-kao | 彭鶴臯 | tan-hu | 蜑(蛋)戶 |
| P'eng Ting-ch'iu | 彭定求 | T'ang Ho-cheng | 唐鶴徵 |
| P'eng Yü-lin | 彭玉麟 | T'ang Kuei | 唐貴 |
| P'eng Yün-chang | 彭蘊章 | T'ang Pao | 唐珤 |
| pi-keng | 筆耕 | T'ang Shun-chih | 唐順之 |
| Pien Kung | 邊貢 | T'ao Chin | 陶潛 |
| pien-shang | 邊商 | T'ao Chu | 陶澍 |

| | | | |
|---|---|---|---|
| T'ao Mo | 陶模 | Wang Ch'i | 王圻 |
| t'i-tu | 提督 | Wang Chüeh-lien | 王覺蓮 |
| to-min | 惰民 | Wang Chung | 汪中 |
| ts'an-chiang | 參將 | Wang Hsien | 汪憲 |
| tsao-chi | 灶籍 | Wang Hsing | 王行 |
| tsao-hu | 灶戶 | Wang Hui-tsu | 汪輝祖 |
| Ts'ao | 曹 | Wang Jih-chang | 汪日章 |
| Ts'ao Chen-huan | 曹振鐶 | Wang Jih-kuei | 汪日桂 |
| Ts'ao Chen-k'ai | 曹振鎧 | Wang Ju-li | 汪汝璸 |
| Ts'ao Chen-ling | 曹振鈴 | Wang K'ai-yün | 王闓運 |
| Ts'ao Chen-lu | 曹振鏴 | Wang Ken | 王艮 |
| Ts'ao Chen-yung | 曹振鏞 | Wang Mien | 王冕 |
| Ts'ao Ching-ch'en | 曹景宸 | Wang Ming-hsiang | 汪鳴相 |
| Ts'ao Ching-t'ing | 曹景廷 | Wang Pang-ch'ing | 王邦慶 |
| Ts'ao En-ying | 曹恩瀅 | Wang Shih-chen | 王世貞 |
| Ts'ao Ming | 曹銘 | Wang Shih-chen | 王士禎 |
| Ts'ao Shih-ch'ang | 曹世昌 | Wang Shih-to | 汪士鐸 |
| Ts'ao Tseng | 曹增 | Wang Shou-jen (Yang-ming) | |
| Ts'ao Tzu-chi | 曹自鎜 | | 王守仁(陽明) |
| Ts'ao Wen-chih | 曹文埴 | Wang Tao-k'un | 汪道昆 |
| Ts'ao Wen-ching | 曹文境 | Wang Tsung-chi | 汪宗姬 |
| Ts'ao Wen-shu | 曹文塾 | Wang Wei-ch'eng | 王維城 |
| ts'e | 策 | Wang Yen-che | 王延喆 |
| tseng-kuang-sheng-yüan | 增廣生員 | wei | 衛 |
| Tseng Kung | 曾鞏 | Wei-ching | 味經 |
| Tseng Kuo-fan | 曾國藩 | Wei Yüan | 魏源 |
| Tso-chuan | 左傳 | Wen Ch'un | 溫純 |
| tso-shang | 坐商 | wen-hsüeh | 文學 |
| tso-tsa | 佐雜 | Weng T'ung-ho | 翁同龢 |
| Tso Tsung-t'ang | 左宗棠 | Wu | 吳 |
| Tsou T'ao | 鄒弢 | Wu Ch'ang-ch'ing | 吳長慶 |
| Tsung-jen-fu | 宗人府 | Wu Ch'eng | 吳城 |
| tsung-ping | 總兵 | Wu Cho | 吳焯 |
| tsung-shih | 宗室 | Wu Chung-liang | 吳中良 |
| tsung-tzu | 宗子 | Wu Ch'ung-yüeh | 伍崇曜 |
| Ts'ung-shu-lou | 叢書樓 | Wu Huai-ch'ing | 吳懷清 |
| T'u Ch'ao | 屠潮 | Wu Hui | 吳恵 |
| t'un | 屯 | Wu K'ai | 吳楷 |
| Tung-lin | 東林 | Wu Liang | 吳良 |
| Wan Hsüeh-chai | 萬雪齋 | Wu Ta-ch'eng | 吳大澂 |
| Wang | 汪 | Wu Yü-ch'ih | 吳玉墀 |
| Wang Ao | 王鏊 | Wu Yü-pi | 吳與弼 |

| | | | |
|---|---|---|---|
| Yang Chi | 楊稷 | Yen Ju-yü | 顏如玉 |
| Yang Chi-sheng | 楊繼盛 | Yen Sung | 嚴嵩 |
| Yang Chüeh | 楊爵 | yen-t'ien | 硯(研)田 |
| Yang Fu | 楊溥 | yin | 蔭 |
| Yang Hua | 楊華 | yin | 引 |
| Yang I-ch'ing | 楊一清 | yu-kung-sheng | 優貢生 |
| Yang Jung | 楊榮 | Yü-lu | 嶽麓 |
| Yang Kung | 楊恭 | Yü Yüeh | 俞樾 |
| Yang Shih-ch'i | 楊士奇 | Yüan Mei | 袁枚 |
| Yang T'ai | 楊泰 | Yüan Ts'ai | 袁采 |
| Yao | 姚 | Yüeh Chi | 樂枅 |
| Yeh Ch'eng-chung | 葉澄衷(成忠) | yüeh-hu | 樂戶 |
| Yeh Liang-ts'ai | 葉良材 | Yüeh-ya-t'ang ts'ung-shu | |
| Yeh Meng-ting | 葉夢鼎 | | 粤雅堂叢書 |
| Yeh Sheng | 葉盛 | Yün-shan | 雲山 |
| Yeh Tzu-ch'i | 葉子奇 | Yung-lo ta-tien | 永樂大典 |
| Yen Ch'en | 嚴辰 | | |

# BIBLIOGRAPHY

## PRIMARY CHINESE SOURCES

MAIN STATISTICAL DATA (each group in chronological order)
The locations of the rare *chin-shih* lists with ancestral information are
indicated by the following abbreviations:
NP —National Library of Peking
NC—National Central Library, Taipei, Taiwan
LC—Library of Congress
LCM—Library of Congress microfilm

*Chin-shih* LISTS
*Hung-wu ssu-nien chin-shih teng-k'o lu*
洪武四年進士登科錄. (1371)
　*I-hai chu-ch'en* 藝海珠塵 ed.
*Yung-lo shih-nien chin-shih teng-k'o lu*
永樂十年進士登科錄. (1412; NP; LCM)
*T'ien-shun yüan-nien chin-shih teng-k'o lu*
天順元年進士登科錄. (1457; NC)
*Ch'eng-hua wu-nien chin-shih teng-k'o lu*
成化五年進士登科錄. (1469; NP; LCM)
*Ch'eng-hua pa-nien chin-shih teng-k'o lu*
成化八年進士登科錄. (1472; NP; LCM)
*Hung-chih chiu-nien chin-shih teng-k'o lu*
弘治九年進士登科錄. (1496; NC)
*Hung-chih shih-pa-nien chin-shih teng-k'o lu*
弘治十八年進士登科錄. (1505; NC)
*Cheng-te shih-lu-nien chin-shih teng-k'o lu*
正德十六年進士登科錄. (1521; NC)
*Chia-ching shih-ssu-nien chin-shih teng-k'o lu*
嘉靖十四年進士登科錄. (1535; NP; LCM)
*Chia-ching shih-ch'i-nien chin-shih teng-k'o lu*
嘉靖十七年進士登科錄. (1538; NP; LCM)

*Chia-ching erh-shih-san-nien chin-shih teng-k'o lu*
嘉靖二十三年進士登科錄. (1544; NC; LC)
*Chia-ching kuei-ssu-k'o chin-shih t'ung-ninen pien-lan lu*
嘉靖癸巳科進士同年便覽錄. (1553; NC)
*Chia-ching ssu-shih-i-nien chin-shih teng-k'o lu*
嘉靖四十一年進士登科錄. (1562; NC; LC)
*Lung-ch'ing erh-nien chin-shih teng-k'o lu*
隆慶二年進士登科錄. (1568; NP; ICM)
*Wan-li pa-nien chin-shih teng-k'o lu*
萬曆八年進士登科錄. (1580; NC)
*Wan-li shih-ssu-nien ping-hsü hui-shih lu*
萬曆十四年丙戌會試錄. (1586; NC)
*Wan-li san-shih-pa-nien keng-hsü-k'o hsü-ch'ih lu*
萬曆三十八年庚戌科序齒錄. (1610; NP; LCM)
*Shun-chih chiu-nien jen-ch'en-k'o chin-shih san-tai lü-li*
順治九年壬辰科進士三代履歷. (1652; NP)
*Shun-chih shih-erh-nien i-wei-k'o chin-shih san-tai lü-li*
順治十二年乙未科進士三代履歷. (1655; NP)
*Shun-chih shih-wu-nien wu-hsü-k'o chin-shih san-tai lü-li*
順治十五年戊戌科進士三代履歷. (1658; NP)
*Shun-chih shih-lu-nien chi-hai-k'o hui-shih chin-shih san-tai lü-li*
順治十六年己亥科會試進士三代履歷. (1659; NP)
*Shun-chih shih-pa-nien hsin-ch'ou-k'o hui-shih ssu-pai-ming chin-shih san-tai lü-li
pien-lan* 順治十八年辛丑科會試四百名進士三代履歷便覽. (1661; NP)
*K'ang-hsi shih-erh-nien kuei-ch'ou-k'o hui-shih chin-shih san-tai lü-li pien-lan*
康熙十二年癸丑科會試進士三代履歷便覽. (1673; NP)
*K'ang-hsi erh-shih-i-nien jen-hsü-k'o t'ung-nien hsü-ch'ih lu*
康熙二十一年壬戌科同年序齒錄. (1682; NP)
*K'ang-hsi erh-shih-ssu-nien i-ch'ou-k'o san-tai chin-shih lü-li*
康熙二十四年乙丑科三代進士履歷. (1685; NP)
*K'ang-hsi ssu-shih-erh-nien kuei-wei-k'o san-tai chin-shih lü-li*
康熙四十二年癸未科三代進士履歷. (1703; NC)
*Tao-kuang jen-wu t'ung-nien ch'ih-lu*
道光壬午同年齒錄. (1822)
*Tao-kuang chi-ch'ou-k'o hui-shih t'ung-nien ch'ih-lu*
道光己丑科會試同年齒錄. (1829)
*Tao-kuang kuei-ssu-k'o hui-shih t'ung-nien ch'ih-lu*
道光癸巳科會試同年齒錄. (1833)
*Tao-kuang i-wei-k'o hui-shih t'ung-nien ch'ih-lu*
道光乙未科會試同年齒錄. (1835)
*Tao-kuang chia-ch'en-k'o hui-shih t'ung-nien ch'ih-lu*
道光甲辰科會試同年齒錄. (1844)

*Hsien-feng chi-wei-k'o hui-shih t'ung-nien ch'ih-lu*
咸豐己未科會試同年齒錄. (1859)
*Hsien-feng shih-nien keng-shen en-k'o hui-shih t'ung-nien ch'ih-lu*
咸豐十年庚申恩科會試同年齒錄. (1860)
*T'ung-chih i-ch'ou-k'o hui-shih t'ung-nien ch'ih-lu*
同治乙丑科會試同年齒錄. (1865)
*T'ung-chih ch'i-nien hui-shih t'ung-nien ch'ih-lu*
同治七年會試同年齒錄. (1868)
*T'ung-chih hsin-wei-k'o hui-shih t'ung-nien ch'ih-lu*
同治辛未科會試同年齒錄. (1871)
*T'ung-chih shih-san-nien chia-hsü-k'o hui-shih t'ung-nien ch'ih-lu*
同治十三年甲戌科會試同年齒錄. (1874)
*Kuang-hsü erh-nien ping-tzu en-k'o hui-shih t'ung-nien ch'ih-lu*
光緒二年丙子恩科會試同年齒錄. (1876)
*Kuang-hsü san-nien ting-ch'ou-k'o hui-shih t'ung-nien ch'ih-lu*
光緒三年丁丑科會試同年齒錄. (1877)
*Kuang-hsü lu-nien keng-ch'en-k'o hui-shih t'ung-nien ch'ih-lu*
光緒六年庚辰科試同年齒錄. (1880)
*Kuang-hsü kuei-wei-k'o hui-shih t'ung-nien ch'ih-lu*
光緒癸未科會試同年齒錄. (1883)
*Kuang-hsü shih-erh-nien ping-hsü-k'o hui-shih t'ung-nien ch'ih-lu*
光緒十二年丙戌科會試同年齒錄. (1886)
*Kuang-hsü chi-ch'ou-k'o hui-shih t'ung-nien ch'ih-lu*
光緒己丑科會試同年齒錄. (1889)
*Kuang-hsü keng-yin en-k'o hui-shih t'ung-nien ch'ih-lu*
光緒庚寅恩科會試同年齒錄. (1890)
*Kuang-hsü shih-pa-nien jen-ch'en-k'o hui-shih t'ung-nien ch'ih-lu*
光緒十八年壬辰科會試同年齒錄. (1892)
*Kuang-hsü erh-shih-i-nien i-wei-k'o hui-shih t'ung-nien ch'ih-lu*
光緒二十一年乙未科會試同年齒錄. (1895)
*Kuang-hsü erh-shih-ssu-nien wu-hsü-k'o hui-shih t'ung-nien ch'ih-lu*
光緒二十四年戊戌科會試同年齒錄. (1898)
*Kuang-hsü san-shih-nien chia-ch'en en-k'o hui-shih t'ung-nien ch'ih-lu*
光緒三十年甲辰恩科會試同年齒錄. (1904)
Note: The above 48 lists supply the data for table 9.

*Chü-jen* AND *kung-sheng* LISTS
*Chia-ch'ing chiu-nien chia-tzu-k'o chih-sheng hsiang-shih t'ung-nien ch'ih-l*
嘉慶九年甲子科直省鄉試同年齒錄. (1804)
*Ting-mou hsiang-shih ch'ih-lu*
丁卯鄉試齒錄. (1807)
Note: The original title does not have the reign period and the list

has been wrongly identified by the Library of Congress as one for
the year 1747.

*Wu-ch'en-k'o hsiang-shih t'i-ming ch'ih-lu*
戊辰科鄉試題名齒錄. (1808)

*Chia-ch'ing ping-tzu-k'o ke-sheng hsiang-shih t'ung-nien ch'ih-lu*
嘉慶丙子科各省鄉試同年齒錄. (1816)

*Tao-kuang hsin-ssu ke-sheng t'ung-nien ch'üan-lu*
道光辛巳各省同年全錄. (1821)

*Tao-kuang wu-tzu-k'o chih-sheng t'ung-nien lu*
道光戊子科直省同年錄. (1828)

*Tao-kuang hsin-mou-k'o ke-chih-sheng t'ung-nien lu*
道光辛卯科各直省同年錄. (1831)

*Tao-kuang jen-ch'en-k'o chih-sheng hsiang-shih t'ung-nien ch'ih-lu*
道光壬辰科直省鄉試同年齒錄. (1832)

*Tao-kuang chia-wu-k'o chih-sheng t'ung-nien lu*
道光甲午科直省同年錄. (1834)

*Tao-kuang i-wei en-k'o chih-sheng t'ung-nien lu*
道光乙未恩科直省同年錄. (1835)

*Tao-kuang kuei-mou-k'o chih-sheng t'ung-nien ch'üan-lu*
道光癸卯科直省同年全錄. (1843)

*Tao-kuang chia-ch'en en-k'o chih-sheng t'ung-nien lu*
道光甲辰恩科直省同年錄. (1844)

*Tao-kuang chi-yu-k'o ke-sheng hsüan-pa ming-ching t'ung-p'u*
道光己酉科各省選拔明經通譜. (1849)

*Hsien-feng i-mou-k'o chih-sheng hsiang-shih t'ung-nien ch'ih-lu*
咸豐乙卯科直省鄉試同年齒錄. (1855)

*T'ung-chih chiu-nien keng-wu-k'o chih-sheng hsiang-shih t'ung-nien ch'ih-lu*
同治九年庚午科直省鄉試同年齒錄. (1870)

*Kuang-hsü chi-mou-k'o chih-sheng t'ung-nien ch'ih-lu*
光緒己卯科直省同年齒錄. (1879)

*Kuang-hsü i-yu-k'o ke-chih-sheng hsüan-pa ming-ching t'ung-p'u*
光緒乙酉科各直省選拔明經通譜. (1885)

*Kuang-hsü ting-yu-k'o ke-chih-sheng hsüan-pa t'ung-nien ming-ching t'ung-p'u*
光緒丁酉科各直省選拔同年明經通譜. (1897)

*Kuang-hsü ping-wu-k'o yu-kung t'ung-nien ch'ih-lu*
光緒丙午科優貢同年齒錄. (1906)

*Hsüan-t'ung keng-hsü-k'o chü-kung k'ao-chih t'ung-nien ch'ih-lu*
宣統庚戌科舉貢攷職同年齒錄. (1910)

Note:    The above 20 lists supply the data for table 11.

STATISTICALLY USEFUL *sheng-yüan* LISTS

*Ching-hsiang t'i-ming lu*
靜庠題名錄. (1933 ed.)

*Kuo-ch'ao yü-yang k'o-ming lu*
國朝虞陽科名錄. (Last ed., printed some time after 1904).
*T'ung-hsiang t'i-ming lu*
通庠題名錄. (1933 ed.)
Note: The above 3 lists supply the data for table 15.

SUPPLEMENTARY 18TH-CENTURY LISTS

*Ch'ien-lung jen-shen-k'o fu-chien hsiang-shih t'ung-nien ch'ih-lu*
乾隆壬申科福建鄉試同年齒錄. (1752)
*Ch'ien-lung chi-yu-k'o ke-sheng hsüan-pa t'ung-nien ch'ih-lu*
乾隆己酉科各省選拔同年齒錄. (1789)
*Ch'ien-lung chia-yin en-ko shun-t'ien hsiang-shih t'ung-nien ch'ih-lu*
乾隆甲寅恩科順天鄉試同年齒錄. (1794)
*Chia-ch'ing wu-nien keng-shen en-k'o shun-t'ien hsiang-shih t'ung-nien ch'ih-lu*
嘉慶五年庚申恩科順天鄉試同年齒錄. (1800)
Note: The above 4 lists supply the data for table 12.

OTHER LISTS OF MINOR STATISTICAL USE

*Chien-wen erh-nien tien-shih teng-k'o lu*
建文二年殿試登科錄. (1400; NP; LCM)
*Wan-li jen-ch'en-k'o chin-shih lü-li pien-lan*
萬曆壬辰科進士履歷便覽. (1592; NC)
*Ch'ung-chen shih-erh-nien shan-hsi hsiang-shih hsü-ch'ih lu*
崇禎十二年山西鄉試序齒錄. (1639; NC)


## OTHER SOURCES

Cha Chi-tso 查繼佐. *Tsui-wei lu* 罪惟錄. SPTK ed.
Chang Ch'ien 張騫. *Se-weng tzu-ting nien-p'u* 嗇翁自訂年譜. 1925 ed.
*Chang-fu-chün hsing-shu* 章府君行述. Undated, by son of Chang Ch'üan (1739–1821) 章銓. (Columbia)
Chang Han 張瀚. *Hsi-nang tu-yü* 奚囊蠹餘. Wu-lin hsien-che i-shu 武林先哲遺書 ed.
——— *Sung-ch'uang meng-yü* 松窗夢語. Wu-lin hsien-che i-shu 武林先哲遺書 ed.
Chang Hsüan 張萱. *Hsi-yüan wen-chien lu* 西園聞見錄 Original preface dated 1627; Yenching University, 1940 reprint.
Chang Huang 章潢. *T'u-shu pien* 圖書編. T'ien-ch'i 天啓 ed.
Chang Hung-tao 張宏道, and Chang Ning-tao 張凝道. *Huang-Ming san-yüan k'ao* 皇明三元攷. Late Ming ed.
Chang Ting-yü 張廷玉. *Ch'eng-huai-yüan yü* 澄懷園語. *Hsiao-yüan ts'ung-shu* 嘯園叢書 ed.
Chang Ying 張英. "Heng-ch'an so-yen" 恒產瑣言, in *Tu-su-t'ang wen-chi* 篤素堂文集. 1897 ed.

———— *Ts'ung-hsün-chai yü* 聰訓齋語. Hsiao-yüan ts'ung-shu 嘯園叢書 ed.

*Ch'ang-chou fu-chih* 常州府志. 1618 ed. and 1794 ed., 1887 reprint.

*Ch'ang-lu yen-fa chih* 長蘆鹽法志. 1726 ed. and 1805 ed.

*Ch'ang-te fu-chih* 常德府志. 1813 ed.

Chao I 趙翼. *Hai-yü ts'ung-k'ao* 陔餘叢攷. *Chao Ou-pei ch'üan-chi* 趙甌北全集 ed.

———— *Nien-erh-shih tsa-chi* 廿二史劄記. Shih-chieh-shu-chü 世界書局 ed.

———— *Yen-p'u tsa-chi* 簷曝雜記. *Chao Ou-pei ch'üan-chi* 趙甌北全集 ed.

Chao Kuan 趙官. *Hou-hu chih* 後湖志. Original preface dated 1531; rev. ed. of 1621.

*Che-chiang t'ung-kuan lu* 浙江同官錄. 1886 ed.

Ch'en Ch'i-yüan 陳其元. *Yung-hsien-chai pi-chi* 庸閒齋筆記. Preface dated 1874; CTPCTK ed.

Ch'en Hung-mou 陳宏謀. *Ch'üan-tien i-hsüeh hui-chi* 全滇義學彙記. 1738 ed.

Ch'en K'ang-ch'i 陳康祺. *Lang-ch'ien chi-wen* 郎潛紀聞. CTPCTK ed.

Ch'en Mao-jen 陳懋仁. *Ch'üan-nan tsa-chih* 泉南雜志. TSCC ed.

Ch'en T'ing-ching 陳廷敬. *Wu-ch'iao wen-pien* 午橋文編. 1708 ed.

Cheng Fang-k'un 鄭方坤. *Pen-ch'ao ming-chia shih-ch'ao hsiao-chuan* 本朝名家詩鈔小傳. 1919 ed.

*Cheng-shih chia-kuei* 鄭氏家規. 1506 ed.

*Chi-an fu-chih* 吉安府志. 1876 ed.

*Chi-hsi Miao-tzu-shan Wang-shih p'u* 績溪廟子山王氏譜. 1935 ed.

*Chi-mo hsien-chih* 即墨縣志. 1873 ed.

*Chi-shih tsung-p'u* 嵇氏宗譜. 1907 ed.

*Chi-shui hsien-chih* 吉水縣志. 1875 ed.

*Chia-hsing fu-chih* 嘉興府志. 1610 ed. and 1878 ed.

*Chia-shan ju-p'an t'i-ming lu* 嘉善入泮題名錄. 1908 ed.

*Chiang-nan t'ung-chih* 江南通志. 1736 ed.

*Chiang-ning hsien-chih* 江寧縣志. 1598 ed.

*Chiang-su t'ung-kuan lu* 江蘇同官錄. 1880 ed.

Chiao Hung 焦竑. *Kuo-ch'ao hsien-cheng lu* 國朝獻徵錄. 1616 ed.

*Chieh-hsiu hsien-chih* 介休縣志. 1924 ed.

Ch'ien Yung 錢泳. *Lü-yüan ts'ung-hua* 履園叢話. Preface dated 1835; CTPCTK ed.

*Chin-chiang shu-yüan chi-lüeh* 錦江書院紀略. 1871 ed.

*Chin-hua hsien-cheng lu* 金華獻徵錄. 1732 ed.

*Chin-ku ch'i-kuan* 今古奇觀. Ya-tung-shu-chü 亞東書局 ed.

*Ch'ing-ch'ao wen-hsien t'ung-k'ao* 清朝文獻通攷. CP ed.

*Ch'ing hua-chia shih-shih* 清畫家詩史. 1930 ed.

*Ch'ing-shih lieh-chuan* 清史列傳. 1928 ed.

Chu K'ung-chang 朱孔彰. *Chung-hsing chiang-shuai pieh-chuan* 中興將帥別傳. SPPY ed.

Chu Kuo-chen 朱國楨. *Huang-Ming k'ai-kuo-ch'en chuan* 皇明開國臣傳. Late Ming ed.

Chu Shih 朱軾. *Chu-wen-tuan-kung chi* 朱文端公集. 1873 ed.

*Chu-yüeh pa-ch'i chih* 駐粤八旗志. Preface dated 1879; printed some time after 1884.

Chu Yün-ming 祝允明. *Yeh-chi* 野記. TSCC ed.

Ch'u Jen-huo 褚人穫. *Chien-hu chi* 堅瓠集. Preface dated 1695; CTPCTK ed.

Ch'ü Yu 瞿祐. *Chü-chia pi-pei* 居家必備. Hang-chou-shu-fang 杭州書坊 undated Ming ed.

*Ch'üan-chou fu-chih* 泉州府志. 1763 ed.

*Chüeh-chih ch'üan-lan* 爵秩全覽. For the years 1764, 1840, 1871, and 1895.

*Chung-chou t'ung-kuan lu* 中州同官錄. 1847 ed. and 1893 ed.

*Fen-yang hsien-chih* 汾陽縣志. 1882 ed.

Feng Ying-ching 馮應京. *Huan-Ming ching-shih shih-yung pien* 皇明經世實用編. 1604 ed.

*Fu-chou fu-chih* 福州府志. 1613 ed. and 1754 ed.

*Fukien t'ung-chih* 福建通志. 1849 ed, revised in 1867, and 1922 ed.

*Hai-ning Po-hai Ch'en-shih tsung-p'u* 海寧渤海陳氏宗譜. 1882 ed.

*Han-fei-tzu* 韓非子. SPPY ed.

*Hang-chou fu-chih* 杭州府志. Compiled between 1879 and 1919. 1923 ed.

Ho Ch'iao-yüan 何喬遠. *Min-shu* 閩書. 1629 ed.

——— *Ming-shan ts'ang* 名山藏. 1636 ed.

*Ho-fei hsien-chih* 合肥縣志. 1803 ed.

Ho Liang-chün 何良俊. *Ssu-yu-chai ts'ung-shuo* 四友齋叢說. Preface dated 1579; Peking 1958 reprint. Also *Ssu-yu-chai tsung-shuo ti-ch'ao* 摘抄, TSCC ed.

*Ho-shuo shu-yüan chih* 河朔書院志. 1839 ed.

*Ho-tung yen-fa chih* 河東鹽法志. 1727 ed.

*Ho-tung yen-fa pei-lan* 河東鹽法備覽. 1789 ed.

*Hsi-chin yu-hsiang lu* 錫金遊庠錄. Printed some time after 1878.

*Hsi-chin yu-hsiang t'ung-jen tzu-shu hui-k'an* 錫金遊庠同人自述彙刊. 1930 ed.

Hsieh Chao-che 謝肇淛. *Wu-tsa-tsu* 五雜俎. 1795 Japanese ed.

*Hsien-feng yüan-nien en-yin t'ung-nien ch'ih-lu* 咸豐元年恩蔭同年齒錄. 1851 ed.

*Hsin-ch'eng hsien-chih* 新城縣志. 1693 ed. and 1933 ed.

*Hsin-ch'eng Wang-shih chia-sheng* 新城王氏家乘. Undated; printed probably in late 17th century.

*Hsin-chiang shu-yüan chih* 信江書院志. 1867 ed.

*Hsin-hua hsüeh-t'ien chih* 新化學田志. 1896 ed.

*Hsin-hui hsien-chih* 新會縣志. 1840 ed.

*Hsing-shih heng-yen* 醒世恒言. Sheng-huo-shu-tien 生活書店 ed.

Hsü Hsi-lin 徐錫麟. *Hsi-ch'ao hsin-yü* 熙朝新語. Preface dated 1832; CTPCTK ed.

Hsü Hsien 徐咸. *Hsi-yüan tsa-chi* 西園雜記. TSCC ed.

Hsü Hsüeh-chü 徐學聚. *Kuo-ch'ao tien-hui* 國朝典彙. 1636 ed.

Hsü Hsüeh-mo 徐學謨. *Shih-miao chih-yü lu* 世廟識餘錄. Preface by the author's grandson, dated 1608.

Hsü K'o 徐珂. ed. *Ch'ing-pai lei-ch'ao* 清稗類鈔. CP ed.

Hsü Kuang-ch'i 徐光啓. *Hsü-wen-ting-kung chi* 徐文定公集. Shanghai, 1933.

Hsü Kuo 許國. *Hsü-wen-mu-kung chi* 許文穆公集. 1923 ed.

*Hsü-wen-hsien t'ung-k'ao* 續文獻通攷. CP ed.

*Hsüan-ch'eng hsien-chih* 宣城縣志. 1888 ed.

*Hsüeh-cheng ch'üan-shu* 學政全書. 1793 ed. and 1812 ed.

Hsüeh Fu-ch'eng 薛福成. *Yung-an pi-chi* 庸盦筆記. CTPCTK ed.

*Hsün-tzu* 荀子. SPTK ed.

*Hu-chou fu-chih* 湖州府志. 1874 ed.

Hu Ch'uan 胡傳. *Tun-fu nien-p'u* 鈍夫年譜. Unpublished manuscript.

*Hu-shih tsung-p'u* 胡氏宗譜. 1880 ed.

*Huan-chiang t'ung-kuan lu* 皖江同官錄. 1871 ed.

Huan K'uan 桓寬. *Yen-t'ieh lun* 鹽鐵論. SPPY ed.

Huang Chün-tsai 黃鈞宰. *Chin-hu ch'i-mo* 金壺七墨. CTPCTK ed.

Huang Fu 黃溥. *Hsien-chung chin-ku-lu ti-ch'ao* 閒中今古錄摘抄. CLHP ed.

Huang-fu Ch'ung 皇甫冲. *Huang-Ming fan-fu cheng-ling* 皇明藩府政令. Late Ming manuscript.

Huang Hsing-tseng 黃省曾. *Wu-feng lu* 吳風錄. *Pai-ling hsüeh-shan* 百陵學山 ed.

Huang Tsung-hsi 黃宗羲. *Ming-ju hsüeh-an* 明儒學案. SPPY ed.

——— *Sung-Yüan hsüeh-an* 宋元學案. SPPY ed.

Huang Yü 黃瑜. *Shuang-huai sui-ch'ao* 雙槐歲鈔. 1495 ed.

*Hui-chou fu-chih* 徽州府志. 1827 ed.

*Hunan t'ung-chih* 湖南通志. 1887 ed.

*Hupei t'ung-chih* 湖北通志. 1911 ed., CP reprint.

*I-chen hsien-chih* 儀眞縣志. 1567 ed.

Juan K'uei-sheng 阮葵生. *Ch'a-yü k'o-hua* 茶餘客話. CTPCTK ed.

*Jui-chou fu-chih* 瑞州府志. 1628 ed.

Ke Shou-li 葛守禮. *Ke-tuan-su-kung chi* 葛端肅公集. 1802 reprint.

*Kiangsi t'ung-chih* 江西通志. 1881 ed.

*K'o-ch'ang t'iao-li* 科場條例. 1790 ed.

*Ku-chin t'u-shu chi-ch'eng* 古今圖書集成. Chung-hua-shu-chü 中華書局 reprint.

*Ku-su chih* 姑蘇志. 1506 ed.

Ku Yen-wu 顧炎武. *Jih-chih-lu chi-shih* 日知錄集釋. SPPY ed.

―――― *T'ing-lin wen-chi* 亭林文集. *T'ing-lin i-shu shih-chung* 亭林遺書十種 ed.

―――― *T'en-hsia chün-kuo li-ping shu* 天下郡國利病書. CP ed.

*Kuan-ch'ang hsien-hsing chi* 官場現形記. Ya-tung-shu-chü ed.

*Kuan-chung t'ung-kuan lu* 關中同官錄. 1894 ed.

*Kuan-tzu* 管子. SPTK ed.

*Kuang-chou fu-chih* 廣州府志. 1879 ed.

*Kuang-hsü yin-sheng t'ung-nien ch'ih-lu* 光緒蔭生同年齒錄. 1904 ed.

Kuei Yu-kuang 歸有光. *Chen-ch'uan hsien-sheng chi* 震川先生集. TSCC ed.

Kung Tzu-chen 龔自珍. *Ting-an wen-chi* 定盦文集. SPPY ed.

K'ung Kuang-t'ao 孔廣陶. *Yü-hsüeh-lou shu-hua lu* 嶽雪樓書畫錄. 1892 ed.

*Kuo-ch'ao hu-chou-fu k'o-ti piao* 國朝湖州府科第表. Printed some time after 1904.

*Kuo-ch'ao shih-liao shih-ling* 國朝史料拾零. 1933 "Manchukuo" ed.

*Kuo-ch'ao su-chou-fu ch'ang-yüan-wu san-i k'o-ti p'u* 國朝蘇州府長元吳三邑科第譜. 1906 ed.

Kuo P'an 郭鑿. *Huang-Ming t'ai-hsüeh chih* 皇明太學志. Preface dated 1557; late Ming revised ed.

Kuo T'ing-hsün 過庭訓. *Kuo-ch'ao ching-sheng fen-chün jen-wu k'ao* 國朝京省分郡人物攷. 1621–25 ed.

*Kuo-tzu-chien chih* 國子監志. 1832 ed.

*Kuo-tzu-chien tse-li* 國子監則例. 1824 ed.

*Kuo-yü* 國語. SPPY ed.

*Lan-hsi hsien-chi* 蘭溪縣志. 1888 ed.

Li Chou-wang 李周望. *Kuo-ch'ao li-k'o t'i-ming pei-lu ch'u-chi* 國朝歷科題名碑錄初集. 1746 ed., expanded from the original 1720 ed.

Li Hsü 李翊. *Chieh-an man-pi* 戒庵漫筆. *Ch'ang-chou hsien-che i-shu* 常州先哲遺書 ed.

Li Huan 李桓. *Kuo-ch'ao ch'i-hsien lei-cheng* 國朝耆類獻徵. 1880 ed.

*Li-pu tse-li* 禮部則例. 1784 ed. and 1844 ed.

Li Shao-wen 李紹文. *Huang-Ming shih-shuo hsin-yü* 皇明世説新語. 1606 ed.

Li Tou 李斗. *Yang-chou hua-fang lu* 揚州畫舫錄. 1795 ed. and Peking, 1959 reprint.

Li Tsung-fang 李宗昉. *Ch'ien-chi* 黔記. TSCC ed.

Li Yin-tu 李因篤. *Shou-ch'i-t'ang wen-chi* 受祺堂文集.  1830–33 ed.

*Liang-che yen-fa chih* 兩浙鹽法志.  1801 ed.

Liang Ch'ing-kuei 梁慶桂. *Shih-hung-t'ang i-kao* 式洪堂遺稿.  1931 ed.

*Liang-huai yen-fa chih* 兩淮鹽法志.  1748 ed. and 1806 ed.

Liu Feng 劉鳳. *Hsü-wu-hsien-hsien tsan* 續吳先賢讚.  CLHP ed.

Liu Shao 劉劭. *Jen-wu chih* 人物志.  SPPY ed.

Lo Ssu-chü 羅思舉. *Lo-chuang-yung-kung nien-p'u* 羅壯勇公年譜. 1908 ed.

*Lo-t'ing Tsun-tao shu-yüan chih* 樂亭遵道書院志.  1876 ed.

Lu Chi 陸楫. *Chien-chia-t'ang tsa-chu ti-ch'ao* 蒹葭堂雜箸摘抄.  TSCC ed.

*Lu-chiang-chün Ho-shih ta-t'ung tsung-p'u* 廬江郡何氏大同宗譜.  1921 ed.

*Lu-ling hsien-chih* 廬陵縣志.  1911 ed.

Lu Yung 陸容. *Chin-t'ai chi-wen ti-ch'ao* 金臺紀聞摘抄.  CLHP ed.

——— *Shu-yüan tsa-chi ti-ch'ao* 菽園雜記摘抄.  CLHP ed.

——— *Yü-t'ang man-pi ti-ch'ao* 玉堂漫筆摘抄.  CLHP ed.

*Lun-yü chu-shu* 論語注疏.  SPPY ed.

*Lung-chiang ch'uan-ch'ang chih* 龍江船廠志.  *Hsüan-lan-t'ang ts'ung-shu* 玄覽堂叢書 ed.

*Lung-hu shu-yüan chih* 龍湖書院志.  Undated late Ch'ing ed.

Ma Ch'i-ch'ang 馬其昶.  *T'ung-ch'eng ch'i-chiu chuan* 桐城耆舊傳.  Preface dated 1886; printed in 1911.

Ma Tuan-lin 馬瑞臨. *Wen-hsien t'ung-k'ao* 文獻通攷.  CP ed.

*Man-Han wen-wu kuan-sheng ming-tz'u lu* 滿漢文武官生名次錄.  1798 ed. (first half only; LC).

*Meng-tzu chu-shu* 孟子注疏.  SPPY ed.

Miao Ch'üan-sun 繆荃孫. *Yün-tzu-tsai-k'an sui-pi* 雲自在龕隨筆.  Peking, 1958 reprint.

*Mien-yang chou-chih* 沔陽州志.  1894 ed.

*Min-chung hui-kuan chih* 閩中會館志.  1942 ed.

*Ming-hsi-tsung shih-lu* 明熹宗實錄, see *Ming-shih-lu*.

*Ming-hsüan-tsung shih-lu* 明宣宗實錄, see *Ming-shih-lu*.

*Ming hui-yao* 明會要.  1887 reprint and Peking, 1956 reprint.

*Ming-shih* 明史.  SPPY ed.

*Ming-shih-lu* 明實錄.  Kiangsu Sinological Library photostat ed.

*Ming-shih-tsung shih-lu* 明世宗實錄, see *Ming-shih-lu*.

*Ming-t'ai-tsu shih-lu* 明太祖實錄, see *Ming-shih-lu*.

*Ming-tao shu-yüan chih* 明道書院志.  1894 ed.

*Ming-ying-tsung shih-lu* 明英宗實錄, see *Ming-shih-lu*.

*Nan-ch'ang fu-chih* 南昌府志.  1873 ed.

*Nan-hai hsien-chih* 南海縣志.  1872 ed.

*Nan-hsün chih* 南潯志.  1922 ed.

*Ning-hsiang Yün-shan shu-yüan chih* 寧鄉雲山書院志.  1874 ed.

*Ning-po fu-chih* 寧波府志.  1730–41 ed., 1846 reprint.

Niu Hsiu 鈕琇. *Hu-sheng* 觚賸. Preface dated 1700; CTPCTK ed.

*Pa-ch'i t'ung-chih* 八旗通志. 1736 ed.

Pan Ku 班固. *Han-shu* 漢書. SPPY ed.

P'an Shih-en 潘世恩. *Ssu-pu lao-jen shou-ting nien-p'u* 思補老人手訂年譜. Undated Ch'ing ed.

*P'an-yü hsien-chih* 番禺縣志. 1871 ed.

*Pao-chin shu-yüan chih* 寶晋書院志. 1880 ed.

*Pao-ch'ing hui-kuan chih* 寶慶會館志. 1903 ed.

*Pao-ting fu-chih* 保定府志. 1607 ed.

P'eng Yün-chang 彭藴章. *Kuei-p'u-an ts'ung-kao* 歸樸盦叢稿, in *P'eng-wen-ching-kung chi* 彭文敬公集. Last preface dated 1868.

*P'ing-hu ts'ai-ch'in lu* 平湖采芹錄. 1915 ed.

*Po-ch'üan shu-yüan chih* 百泉書院志. 1533 ed.

*Po-lu-tung shu-yüan chih* 白鹿洞書院志. 1525 ed. and 1673 ed.

P'u Sung-ling 蒲松齡. *Hsing-shih yin-yüan* 醒世姻縁. Kuang-i-shu-chü 廣益書局 ed.

*Shan-kan wei-ching shu-yüan chih* 陝甘味經書院志. 1894 ed.

*Shantung t'ung-chih* 山東通志. 1911 ed., CP reprint.

*Shan-tung t'ung-kuan lu* 山東同官錄. 1859 ed.

*Shan-tung yen-fa chih* 山東鹽法志. 1725 ed. and 1808 ed.

*Shang-ch'eng hsien-chih* 商城縣志. 1803 ed.

*Shang-tzu* 商子. SPPY ed.

*Shao-hsing fu-chih* 紹興府志. 1586 ed. and 1792 ed.

*Shao-yang hsien-chih* 邵陽縣志. 1875 ed.

*Shao-yang Wei-fu-chün shih-lüeh* 邵陽魏府君事略. Undated, by son of Wei Yüan 魏源. (Columbia)

*She-hsien hui-kuan lu* 歙縣會館錄. 1834 ed.

Shen Te-fu 沈德符. *Wan-li yeh-huo pien* 萬曆野獲編. Preface dated 1607; Peking, 1958 reprint; also an earlier edition, *Yeh-huo pien* and *Yeh-huo pien pu-i* 野獲編補遺. 1870 ed.

Shen Yao 沈堯. *Lo-fan-lou wen-chi* 落帆樓文集. Liu-shih chia-yeh-t'ang 劉氏嘉業堂 ed.

*Shensi t'ung-chih* 陝西通志. 1735 ed.

*Shensi t'ung-chih-kao* 陝西通志稿. 1934 ed.

*Shih-ch'ü pao-chi* 石渠寶笈. Printed 1918.

*Shih-ch'ü pao-chi hsü-pien* 石渠寶笈續編. Printed 1918.

*Shih-ch'ü san-pien* 石渠三編. Printed 1918.

*Shun-te hsien-chih* 順德縣志. 1854 ed.

*Shun-t'ien fu-chih* 順天府志. 1885 ed.

*Ssu-ch'uan yen-fa chih* 四川鹽法志. 1883 ed.

*Ssu-hui hsien-chih* 四會縣志. 1896 ed.

Ssu-ma Ch'ien 司馬遷. *Shih-chi* 史記. SPPY ed.

*Su-chou fu-chih* 蘇州府志. 1862 ed.

Sun Ch'eng-tse 孫承澤. *Ch'un-ming meng-yü lu* 春明夢餘錄. Ku-hsiang-chai 古香齋 pocket ed.

Sun I-jang 孫詒讓. *Mo-tzu chien-ku* 墨子間詁. Peking, 1954, reprint.

*Sung-chiang fu-chih* 松江府志. 1819 ed. and 1883 ed.

*Sung-shih* 宋史. SPPY ed.

*Ta-Ch'ing hui-tien shih-li* 大清會典事例. 1818 ed. and 1899 ed.

*Ta-kao* 大誥. 1385 ed.

*Ta-Ming hui-tien* 大明會典. 1502 ed. and 1587 ed.

*Ta-Ming i-t'ung chih* 大明一統志. 1559 ed.

*T'ai-yüan fu-chih* 太原府志. 1612 ed.

*T'ang hui-yao* 唐會要. Palace ed.

T'ao Chu 陶澍. *T'ao-wen-i-kung ch'üan-chi* 陶文毅公全集. Printed some time after 1839.

*Tao-kuang yüan-nien en-yin t'ung-nien lu* 道光元年恩蔭同年錄. 1821.

*T'ao-ch'in-su-kung hsing-shu* 陶勤肅公行述. 1902. (Columbia)

*Ti-hsi Chang-shih chi-sheng* 荻溪章氏家乘. 1894 ed.

T'ien Ju-ch'eng 田汝成. "Ah Chi Chuan" 阿寄傳, in *Shuo-fu* 説郛, vol. 165.

Ts'ao Wen-chih 曹文埴. *Shih-ku-yen-chai wen-ch'ao* 石鼓硯齋文鈔. 1800 ed.

Tsou T'ao 鄒弢. *San-chieh-lu pi-t'an* 三借廬筆談. Prefaces dated 1871 and 1875; CTPCTK ed.

*Tsung-jen-fu tse-li* 宗人府則例. 1812 ed. and 1840 ed.

Tu Yu 杜佑. *T'ung-tien* 通典. CP ed.

*Tung-p'o shu-yüan chih-lüeh* 東坡書院志略. 1849 ed.

*T'ung-ch'eng Chang-shih tsung-p'u* 桐城張氏宗譜. 1890 ed.

*T'ung-chih yüan-nien en-yin-sheng t'ung-nien ch'ih-lu* 同治元年恩蔭生同年齒錄 1862.

Wang Ch'i 王圻. *Wang-shih-yü lei-kao* 王侍御類稿. Preface dated 1585; 1620 ed.

Wang Chia-hsiang 王家相. *Ch'ing-mi shu-wen hsü* 清秘述聞續. 1889 ed.

Wang Chih-yüan 王之垣, and Wang Hsiang-chin 王象晋. *Ta-huai Wang-shih nien-tsu yüeh-yen shih-chi* 大槐王氏念祖約言世記. Preface dated 1601, but probably printed in the mid-17th century.

Wang Ch'ung 王充. *Lun-heng* 論衡. SPPY ed.

Wang Hui-tsu 汪輝祖. *Ping-t'a meng-hen lu* 病榻夢痕錄. In *Wang Lung-chuang hsien-sheng i-shu* 汪龍莊先生遺書. 1826 ed.

——— *Meng-hen yü-lu* 夢痕餘錄. In *Wang Lung-chuang hsien-sheng i-shu*. 汪龍莊先生遺書. 1826 ed.

——— *Shuang-chieh-t'ang yung-hsün* 雙節堂庸訓. In *Wang Lung-chuang hsien-sheng i-shu* 汪龍莊先生遺書. 1826 ed.

Wang K'ai-yün 王闓運. *Hsiang-i-lou wen-chi* 湘綺樓文集. 1900 ed.
——— *Wang Hsiang-i hsien-sheng ch'üan-chi* 王湘綺先生全集. 1923 ed.
Wang Shih-chen 王世貞. *Feng-chou tsa-pien* 鳳洲雜編. CLHP ed.
——— *Yen-chou shan-jen ssu-pu kao* 弇州山人四部稿. 1577 ed.
——— *Yen-chou shih-liao* 弇州史料. 1st and 2d series, 1614 ed.
Wang Shih-chen 王士禎. *Ch'ih-pei ou-t'an* 池北偶談. Preface dated 1691; CTPCTK ed.
——— *Chü-i lu t'an* 居易錄談. TSCC ed.
——— *Hsiang-tsu pi-chi* 香祖筆記. CTPCTK ed.
Wang Shou-jen 王守仁. *Yang-ming ch'üan-shu* 陽明全書. SPPY ed.
Wang Shu 王恕. *Wang-tuan-i-kung tsou-i* 王瑞毅公奏議. 1534 ed.
Wang Tao-k'un 汪道昆. *T'ai-han chi* 太函集. 1591 ed.
——— *T'ai-han fu-mo* 太函副墨. 1633 ed.
Wang Ting-pao 王定保. *T'ang chih-yen* 唐撫言. Shanghai, 1957, reprint.
Wang Wan 汪琬. *Shuo-ling* 説鈴. Preface dated 1659; Hsiao-yüan ts'ung-shu 嘯園叢書 ed.
Wang Yu-tun 汪由敦. *Sung-ch'üan shih-wen chi* 松泉詩文集. 1778 ed.
Wen Ch'un 温純. *Wen-kung-i-kung wen-chi* 温恭懿公文集. *Wen-shih ts'ung-shu* 温氏叢書 ed.
Wen T'ien-hsiang 文天祥. *Wen-shan hsien-sheng ch'üan-chi* 文山先生全集. SPTK ed.
*Wu-chin-yang-hu-hsien ho-chih* 武進陽湖縣合志. 1879 ed.
Wu Ching-tzu 吳敬梓. *Ju-lin wai-shih* 儒林外史. Ya-tung ed.
*Wu-hsi chin-k'uei hsien-chih* 無錫金匱縣志. 1883 ed.
*Wu-hsien chih* 吳縣志. 1642 ed.
Wu Huai-ch'ing 吳懷清. *Kuan-chung san-Li-hsien-sheng nien-p'u* 關中三李先生年譜. 1928 ed.
Wu Te-hsüan 吳德璇. *Ch'u-yüeh-lou wen-chien lu* 初月樓聞見錄. Undated 19th-century work; CTPCTK ed.
Yang Chi-sheng 楊繼盛. *Yang-chung-min-kung chi* 楊忠愍公集. 1673 ed
Yang I 楊儀. *Ming-liang chi* 明良記. TSCC ed.
Yang Shih-ts'ung 楊士聰. *Yü-t'ang k'uei-chi* 玉堂薈記. Liu-shih chia-yeh-t'ang 劉氏嘉業堂 ed.
Yeh Ch'ang-chih 葉昌熾. *Ts'ang-shu chi-shih shih* 藏書紀事詩. Shanghai, 1958, reprint.
*Yeh-kung-Ch'eng-chung ai-yung lu* 葉公澄衷哀榮錄. 1902. (Columbia)
Yeh T'ing-kuan 葉廷琯. *Ou-p'o yü-hua* 甌波漁話. CTPCTK ed.
Yeh Tzu-ch'i 葉子奇. *Ts'ao-mu tzu* 草木子. 1529 ed.
Yen Ch'en 嚴辰. *T'ung-hsi ta-sou tzu-ting nien-p'u* 桐溪達叟自訂年譜. Undated late Ch'ing ed.
*Yen-cheng chih* 鹽政志. 1529 ed.

Yü Chi-teng 余繼登. *Tien-ku chi-wen* 典故紀聞. TSCC ed.

Yü Ju-chi 俞汝楫. *Li-pu-chih kao* 禮部志稿. *Ssu-k'u chen-pen ch'u-chi* 四庫珍本初集 ed.

*Yü-lu shu-yüan chih* 嶽麓書院志. 1687 ed., 1868 reprint.

Yü Yüeh 俞樾. *Ch'un-tsai-t'ung sui-pi* 春在堂隨筆. CTPCTK ed.

*Yüan-jen shun-t'ien fu-yin hou-pu ssu-p'in ching-t'ang Liang-kung chia-chuan* 原任順天府尹後補四品京堂梁公家傳. Undated. (Columbia)

*Yüan-jen shun-t'ien fu-yin Liang-kung mu-piao* 原任順天府尹梁公墓表. By Ch'en Li 陳澧. (Columbia)

Yüan Ts'ai 袁采. *Yüan-shih shih-fan* 袁氏世範. *Chih-pu-tsu-chai ts'ung-shu* 知不足齋叢書 ed.

*Yüan-t'ung yüan-nien chin-shih teng-k'o lu* 元統元年進士登科錄, in *Sung-Yüan k'o-chü san-lu* 宋元科舉三錄. 1333 ed., 1923 reprint.

# SECONDARY CHINESE AND JAPANESE SOURCES

Aoyama Sadao 青山定雄. "Godai-sō ni okeru Kōsei no shinkō kanryō" 五代宋に於ける江西の新興官僚, in *Wada Hakase Kanreki Kinen Tōyōshi Ronsō* 和田博士還曆紀念東洋史論叢. Tokyo, 1951.

Chang Hsiao-jo 張孝若. *Nan-t'ung Chang Chi-chih hsien-sheng chaun-chi* 南通張季直先生傳記. Shanghai, 1930.

Chang Yüeh-hsiang 張耀翔. "Ch'ing-tai chin-shih chih ti-li ti fen-pu" 清代進士之地理的分佈, *Hsin-li* 心理, IV (no. 1, March), 1926.

Chao T'ieh-han 趙鐵寒. "Sung-tai ti t'ai-hsüeh" 宋代的太學, *Ta-lu tsa-chih* 大陸雜誌, VII (nos. 4–5, 1953).

——— "Sung-tai ti chou-hsüeh" 宋代的州學, *Ta-lu tsa-chih* (nos. 10–11, 1953).

Ch'en Mao-heng 陳懋恒. *Ming-tai wo-k'o k'ao-lüeh* 明代倭寇攷略. Harvard-Yenching Monograph Series, 1934.

Ch'en Yin-k'o 陳寅恪. *T'ang-tai cheng-chih-shih lüeh-lun kao* 唐代政治史略論稿. Chungking, 1942.

Chia Ching-te 賈景德. *Hsiu-ts'ai chü-jen chin-shih* 秀才舉人進士. Hong Kong, 1946.

Ch'ien Mu 錢穆. *Kuo-shih ta-kang* 國史大綱. 2 vols. Shanghai, 1940.

Chu Chün-i 朱君毅. *Chung-kuo li-tai jen-wu chihti-li ti fen-pu* 中國歷史人物之地理分佈. Shanghai, 1932.

Chu Shih-chia 朱士嘉. *Chung-kuo ti-fang-chih tsung-lu* 中國地方志綜錄. Shanghai, 1958.

Ch'ü T'ung-tsu 瞿同祖. *Chung-kuo fa-lü yü Chung-kuo she-hui* 中國法律與中國社會. Shanghai, 1947.

——— *Chung-kuo feng-chien she-hui* 中國封建社會. Shanghai, 1937.

Ch'üan Han-sheng 全漢昇. *T'ang-Sung ti-kuo yü yün-ho* 唐宋帝國與運河. Shanghai, 1946.

―――― "Pei-Sung Pien-liang ti shu-ch'u-ju mao-i" 北宋汴梁的輸出入貿易, *Chung-yang yen-chou-yüan li-shih yü-yen yen-chiu-so chi-k'an* 中央研究院歷史語言研究所集刊, VIII (part 2, 1939).

―――― "Sung-tai kuan-li chih ssu-ying shang-yeh" 宋代官吏之私營商業, VII (part II, 1936).

*Chung-kuo tzu-pen-chu-i meng-ya wen-t'i t'ao-lun chi* 中國資本主義萌芽問題討論集. 2 vols. Peking, 1957.

*Chung-kuo yin-pen shu-chi chan-lan mu-lu* 中國印本書籍展覽目錄. Peking, 1952.

Fang Chao-ying 房兆楹, and Tu Lien-che 杜聯喆. *Tseng-chiao Ch'ing-ch'ao chin-shih t'i-ming pei-lu* 增校清朝進士題名碑錄. Harvard-Yenching Index Series, 1941.

Fang Hao 方豪. *Chung-hsi chiao-t'ung shih* 中西交通史. 5 vols. Taipei, 1955.

―――― *Hsü Kuang-ch'i* 徐光啓. Chungking, 1944.

―――― *Sung-shih* 宋史. 2 vols. Taipei, 1944.

Fu I-ling 傅衣凌. *Ming-Ch'ing shih-tai shang-jen chi shang-yeh tzu-pen* 明清時代商人及商業資本. Peking, 1956.

Fujii Hiroshi 藤井宏. "Shinan shōnin no kenkyū" 新安商人の研究, *Tōyō gakuhō* 東洋學報, XXXVI-VIII.

―――― "Mindai enshō no ichi kōsatsu" 明代鹽商の一攷察, *Shigaku zasshi* 史學雜誌, LIV (no. 5-6, 1943).

Ho Wei-ning 何維凝. "Ming-tai ti yen-hu" 明代的鹽戶, *Chung-kuo she-hui-ching-chi-shih chi-k'an* 中國社會經濟史集刊, VII (no. 2, 1946).

Ho Yu-shen 何祐森. "Liang-Sung hsüeh-feng chih ti-li fen-pu" 兩宋學風之地理分佈, *Hsin-ya hsüeh-pao* 新亞學報, I (no. 1, August, 1955).

―――― "Yüan-tai hsüeh-shu chih ti-li fen-pu" 元代學術之地理分佈, *Hsin-ya hsüeh-pao* 新亞學報, I (no. 2, February, 1956).

―――― "Yüan-tai shu-yüan chih ti-li fen-pu" 元代書院之地理分佈, *Hsin-ya hsüeh-pao* 新亞學報, II (no. 1, August, 1956).

Hsiao Kung-ch'üan 蕭公權. *Chung-kuo cheng-chih ssu-hsiang shih* 中國政治思想史. 2 vols. Shanghai, 1946.

Hsieh Kuo-chen 謝國楨. "Ch'ing-tai shu-yüan hsüeh-hsiao chih-tu pien-ch'ien k'ao" 清代書院學校制度變遷攷, in *Chang Chü-sheng hsien-sheng ch'i-shih sheng-jih chi-nien lun-wen chi* 張菊生先生七十生日紀念論文集. Shanghai, 1935.

Hsü Ta-ling 許大齡. *Ching-tai chüan-na chih-tu* 清代捐納制度. Harvard-Yenching Monograph Series, 1947.

Hu Shih 胡適, Li Chin-hsi 黎錦熙, and Teng Kuang-ming 鄧廣銘. *Ch'i Po-shih nien-p'u* 齊白石年譜. Shanghai, 1949.

Kato Shigeshi 加藤繁. *Shina keizaishi kōshō* 支那經濟史攷證. 2 vols. Tōyō Bunko 東洋文庫, 1953.

*Kuo-hui t'u-shu-kuan ts'ang Chung-kuo shan-pen shu-lu* 國會圖書館藏中國善本書錄. 2 vols. Washington, D.C., 1957.

*Kuo-li chung-yang t'u-shu-kuan shan-pen shu-mu* 國立中央圖書館善本書目. 3 vols. Taipei, 1957.

*Kuo-li pei-p'ing t'u-shu-kuan shan-pen shu-mu* 國立北平圖書館善本書目. Peiping, 1933.

*Kuo-li pei-p'ing t'u-shu-kuan shan-pen shu-mu i-pien* 國立北平圖書館善本書目乙編. Peiping, 1935.

Kuwabara Jitsuzō 桑原隲藏. *P'u Shou-ken k'ao* 蒲壽庚攷. Chinese translation, Shanghai, 1954.

Lao Kan 勞幹. "Han-tai ch'a-chü chih-tu" 漢代察舉制度, *Bulletin of the Institute of History and Philology*, XVII (1948).

Lei Hai-tsung 雷海宗. *Chung-kuo wen-hua yü Chung-kuo ti ping* 中國文化與中國的兵. Shanghai, 1940.

——— "Ch'un-ch'iu shih-tai cheng-chih yü she-hui" 春秋時代政治與社會, *She-hui k'o hsüeh* 社會科學, IV (no. 1, October, 1947).

Li Kuang-ming 黎光明. *Chia-ching yü-wo chiang-che chu-k'o-chün k'ao* 嘉靖禦倭江浙主客軍攷. Harvard-Yenching Monograph Series, 1933.

Li Shu-hua 李書華. "Yin-shua fa-ming ti shih-ch'i wen-t'i" 印刷發明的時期問題, *Ta-lu tsa-chih* 大陸雜誌, XII (no. 5–6, 1958).

Ling Chia-pin 梁嘉彬. *Kuang-tung shih-san-hang k'ao* 廣東十三行攷. Shanghai, 1937.

Liang Fang-chung 梁方仲. "Ming-tai kuo-chi mao-i yü yin ti shu-ch'u-ju" 明代國際貿易與銀的輸出入, *Chinese Social and Economic History Review*, VI (no. 2, 1939).

——— "Ming-tai ti min-ping" 明代的民兵, *Chinese Social and Economic History Review*, V (no. 2, 1937).

Liu Po-chi 劉伯驥. *Kuang-tung shu-yüan chih-tu yen-ke* 廣東書院制度沿革. Shanghai, 1937.

Lo Erh-kang 羅尔綱. *Hsiang-chün hsin-chih* 湘軍新志. Shanghai, 1939.

Lü Ssu-mien 呂思勉. *Ch'in-Han shih* 秦漢史. 2 vols. Shanghai, 1947.

Meng Shen 孟森. "Chi-wei tz'u-k'o-lu wai-lu" 己未詞科錄外錄, in *Chang Chü-sheng hsien-sheng ch'i-shih sheng-jih chi-nien lun-wen chi* 張菊生先生七十生日紀念論文集. Shanghai, 1935.

Meng Ssu-ming 蒙思明. *Yüan-tai she-hui cheih-chi chih-tu* 元代社會階級制度. Harvard-Yenching Monograph Series, 1938.

P'an Kuang-tan 潘光旦. *Ming-Ch'ing liang-tai chia-hsing ti wang-tsu* 明清兩代嘉興的望族. Shanghai, 1947.

———, and Fei Hsiao-t'ung 費孝通. "K'o-chü yü she-hui liu-tung" 科舉與社會流動, *She-hui k'o-hsüeh*, IV (no. 1, October, 1947).

Shang Yen-liu 商衍鎏. *Ch'ing-tai k'o-chü k'ao-shih shu-lu* 清代科舉攷試述錄. Peking, 1958.

Sheng Lang-hsi 盛朗西. *Chung-kuo shu-yüan chih-tu* 中國書院制度. Shanghai, 1934.

Shimizu Morimitsu 清水盛光. *Chūgoku zokusan seido kō* 中國族産制度攷. Tokyo, 1949.

Sun Kuo-tung 孫國棟. "T'ang-Sung chih-chi she-hui men-ti chih hsiao-yung" 唐宋之際社會門第之消融, *Hsin-ya hsüeh-pao*, IV (no. 1, August, 1959).

Sung Hsi 宋晞. "Sung-tai fu-shang ju-shih ti t'u-ching" 宋代富商入仕的途徑, *Ta-lu tsa-chih*, IV (no. 11, 1952).

T'ang Chang-ju 唐長孺. *Wei-Chin-Nan-Pei-Ch'ao shih lun-ts'ung* 魏晋南北朝史論叢. Peking, 1955.

——— *Wei-Chin-Nan-Pei-Ch'ao shih lun-ts'ung hsü-pien* 魏晋南北朝史論叢續編. Peking, 1959.

T'ang Hsiang-lung 湯象龍. "Tao-kuang-ch'ao chüan-chien t'ung-chi" 道光朝捐監統計, *She-hui k'o-hsüeh tsa-chih* 社會科學雜誌, II (no. 4, December, 1931).

Ting Fu-pao 丁福保. *Fo-hsüeh ta-tz'u-tien* 佛學大詞典. Shanghai, 1925.

Ts'en Chung-mien 岑仲勉. *Sui-T'ang shih* 隋唐史. Shanghai, 1957.

*T'ung-hsiang tsu-chih chih yen-chiu* 同鄉組織之研究. Chungking, Ministry of Social Affairs, 1943.

Wang Ch'ung-wu 王崇武. "Ming-tai shang-t'un tsu-chih" 明代商屯組織, *Yü-kung* 禹貢, V (no. 12, August, 1936).

Wang I-t'ung 王伊同. *Wu-ch'ao men-ti* 五朝門第. Harvard-Yenching Monograph Series, Ch'eng-tu 成都, 1943.

Wang Yü-ch'üan 王毓銓. "Ming-tai ti chün-hu" 明代的軍戶, *Li-shih yeh-chiu* 歷史研究, 1959, no. 8.

Wu Ching-ch'ao 吳景超. "Hsi-Han she-hui chieh-chi chih-tu" 西漢社會階級制度, *Ch'ing-hua hsüeh-pao* 清華學報, IX (no. 1, October, 1935).

Wu Han 吳晗. *Chu Yüan-chang chuan* 朱元璋傳. Shanghai, 1949.

——— "Ming-tai ti chün-ping 明代的軍兵," *Chinese Social and Economic History Review*, V (no. 2, 1937).

Yang Lien-sheng 楊聯陞. "K'o-chü shih-tai ti fu-k'ao lü-fei wen-t'i" 科舉時代的赴考旅費問題, *Ch'ing-hua hsüeh-pao* 清華學報, new series, II (no. 2, June, 1961).

Yang Yün-ju 楊筠如. *Chiu-p'in chung-cheng yü liu-ch'ao men-fa* 九品中正與六朝門閥. Shanghai, 1930.

Yen Keng-wang 嚴耕望. "T'ang-jen tu-shu shan-lin ssu-yüan chih feng-shang" 唐人讀書山林寺院之風尚, *Bulletin of Institute of History and Philology*, XXX (1960).

Yung Chao-tsu 容肇祖. *Li Chih nien-p'u* 李贄年譜. Peking, 1957.

# WORKS IN WESTERN LANGUAGES

Barber, Bernard. *Social Stratification, a Comparative Analysis of Structure and Process.* New York, 1956.

Barber, Elinor. *The Bourgeoisie in 18th-Century France.* Princeton, 1955.

Bendix, Reinhard. *Higher Civil Servants in American Society, a Study of the Social Origins, the Careers, and Power-Position of Higher Federal Administration.* Boulder, Colorado, 1949.

Bottomore, Thomas B. "La Mobilité Sociale dans la Haute Administration Française," *Cahiers Internationaux Sociologie,* XIII (September, 1952).

—— "Higher Civil Service in France," *Transactions of the Second World Congress of Sociology,* 1954.

Carter, Thomas F. *The Invention of Printing in China and Its Spread Westward.* Rev. by L. Carrington Goodrich. New York, 1955.

Chang Chung-li. *The Chinese Gentry, Studies in Their Role in Nineteenth-Century Chinese Society.* Seattle, 1955.

Ch'ü T'ung-tsu. "Chinese Class Structure and Its Ideology," in J. K. Fairbank, ed., *Chinese Thought and Institutions.* Chicago, 1957.

Dibble, Vernon K., and Ping-ti Ho. "The Comparative Study of Social Mobility" (Debate), *Comparative Studies in Society and History,* III (no. 3, April, 1961).

Dubs, Homer H., tr. *The Works of Hsuntze.* London, 1928.

—— *History of the Former Han Dynasty,* Vol. II. Baltimore, 1944.

Duyvendak, J. J. L., tr. *The Book of Lord Shang, a Classic of the Chinese School of Law.* London, 1928.

Feng Yu-lan. *A History of Chinese Philosophy.* Vol. I, Peiping, 1937; vol II, Princeton, 1954.

Forke, Alfred, tr. *Lun-heng.* 2 vols. Leipzig, 1907.

Geiger, Theodor. "An Historical Study of the Origins and Structure of the Danish Intelligentsia," *British Journal of Sociology,* I (no. 3, September, 1950).

Goodrich, L. C. "The World's Greatest Book," *Pacific Affairs,* VII (no. 1, March, 1934).

Ho, Ping-ti. "The Salt Merchants of Yang-chou: A Study of Commercial Capitalism in Eighteenth-Century China," *Harvard Journal of Asiatic Studies,* XVII (nos. 1–2, June, 1954).

—— "Early-Ripening Rice in Chinese History," *Economic History Review,* 2d series, IX (no. 2, December, 1956).

—— "The Examination System and Social Mobility in China, 1368–1911," in *Proceedings of the 1959 Annual Spring Meeting of the American Ethnological Society.*

―――― "Aspects of Social Mobility in China, 1368–1911," *Comparative Studies in Society and History,* I (no. 4, June, 1959).

―――― *Studies on the Population of China,* 1368–1953. Cambridge, Massachusetts, 1959.

Hu, Hsien-chin. *The Common Descent Group in China and Its Functions.* New York, 1948.

Hu Shih. Oral autobiography. Incomplete manuscript. Oral History Project, East Asian Institute, Columbia University.

Hucker, Charles O. "The Tung-lin Movement of the Late-Ming Period," in J. K. Fairbank, ed., *Chinese Thought and Institutions.* Chicago, 1957.

Hummel, Arthur W. *Eminent Chinese of the Ch'ing Period.* 2 vols. Washington, D.C., 1943–44.

Jenkins, Hester, and D. Caradog Jones. "Social Class of Cambridge University Alumni of the 18th and 19th Centuries," *British Journal of Sociology,* I (No. 2, June, 1950).

Kelsall, R. K. "The Social Origin of Higher Civil Servants in Great Britain, Now and in the Past," *Transactions of the Second World Congress of Sociology,* 1954.

―――― *Higher Civil Servants in Britain, from 1871 to the Present Day.* London, 1955.

Kracke, Edward A. "Family vs. Merit in Chinese Civil Service Examinations under the Empire," *Harvard Journal of Asiatic Studies,* X (no. 2, September, 1947).

―――― *Civil Service in Early Sung China.* Cambridge, Massachusetts, 1953.

Legge, James, tr. *The Chinese Classics,* vol. 2, *The Works of Mencius.* Hong Kong, 1861.

Liao, W. K., tr. *The Complete Works of Han Fei-tzu, a Classic of Chinese Legalism.* London, 1939.

Lipset, Seymour M., and Reinhard Bendix. "Ideological Equalitarianism and Social Mobility in the United States," *Transactions of the Second World Congress of Sociology,* 1954.

―――― *Social Mobility in Industrial Society.* Berkeley, 1959.

Liu, Hui-chen (Wang). *The Traditional Chinese Clan Rules.* New York, 1959.

Liu, James T. C. "An Early Sung Reformer: Fan Chung-yen," in J. K. Fairbank, ed., *Chinese Thought and Institutions.* Chicago, 1957.

Marsh, Robert M. "Mandarin and Executive : Elite Mobility in Chinese and American Societies." Unpublished doctoral dissertation, Columbia University, 1959.

Mathew, David. *The Social Structure of Caroline England.* Oxford, 1948.

Maverick, L. A., ed. *Economic Dialogues in Ancient China, Selections from the Kuan-tzu.* New York, 1954.

Mei, Yi-pao, tr. *The Ethical and Political Works of Motse.* London, 1932.

Namier, Sir Lewis B. *The Structure of Politics at the Accession of George III.* London, 1957.

Porter, John. "The Economic Elite and the Social Structure in Canada," *Canadian Journal of Economics and Political Science*, XXIII (no. 3, August, 1957).

——— "Higher Public Servants and the Bureaucratic Elite in Canada," *Canadian Journal of Economics and Political Science*, XXIV (no. 4, November, 1958).

Pulleyblank, E. G. *The Background of the Rebellion of An Lu-shan.* Vol. 1, Oxford, 1955.

——— "The Origins and Nature of Chattel Slavery in China," *Journal of Economic and Social History of the Orient*, I (part 2, April, 1958).

Swann, Nancy Lee. "Seven Intimate Library Owners," *Harvard Journal of Asiatic Studies*, I (1936).

——— *Food and Money in Ancient China.* Princeton, 1949.

Tawney, R. H. "The Rise of the Gentry, 1558–1640," *Economic History Review*, XI (no. 1, 1941).

Thrupp, Sylvia L. "Hierarchy, Illusion and Social Mobility: A Comment on Ping-ti Ho, 'Aspects of Social Mobility in China, 1368–1911,'" *Comparative Studies in Society and History*, II (no. 1, October, 1959).

Twitchett, Denis C. "The Fan Clan's Charitable Estate, 1050–1760," in David S. Nivison and Arthur F. Wright, eds., *Confucianism in Action.* Stanford, California, 1959.

Watson, Burton, tr. *Records of the Grand Historian of China, Translated from the Shih chi of Ssu-ma Ch'ien.* Vol. II, *The Age of Emperor Wu, 140 to circa 100 B.C.* New York, 1960.

Wittfogel, Karl A. *New Light on Chinese Society.* New York, 1938.

———"Public Office in the Liao Dynasty and the Chinese Examination System," *Harvard Journal of Asiatic Studies*, X (June, 1947).

——— *Oriental Despotism.* New Haven, 1957.

——— and Feng Chia-sheng. *History of Chinese Society—Liao, 907–1125.* Philadelphia, 1949.

Wu, K. T. "Ming Printing and Printers," *Harvard Journal of Asiatic Studies*, (1942–43).

# INDEX

Ah Chi, 78
An Ch'i, 82, 155–56
An Kuo, 213
An Shang-i, 81
Anhwei: total *chin-shih* in Ming-Ch'ing, 227–28 (*tables*); high mobility rates in Ming, 233–34; *see also* Hui-chou
Artisans: in feudal and post-feudal stratification, 18, 20; as a special-service status in Ming, 56–59

*Bithesi* (Manchu clerks), 23; sale of office, 47
Board of Civil Appointments, 27, 35, 65, 89, 148
*Booi* (bond servants of Eight Banners), educational facilities for, 242
Bureaucracy: Mencian definition, 19–20; education of, 21; strata and ranks, Ming-Ch'ing, 24–26; *see also* Officialdom

Chang Ch'ien, 193; case study of, 310–13
Chang Chü-cheng, 191
Chang Ch'üan, case study of, 294–95
Chang Ch'un, 59
Chang Chung-li: criticism of his "gentry" definition, 30–31; criticism of his "gentry" family-background data, 93–94
Chang clan of T'ung-ch'eng, 127, 137–38, 139 (*table*), 140, 141; *yin* privilege, 149–50
Chang Feng, case study of arrested mobility, 273
Chang Han, case of successful mobility of a descendant of weavers, 76, 89

Chang Hsün, 82
Chang Huan, 82
Chang Jo-ai, 149–50
Chang Jo-ch'eng, 148–50
Chang Jo-shu, 149–50
Chang Jo-t'ing, 149–50
Chang Lin, 82
Chang Mao, 75
Chang Shih-i, case showing crucial nature of *chü-jen* degree in social stratification, 27
Chang T'ing-yü, 137, 157
Chang Tseng-i, 150
Chang Ying, and his descendants, 137–40, 149–50
Ch'ang-chou Prefecture, academic success, 246–47 (*tables*)
Chao I, on difficulty of *yin* transference, 151–52
Ch'ao Ssu-hsiao, 43
Chekiang: *chü-jen* quotas, 184–85; *chin-shih* ratios, 187–88; numbers of *chin-shih* in Ming-Ch'ing, 227–28 (*tables*); cultural advantages since Sung, 230–31; mobility rates in Ming-Ch'ing, 239–40; changes of prefectural distribution of academic success, 251–53; permeation of Confucian social ideology, 251–52; *see also:* Chia-hsing, Hang-chou, Hu-chou, Ning-po, Shao-hsing Prefectures
Ch'en Chi, 78–79
Ch'en Chih-lin, 137
Ch'en Eng, 218
Ch'en Mao-jen, rational explanation of rise and fall of families, 146–47
Ch'en Shih-kuan, 137
Ch'en Sung, 109–10
Ch'en Yü-hsiang, 138
Cheng Te-shu, 110
Ch'eng Chin-fang, 161